OXFORD THEOLOGICAL MONOGRAPHS

OXFORD THEOLOGICAL MONOGRAPHS

ST GREGORY OF NAZIANZUS
Poemata Arcana

EDITED WITH A TEXTUAL INTRODUCTION BY
C. MORESCHINI

INTRODUCTION, TRANSLATION, AND
COMMENTARY BY
D. A. SYKES

ENGLISH TRANSLATION OF TEXTUAL
INTRODUCTION BY
LEOFRANC HOLFORD-STREVENS

CLARENDON PRESS · OXFORD
1997

Oxford University Press, Great Clarendon Street, Oxford OX2 6DP

Oxford New York
Athens Auckland Bangkok Bogota Bombay
Buenos Aires Calcutta Cape Town Dar es Salaam Delhi
Florence Hong Kong Istanbul Karachi
Kuala Lumpur Madras Madrid Melbourne
Mexico City Nairobi Paris Singapore
Taipei Tokyo Toronto
and associated companies in
Berlin Ibadan

Oxford is a trade mark of Oxford University Press

Published in the United States
by Oxford University Press Inc., New York

British Library Cataloguing in Publication Data
Data available

Library of Congress Cataloging in Publication Data
Poemata arcana / St. Gregory of Nazianzus; edited with a textual
introduction by C. Moreschini; introduction, translation and
commentary by D. A. Sykes; English translation of textual
introduction by Leofranc Holford-Strevens.
Includes bibliographical references and index.
1. Christian poetry, Greek—Translations into English.
2. Theology—Early church, ca. 30–600—Poetry. I. Moreschini,
Claudio. II. Sykes, D. A. III. Title. IV. Series.
PA3998.G73A2613 1996 230´.14—dc20 95-40276
ISBN 0-19-826732-0

1 3 5 7 9 10 8 6 4 2

Typeset by Joshua Associates Ltd., Oxford
Printed in Great Britain on acid-free paper by
Bookcraft (Bath) Ltd., Midsomer Norton

Contents

CONTENTS

Abbreviations

AC	*Antike und Christentum*
ACO	*Acta Conciliorum Oecumenicorum*, ed. E. Schwartz, J. Straub, and R. Riedinger (Berlin and Leipzig, 1924–)
ACW	Ancient Christian Writers, ed. J. Quasten and J. C. Plumpe (Westminster, Md., and London, 1946–)
BTAM	*Bulletin de théologie ancienne et médiévale*
BZ	*Byzantinische Zeitschrift*
CC	Corpus Christianorum
CCSL	Corpus Christianorum, series Latina
CHLGEMP	*Cambridge History of Later Greek and Early Medieval Philosophy*, ed. A. H. Armstrong (Cambridge, 1967)
CSEL	Corpus Scriptorum Ecclesiasticorum Latinorum
DCB	*Dictionary of Christian Biography, Literature, Sects and Doctrines*, ed. W. Smith and H. Wace (London, 1877–87)
DK	H. Diels, rev. W. Kranz, *Die Fragmente der Vorsokratiker*, 6th edn. (Berlin, 1951)
DOP	*Dumbarton Oaks Papers*
Dox.	*Doxographi Graeci*, ed. H. Diels (Berlin, 1879)
DTC	*Dictionnaire de théologie catholique*, ed. A. Vacant, E. Mangenot, and E. Amann (Paris, 1903–72)
ECQ	*Eastern Churches Quarterly*
ETL	*Ephemerides Theologicae Lovanienses*
GCS	Die griechischen christlichen Schriftsteller der ersten drei Jahrhunderte
HTR	*Harvard Theological Review*
ICC	*International Critical Commentary*
JAC	*Jahrbuch für Antike und Christentum*
JEH	*Journal of Ecclesiastical History*
JTS	*Journal of Theological Studies*
LCC	Library of Christian Classics, ed. J. Baillie, J. T. McNeill, and H. P. van Dusen (Philadelphia and London, 1953–)
LNPF	A Select Library of Nicene and Post-Nicene Fathers of the Christian Church, ed. P. Schaff and H. Wace (Edinburgh, 1860–1900; repr. Grand Rapids, Mich., 1952–)
LSJ	H. G. Liddell and R. Scott, rev. H. S. Jones with

	R. McKenzie, *Greek–English Lexicon*, 9th edn. (Oxford, 1940)
M.	J. P. Migne, *Patrologia Graeca* (Paris, 1857–66)
M. *PL*	J. P. Migne, *Patrologia Latina* (Paris, 1844–64)
MSLC	*Miscellanea di studi di letteratura cristiana antica*
MSR	*Mélanges de science religieuse*
ODC	*Oxford Dictionary of the Christian Church*, ed. F. L. Cross, 2nd edn. rev. F. L. Cross and E. A. Livingstone (Oxford, 1974)
PGL	*A Patristic Greek Lexicon*, ed. G. W. H. Lampe (Oxford, 1968)
PPF	*Poetarum philosophorum fragmenta*, ed. H. Diels (Berlin, 1901)
RAC	*Reallexikon für Antike und Christentum*, ed. Th. Klauser and E. Dassmann (Stuttgart, 1950–)
RE	*Real-Encyklopädie der classischen Altertumswissenschaft* (Stuttgart, 1894–1980)
RHR	*Revue de l'histoire des religions*
RSR	*Recherches de science religieuse*
RTAM	*Recherches de théologie ancienne et médiévale*
SC	Sources chrétiennes
SJT	*Scottish Journal of Theology*
Stud. Patr.	*Studia Patristica*
SVF	*Stoicorum veterum fragmenta*, ed. H. von Arnim (Leipzig, 1903–24)
ThQ	*Theologische Quartalschrift*
TU	Texte und Untersuchungen
VC	*Vigiliae Christianae*
ZTK	*Zeitschrift für Theologie und Kirche*

Textual Introduction
by Claudio Moreschini

THE manuscript tradition of the *Poemata Arcana* falls into two main groups, one comprising the direct tradition of Gregory's poetry, which in turn forms two families Ω and Ψ,[1] the other the 'Fourteen-Paraphrase Corpus' of Nicetas David (Π). This corpus, the object of previous scholarly investigation,[2] consists of fourteen poems (seventeen in the arrangement of M. 37), accompanied by a paraphrase, or rather commentary, by the Byzantine commentator Nicetas David (ss. ix–x). The poems on which he wrote are (in Migne's numeration) I. I. 1–5, 7–9; I. 2. 9, 14, 15+16, 17(+2. I. 2), 31, 33. Nicetas gave them the title of τὰ ἀπόρρητα; we do not know whether he invented it or found it already in use. In the sixteenth century it was translated, in circumstances we shall consider in due course, as *Arcana*. The title *Poemata Arcana* used in the present edition for Migne's I. I. 1–5, 7–9, in our numeration *Arc.* 1–8, is therefore derived from Nicetas, even if strictly speaking it applies not only to this collection but also to the other poems noted above. All the same, our *Poemata Arcana*, the first part of Nicetas' corpus, must have constituted a homogeneous grouping even before his day, since they stand together in the same order in the manuscripts of the two families Ω and Ψ, albeit with the addition of I. I. II. Nicetas may have omitted this latter and added the other poems, which are on moral subjects.[3]

This introduction summarizes the findings set out in C. Moreschini, 'La tradizione manoscritta dei *Carmina Arcana* di Gregorio Nazianzeno', *Atti della Accademia Pontaniana*, NS 44 (1995), 99–120.

[1] These symbols have been in general use ever since they were first proposed by L. Sternbach, 'Cercidea', *Eos*, 30 (1927), 347–60, in connection with his projected edition of Gregory of Nazianzus' works for the Polish Academy of Sciences in Kraków, on which see now M. Plezia, *L'incompiuta edizione delle opere di Gregorio Nazianzeno progettata a Cracovia* (Naples, 1991): cf. e.g. *Gregor von Nazianz: De vita sua*, ed. Ch. Jungck (Heidelberg, 1974), 39; *Gregor von Nazianz: Carmina de virtute Ia/Ib*, ed. R. Palla, tr. and comm. M. Kertsch (Graz, 1985), 39.

[2] See Fr. Lefherz, *Studien zu Gregor von Nazianz: Mythologie, Überlieferung, Scholiasten* (Bonn, 1958), 161–8 *et alibi*; Palla, edn. 9.

[3] His commentary on *Arc.* 1–5 is available in the recent edition by C. Moreschini and I. Costa, *Niceta David: Commento ai Carmina Arcana di Gregorio Nazianzeno* (Naples, 1992), that on the rest in the older edition by E. Dronke (Göttingen, 1840), reprinted in M. 38. 681–842.

1. The oldest manuscript in the Ω family is Bodleianus Clarkianus 12
(C), s. x, fos. 151ʳ–166ʳ, which owing to the loss of one leaf lacks *Arc.* 1.
1–24. It divides the longer poems into sections: thus it breaks *Arc.* 4
into (*a*) vv. 1–88, entitled περὶ κόσμου, and (*b*) vv. 89–100, entitled περὶ
ἀγγέλων, and similarly *Arc.* 8 into (*a*) vv. 1–30 περὶ διαθηκῶν, (*b*) vv.
31–81 περὶ ἐπιφανείας Χριστοῦ, (*c*) vv. 82–99 περὶ βαπτίσματος.

The same division of *Arc.* 8, into the same sections with identical
titles, is found in Neapolitanus Graecus 24 (N), ss. xiv–xv, fos. 148ᵛ–
165ʳ, but this manuscript does not divide *Arc.* 4.[4] Like C and N, Vat-
icanus Graecus 482 (Va), s. xiv, fos. 79ᵛ–96ᵛ, divides *Arc.* 8, into vv.
1–30, 31–81, and 82–99, but not *Arc.* 4; it omits *Arc.* 7.

Marcianus Graecus 82 (Ma), s. xii, also belongs to the Ω family. It
includes our poems (fos. 86ʳ–127ᵛ), accompanied by a paraphrase (not
Nicetas David's), but omits *Arc.* 8. 19–33, so that we cannot tell
whether it exhibited C's first break, between vv. 30 and 31. The second
is indeed indicated, but in a later hand (possibly s. xiv), which adds a
marginal note περὶ τοῦ θείου βαπτίσματος; however, the beginning of
section (*c*) at v. 82 constitutes the first line of a new pericope.

Within the Ω family we may observe a series of agreements in error
between Ma and N:[5] *Arc.* 2. 1 δὲ] δή; 2. 51 μιν] μιν αὐτὸν (an inter-
linear gloss entered into their hyparchetype); 3. 7 μένος] σθένος; 5. 67
prius τε om.; 6. 44 μὲν] μὴν; 7. 58 οὐρανὸς] οὐρανοὶ MaNᵐᵍ; 7. 91 ἐνὶ]
ἐν; 7. 126 ὡς ἡμεῖς] ὡς καὶ ἡμεῖς. The tradition from which N derives
appears from its readings to be radically contaminated from the Ψ
tradition of Laurentianus VII. 10 (L), a manuscript to be examined
later: *Arc.* 5. 39 τὸ μὲν . . . τὸ δ᾽ ἐν] τὰ μὲν . . . τὰ δ᾽ ἐν LN, corr. N²; 5.
70 ἄνιμεν SVa²Nᵞᵖ]ἄνομεν alii, ἄννομεν CMaVa, ἴομεν LN; 6. 69 ἐδί-
δαξεν ΠLN] ἐξεδίδαξεν CMaVa; 7. 6 γε ΠLN] τε CMaN² (Va *deest*).[6]
Furthermore, N seems to be contaminated from a tradition detectable
in Vaᵐᵍ: thus only N and Va know the title περὶ τριάδος for *Arc.* 1 περὶ
ἀρχῶν, which is found both in the rest of the Ω tradition (Ma and Va
itself; C *deest*) and in one branch of the manuscripts containing
Nicetas' commentary (the other, like Ψ, omits the titles): *Arc.* 4. 36
ἐγὼ ΠVaᵞᵖN] e᾽gvge CMaVaL; ibid. ἔμπεδος ΠLVaᵞᵖN] ἔμπεδον

---

[4] N is a composite MS, of prime importance for the *Arcana*, but for other poems of
Gregory's embodying no independent tradition; cf. in greater detail Palla, edn. 54 ff. Cf.
also C. Moreschini, 'Studi sulla tradizione manoscritta di Gregorio Nazianzeno: la
Gedichtgruppe II', in *Miscellanea in onore di Giovanni Tarditi* (Milan, 1995), 1235–55.
[5] Cf. Palla, edn. 61.
[6] Cf. Palla, edn. 61–2. It is probable that contamination by a MS of the Ψ family took
place in the exemplar from which N was copied.

CMaVa; ibid. οὐκέτ᾽ ΠLVa^{γρ}N] οὐδὲν CMaVa; 5. 33 ἦ γὰρ δὴ θεὸς
ΠVa²N] ἤδη γὰρ θεὸς CMaVaL.

Agreement between C and Va is found in *Arc.* 2. 41, where both read
νόον instead of δέος as in the other manuscripts, and in *Arc.* 8, where
both transpose v. 26 to follow v. 28. Moreover, in both manuscripts
v. 66 is omitted, and then added in the margin by the scribe; which
indicates that the hyparchetype of C and Va, designated η by Palla,
exhibited this line in the margin. However, for the *Poemata Arcana*, as
for Gregory's other poems, Va appears to be akin to L.[7] In *Arc.* 3. 77
both L and Va (like Π) read εὖτε instead of the οὖτε of CMaN, and
μνῆστιν instead of their μνῆστον; in 4. 6 ἔσαν (with ΠL) against the
other Ω manuscripts' ἔαν; in 1. 1. 11. 2 (not part of the *Poemata Arcana*)
both L and Va read οὐ σέβετ᾽ ἰσοθέως οὐρανίου λόγον *contra metrum*.

Va also presents a certain number of readings derived from the Π
family; but Palla has observed, precisely on the basis of certain of the
Poemata Arcana (3. 31, 8. 98), that the marginal readings and correc-
tions inserted into the text of Va over erasures in a different ink derive
specifically from δ, the hyparchetype of S and Mb, to be examined in a
moment.[8] At all events, to complete our demonstration that the
marginal readings and corrections in Va derive from the Π family, we
may adduce the following instances: *Arc.* 1. 19 τε om. Ω, add. Va²; 1. 26
μετέπειτα ΠLVa²] μετόπισθεν Ω; 2. 10 om. MaNVa, add. Va²ᵐᵍ; 2. 19
ἄναρχος Ω] ἀνάρχου ΠVa²; 3. 36 αὐτὸς ἐπελθών ΠVaᵐᵍ] ἐλθὼν ἐπί-
κουρος Ma, ἔλθ᾽ ἐπίκουρος CNVaL; 3. 63 δὲ Π] om. Ω, add. Va²ᵐᵍ; 5.
68 ἄτροφος ΠΝ^{γρ}Va²] ἄτροπος MaNVa; 8. 14 τρέψατο ΠVa²]
στρέψατ᾽ MaNVa; 8. 35 λεύσσων ΠΝVa²] λεύσων CMaVa. We may
also cite the two passages indicated by Palla to show the derivation of
Va² from δ, *Arc.* 3. 31 σαωτὴρ Va (with the other Ω MSS)] ἀωτὴρ
SMbVa^{γρ}; 8. 98 ἄθ᾽ ὤρια κύκλος ἐλίσσει Va cett.] ἅμα τ᾽ ἠελίῳ σελήνῃ
τε SMbVaᵐᵍ.

2. In the second family of manuscripts, that designated Ψ, the *Poemata
Arcana* are present only in Laurentianus VII. 10 (L), s. xi; this is one of
the most authoritative witnesses to the tradition, and the one contain-
ing the largest number of Gregory's poems. The *Arcana* are found on
fos. 45ᵛ–53ᵛ. However, L shows closer kinship to Ω than to Π in that

---

[7] Va, as Palla, edn. 46 observes, is a particularly contaminated MS, with a corres-
ponding disorder in the sequence of poems; proof lies, so far as the *Arcana* are con-
cerned, in the omission of *Arc.* 7, περὶ ψυχῆς. Cf. Moreschini, 'Studi', 105–6.

[8] Palla, edn. 48–50.

(i) it adds 1. 1. 11 after *Arc.* 8, (ii) after *Arc.* 8. 30, 81 it signals the beginning of a new poem (albeit without inserting headings), dividing *Arc.* 8 into three parts like C, N, and Va. For the rest, L (i.e. Ψ) agrees in turn with Ω and Π, as is evident from the apparatus criticus. A further characteristic of L, already noted by previous scholars,[9] is that it demonstrates a marked reworking of form and grammar. So far as the *Poemata Arcana* are concerned such scholarly revision is evident in L from the following examples:

Arc. 4. 97 θνητός] φθιτός NC², βροτός L, θνατός Caillau; 5. 5 ἐπειγόμενον] ἐλισσόμενον L; 5. 22 ὁμὸς μόρος] ὁμόσπορος L; 5. 39 ἡμῖν] ἄμμιν L; 5. 50 ἐποίσει] ἐλίσσει L; 6. 5 λυομένοισι] δυομένοισι L (or is this an error in transcribing from capitals?); 6. 44 μέν Π] μήν Ω, τιν' L; 6. 50 μεγάλοι] μεγάλου L; 7. 38 ἰξίονος κύκλοισιν Π] ἰξίονος κύκλον τιν' Ω, ἰξίονός τινα κύκλον L; 7. 42 οὐδὲ θάμνον] οὐ θάμνον L; 7. 49 τόδε] τάδε L; 7. 53 ἄριστον] ἄριστε L; 7. 78 δέσις] φύσις L; 7. 112 παλαίσμασιν] κακόφρονος L; 8. 4 ἔπειτα] μετέπειτα L; αἴης] γαίης L; 8. 85 ἐρείδει] μ' ἐρείδει L.

A further feature of L should perhaps also be ascribed to a similar learned initiative: the insertion on fo. 52^(r-v) of sixty lines, not found in the rest of the manuscript tradition, within *Arc.* 8, after v. 18. They have been transcribed by Bandini,[10] again by Vári,[11] and most recently by Wyss;[12] the last-named has sought to demonstrate their authenticity by comparison with other poems of Gregory's, and by the observation that he habitually repeats himself or reuses in different contexts passages, phrases, or syntagms already employed elsewhere. But in that case, why should Nicetas and the Ω hyparchetype independently omit these lines? Indeed, I am quite ready to believe that this substantial insertion, stitched together in cento fashion from other poems by Gregory, was also due to scholarly activity of this sort.

3. By virtue of its antiquity a considerable significance also attaches to an ancient Syriac translation of some of Gregory's poems,[13] preserved

[9] Cf. e.g. Jungck, edn. 39.

[10] A. M. Bandini, *Catalogus codicum manuscriptorum Bibliothecae Laurentianae*, i (Florence, 1764), 219–20.

[11] R. Vári, 'Sancti Gregorii Nazianzeni codicis Mediceo-Laurentiani celeberrimi collatio', *Egyetemes philologiai közlöny*, 20 (1896), 759–72, esp. 770–2.

[12] B. Wyss, 'Zu Gregor von Nazianz', in *Phyllobolia für Peter Von der Mühll* (Basel, 1946), 153–83, esp. 159–72.

[13] This translation appears to be the work of Theodosius, later metropolitan of

in Vaticanus Syriacus 105.[14] As regards the disposition of the *Poemata Arcana*, however, the translator seems to have allowed himself remarkable freedom. Thus he singled out only a short section of *Arc.* 7 (vv. 1–25) to form poem 129 (p. 164). Moreover, in order to give the poem a coherent sense he altered the text of vv. 24–5 as we read it in the rest of the manuscript tradition, namely ψυχὴ πλαζομένη τε δι᾽ ἠέρος. ὦδ᾽ ἂν ὁμοίη | πᾶσι πέλοι, rendering instead 'anima pervadens per aerem *eum qui ei similis est*.'[15] In other words, his Greek text is something like ᾧ δ᾽ ἂν ὁμοίη πέλοι, and πᾶσι appears to be left untranslated; of course we cannot say whether the change was his own, or was already present in the Greek source he was using. *Arc.* 1 ('Aliud Sancti Gregorii Theologi e libro poematum de principatibus') and 2 ('Aliud, de Filio'), are moved elsewhere (pp. 8 ff.). The translation seems to be by turns very free and extremely literal, not that I am in a position to assess the potentialities of Syriac for translating in accordance with criteria we generally define as 'literal', 'free', or 'paraphrastic'. It is therefore difficult to judge the readings that we should call isolated in the Greek tradition, among them *Arc.* 1. 6 πολλάκις om. Syr.; 1. 13 ῥηγνύμενοι ~ *cadentes*; 1. 32 μονώτατος ~ *solitarie*; 2. 7 θεοῦ] *deus*; 2. 32 ἀγένητος sive ἀγέννητος] *ingenerationis*; 2. 45 θεοῖο om.; 2. 53 ἔμ᾽] *te*; 2. 59 πλεῖον om.; 2. 63 σώματος] *carni*.

One of the hardest passages to interpret is *Arc.* 2. 6, where the manuscript tradition gives us ἀπήορος οἶδεν ΠMaNVa] ἀπήορος οὐδὲν CVa²L (ὑπέρτερον οὐδὲν Caillau). The Syriac translation reads (vv. 5–7) 'nihil [sc. erat] quod praecederet Patrem magnum, hic enim omnia tenet, *et alienum a Patre etiam nihil*', giving the overall sense 'nothing is detached, separated from the Father. He who is begotten of the Father (is) the Logos of the great God.' The translator presumably read ἀπήορον neuter, agreeing with οὐδέν, and in his understanding of this rare word gave the prefix ἀπ- more weight than the verb αἴρω.

Edessa, *c.*804: cf. A. Baumstark, *Geschichte der syrischen Literatur* (Bonn, 1922), 276. On Syriac translations see Sebastian Brock, 'The Limitations of Syriac in Representing Greek', in Bruce M. Metzger, *The Early Versions of the New Testament: Their Origin, Transmission, and Limitations* (Oxford, 1977), 83–98, and the articles reprinted in the Variorum collections *Syriac Perspectives on Late Antiquity* (London, 1984), nos. II–IV and *Studies in Syriac Christianity* (London, 1992), no. X.

[14] *Sancti Gregorii Theologi liber carminum iambicorum: Versio syriaca antiquissima e cod Vat. CV*, i, ed. P. J. Bollig, SJ (Beirut, 1895).

[15] We quote the readings of this Syriac version according to the translation kindly supplied to us by Fr J. Guirau of the Istituto Patristico Augustinianum, Rome, whose help we are very glad to acknowledge.

This points to agreement between Syr, L, and C(Va²): *nihil* = οὐδέν. In other instances too the Syriac version agrees with L against Ω: *Arc.* 1. 6 δ' ΠLVQ², *quidem* Syr.] om. MaNVa (deest C); 2. 10 habent ΠLVa²Syr.] om. Ω; 2. 80 ἀσάρκου ΠLN², *incorporei* Syr.] ἀνάρχου Ω; 7. 16 ἀλόγοισιν] ἀλόγοιο L, *harmonia... formae non rationalis* Syr. This last, an agreement in error, leads us to suppose that the Ψ family is older than Ω.

4. The commentary on Gregory's *Poemata* by Cosmas of Jerusalem takes us back to a very early stage of the tradition. It was published by Mai from the *codex unicus* Vaticanus Graecus 1260, s. xii as *Collectio et interpretatio Historiarum quarum meminit Divus Gregorius in Carminibus suis tum ex S. Scriptura tum ex profanis poetis atque scriptoribus: Opus Cosmae Hierosolymitani cognomento Philogregorii* = M. 38. 341–680. The part that interests us here comes in cols. 452–66 (fos. 78ʳ–87ʳ in the Vatican manuscript).[16] The *Arcana* group, however, is incomplete, for Cosmas does not comment on *Arc.* 4 and 6 (which is not to say he did not have them at his disposal). The title is περὶ ἀρχῶν; the regrettably few textual pericopae, comprising very few lines or passages, are:

Arc. 1. 11–13 (12 λαμπομένου Cosmas cett.] λαμπόμενοι L); 2. 62–3; 2. 65–6 (65 μιν codd. ~ μὲν Cosmas); 2. 67–8 (ὑπέρσχεθε δ' ὡς Cosmas CMaNCuCoMb] ὑπάνσχεθε δ' ὡς S, ὑπέρσχεθ' ὡς LVa); 2. 68–9 (68 ἄμειψε] ἀνάμειψε Cosmas); 2. 70–1 (πνεύματι ~ πνεύματος Cosmas); 2. 72; 2. 73–4 (γοῦνα κάμεν] γούνατα μὲν Cosmas); 3. 30–1 (31 ὅτ' ἐκ] ὅτε Cosmas); 3. 37–9; 5. 27–33 (29 εἰ δὲ Π] εἰ μὲν ΩL Cosmas; 30 ἐλίξεις Cosmas; 31 τις] τι Cosmas); 5. 32–40 (33 ἢ γὰρ δὴ ΠΝVa²] ἤδη γὰρ CMaVaL Cosmas; 40 ἧς om. Cosmas); 5. 53–7 (56 ὅσσων] ὅσων Cosmas); 7. 38–9.

More remarkably, he too makes three poems out of *Arc.* 8, just like the Ω manuscripts CNVa (see §1 above). Thus Cosmas' commentary affords us a series of isolated readings (most likely attributable to the copyist of Vaticanus Graecus 1260) and general agreement with the Ω family. Significant agreement with L, by contrast, cannot be established.

---

[16] Mai's edition is, like all his editions, very much wanting from a philological standpoint. Despite the labour involved, a new edition of the text would be extremely useful.

5. Even earlier is the anthology generally known as *Doctrina Patrum de incarnatione Verbi*, which goes back to *c.*700. It includes two excerpts from the *Poemata Arcana*: 1. 25–35 (= *Doctrina Patrum* 1. 3, p. 2 Diekamp), 2. 47–50 (= 40. 16, p. 302). In 1. 26 the *Doctrina Patrum* exhibits the reading μετόπισθεν as in Ω, instead of μετέπειτα as in Nicetas and L.

6. The oldest manuscripts in the Π family number two: Vaticanus Graecus 488 (Vl), s. x, which includes our portion of the *Arcana* together with Nicetas' paraphrase at fos. 1ʳ–63ᵛ, and Cusanus 48 (Cu), also s. x, 1–124.[17] They are two completely independent copies, each showing isolated readings not shared with the other. Those in Cu include *Arc.* 1. 14 ὧσε] ὧσσε; 1. 32 om.; 2. 22 μέγαν] μέγα; 3. 39 τεκτός] τικτός; 3. 58 ῥίζαν] ῥίζην; 4. 52 κρατεροῖο] καρτεροῖο; 5. 29 θεός] θεόν; 7. 16 καὶ] τε καὶ. In Vl, note e.g. 1. 17 πάροιθε] πάρος; 2. 71 υἱός] πατρός; 3. 55 θείοισι] θείοις; 5. 61 ἠέρος] ἤρεος; 6. 31 καὶ om.; 8. 33 ἔργμασι] ἔρμασι.

A relationship can also be established between Vl and the manuscripts Marcianus Graecus 494 (Md), s. xiii (as Palla has demonstrated), fos. 203ʳ–206ᵛ,[18] and Parisinus Coislinianus Graecus 262 (Co), s. xii, fos. 164ʳ–175ᵛ, each of which contains a short paraphrase. Co's text is incomplete, breaking off abruptly after *Arc.* 7. 12. It is above all the paraphrase that links Co to Md: however, it is not Nicetas', even though Md attributes it to him. This leads us to believe that Co and Md descend from the same hyparchetype, which, moreover, may be derived from the source of Vl (Palla's γ), on the basis of agreements between Vl, Md, and Co, as in the following instances: *Arc.* 2. 71 υἱός] πατρός; 4. 70 ἄτ'] ἄπ'; 6. 11 τεινώμεσθα] τεινώμεθα VlCo, τεινόμεθα Md. Agreement between Co and Md can be found in many other places as well: 3. 43 τρισσοῖς] τρισίν; 3. 55 θεοφόροισιν] θεοφόροισιν; 4. 67 λεύσσων] λεύσων; 6. 2 περιωγαῖς] περιωπαῖς; 6. 41 τιν'] τε; 6. 55 τόσον] τόσσον; 6. 98 αὖ θεός] αὖθις; 6. 99 τοσσάτιον] τοσάτιον; 7. 1 δ'] δέ.

For this group we must also consider another manuscript of the same period, Monacensis Graecus 488 (Mn), s. xiii, fos. 160ᵛ–162ᵛ, which, however, exhibits only *Arc.* 1. 1–3. 68, all set out continuously as though in prose. This manuscript has no paraphrases; it must belong to the class whose earliest representative is Vl, for like Co and

---

[17] On these Π MSS cf. Palla, edn. 1–17.   [18] Ibid. 27.

Md it contains the error *Arc.* 2. 71 υἱός] πατρός. Since, moreover, Mn shares certain isolated readings with Md and Co (*Arc.* 1. 6 δ' om.; 2. 32 ἀγένητος] ἀγέννητος), it may be taken to derive from the same hyparchetype. Indeed, it seems to have more in common with Md than with Co, as appears from the following instances: *Arc.* 1. 2 πτερύγεσσι] πτερύγεσι; 2. 25 μεσσηγύ] μεσηγύ. For all that they are independent copies, we have not relied on Md and Mn because their texts are so poor.

To Π also belong Marcianus Graecus (Mb), written in 1327, fos. 88ᵛ–108ʳ, which omits Nicetas' paraphrase, and Oxoniensis Baroccianus 96 (S), s. xiv, fos. 1ʳ–42ʳ, which retains it. These two manuscripts have a common bond in a series of errors and isolated readings that set them apart from the other manuscripts in the Π family. Shared errors include *Arc.* 1. 17 ἄνδρες] ἴδρες; 2. 59 ἀγητός] ἀγαπητός; 2. 66 δωροφόροι] δωροφόρος; 3. 31 σαωτὴρ] ἀωτὴρ; 4. 49 ἀνδροφόνοιο] ἰδροφόνοιο; 6. 2 ἀντομένη] ἀντομένην; 8. 98 ἄθ' ὥρια κύκλος ἐλίσσει] ἅμα τ' ἠελίῳ σελήνη τε. Among the isolated readings in S are 2. 12 μερόπεσσιν] μερόπεσιν; 2. 17 εἰ] εἴ γε; 2. 19 ὁ χρόνος] οὐ χρόνος; 2. 67 ὑπέρσχεθε] ὑπάνσχεθε; 3. 42 ἄκτιστον] ἄκτιτον; 4. 10 διέκρινεν] δ' ἔκρινεν; 5. 46 ζωοφόρους] ζωηφόρους; 7. 22 δὲ om.; 8. 45 ἀνδρομέοισι] ἀδρομέοισι; among those in Mb are 2. 37 ἐπιδέξεται] ἐπιδέξηται; 2. 53 ἔμ'] ἐμόν; 2. 80 εἰ κεῖνα] ἐκεῖνα (ut VaCo); 3. 20 πυρός] πρός; 3. 30 om.; 4. 9 ἄχροον] ἄχρονον; 5. 13 χορός] χοός; 6. 58 ὤλεσεν] ὤλεσας; 7. 103 θῆκε] θῆκε δὲ.

We follow Palla in employing the symbol δ to indicate the hyparchetype of S and Mb.[19] Palla was obliged to admit that there were only a few conjunctive errors in γ and δ opposed to correct readings in Cu.[20] On the basis of an error common to γ and δ in 1. 2. 3. 47 (ἀνήφθω] ἀνήφθων), he postulated a genealogy along the lines shown in the stemma in Fig. 1.

Parisinus Graecus 1220 (Pj), s. xiv, fos. 191ᵛ–202ᵛ, lacking the paraphrase, also belongs among the δ manuscripts, concurring in its errors (e.g. *Arc.* 1. 34 νωμεύς] νομεύς; 2. 59 ἀγητός] ἀγαπητός; 4. 49 ἀνδροφόνοιο] ἰδροφόνοιο), and within it generally agreeing with Mb rather than S (2. 53 θεός] θεοί; ἔμ'] ἐμόν; 2. 80 εἰ κεῖνα] ἐκεῖνα; 3. 20 πυρός] πρός; 3. 30 om.; 4. 9 ἄχροον] ἄχρονον; 6. 58 ὤλεσεν] ὤλεσας. On the other hand, the absence from Pj of many of the errors in Mb (e.g. *Arc.* 1. 2 πτερύγεσσι] πτερύγεσι; 1. 28 μουνογενοῦς] μονογενοῦς;

---

[19] Palla, edn. 26 ff.   [20] Ibid. 30.

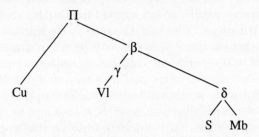

FIG. 1. Stemma of Π family according to Palla

4. 22 ἐγείρειν] ἀγείρειν; 4. 53 αὐτοδάϊκτος] αὐτοδάϊκτον; 5. 12 οὔτ᾽ ἄν] οὔτ᾽ ἄρ᾽; 5. 13 χορός] χοός) proves that it is not descended from Mb, but probably from the same manuscript from which the latter was copied. In his *editio princeps* of the *Arcana*, published in Paris in 1575, Billius is known to have made use of a manuscript belonging to Cardinal Sirleto (the 'Codex Sirletanus'), now lost; he compared it where necessary with the 'Codex Reginae Matris', no further identified.[21] Palla has demonstrated that we have very good grounds for taking Pj to be the Codex Reginae Matris used by Billius to correct, so far as possible, the errors in his copy-text, the Codex Sirletanus.[22]

However, the reading ἄφθιτος at *Arc.* 5. 55, common to Pj and the Codex Reginae Matris, merits attention: it is typical not of Π, which is agreed on ἄχρονος, but of Ω (Ψ has ἄχρονος like Π). Influence from Ω on Pj may also be detected in *Arc.* 4. 36 ἐγώ Π] ἔγωγε ΩL, ἐγώ Pj, γε γρ. s.v.; 4. 67 λεῦσσεν LVa] λεῦσεν CMaN, λεύσσων Π, λεύσσειν Pj; 6. 2 ἀντομένη ΩLCuVlCoPj] ἀντομένην SMb; 7. 97 τεῦξε νέον ΩPj] τεῦξει ἑὸν ΠLN² and, significantly, the omission of *Arc.* 2. 10 from Pj and the entire Ω tradition. At all events Pj is of mixed origin; we have not made use of its readings in establishing the text, since it adds nothing new with respect to Mb.

There is another sixteenth-century edition, that of D. Hoeschel, *S. Gregorii Nazianzeni, Theologi, Arcana; seu de Principiis, versus CCCC*

---

[21] Palla, edn. 32 ff. gives more details on the Sirletanus and its place in the tradition.

[22] This results from Palla's own recent researches, 'Alle fonti della prima edizione billiana dei carmi di Gregorio Nazianzeno', in *Polyanthema: Studi di letteratura cristiana antica offerti a Salvatore Costanza* (Messina, 1990).

*XXCII cum Paraphrasi Graeca. Eiusdem Carmen contra Apolinarium. Item
... Graecè nunc primùm publicata studio et operâ Davidis Hoeschelij, A.M. ...
Lugduni Batavorum ... MDCXI*; this rests on the Π tradition, but on a
different branch from Billius' text. Palla has recognized that the
pericopae of Gregory's text and the accompanying paraphrase in
Hoeschel's edition are very similar to those in Md.[23] It is unlikely,
however, that Hoeschel used Md or a manuscript closely resembling
it, since the paraphrase is there explicitly ascribed to Nicetas, even
though falsely. Hoeschel, by contrast, attributes it to him with hesita-
tion, and even then not on the title-page ('cum Paraphrasi Graeca')
but in the preface ('Hunc tractatum, cum perspicua paraphrasi, quam
Nicetae *arbitror esse*', 7; my emphasis). Probably, knowing the exist-
ence of a paraphrase by Nicetas, he attributed to him the paraphrase
he had discovered, which he could not have done unless it had been
anonymous. Now the same paraphrase is given anonymously in Co, a
manuscript of the same subfamily as Md. There are several other
factors besides that persuade us to attach Hoeschel's edition to the Co
tradition:

(i) Like Co, Hoeschel's edition contains only *Arc* 1–6. To be sure,
Co includes the first twelve lines of *Arc.* 7, which Hoeschel did not,
but there is a logical explanation: he did not see fit to publish a mani-
festly mutilated poem.[24] He occasionally splits a pericope in two, but
that was one of the licences permitted to an editor; the fact remains
that none of his pericopae is longer than in Co. That is to say,
Hoeschel felt entitled to a degree of licence only within a pericope
already extant in his model.

(ii) Co and Hoeschel agree in a great number of errors, against dis-
crepancies attributable easily enough to a sixteenth-century editor.
Chief among the errors is the omission within *Arc.* 1. 38–9, which
makes the text run ἡμιφαεῖς φθονεροί τε, λύχνος σκοτίοις ἐνὶ κόλποις.
Another, to be attributed purely to a false reading found in Co, is the
saut du même au même in 5. 62–3, reducing the two lines to Ἐβραίων
τέχνης. Other shared errors include *Arc.* 1. 3 ἀναφαίνειν] ἀμφαίνειν;

---

[23] Edn. 24 n. 22.
[24] This also explains why Hoeschel published a total of only 482 (continuously
numbered) lines of the *Arcana*, as stated on his title-page. By adding up the lines in *Arc.*
1–6 we obtain 485 lines; from this total we deduct those omitted outright (3. 71, 5. 31) or
reduced from two to one (1. 38–9, 5. 62–3), which brings us down to 481 lines. But in the
printed text, *Arc.* 1. 9 is misnumbered 10, so that an extra line is assigned to that poem;
we thus arrive at a total of 482 lines.

2. 73 παρέτοις] παρέτας; 4. 13 ἐστάμεν] ἐστάναι; ἄνδιχα πάντα om.;
6. 71 om.

Hoeschel frequently used another manuscript ('alter') to correct the
text he was printing, or to indicate variant readings. Since as a rule he
was extremely scrupulous and precise in his work, it should be
possible to identify this supplementary 'alter'. At *Arc.* 3. 67 Hoeschel
notes in the margin 'Hactenus alter recentior'; this remark is very
valuable, directing us at once to Mn, which as we have seen breaks off
precisely at *Arc.* 3. 68. This hypothesis is confirmed by the agreements
in isolated readings or in error between Mn and the *alter codex* in the
margin of Hoeschel's edition, e.g. *Arc.* 1. 31 κινουμένη in textu, οὐ
κινουμένη alter (= Mn); 2. 7 ἐκπεφυώς in textu, ἐκπεφυκώς alter (=
Mn); 2. 8 γεννήτορι ἴση in textu, γεννητῆρος ἴση τε alter (= Mn); 2. 17
γεννήσιες ἄλλαι in textu, γεννήσιες ἄλλαι τε alter (= Mn); 2. 21
ἄχρονον in textu, ἄναρχον alter, mendose (= Mn); 2. 55 πολλόν in
textu, πολλῷ alter (= Mn).

Nevertheless, we cannot set down Hoeschel's edition as a straight-
forward transcript of Co, for a certain number of the latter's errors
have not passed into the printed text. We may of course ignore those
obvious mistakes in grammar or metre that should (and above all
could) have been corrected by a modern editor. Hoeschel would, how-
ever, have found it difficult to correct certain errors in Co such as the
following, which are not found in his edition: *Arc.* 4. 61 ἐστιν Hoeschel
cett.] om. Co.; 5. 23 συνέδησαν ὁμὸν τέλος οὐ Hoeschel cett.] om. Co;
6. 24 ἐπιστασίην Hoeschel cett.] ἐπιστασίαν Co; 6. 54 τὸ τρίτον
Hoeschel cett.] τρίτον Co. From this it follows that Hoeschel used a
manuscript closely akin to Co, but not identical with it; furthermore,
he states (p. 66) that he used a 'codex Augustanus'. His edition is in
any case of no value in establishing the text of the *Arcana*.

7. The *Poemata Arcana* were published for the first time together with
others by Billius (Jacques de Billy) in 1575. They occupy a separate
section within his edition; it may be noted that he published not only
Arc. 1–8, but also the remaining poems in the Nicetas corpus, in the
same order as indicated in § 1. It has been rightly inferred, therefore,
that the manuscript used by Billius for this part of the edition—that
given him by Cardinal Sirleto, now lost—belonged to the Π tradition.
This has been demonstrated by Palla, who has allocated the Codex
Sirletanus to a class within this tradition created during the human-
istic era. Billius himself informs us that where necessary he has

corrected unsatisfactory readings in this manuscript from another copy, the Codex Reginae Matris, which Palla has shown can most probably be identified with Pj. The origin of the *editio princeps* in a manuscript of the Nicetas tradition explains why the text of the *Arcana*, as we have read it so far, is essentially a Π text; it also explains why this group of poems bears the title of *Arcana*, the Latin translation of τὰ ἀπόρρητα. No subsequent editor, indeed, has made systematic use of manuscript sources, which is why the text most often cited up to now, that in M. 37. 397–429, 438–64, preserves the same characteristics, departing only slightly from Billius. The next edition, by Morellus, is merely an aggregate of the sixteenth-century editions and reprints; the textual modifications are few and insignificant, for the most part suggested by Billius' own notes. Caillau, the last editor of Gregory's poems, relied, so far as the *Arcana* are concerned, on certain manuscripts from the Bibliothèque nationale, and then only sporadically (Parisinus Graecus 991, a late and worthless apograph, and also Co), and probably also Va.

The apparatus criticus presented here in support of our edition is selective: the isolated readings are omitted, except for those in L, which as indicated above may often be interpreted as the result of scholarly revision during the Byzantine era. We have ignored other manuscripts that were not in the strict sense *descripti*, if they offered what was clearly a mediocre or interpolated text (e.g. Pj and MnMd). Besides the isolated readings, we have omitted variants of spelling, accentuation, or punctuation.

Conspectus Siglorum

Ex familia Ω
C   Oxoniensis Bodl. Clark. 12, saec. x
Ma   Marcianus gr. 82, saec. xii
Va   Vaticanus gr. 482, saec. xiv
N   Neapolitanus gr. 24, saec. xv

Ex familia Ψ
L   Laurentianus pl. vii. 10, saec. xi

Ex familia Π
Cu   Cusanus gr. 48, saec. x
Vl   Vaticanus gr. 488, saec. x
Mb Marcianus gr. 83, a. 1327
S   Oxoniensis Bodl. Barocc. gr. 96, saec. xiv
Co   Parisinus Coislin. gr. 262, saec. xii

Syr   interpretatio Syriaca
Doct   Doctrina Patrum, ex recensione Fr. Diekamp (Monasterii, 1907)
Cosmas Cosmas Hierosolymitanus, ex Vat. gr. 1260

Bill.   editio Iac. Billii (Lutetiae, 1575)
Morel.   editio Fed. Morelli (Lutetiae, 1611)
Caill.   editio A. B. Caillau (Lutetiae, 1842 = M. 37. 397–429, 438–64)

ΓΡΗΓΟΡΙΟΥ ΤΟΥ ΘΕΟΛΟΓΟΥ
ΤΑ ΑΠΟΡΡΗΤΑ

α΄. Περὶ ἀρχῶν

397A   Οἶδα μὲν ὡς σχεδίῃσι μακρὸν πλόον ἐκπερόωμεν,
  ἢ τυτθαῖς πτερύγεσσι πρὸς οὐρανὸν ἀστερόεντα
398A   σπεύδομεν, οἷσιν ὄρωρε νόος Θεότητ᾽ ἀναφαίνειν,
  ἢν οὐδ᾽ οὐρανίοισι σέβειν σθένος, ὅσσον ἐοικός,
  ἢ μεγάλης θεότητος ὅρους καὶ οἴακα παντός.   5
399A   ἔμπης δ᾽ (οὐδὲ Θεὸν γὰρ ἀρέσσατο πολλάκι δῶρον
  πλειοτέρης ἀπὸ χειρὸς ὅσον φιλίης ὀλίγης τε),
  τοὔνεκα θαρσαλέως ῥήξω λόγον. ἀλλ᾽ ἀπὸ τῆλε
  φεύγετε, ὅστις ἀλιτρός· ἐμὸς λόγος ἢ καθαροῖσιν
  ἠὲ καθαιρομένοισιν ὅδ᾽ ἔρχεται· οἱ δὲ βέβηλοι,   10
  ὡς θῆρες, Χριστοῖο κατ᾽ οὔρεος ἀκροτόμοιο
  λαμπομένου, Μωσῆϊ νόμον τ᾽ ἐνὶ πλαξὶ γράφοντος,
  αὐτίκα ῥηγνυμένοισιν ὑπὸ σκοπέλοισι δαμεῖεν.
  κεῖνοι μὲν δὴ τοῖα· καὶ ὣς Λόγος ὦσε κακίστους
  ἡμετέροιο χοροῖο θεημάχον ἦτορ ἔχοντας.   15
  αὐτὰρ ἐγὼν ὄπα τήνδε προοίμιον ἐν σελίδεσσι
  θήσομαι, ἢν τὸ πάροιθε θεόφρονες ἄνδρες ἔηκαν,
  λαῷ τάρβος ἄγοντες ἀπηνέϊ μάρτυρε μύθων,
400A   Μωσῆς Ἡσαΐας τε (ἐπισταμένοις δ᾽ ἀγορεύσω),
  ἤτοι ὁ μὲν νεόπηγα διδοὺς νόμον, ὃς δὲ λυθέντος·   20
  "οὐρανὸς εἰσαΐοι, χθὼν δέχνυσο ῥήματ᾽ ἐμεῖο."
  Πνεῦμα Θεοῦ, σὺ δ᾽ ἔμοιγε νόον καὶ γλῶσσαν ἐγείροις
  ἀτρεκίης σάλπιγγα ἐρίβρομον, ὣς κεν ἅπαντες
  τέρπωνται κατὰ θυμὸν ὅλῃ Θεότητι μιγέντες.
  εἷς Θεός ἐστιν ἄναρχος, ἀναίτιος, οὐ περίγραπτος   25
  ἤ τινι πρόσθεν ἐόντι ἢ ἐσσομένῳ μετόπισθεν,
  αἰῶν᾽ ἀμφὶς ἔχων, καὶ ἀπείριτος, Υἱέος ἐσθλοῦ
  μουνογενοῦς μεγάλοιο Πατὴρ μέγας, οὔ τι πεπονθὼς
  Υἱέϊ τῶν ὅσα σαρκός, ἐπεὶ Νόος. εἷς Θεὸς ἄλλος,

---

1 tit. περὶ ἀρχῶν MaCuSMb, περὶ τριάδος N, περὶ ἀρχῶν ἤτοι περὶ τριάδος Va, α΄
τῶν ἀπορρήτων add. Va², titulum omittunt LVlCo, a versu 25 incipit C, *Carmen de Patre*
Syr., λόγος A tantum Bill. τὰ ἀπόρρητα περὶ ἀρχῶν λόγος A Morel. Α΄ Περὶ τοῦ
Πατρὸς Caill.   6 δ᾽ om. MaNVaCo, add. Va²   οὐδὲ θεὸν] οὐ θεόθεν L   πολ-
λάκις VlCo   9 φεύγετε] φευγέτω MaNVa   10 καταιρομένοισιν VlCu,
καθαιρομένοις Va   12 λαμπόμενοι L   16 ἐγὼ L   17 ἄνδρες] ἴδρες
SMb   ἔειπαν S²   19 τε om. MaNVa, add. Va²   21 ἐμεῖο] ἐμοῖο CuMb
23 ἀτρεκίη L   σάλπιγγον L   24 τέρπονται vel τέρπωνται Cu   26 μετό-
πισθεν Ω Doct] μετέπειτα ΠLVa²ᵐᵍʸʳ   27 καὶ om. L   28 μονογενοῦς SMb

1. On First Principles

I KNOW that it is upon a flimsy raft that we set out on a great voyage, or upon frail wings we hasten towards the starry heaven. On these the mind stirs itself to proclaim a Divinity which not even heavenly beings have power to worship fittingly, nor can they revere the ordinances of great Divinity and its governance of the universe. Yet (for often God is pleased not with a gift from the hand of a wealthy man so much as with the offering of a humble and loving giver), I shall break into confident speech. But get you far away, any who are sinful. This discourse of mine is meant for the pure or for those moving towards purity. As for the profane, like wild beasts, when Christ coming from the peak clothed in light wrote the Law for Moses upon tablets, let them be crushed by the rending of rocks. That is how the Hebrews acted and that is how the Word drove from our assembly rascally men with hearts set against God. But I shall set this word upon the page as a prologue, a word which before now godly men have uttered to bring fear to a harsh-minded people, those two witnesses of divine sayings, Moses and Isaiah (I shall address the perceptive), the one when he gave the newly enunciated law, the other when it had been broken: 'Let heaven hear and earth receive my words!' Spirit of God, in your truthfulness, come rouse my mind and stir my tongue to be a loud-sounding trumpet, that all who are fused with the fullness of Godhead may heartily rejoice.

The one God is without beginning, without cause, not circumscribed by anything existing before or in time to come. He encompasses eternity, he is infinite, the great Father of the great and excellent Son, his only-begotten, the Father who experiences through the Son nothing corporeal, since he is Mind. There is one other who is God,

οὐκ ἄλλος θεότητι, Θεοῦ Λόγος· οὗτος ἐκείνου   30
σφρηγὶς κινυμένη πατρώϊος, Υἱὸς ἀνάρχου
401Α οἷος, καὶ μούνοιο μονώτατος, ἰσοφέριστος,
ὥς κεν ὁ μὲν μίμνῃ γενέτης ὅλον, αὐτὰρ ὅ γ᾽ Υἱὸς
κοσμοθέτης νωμεύς τε, Πατρὸς σθένος ἠδὲ νόημα.
ἓν Πνεῦμ᾽ ἐξ ἀγαθοῖο Θεοῦ Θεός. ἔρρετε πάντες,   35
οὓς μὴ Πνεῦμ᾽ ἐτύπωσεν ἑὴν θεότητ᾽ ἀναφαίνειν,
ἀλλ᾽ ἢ βένθος ἔχουσι κακῶς ἢ γλῶσσαν ἄναγνον,
ἡμιφαεῖς φθονεροί τε, νοήμονες αὐτοδίδακτοι,
πηγὴ κευθομένη, λύχνος σκοτίοις ἐνὶ κόλποις.

β΄. Περὶ Υἱοῦ

Υἱέα δὲ πρώτιστον ἀείσομεν, αἷμα σέβοντες
ἡμετέρων παθέων τὸ καθάρσιον. ἡ γὰρ ἀνάγκη
402Α καὶ βροτὸν οὐρανίοισιν ἀρηγέμεν εἵνεκα γλώσσης
μαρναμένης θεότητι, κακόφρονος, αὐτοφόνοιο.
οὐδὲν ἔην μεγάλοιο Πατρὸς πάρος· ὃς γὰρ ἅπαντα   5
ἐντὸς ἔχει καὶ Πατρὸς ἀπήορος οἶδεν, ὁ Πατρὸς
ἐκπεφυὼς μεγάλοιο Θεοῦ Λόγος, ἄχρονος Υἱός,
εἰκὼν ἀρχετύποιο, φύσις γεννήτορι ἴση.
πατρὸς γὰρ κλέος ἐστὶ πάϊς μέγας, ἐκ δὲ φαάνθη
ὡς μόνος οἶδε Πατήρ τε καὶ ὃς Πατρὸς ἐξεφαάνθη,   10
οὐδὲν γὰρ θεότητος ἔην πέλας, ἀλλὰ τόδ᾽ ἔμπης
πᾶσιν ὁμῶς μερόπεσσιν ἀριφραδὲς ὥσπερ ἐμοί γε·
οὐδὲν ἐμῆς θέμις ἐστὶ φέρειν θεότητι γενέθλης,
οὐ ῥύσιν, οὐδὲ τομὴν κακοαισχέα. εἰ γὰρ ἔγωγε
403Α οὐκ ἀπαθὴς γενέτωρ (καὶ γὰρ δετός), οὔτι παθητὸς   15
ὅς τις πάμπαν ἄπηκτος ἀσώματος. ὢν γὰρ ἄπωθεν

31 κινυμένη S², κινουμένη MaCo, μὴ κινυμένη Vl² (ex κινυμένη)   32 om. Cu,
add. in mg. Cu³   μούνοι L   33 ὅλον] ὅλος LVl² (totaliter Syr.)   34 νομεὺς
SMb   περὶ ἀρχῶν λόγος α΄ VlCu, subscriptionem omittunt ceteri
  2 tit. περὶ υἱοῦ MaNVaSMb, περὶ υἱοῦ δι᾽ ἐπῶν C, περὶ υἱοῦ λόγος β΄ CuVl, λόγος
δεύτερος περὶ υἱοῦ Co, aliud (sc. carmen) de Filio Syr., περὶ τοῦ υἱοῦ λόγος B Bill., B΄
Περὶ τοῦ Υἱοῦ Caill., inscriptionem om. L   1 δὲ] δὴ MaN   4 αὐτο-
φόνοιο Π] αὐτοφονῆος ΩL   6 ἀπήορος] ὑπέρτερον Caill.   οἶδεν] οὐδὲν
LCVa²L, alienum nihil Syr.   8 γεννήτορι SMb (corr. S²), γεννήτορος edd.
9 ἐκ δ᾽ ἐφαάνθη L   10 om. MaNVa, add. in mg. Va²

though not other in point of Godhead, the Word of God. He, the living image of his Father, is alone Son of the one who is without beginning, unique Son of the only God, equal in excellence, so that the one should remain entirely Father, while the Son should be the founder of the universe who steers its course, at once the strength and understanding of the Father. There is one Spirit, God from the good God. Be gone, all you on whom the Spirit has not left his mark to make you proclaim his Godhead, those who are instead evil to the core and who sport an evil tongue, only half-enlightened, full of ill-will, minds taught merely by themselves, like a hidden spring or a lamp lost in dark recesses.

2. On the Son

WE shall sing first of the Son, revering the blood which cleanses our passions. For it is needful that even a mortal man should assist heavenly beings, because of a tongue at war with Godhead, a malicious and self-destructive tongue.

Nothing ever existed before the great Father. For he who contains the universe and is dependent on the Father knows this, the one who is sprung from the great Father, the Word of God, the timeless Son, the image of the original, a nature equal to his who begot him. For the Father's glory is his great Son and he was manifested in a way known only to the Father and to the Son made known by him. For there was nothing which came close to Godhead. Yet this is as clear to all mortal beings as it is to me, that it is wrong to ascribe to Godhead anything relating to human birth, like flux or shameful sundering. For if I experience passion in the act of generation (being bound to flesh), one who is totally uncompounded and bodiless is quite free of such passion. Where natures are so far apart, is it surprising if modes of

εἰσὶ φύσεις, τί τὸ θαῦμα καὶ εἰ γεννήσιες ἄλλαι;
εἰ χρόνος ἐστὶν ἐμεῖο παροίτερος, οὐ πρὸ Λόγοιο
ὁ χρόνος, οὐ γενέτης ἔστ᾽ ἄχρονος. ἦμος ἄναρχος
ἦε Πατήρ, θεότητος ὑπέρτερον οὔ τι λελοιπώς,   20
τῆμος καὶ Πατρὸς Υἱός, ἔχων Πατέρ᾽ ἄχρονον ἀρχήν,
ὡς φάος ἠελίοιο μέγαν περικαλλέα κύκλον
(εἰ καὶ εἴδεα πάντα κάτω μεγάλοιο Θεοῖο),
ὄφρα κε μή τι Πατρὸς καὶ Υἱέος αἰὲν ἐόντων
μεσσηγὺ στήσαντες, ἀπορρήξωμεν ἄνακτα   25
Υἱόν Πατρὸς ἄνακτος. ὃ γὰρ πάρος ἐστὶ Θεοῖο,
ἢ χρόνος ἠὲ ἤελησις, ἐμοὶ τμῆξις θεότητος.
404α ὡς Θεός, ὡς γενέτης, γενέτης μέγας. εἰ δὲ μέγιστον
Πατρὶ τὸ μή τιν᾽ ἔχειν κεδνῆς θεότητος ἀφορμήν,
οὐχ ἧσσον μεγάλοιο Πατρὸς γεννήματι σεπτῷ   30
τοίην ῥίζαν ἔχειν. τῷ μὴ Θεὸν εἶργε Θεοῖο.
οὐ γὰρ ἀπόπροθι Πατρὸς ἔγνως Πάϊν. ἡ δ᾽ "ἀγένητος"
φωνὴ "γέννησίς τε Πατρὸς ἄπο", οὐ θεότητος
ἔπλετο εἴδεα δισσά (τίς ἔπλασεν;), ἀμφὶ δ᾽ ἐκείνην
ἀμφότερ᾽ ἐκτὸς ἐόντα, φύσις δ᾽ ἀκέαστος ἔμοιγε.   35
εἰ μὲν δὴ γέννησιν ἔχει Λόγος, οὔτε Πατήρ τι
σαρκός, ἄσαρκος ἐών, ἐπιδέξεται (οὔποτε τόσσον
ἀνθρώπων νόος ἐστὶν ἀτάσθαλος ὡς τὸ νοῆσαι),
καὶ Θεὸν Υἱὸν ἔχεις, γεννήτορος ἄξιον εὖχος.
εἰ δ᾽ ἐπίηρα φέρων Πατρὸς μεγάλου θεότητι   40
μαψιδίως, κενεόν τε δέος πραπίδεσσι χαράσσων,
405α τὴν μὲν ἀπαρνήσαιο, βάλοις δ᾽ ἐς κτίσματα Χριστόν,
ἀμφοτέρων θεότητα καθύβρισας, ὢ κενεόφρον,
τὸν μὲν Παιδὸς ἄμερσας, ὁ δ᾽ οὐ Θεός, εἴπερ ἐτύχθη.
πᾶν γὰρ ὃ μή ποτ᾽ ἔην, λυτὸν τόδε, κἂν τι Θεοῖο   45
τοῖς μεγάλοισι λόγοισι μένῃ, καὶ ἔμπεδον εἴη.
τίς δὲ λόγος, σὲ μὲν ἔνθεν ἀφορμηθέντα, φέριστε,
τοῖς Χριστοῦ παθέεσσι Θεὸν μετέπειτα γενέσθαι,

---

17 γεννήσεες L, γενήσιες S   18 ἐμεῖο] ἐμοῖο Bill.   19 ἄναρχος ΩL]
ἀνάρχου ΠVa² sine initio Pater Syr.   20 ἦεν C²Ma²Va   22 μέγα CuCo
26 ὃ] οὐ L   30 οὐχ] οὔθ᾽ Morel.   32 ἀγένητος CLVa²CuVlS] ἀγέννητος
MaNVaMbCo   33 τε ΠLCVa²] δέ τε MaNVaᵘᵛ   ἄπο ΠLCVa²] ἀπ᾽ MaNVa,
ἄπω Co   34 dist. Holford-Strevens   36 ἔχει LVa] ἔχοι cett.   38 ὡς
τὸ ΩL] ὥστε Π   39 υἱὸν] οἷον L   ἔχεις] ἔχειν Bill.   41 δέος] νόον CVa,
corr. Va²   42 βάλλοις L, βάλῃς Sᵐᵍ   43 ἀμφοτέρων ΩLCoSᵐᵍ] ἀμφότερον
Π praeter Co, ἀμφοτέροιν Vl², amborum Syr.   45 ποτ᾽ ἦν edd.   λυτὸν ΩL]
αὐτῶν Π   46 λόγοις L   μένῃ] μένοι S², μένει Vl, corr. Vl²

generation also differ? If time precedes my human existence, time is not prior to the Word whose begetter is timeless. When there existed the Father who is without beginning, the Father who left nothing beyond his Godhead, then there also existed the Son of the Father, having that Father as his timeless beginning, as light originates from that beautiful great circle of the sun (though all images fall short of the great God), lest interposing anything between Father and Son, both everlasting beings, we should sever the royal Son from the royal Father. For what is prior to God, be it time or will, is to me a division of Godhead. As God, as progenitor, he is a mighty progenitor. But if it is a great thing for the Father to have no point of origin for his noble Godhead, it is no lesser glory for the revered offspring of the great Father to come from such a root. So do not sever God from God. You have not recognized the Son apart from the Father. The expressions 'ingenerate' and 'generation from the Father' do not constitute two different forms of Godhead (who invented that notion?), but both are externals around Godhead. But to my mind, the nature of Godhead is indivisible. If the Word indeed experiences generation, the Father, who is free of flesh, will take on nothing which pertains to flesh. (Never would a human mind be foolhardy enough to imagine such a thing.) Then you have God the Son also, a worthy source of pride to his Father who begot him.

But if idly seeking to find favour with the Godhead of the mighty Father, meaning to strike into people's hearts an empty awe, you should deny generation and consign Christ to the realm of creatures, dishonouring, empty-minded person that you are, the Godhead of both Father and Son, then you have robbed the Father of his Son, while the Son is not God, if he has been created. For everything which once lacked existence is subject to dissolution again into nothing, even if it should maintain some place in the mighty plans of God and were to be firmly established. For what reason would you, my friend, having a creaturely origin, hereafter become God through the sufferings of

τὸν δ' ὑπὸ δεσμὰ φέρειν, καὶ σὸν καλέειν ὁμόδουλον
δουλοσύνης γεράεσσι τιμώμενον ἀντὶ Θεοῖο;   50
εἴ μιν ἔτευξεν ἔπειτα Θεὸς μέγας ὄργανον ἐσθλὸν
(χαλκεὺς ὡς ῥαιστῆρα πονησάμενος δι' ἄμαξαν),
ὥς κεν ἔμ' Ἀρχεγόνοιο Θεοῦ χειρὶ κτεατίσσῃ,
ὧδ' ἂν καὶ Χριστοῖο πέλοι κτίσις οὐρανίοιο
406A   πολλὸν ἀρειοτέρη, κείνης Λόγος εἴ περ ἔκητι   55
οὐ κείνη Χριστοῖο. τίς ἂν τάδε μυθήσαιτο;
εἰ δ' ὅτι σῶμ' ὑπέδεκτο τεοῖς παθέεσσιν ἀρήγων,
τοὔνεκα καὶ θεότητι μεγακλέϊ μέτρ' ἐπιθήσεις,
ἤλιτεν ὅς σ' ἐλέηρεν; ἐμοὶ δέ τε πλεῖον ἀγητός·
οὔτε τι γὰρ θεότητος ἀπέξεσε, καί μ' ἐσάωσεν,   60
ἰητὴρ δυσόδμοισιν ἐπικύψας παθέεσσιν.
ἦν βροτός, ἀλλὰ Θεός· Δαβὶδ γένος, ἀλλ' Ἀδάμοιο
πλάστης. σαρκοφόρος μέν, ἀτὰρ καὶ σώματος ἐκτός.
μητρός, παρθενικῆς δέ· περίγραφος, ἀλλ' ἀμέτρητος.
καὶ φάτνη μιν ἔδεκτο, Μάγοις δέ τε ἡγεμόνευεν   65
ἀστήρ, δωροφόροι δ' ἄρ' ἔβαν, καὶ γούνατ' ἔκαμψαν.
ὡς βροτὸς ἦλθ' ἐπ' ἀγῶνα, ὑπέρσχεθε δ' ὡς ἀδάμαστος
407A   πειραστὴν τρισσοῖσι παλαίσμασιν· εἶδαρ ὑπέστη,
θρέψε δὲ χιλιάδας, ὕδωρ τ' εἰς οἶνον ἄμειψε.
λούσατο, ἀλλ' ἐκάθηρεν ἁμαρτάδας, ἀλλ' ἐβοήθη   70
πνεύματι βρονταίης φωνῆς ὕπο Υἱὸς Ἀνάρχου·
ὡς βροτὸς ὕπνον ἔδεκτο, καὶ ὡς Θεὸς εὔνασε πόντον.
γοῦνα κάμεν, παρέτοις δὲ μένος καὶ γούνατ' ἔπηξεν.
εὔξατο· τίς δ' ἐσάκουσε λιταζομένων ἀμενηνῶν;
ἦν θύος, ἀρχιερεὺς δέ· θυηπόλος, ἀλλὰ Θεός περ.   75
αἷμ' ἀνέθηκε Θεῷ, κόσμον δ' ἐκάθηρεν ἅπαντα.
καὶ σταυρός μιν ἄειρε, πάγη δ' ἥλοισιν ἁμαρτάς.
ἀλλὰ τί μοι τὰ ἕκαστα λέγειν; νεκύεσσιν ἐμίχθη,
ἔγρετο δ' ἐκ νεκύων, νεκροὺς δ' ἀνέγειρε πάροιθεν.
εἰ κεῖνα βροτέης πενίης, ὅδε πλοῦτος ἀσάρκου·   80

50 ἀντιθεοῖο L, corr. Bill. in comm.   51 μιν αὐτὸν MaN   53 θεοῦ
ΩLVCo Syr.] θεοὶ SMb, θεὸς CuS², θείου Vl^{uv}   54 πέλῃ Ma, πέλει N
55 πολλῷ Vl²   59 τε] γε edd.   ἀγητός] ἀγαπητὸς SMb   61 δυσόδοισιν L
63 αὐτὰρ VaS, corr. S²   65 μιν] μὲν CuVlCo² Cosmas   ἡγεμονεύειν SMb,
ἡγεμονεύει S²   66 δωροφόρος SMb   67 ὑπέρσχεθε CMaNCuCoMb
Cosmas] ὑπέρσχε** (rasura) HVl, ὑπάνσχεθε S, ὑπέρσχεθ' LVa   δ' ὡς] ὡς LVa
69 τ' εἰς] δ' εἰς Ma, εἰς Va   70 ἀλλ' ἐκάθηρεν ΩL] ἀλλὰ κάθηρεν Π, ἀλλὰ
κάθαρεν Bill.   71 υἱὸς] πατρὸς VlCo   77 μιν] μὲν Bill.   ἄειρεν L
80 εἰ κεῖνα CMaNCuVlSL Syr.] ἐκεῖνα VaMbCo, ἦν κεῖνα N^{γρ}, κἀκεῖνα coni. Caill.
βροτέης] βροτέοις Bill.   ὅδε] τό δε L   ἀσάρκου PN²L Syr.] ἀνάρχου Ω

8

Christ, should you throw him in chains and call him your fellow-slave, one respected by the privileges of servitude rather than of God? If the great God created him later in time to be his reliable instrument (as a smith might fashion a hammer merely to make a cart), that he might have me as his own, made by the hand of the divine first author, then creation would be far superior to the heavenly Christ, since the Word would have been brought into existence for its sake, rather than creation for the sake of Christ. Who would fabricate such a tale?

But if his reason for submitting to a body was to help your sinful passions, you will subject to limitation even the Godhead in all its glory. Was it an offence that he showed mercy to you? I find him the more admirable. For he stripped off none of his Godhead in bringing my salvation, a physician who descended to the world of evil-smelling passions. He was mortal, yet God, of the seed of David, but still the moulder of Adam's form. He bore flesh, yet existed outside a body. He is son of a mother, yet she is a virgin. He was subject to limitation, yet beyond measure. A manger received him, while the Magi were led by a star, as they came bringing gifts and bending their knees in worship. As a mortal man he came to the struggle, yet unconquered he prevailed over the tempter in the threefold conflict. Food was laid before him, yet he it was who fed thousands and turned water into wine. He was baptized, but himself cleansed sins and was proclaimed Son of the Eternal by the thundering voice of the Spirit. As a human being he took sleep, while as God he lulled the sea to sleep. He bent his knees in weariness, but to the knees of the palsied he restored strength. He prayed. Yet who was it who heard the supplications of the weak? He was both sacrifice and High Priest, an offerer of sacrifice, yet God. He dedicated his blood to God and cleansed the whole world. Even when a cross raised him up, it was sin which was fixed by its nails.

But why should I review each detail? He mingled with the dead but was raised from the dead, raising some who had previously died. If those are aspects of mortal poverty, here is found the wealth of the

408A   μὴ σύ γε τοῖς βροτέοισιν ἀτιμάζειν θεότητα·
      κείνη δὲ χθονίην μορφὴν ἐρικυδέα τεύχει,
      ἥν, σοί γ᾽ εὐμενέων, μορφώσατο ἄφθιτος Υἱός.

γ΄. Περὶ Πνεύματος

408A   Θυμέ, τί δηθύνεις; καὶ Πνεύματος εὖχος ἄειδε,
      μηδὲ τέμῃς μύθοισιν ὃ μὴ φύσις ἐκτὸς ἔθηκε.
      Πνεῦμα μέγα τρομέωμεν, ὅ μοι Θεός, ᾧ Θεὸν ἔγνων,
      ὃς Θεός ἐστιν ἔναντα, καὶ ὃς Θεὸν ἐνθάδε τεύχει·
      πανσθενές, αἰολόδωρον, ἁγνῆς ὕμνημα χορείης,   5
      οὐρανίων χθονίων τε φερέσβιον, ὑψιθόωκον,
      Πατρόθεν ἐρχόμενον, θεῖον μένος, αὐτοκέλευστον,
      οὔτε Πάϊς (μοῦνος γὰρ ἑνὸς Πάϊς ἐσθλὸς ἀρίστου),
409A   οὔτ᾽ ἐκτὸς θεότητος ἀειδέος, ἀλλ᾽ ὁμόδοξον.
      ὅστις δ᾽ ἐν σελίδεσσι θεοπνεύστοιο νόμοιο   10
      Πνεύματος οὐρανίοιο λαβεῖν ποθέει θεότητα,
      πολλὰς μὲν πυκινάς τε τρίβους εἰς ἓν συνιούσας
      ὄψεται, ἣν ἐθέλῃσι, καὶ εἴ τι Πνεύματος ἁγνοῦ
      εἴρυσεν ἢ κραδίη, καί οἱ νόος ὀξὺ δέδορκεν.
      εἰ δὲ γυμνὴν ποθέει φωνὴν θεότητος ἐραννῆς,   15
      ἴστω μὴ πινυτὸν ποθέων λόγον. οὐ γὰρ ἐῴκει,
      μή πω τῆς Χριστοῖο βροτῶν πλεόνεσσι φανείσης,
      ἄχθος ἄγειν κραδίῃσιν ἀφαυροτάτῃσιν ἄπιστον.
      οὐδὲ γὰρ ἀρχομένοισι τελειοτέροιο λόγοιο
      καιρός. τίς δ᾽ ἀμυδροῖσιν ἔτ᾽ ὄμμασιν ἢ πυρὸς αὐγὰς   20
      δεῖξεν ὅλας ἢ φωτὸς ἀπληστοτέροιο κόρεσσεν;
      λώϊον, ἢν κατὰ μικρὸν ἄγῃς πυριθαλπέας αὐγάς,
410A   μή πως καὶ γλυκεροῖο φάους πηγάς τι χαλέψῃς.
      ὡς γὰρ Πατρὸς ἄνακτος ὅλην θεότητα προφαίνων

---

81 τοῖς in codd. suis om. rest. Bill.   ἀτιμάζοις Morel.   82 κείνη (sc.
θεότης)] κείνη Vl Caill.   τεύχει ΩL Syr.] τεύχειν ΠVa   περὶ υἱοῦ λόγος β΄
CuVl, subscriptionem omittunt ceteri
    3 tit. περὶ πνεύματος MaNSMb, περὶ τοῦ πνεύματος Va, περὶ πνεύματος δι᾽ ἐπῶν
C, λόγος γ΄ περὶ τοῦ ἁγίου πνεύματος CuVlCo, Γ΄ Περὶ τοῦ ἁγίου πνεύματος Caill., περὶ
τοῦ ἁγίου πνεύματος λόγος γ΄ Bill., inscriptionem om. L   3 ὁμόιθεον edd.
4 καὶ ὡς Bill.   5 αἰολόδωρον Π] ὀλβιόδωρον ΩL   7 μένος] σθένος
MaN   13 ἐθέλῃ L   14 καρδίη L καί οἱ] καὶ εἰ Caill.   20 πυρὸς]
πρὸς SMbCu³, corr. S², πατρὸς Bill., qui πυρὸς coniecit

incorporeal one. Do not use these mortal traits to dishonour his Godhead. It is that Godhead which makes glorious the earthly form which the everlasting Son took upon himself in gracious love for you.

3. On the Spirit

MIND, why do you hesitate? Sing also the praise of the Spirit and do not in a form of words divide that which inherent nature has not dissevered. Let us bow in awe before the mighty Spirit, who is God in heaven, who to me is God, by whom I came to know God, and who in this world makes me God. All-powerful, manifold in gifts, theme of the hymn sung by the heavenly choir, giving life to heavenly and earthly beings, seated on high, coming from the Father, divine might, a self-determined being. He is not the Son (for there is a single good Son of the one supreme excellence), nor is he outside the invisible Godhead, but is of equal glory.

Whoever desires in the tables of divinely inspired law to understand the divinity of the heavenly Spirit will see, if he is willing, many manifold ways converging on one point, if he draws anything of the Holy Spirit into his heart and his mind enjoys clear perception. But if what he longs for is a plain word concerning lovely Godhead, let him know that the expression he seeks is unwise. For it was not fitting, when the Godhead of Christ was not yet clear to most mortal men, to impose upon feeblest minds a burden of what was not credible. Nor is the more complete account appropriate for beginners. Who ever exposes the full beams of fire to eyes still weak or overstrains them with excessive light? You would do better to introduce gradually the glowing beams of fire, in case you should damage in any way the body's sources of sweet light.

For, just as in former times teaching brought to light the full God-head of the sovereign Father, while enlightening only a few wise

Γ΄. ΠΕΡΙ ΠΝΕΥΜΑΤΟΣ

πρόσθε λόγος, Χριστοῖο μέγα κλέος αὐγάζεσκε   25
παύροισιν πινυτοῖσι φαεινόμενον μερόπεσσιν,
ὣς καὶ Παιδὸς ἔπειτα φαεινοτέρην ἀναφαίνων,
πνεύματος αἰγλήεντος ὑπήστραψεν θεότητα.
βαιὸν τοῖσδ᾽ ὑπέλαμψε, τὸ δὲ πλέον ἡμῖν ἔλειπεν,
οἷς ῥα καὶ ἐν γλώσσῃσι πυρὸς μετέπειτ᾽ ἐμερίσθη,   30
σῆμα φέρον θεότητος, ὅτ᾽ ἐκ χθονὸς ἆλτο Σαωτήρ.
καὶ γὰρ πῦρ Θεὸν οἶδα κακοῖς, ὡς φῶς ἀγαθοῖσιν.
οὕτω σοι θεότητα συνήγαγον. εἰ δὲ τέθηπας
Υἱόν τ᾽ οὐχ Υἱόν τε μιῆς θεότητος ἀκούων,
μύθοις τ᾽ ἀντιθέτοισιν ἐϋστρεφέεσσι πέποιθας,   35
δώσει κἀνθάδ᾽ ἔμοιγε Θεὸς λόγον αὐτὸς ἐπελθών.
411A   ἐξ ἑνὸς ἀρχεγόνοιο δάμαρ καὶ Σῆθ ἐγένοντο,
ἡμίτομος, δυάδος τε γόνος θεσμοῖσι γάμοιο·
οὐ τεκτή, τεκτός τε, βροτοί γε μὲν ἔσκον ὁμοίως.
τῶν σὺ μνωόμενος μηδὲν Θεότητος ἀτίζειν,   40
πρόσθε φέρων τόδ᾽ ἔνερθεν. ἵη φύσις ἐστίν, ἄμετρον,
ἄκτιστον, ἄχρονον, ἐσθλόν, ἐλεύθερον ἠδ᾽ ὁμόσεπτον,
εἷς Θεὸς ἐν τρισσοῖς ἀμαρύγμασι κόσμον ἑλίσσων.
τοῖσιν ἐγὼ νέος ἄλλος ἐγείρομαι, εὖτε λοετρῷ
θαπτομένου θανάτοιο παλίσσυτος ἐς φάος ἔλθω·   45
τρισσὴ γὰρ θεότης με φαεσφόρον ἐξανέτειλεν.
οὗ σε, κάθαρσι φίλη, οὐ ψεύσομαι. εἰ θεότητι
412A   λουσάμενος θεότητα διατμήξαιμι φαεινήν,
λώϊον ἦν . . . τρομέω δὲ κακοῦ μύθοιο τελευτήν,
ἐλπωρῇ θείοιο χαρίσματος ἠὲ λοετρῶν.   50
εἴ μ᾽ ὅλον ἐξεκάθηρεν, ὅλος καὶ σεπτὸς ἔμοιγε
ἔστι Θεός. τὸ δ᾽ ἂν ἴσον ἔχοι βροτὸς ὅστις ἀλιτρός,
αὐτὸς ἑὴν θεότητα, Θεοῦ γέρας, ἄνδιχα τέμνων.
εἴ τινα δ᾽ ἢ περὶ Παιδὸς ἀκούομεν, ἢ ἀγαθοῖο
Πνεύματος ἐν θείοισι λόγοις καὶ θειοφόροισιν   55
ἀνδράσιν, ὣς ῥα Θεοῖο τὰ δεύτερα Πατρὸς ἔχουσιν,
ὧδε νοεῖν κέλομαί σε λόγους Σοφίης βαθυκόλπου,
ὡς εἰς ῥίζαν ἄναρχον ἀνέρχεται, οὐ θεότητα

---

26 φαεινομένην L   μερόπεσσιν . . .   27 faeinotérhn om. L   29 ἡμῖν]
ἄμμιν L   31 σαωτήρ] ἀωτήρ SMbVa²ᵐᵍʸʳ   35 ἐϋστροφέεσσι Caill.
36 αὐτὸς ἐπελθὼν Π (αὐτὸς ex corr. VI²) Va²ᵐᵍ] ἐλθ᾽ ἐπίκουρος CNVaL, ἐλθὼν ἐπί-
κουρος Ma   37 ἐγένετο (sed corr. s.v.) Lʸʳ   42 ἄκτιτον CLS   50 ἠὲ]
ἠδὲ Caill.   λοετρῶν Π] λοετρὸν ΩL   51 ὅλον] ὅλος L   52 τὸ δ᾽ ἄνισον
Bill.   ἔχει Bill.   57 λόγους ΩL] λόγοις Π

mortals by showing the great glory of Christ, so later, when revealing more clearly the Godhead of the Son, it manifested only half-hidden gleams of the shining Spirit's Godhead. Gradually the Spirit began to shine for these people, but he reserved the greater part for us, for whom in later times he was divided in tongues of fire, bringing a token of his divinity when the Saviour had leapt up from the earth. For I know that God is fire to the wicked, as he is light to the good. This is how I sum up for you the case for Godhead. But if you are astonished to hear that the Son and one who is not Son are of one Godhead and trust in neatly turned contrary arguments, God himself will come to my help in giving me utterance at this point also.

His wife and Seth came into existence from Adam, the one progenitor, she cut from Adam's side and he the offspring of a couple joined by the laws of marriage. Eve was not begotten, while Seth was, yet both were equally human. With these in mind, refrain from dishonouring Godhead in any way, bearing in front of you this analogy drawn from below. There exists a single nature, beyond measuring, uncreated, timeless, excellent, free, and to be worshipped equally, one God in his three gleaming facets keeping the universe on its whirling course. Through these I am raised to a new and different life, when in baptism I spring again into light after the burial of death. For the threefold Godhead has made me shoot up as a bearer of light. No, I shall not deny you, dear cleansing power of baptism. If, being washed by Godhead, I should tear asunder that shining Godhead, then it were better ... But I tremble at the dreadful words which would follow, relying on the hope of divine grace in baptism. If he has cleansed me fully, then God is to me a single whole calling for my worship. It would be a just recompense for any mortal who gives way to sin that he should divide his own Godhead, God's gift.

But if we hear anything about the Son or about the good Spirit in Scripture or among inspired writers, to the effect that they hold second place to God the Father, then I bid you recognize the words of profound Wisdom which show that that which goes back to the unoriginate root does not divide Godhead, that you may have one

τέμνει, ὄφρα κεν οἷον ἔχῃς κράτος, οὐ πολύσεπτον.

413A ἐκ μονάδος Τριάς ἐστι, καὶ ἐκ Τριάδος μονὰς αὖθις,   60
οὔτε πόρος, πηγή, ποταμὸς μέγας, ἔν τε ῥέεθρον
ἐν τρισσοῖσι τύποισιν ἐλαυνόμενον κατὰ γαίης·
οὔτε δὲ πυρκαϊῆς λαμπὰς πάλιν εἰς ἓν ἰοῦσα,
οὔτε λόγος προϊών τε νόου καὶ ἔνδοθι μίμνων,
οὔτε τις ἐξ ὑδάτων κινήμασιν ἡλιακοῖσι   65
μαρμαρυγή, τοίχοισι περίτρομος, ἀστατέουσα,
πρὶν πελάσαι φεύγουσα, πάρος φυγέειν πελάουσα.
οὐδὲ γὰρ ἄστατός ἐστι Θεοῦ φύσις ἠὲ ῥέουσα
ἠὲ πάλιν συνιοῦσα· τὸ δ᾽ ἔμπεδόν ἐστι Θεοῖο.
ἀλλ᾽ ὧδ᾽ ἂν φρονέων καθαρὸν θύος ἔνδοθι ῥέζοις.   70
ἐν τρισσοῖς φαέεσσιν ἴη φύσις ἐστήρικται·
414A οὔτε μονὰς νήριθμος, ἐπεὶ τρισὶν ἵστατ᾽ ἐν ἐσθλοῖς,
οὔτε Τριὰς πολύσεπτος, ἐπεὶ φύσις ἔστ᾽ ἀκέαστος.
ἡ μονὰς ἐν θεότητι, τὰ δ᾽ ὦν θεότης τρισάριθμα.
εἷς Θεός ἐστιν ἕκαστον, ἐπὴν μόνον ἐξαγορεύῃς,   75
εἷς Θεὸς αὖθις ἄναρχος, ὅθεν πλοῦτος θεότητος,
εὖτε τριῶν τινα μνῆστιν ἔχῃ λόγος, ὡς τὸ μὲν εἴη
τῶν τρισσῶν φαέων σεπτὸν κήρυγμα βροτοῖσι,
τῷ δὲ μονοκρατίην ἐριλαμπέα κυδαίνωμεν,
μηδὲ θεῶν ἀγορῇ τερπώμεθα τῇ πολυάρχῳ·   80
ἶσον γὰρ πολύαρχον ἐμοὶ καὶ πάμπαν ἄναρχον
μαρνάμενον. δῆρις δὲ διάστασις· ἡ δ᾽ ἐπὶ λύσιν
σπεύδει. τῷ Θεότητος ἑκὰς πολύαρχον ἔμοιγε.
τρεῖς δὲ θεοὺς καλέοιεν ἢ οὓς χρόνος ἠὲ νόημα,
415A ἢ κράτος ἠὲ θέλησις ἀπ᾽ ἀλλήλων ἐκέασσεν,   85
αὐτοῦ ταυτὸν ἕκαστον ἀδήριτον οὔ ποτ᾽ ἐόντα.
τῆς δ᾽ ἄρ᾽ ἐμῆς Τριάδος ἓν μὲν σθένος, ἓν δὲ νόημα,
ἓν κλέος, ἓν δὲ κράτος. τῷ καὶ μονάς ἐστιν ἄρευστος,
ἁρμονίῃ θεότητος ἰῇ μέγα κῦδος ἔχουσα.
τόσσον ἐμοῖς φαέεσσι Τριὰς σέλας ἐξεκάλυψεν,   90
ἐκ πτερύγων θείου τε πετάσματος ἔνδοθι νηοῦ,
τοῖς ὕπο κεύθετ᾽ ἄνασσα Θεοῦ φύσις. εἰ δὲ πλέον τι,
ἀγγελικοῖσι χοροῖσι· τὸ δὲ πλέον ἡ Τριὰς ἴστω.

59 τέμνῃ MaL   ἔχεις LMb   62 τρισσοῖς CuSMb   63 δὲ Π
om. ΩL, add. Va²   66 περίτρομος ΠL] περίδρομος Ω   73 οὔτε ΠLVa] οὐ
CNVa, corr. Va²   74 ἰσάριθμα L   75 μόνον] θεὸν L   77 εὖτε] οὔτε
CMaN, εὖτε N²ˢᵛ   μνῆστιν ΠLNˢᵛVa] μνῆστον CMaN   ἔχῃ MaΠ] ἔχοι N², ἔχει
CNVaLVI²   84 ἢ οὓς Ω] ὅσους ΠLVa²   85 ἐκέασσεν CuS] ἐκέασεν cett.
86 θ᾽ αὑτὸν L   93 τὸ δὲ] τόδε Caill.   περὶ τοῦ ἁγίου πνεύματος λόγος γ΄ Vl,
λόγος γ΄ Cu, subscriptionem omittunt ceteri

single power not worshipped in plurality. Trinity comes from unity and unity again from Trinity. It is not a case of an underground passage, a spring, and a great river, one current directed down into the earth in three forms. Nor again is it like a torch from the pyre returning to its point of origin, nor like the word proceeding from the mind while remaining within it. Neither is it to be compared to some glint from the sun's rays moving off the water, reflected on a wall in its ceaseless motion, fleeing as it approaches and approaching in advance of its flight. For God's nature is not unstable, in flux, having to reassemble itself. Stability belongs to God. In thinking thus you would be offering a pure sacrifice in your heart.

The single nature is firmly established in three lights. It is not a unity unrelated to number, since it consists in three excellent forms. Nor is it a Trinity to be worshipped as plural, since its nature is indivisible. The oneness inheres in Godhead; those to whom Godhead belongs are three in number. Each of them is the one God, when you mention only one. Again, the one God is unoriginate, whence comes the rich quality of Godhead, when there is any reference to three, so as to bring about among mortal men a reverent proclamation of the three lights and also that we may glorify the clear-shining unity of rule, rather than finding pleasure in some Babel governance by a host of gods. For, as I see it, the rule of many in their strife amounts to no rule at all. Contest involves separation. Separation rushes towards dissolution. Thus, I think, the rule of many must be banished from all thought of Godhead. Let people call three gods those who are divided from one another by time or understanding, power, or will. For each would never be at one with himself nor free from strife. In the Trinity I teach there is one power, one understanding, one glory, one might. That is why the unity is beyond flux, possessing great glory in the single harmony of Godhead. So great is the splendour which the Trinity has revealed to my eyes, from the wings of the cherubim and within the veil of the temple, under which the sovereign nature of God is hidden. If there is anything beyond this, it is for choirs of angels. What is beyond, let the Trinity have knowledge.

δ΄. Περὶ κόσμου

Εἰ δ᾽ ἄγε καὶ μεγάλοιο Θεοῦ κτίσιν ὑμνείωμεν,
δόξαις ψευδομένῃσιν ἐναντία δηριόωντες.

416ᴀ εἷς Θεός· ὕλη δ᾽ αὖτε καὶ εἴδεα μῦθος ἀφαυρός,
Ἑλλήνων πινυτοῖσι νοεύμενα ὡς συνάναρχα.
τῶν μὲν ὅσα πλάσσουσι θεοὺς μορφώματα σεπτὰ   5
οὐκ ἔσαν, ἀλλ᾽ ἐγένοντο, Θεοῦ μεγάλοιο θέλοντος.
τίς δ᾽ ὕλην ποτ᾽ ὄπωπεν ἀνείδεον ἢ τίς ἄϋλον
μορφήν, καὶ μάλα πολλὰ νόου στροφάλιγξι μογήσας;
οὐδὲ γὰρ ἄχροον εὗρον ἐγὼ δέμας ἤ τιν᾽ ἄσωμον
χροιήν. τίς διέκρινεν ἃ μὴ φύσις, εἰς ἓν ἄγουσα;   10
ἀλλ᾽ ἔμπης τέμνωμεν· ἄθρει δέ μοι, εἰ μὲν ἄμικτα
πάμπαν ἔην, πῶς εἰς ἓν ἐλήλυθεν, ἢ τίς ὁ κόσμος
ἐστάμεν ἄνδιχα πάντα διαμπερές; εἰ δ᾽ ἐπίμικτα,
πῶς μίχθη; τίς ἔμιξε Θεοῦ δίχα; εἰ δ᾽ ὁ κεραστὴς
ἐστι Θεός, τοῦτον καὶ κτίστορα δέχνυσο πάντων.   15

417ᴀ εἶδος καὶ κεραμεὺς πηλῷ βάλε κύκλον ἑλίσσων,
χρυσῷ χρυσοχόος, λαοξόος οἷσι λίθοισι.
δὸς πλέον ἡμετέρης τι Θεῷ φρενός, ὦ φιλάναρχε·
ὕλη τὸ πλέον ἐστὶ σὺν εἴδεσι κινυμένοισι.
νώσατο, καὶ τὰ γένοντο ἐνειδέα· θεία νόησις,   20
ἡ πάντων γενέτειρα πολύπλοκος. οὐ γὰρ ἔοικε
ζωγράφον ὥς τιν᾽ ἐοικὸς ἀπ᾽ εἴδεος εἶδος ἐγείρειν
δερκόμενον προπάροιθε τὰ μὴ νόος ἔγραφεν οἷος.
καὶ σύ, Μανιχαίοιο κακὸν σκότος, οὐ πάρος ἦες
ἀκροτάτοιο φάους ἀντίθρονον. εἰ Θεὸς ἦεν,   25
οὐ σκότος· οὐ γὰρ ἔοικε Θεῷ κακὸν ἀντιφερίζειν.
εἰ σκότος, οὐ Θεὸν οἶδας. ὁμοφρονέειν μὲν ἄκοσμον·
μαρναμένων δέ, τὸ κάρτος ἀρείονος. ἰσοπαλεῖς δέ,

418ᴀ τίς τρίτος εἰς ἓν ἄγων σοφίῃ καὶ νείκεα λύων;
καὶ τόδε θαῦμα μέγιστον· ἐπεὶ μόθον αἰνὸν ἔγειρας,   30
αὖθις ὁμοφρονέοντα τιθεὶς ἐπελήσαο χάρμης.

---

4 tit. περὶ κόσμου MaNVaSMb, περὶ κόσμου δι᾽ ἐπῶν C, περὶ κόσμου λόγος δ΄
CuVlCo, Δ΄ Περὶ κόσμου Caill., inscriptionem om. L   1 ὑμνήσωμεν L
4 νοούμενα Morel.   5 μὲν] ἓν L   6 ἔσαν] ἔαν CMaN, corr. N²   ἀλλὰ
γένοντο edd.   8 νόον Bill.   9 ἄχροον] ἄχρονον MaMb, corr. Ma²
13 ἐστάμεν] ἑστάναι Co, ἑστακεν edd.   14 δ᾽ ὁ κεραστὴς ΩL· δὲ κεραστὴς Π (et
Vaᵘᵛ)   15 τούτων L   19 ὕλη τὸ] ὑλητὸς L   30 ἔγειρας] ἔγειραι Cu,
ἄγειραι MbSᵘᵛ, sed corr. S², ἐγείρεις edd.

4. On the Universe

COME, let us celebrate creation by the mighty God, opposing lying opinions with contending argument. There is one God. It is a feeble tale to suggest, as was thought by some wise Greeks, that matter and forms should be conceived as sharing his unoriginate status. Such of those revered shapes as they imagine to be gods never were so, but came into existence through the will of the mighty God. Now who has ever seen matter without form or an immaterial shape, even if he has toiled over many concepts whirling about in his mind? I have never discovered a body devoid of colour, any more than a disembodied hue. Who has made a distinction where nature does not, but firmly unites? But suppose we do make a division. Consider, I ask you, if things were once totally separate, how did they ever come together in a unity, or what world order came to stand in respect of a totality of things utterly divided in two? But if the elements were mixed, how did they come to be mixed? Who brought about the mixing, apart from God? If it is God who combines them, then accept that he is also the creator of the universe. Even the potter imparts form to the clay when he whirls his wheel, as the goldsmith with his gold and sculptor with his stone. Allow to God something more than our human mind, you who favour uncaused principles. Matter amounts to something more when joined to forms in motion. God exercised his mind and objects came into existence complete with their forms. It was divine intelligence, the subtle mother of the universe. For it is not likely that God, as if he were some painter, should produce a form resembling some other form, while observing before him objects which his mind alone did not paint.

As for you, evil Manichaean darkness, you were never originally a rival for the throne of supreme light. If God was in existence, darkness was not. For it is not fitting that evil should set itself against God. If you recognize darkness, you do not recognize God. Any agreement spells an end of order. If powers are in conflict, the better opponent will win. But if they are equally matched, what third force is there to bring unity through its wisdom and resolve the conflict? It would surely be very surprising, when once you had roused this deadly strife, if you should then restore agreement and forget the battle. I am made

17

ψυχὴ καὶ δέμας εἰμί. τὸ μὲν θεότητος ἀπορρὼξ
φωτὸς ἀπειρεσίοιο· τὸ δὲ σκοτίης ἀπὸ ῥίζης
σοὶ πλάσθη. τὰ δὲ πολλὸν ἀπόπροθεν εἰς ἓν ἄγειρας·
εἰ ξυνὴ φύσις εἰμί, λύω μόθον. εἰ μόθος αἰνός,   35
ἔμπεδος, οὐκέτ᾽ ἐγὼ πλεκτὴ φύσις ἀμφοτέρωθεν.
οὐ γὰρ μαρναμένων ξυνὸς γόνος, ἀλλὰ φιλεύντων.
τοῖος μὲν κραδίης τῆς σῆς ζόφος. αὐτὰρ ἔμοιγε
εἷς Θεός ἐστιν ἄναρχος, ἀδήριτος, ἓν φάος ἐσθλόν,
ἁπλῶν τε πλεκτῶν τε νοῶν σθένος ὑψιθεόντων,   40
419A   οὐρανίων χθονίων τε· τὸ δὲ σκότος ὕστατον ἦλθεν,
οὐ φύσις ἑστηκυῖα περίγραφος, ἡμετέρη δὲ
τοῦτο πέλει κακίη. κακίη δέ τε λύσις ἐφετμῆς,
ὡς νὺξ ἠελίοιο δύσις, νεότητος ἀφαυρὸν
γῆρας, χεῖμα δ᾽ ἔνεικεν ἄνω δρόμος ἠελίοιο   45
φρικτόν. ὁ μὲν πρώτιστος ἐν οὐρανίοις φαέεσσιν
ἧς ὑπεροπλίῃσι φάος καὶ κῦδος ὀλέσσας,
αἰὲν ἀπεχθαίρει μερόπων γένος. ἐκ δ᾽ ἄρ᾽ ἐκείνου
γεύσατο καὶ κακίης πρῶτος βροτὸς ἀνδροφόνοιο,
καὶ θανάτου, ῥιπίσαντος ἐμὴν φλόγα οἷσι δόλοισιν.   50
ἥδε μὲν ὀψιγόνοιο κακοῦ φύσις, ἧς περ ἐκεῖνος
ἔστι πατήρ. λώβη μὲν ἰὸς κρατεροῖο σιδήρου·
420A   λώβην δ᾽ αὐτοδαϊκτος ἐγὼ κακίην ἐφύτευσα,
ἑσπόμενος φθονεροῖο παλαίσμασιν ἣν διὰ μῆτιν.
κόσμε, σὺ δ᾽ εἰ μὲν ἔῃς τῆμος Τριάς, ἐγγὺς ἀνάρχου   55
κύδεϊ, πῶς δέ σε τόσσον ἀπόπροθι φῶτες ἔθηκαν
Χριστοφόροι θείων τε δαήμονες, ὥστε μετρεῖσθαι
οὐ μάλα πολλὸν ἀριθμὸν ἑλισσομένων ἐνιαυτῶν,
ἐξότε πῆξε μέγας σε Θεοῦ Λόγος; εἰ δ᾽ ἄρ᾽ ἔπειτα
πήχθης, φραζώμεσθ᾽ ὅ τι κίνυτο θεία νόησις   60
(οὐδὲ γάρ ἐστιν ἄπρηκτος ἐμοὶ Θεὸς οὐδ᾽ ἀτέλεστος),
πρὶν τόδε πᾶν στῆναί τε καὶ εἴδεσι κοσμηθῆναι.
αἰῶσιν κενεοῖσιν ὑπέρτατος ἐμβασιλεύων,
κίνυτο κάλλεος οἷο φίλην θηεύμενος αἴγλην,

34 πλάσθη CMaVaL] πλάστη NΠ   36 ἔμπεδος ΠLNVa^γρ] ἔμπεδον
CMaVa   οὐκέτ᾽] οὐδὲν CMaVa, corr. Va²ᵐᵍγρ   ἐγὼ ΠΝVa²γρ: ἔγωγε
CMaVaL   37 ξυνὸν L   γόνος] γένος L   42 φύσις] φύσιν L
45 ἔνεικεν] εἴνεκεν Cu, ἔ✝νεικεν Vl, ἔνεγκεν Ν, ἤνεγκεν Co   47 ὑπερ-
οπλείῃσι CuVlCoL   49 ἰδροφόνοιο SMb   50 ἐμήν] ἐμοὶ edd.
56 φῶτες ἀπόπρωθι τόσσον ἔθηκαν L   60 φραζώμεσθ᾽ ὅτι MaNVaL] φραζώ-
μεσθα τί CS², φραζώμεθα τί VlCoSMb, φραζόμεσθα τί Cu   κίννυτο S²
64 κίννυτο S²   οἷο] ἑοῖο Bill.

18

up of soul and body; the one is a particle of the boundless light of Godhead, while the other, you would have it, has been formed from the root of darkness. You have brought together into a unity elements which lie far apart. If I am a common nature, then I resolve conflict. If there is dreadful and unremitting conflict, then I am no longer a nature interwoven of both these elements. For there is no common offspring of two warring elements; rather must it come from mutual love. Such is the murky state of your mind. But I hold that there is one God, who is without beginning, beyond reach of strife, one perfect light, the strength of simple and composite minds, those moving swiftly on high in heaven and others here on earth. But darkness came late on the scene, not a self-existent nature with its own boundaries, but evil on our part. Now evil comes with breaching of the commandment, as night comes with the setting of the sun and feeble age with the fading of youth and as the sun's course in the north brings awful winter. But he who was first among the heavenly lights and who by his insolence forfeited his glorious light maintains constant hatred of the human race. For it was through his murderous agency when he fanned my human flame by his trickery that the first mortal came to taste evil and death.

This is the nature of evil born late in time of which he is the father. It is the contagion rust brings to strong iron. In acts of self-destruction I have produced the contagion of evil, deceived by his cleverness into falling in with my envious enemy's tricks. World, if you had been in existence as long as the Trinity, being close to the glory of the God who has no beginning, how is it that men inspired by Christ and those endowed with knowledge of divine matters have assigned you a place so far distant from it that no great number of circling years can be counted since the mighty Word of God established you? If then you were at that point established, let us ponder to what concern divine reflection was stirred (for I believe that God is neither idle nor ineffectual), before this universe stood in place and had been ordered by visible forms. He who was ruling in highest power over empty ages was active in contemplating his own splendour of beauty, one equal gleam of

421A τρισσοφαοῦς Θεότητος ὁμὸν σέλας ἰσοφέριστον,   65
ὡς μούνῃ Θεότητι καὶ ὢν Θεὸς ἔστ᾽ ἀρίδηλον.
κίνυτο καὶ κόσμοιο τύπους οὓς στήσατο λεῦσσεν
οἷσιν ἐνὶ μεγάλοισι νοήμασι κοσμογόνος Νοῦς
ἐσσομένου μετέπειτα, Θεῷ δέ τε καὶ παρεόντος.
πάντα Θεῷ προπάροιθεν, ἅτ᾽ ἔσσεται, ὅσσ᾽ ἐγένοντο,   70
ὅσσα τε νῦν παρέασιν. ἐμοὶ χρόνος ὧδ᾽ ἐκέασσε,
πρόσθε τὰ μέν, τὰ δ᾽ ὄπισθε· Θεῷ δέ τε εἰς ἓν ἅπαντα,
καὶ μεγάλης Θεότητος ἐν ἀγκοίνῃσι κρατεῖται.
τοὔνεκεν ὅσσον ἔτετμεν ἐμὸς νόος εἰσαΐοιτε.
Νοῦς ὤδινεν ἅπαντα, ῥάγη δ᾽ εἰς ὕστερον ὠδίς,   75
ὥριος, εὖτε Θεοῖο μέγας Λόγος ἐξεκάλυψεν.

422A ἤθελε μὲν νοερὰν στῆσαι φύσιν, οὐρανίην τε
καὶ χθονίην, πρώτοιο διαυγέα φωτὸς ἔσοπτρα,
τὴν μὲν ἄνω στίλβουσαν, ὑποδρήστειραν ἄνακτος,
πλησιφαῆ, μεγάλην, τὴν δ᾽ ἐνθάδε κῦδος ἔχουσαν,   80
πηγάζων θεότητα, ὅπως πλεόνεσσιν ἀνάσσῃ
οὐρανίοις, πλεόνων τε πέλῃ φάος ὀλβιόδωρον.
ἥδε γάρ ἐστιν ἄνακτος ἐμοῦ φύσις, ὄλβον ὀπάζειν.
ὄφρα δὲ μὴ πελάουσα Θεῷ κτίσις ἀντιθέοιο
κύδεος ἱμείρουσα, φάος καὶ κῦδος ὀλέσσῃ   85
(μέτρα φέρειν γὰρ ἄριστον, ἀμετρίη δὲ κάκιστον),
τοὔνεκεν ἐσσομένοισι φίλα φρονέων Λόγος αἰπὺς
τῆλε βάλε Τριάδος μὲν ὅσον φάος ἀμφιθόωκον,
ἀγγελικῶν τε χορῶν βροτέην φύσιν· ἀγγελικὴν μὲν

423A οὐ μάλα πολλὸν ἄνευθε παραστάτιν, ἡμετέρην δὲ   90
καὶ μάλα πολλὸν ἄνευθεν, ἐπεὶ χθονὸς ἐκγενόμεσθα
μιχθείσης Θεότητι· ἁπλῆ δέ τε φύσις ἀρείων.
κόσμων δ᾽ ὃς μὲν ἔην προγενέστερος οὐρανὸς ἄλλος,
θειοφόρων χώρημα, μόνοις τε νόεσσι θεητόν,
παμφαές, εἰς ὃν ἔπειτα Θεοῦ βροτὸς ἔνθεν ὁδεύει,   95
εὖτε Θεὸς τελέθῃσι, νόον καὶ σάρκα καθήρας·
αὐτὰρ ὅ γε θνητοῖσι πάγη θνητός, ἡνίκ᾽ ἔμελλε

---

67 κίννυτυ S²   λεῦσσεν LVa] λεῦσεν CMaN, λεύσσων Π (λεύσων Co)
71 ὧδε edd.   ἐκέασσεν CVaCuVlCoMbLˢᵛ] ἐκέασεν MaNLS, κέασσεν edd.
77 στῆναι edd.   82 οὐρανίοις] οὐρανίων Co   πέλει Bill.   84 θεῷ]
θεοῦ Bill.   85 ὀλέσσῃ ΩS² in ras., con. Bill.] ὀπάζει Π   89 τε]
δὲ L   90 παράστασιν L   91 ἐκγενόμεθα VlSMb, ἐγενόμεθα Co
95 ἔνθεν] ἔνδον Cu   97 ὅ γε] ὅ τε Cu   θνητὸς] βροτὸς L, φθιτὸς C²N, θνατὸς
Caill.

20

excellence expressed in the threefold light of Godhead, as is manifest to that Godhead alone and to those whose God he is. The world-creating Mind was stirred and gazed within his mighty thoughts upon the forms of the world to come into existence later, a world present to God. All things stand before God, future, past, and presently existing. For me, time has created division between events which come before and after. But where God is concerned, all things come together into unity and within the arms of his powerful Godhead they are supported. Therefore, I ask you, my listeners, to be aware of the point my mind has reached. It was Mind which brought forth the universe when later, at the right time, the fruit of travail burst into existence, the mighty Word of God revealing it. He willed to establish intelligent nature, both heavenly and earthly, a translucent mirror of the primal light. The one nature gleams above, servant of the heavenly King, great and full of light, whereas the other has its glory in this world. He poured forth from its source his own Godhead, that it might rule over more numerous heavenly beings and reach to more beings as the blissful gift of light. For it is the nature of my Lord to bestow happiness. But lest a created being in approaching God should yearn for a nature like God's and thus lose the light and glory already granted (to keep within set bounds is best and the worst conduct is to stray beyond them), for this reason the lofty Word, with kindly thought for generations to come, firmly placed at a distance from the Trinity whatever light surrounds the throne, separating human nature from the angelic choirs. The angelic he set at a lesser distance, to assist him, whereas our nature was placed much farther away, since we came into existence out of earth mingled with Godhead. Uncompounded nature is better. Of the worlds, one is older, that is heaven, the place visible to minds alone, occupied by those who possess God, the world, full of light, to which the mortal who belongs to God journeys when he leaves this world to become God, once he has cleansed mind and flesh. This world of ours, however, was established as mortal for mortal beings, when the beauty of heavenly lights was intended to find its place and

στήσεσθαι φαέων τε χάρις κῆρύξ τε Θεοῖο,
κάλλεΐ τε μεγέθει τε, καὶ εἰκόνος ἐμβασίλευμα·
πρῶτος δ' ὑστάτιός τε Θεοῦ μεγάλοιο λόγοισι.   100

424A   ε'. Περὶ Προνοίας

Ὧδε μὲν εὐρυθέμειλον ἐπήξατο κόσμον ἀπείρων
Νοῦς μέγας, ἐντὸς ἅπαντα φέρων καὶ παντὸς ὕπερθεν
αὐτὸς ἐών· τί δὲ μῆχος ἀχωρήτοιο λαβέσθαι;
αὐτὰρ ἐπεί μιν ἔτευξεν, ἄγει πρώτης ὑπὸ ῥιπῆς,
πληγῆς ὡς ὗπο ῥόμβον ἐπειγόμενον στροφάλιγξι,   5
κινύμενον μεγάλοισιν ἀκινήτοισι λόγοισιν.
οὔτε γὰρ αὐτομάτη φύσις κόσμοιο τοσούτου
καὶ τοίου, τῷ μηδὲν ὁμοΐϊον ἔστι νοῆσαι·
μὴ τόσον αὐτομάτοισιν ἐπιτρέψητε λόγοισι.
τίς δὲ δόμον ποτ' ὄπωπεν, ὃν οὐ χέρες ἐξετέλεσσαν;   10
425A   τίς ναῦν ἢ θοὸν ἅρμα; τίς ἀσπίδα καὶ τρυφάλειαν;
οὔτ' ἂν τόσσον ἔμεινεν ἐπὶ χρόνον, εἴπερ ἄναρχος,
καὶ χορὸς ἂν λήξειεν ἀνηγεμόνευτος ἔμοιγε.
οὔτ' ἄλλον τιν' ἐοικὸς ἔχειν σημάντορα παντὸς
ἠὲ τὸν ὅς μιν ἔτευξεν. ὁ δ' ἀστέρας ἡγεμονῆας   15
ἡμετέρης γενεῆς τε βίου θ' ἅμα παντὸς ὀπάζων,
αὐτοῖς ἀστράσιν εἰπὲ τίν' οὐρανὸν ἄλλον ἑλίξεις;
καὶ τῷ δ' αὖ πάλιν ἄλλον, ἀεί τ' ἐπ' ἄγουσιν ἄγοντας;
εἷς βασιλεὺς πλεόνεσσι συνάστερος, ὢν ὁ μὲν ἐσθλὸς
ὃς δὲ κακός, ῥητήρ τις, ὁ δ' ἔμπορος, ὃς δ' ἄρ' ἀλήτης,   20
τὸν δὲ φέρει θρόνος αἰπὺς ὑπέρφρονα. ἐν δέ τε πόντῳ
καὶ πολέμῳ πλεόνεσσιν ὁμὸς μόρος ἀλλογενέθλοις.
ἀστέρες οὓς συνέδησαν, ὁμὸν τέλος οὐ συνέδησε,
426A   κείνους δ' οὓς ἐκέασσαν, ὁμῇ συνέδησε τελευτή.

98 στήσεσθαι Cu²Ω] στησεῖσθαι ΠVa²ˢᵛ   100 δ' ΠL] θ' Ω, γ'
Vl²   περὶ κόσμου λόγος δ' VlCu, subscriptionem omittunt ceteri
5 tit. περὶ προνοίας MaNVaSMb, περὶ προνοίας δι' ἐπῶν C, περὶ προνοίας λόγος ε'
CuVlCo, E' Περὶ προνοίας Caill., inscriptionem om. L   1 εὐρυθέμεθλον N
ἄπειρον N², ἀπείρω L   4 ἔτευξεν] ἔπηξεν N, corr. N²   5 ἐπειγό-
μενον] ἐλισσόμενον L   6 κιννύμενον S²   8 τοίου τῷ ΠNL] τοιοῦθ' ᾧ
MaVa, τοιούτ' ᾧ C, τοιούτου τῷ Co   10 ἐξετέλεσσαν C²MaVaNVlS] ἐξετέλεσαν
CuCoMbC   15 ἠὲ] ἢ L   16 τε om. L   17 αὐτοῖς ΩL] αὐτοῖς δ'
ΠVa²   18 ἐπ' ἄγουσιν MaNCuS²] ἐπάγουσιν cett.   22 ὁμὸς μόρος] ὁμό-
σπορος L

to be God's herald in its splendid expanse, a royal palace to house God's image. But the first world and the last are alike based on the counsels of the great God.

5. On Providence

THUS did the infinite great Mind set the world on its broad foundations, bearing the universe within himself, while being himself above it all. What means is there to lay hold upon what cannot be contained? But when he fashioned it he drove it with initial impetus, as a top spins, urged on its whirling course by a whiplash, the world thus set in motion by his great unmoved counsels. For it is not the nature of such a great and wonderful world to be self-generating, a world whose like cannot be imagined. Do not commit such a world to theories of chance causation. Who has ever seen a house without hands to bring it to completion? Or a boat? A swift chariot? A shield or a helmet? The world would not have lasted so long if it had lacked an originator, as I believe a choir would cease without a conductor. Nor is it likely that the universe would have a governor different from its creator. But you who assign stars to be directors both of our birth and of our entire life, tell me what other heaven will you set in motion for these very stars? Again, to what further heaven do you supply a director, for ever piling leader on leader? The sole king shares his star with many of his subjects, one a fine man, another a rascal, this one an orator, that a merchant, yet another a vagabond. But he is the one borne up in pride on the lofty throne. At sea and in war a single death overwhelms many who are born under different nativities. People bound together by a common star are not conjoined in a common death and those the stars held apart at birth are bound together in a

εἰ μὲν δὴ καθ᾽ ἕκαστον ἔχει πρώτη τις ἀνάγκη,   25
μῦθος ὅδ᾽· εἰ δ᾽ ἄρα τῆς κρατέει ξυνή τις ἀρείων,
τείρεα τείρεσίν ἐστιν ἐναντία. τίς δ᾽ ἄρ᾽ ὁ μίξας;
ὃς γὰρ δὴ συνέδησε, καὶ ἦν ἐθέλησιν ἔλυσεν.
εἰ δὲ Θεός, πῶς πρῶτον, ὅ μοι Θεὸν ἐξετίναξεν;
εἰ μὴ καὶ Θεὸν αὐτὸν ὑπ᾽ ἄστρασι σοῖσιν ἑλίξεις.   30
εἰ δ᾽ οὔ τις κρατέων, πῶς στήσεται; οὐ γὰρ ὄπωπα.
κεῖνοι μὲν τοίοισι λόγοις Θεὸν ἐκτὸς ἔχοιεν·
ἢ γὰρ δὴ Θεός ἐστιν ἢ ἀστέρες ἡγεμονῆες.
αὐτὰρ ἐγὼ τόδε οἶδα· Θεὸς τάδε πάντα κυβερνᾷ,
νωμῶν ἔνθα καὶ ἔνθα Θεοῦ Λόγος ὅσσα θ᾽ ὕπερθεν,   35
ὅσσα τ᾽ ἔνερθεν ἔθηκε νοήμασι· τοῖς μὲν ἔδωκεν
427Α   ἁρμονίην τε δρόμον τε διαρκέα ἔμπεδον αἰεί,
τοῖς δὲ βίον στρεπτόν τε καὶ εἴδεα πολλὰ φέροντα·
ὧν τὸ μὲν ἡμῖν ἔφηνε, τὸ δ᾽ ἐν κευθμῶσι φυλάσσει
ἧς σοφίης, θνητοῦ δ᾽ ἐθέλει κενὸν εὖχος ἐλέγχειν.   40
καὶ τὰ μὲν ἐνθάδ᾽ ἔθηκε, τὰ δ᾽ ἤμασιν ὑστατίοισιν
ἀντήσει, κείρει δὲ γεημόρος ὥρια πάντα.
ὡς καὶ Χριστὸς ἄριστος ἐμοῦ βιότοιο δικαστής.
οὗτος ἐμὸς λόγος ἐστὶν ἀνάστερος, αὐτοκέλευθος.
ὡροθέτας δὲ σύ μοι καὶ λεπταλέας ἀγόρευε   45
μοίρας, ζωοφόρους τε κύκλους καὶ μέτρα πορείης·
λῦε δέ μοι ζωῆς τε νόμους, καὶ τάρβος ἀλιτροῖς,
ἐλπωρήν τ᾽ ἀγαθοῖσιν ἐς ὕστερον ἀντιόωσαν.
428Α   εἰ γὰρ κύκλος ἅπαντα φέρει, κείνου περιωγῇ
ῥοιζοῦμαι, τὸ θέλειν δὲ καὶ αὐτόγε κύκλος ἐποίσει,   50
οὐδέ τίς ἐστιν ἐμεῖο ῥοπὴ πρὸς κρεῖσσον ἄγουσα,
βουλῆς ἠδὲ νόοιο, πόλος δέ με τῇδε κυλίνδει.
σιγάσθω Χριστοῖο μέγα κλέος ἄγγελος ἀστὴρ
ἀντολίηθε Μάγοισιν ἐπὶ πτόλιν ἡγεμονεύσας,
ἔνθα Χριστὸς ἔλαμψε βροτοῦ γόνος ἄχρονος Υἱός.   55
οὐ γὰρ τῶν τις ἔην ὅσσων φραστῆρες ἔασιν
ἀστρολόγοι, ξεῖνος δὲ καὶ οὐ πάρος ἐξεφαάνθη,
Ἑβραϊκῇσι βίβλοισιν ὁρώμενος, ὧν ἄπο παῖδες

26 τῆς MaNCuVlSMb] τίς Vl²CoCVaL   κρατέει] κραταίη L   29 εἰ δὲ Π] εἰ
μὲν ΩL Cosmas   θεὸν] θεὸς Caill.   30 ἑλίξεις] ἑλίξῃς edd.   33 ἢ γὰρ δὴ
ΠΝVa²] ἤδη γὰρ CMaVaL   36 νοήμασι] σήμασι Bill.   39 τὸ μὲν] τὰ μὲν
NL, corr. N²   ἡμῖν] ἄμμιν L   τὸ δ᾽ ἐν] τὰ δ᾽ ἐν NL, corr. N²   φυλάττει L
42 γεημόρος ΠVa²] γεωμόρος ΩL   50 ἐποίσει] ἑλίσσει L   51 οὐδὲ
ΠVa²NL] εἰ δὲ CMaVa   ἐμεῖο] ἔμοιγε Caill.   52 νόοιο] νόμοιο L
55 ἄχρονος ΠL] ἄφθιτος Ω

single moment of death. If some primary necessity is supposed to hold in each case, this is nonsense. But if there is some superior necessity in common taking precedence over this necessity, then the signs in heaven are in conflict. Who then has combined them? For the one who bound them together has also by an act of will loosened the bonds. But if it is God who does this, what becomes of the first argument, which, I think, expelled him? Unless of course you will make God himself revolve under the influence of these stars of yours. But if there is no one in control, how will this world stay in existence? This is something I cannot see. I presume those who think this way would exclude God by such arguments. For either God directs or the stars do.

But this much I do know: it is God who steers the course of this universe, the Word of God guiding here and there what his designs have placed above and below. To the world above he has granted concord and a fixed course lasting firm for ever. To the lower world he has assigned a life of change which involves many varying forms. Some part of these he has revealed to us, the other he preserves in the hidden depths of his wisdom, willing to prove empty the boast of mortal man. Part of his design he has placed here and now, part will encounter later times. The farmer cuts all the crop in its season, as Christ is also the superlative judge of life. This then is my account, uninfluenced by the stars, going its own independent way.

Now you must tell me about ascendant signs and fine degrees, the circle of the Zodiac and the measurement of the path of heavenly bodies. Let us have no more, I beg you, of laws governing life or fear in the heart of sinners or hope which will come later to good men. For if it is the circle which carries all along, then I am whirled in its rotation and the circle will impose the very act of willing, nor is there any inclination on my part towards a better course of counsel and under-standing. Rather is it the orbit of a star which makes me roll upon my course.

Let us have no talk of that great glory of Christ, the star in the east giving its message to the Magi, leading them to the town where Christ shone forth, the timeless Son as child of a mortal. For this is not the kind of star dealt with by expounders of astrology, but rather a star without precedent which had never previously appeared, though foreseen in Hebrew scriptures, from which certain Chaldaeans had

Χαλδαίων προμαθόντες, ὅσοις βίος ἀστροπολεύειν,
μοῦνον ἀπὸ πλεόνων θηεύμενοι, οὓς ἐδόκευον,　　　　60
429Α　ἀρτιφαῆ τροχάοντα κατ᾽ ἠέρος ἀντολίηθεν
Ἑβραίων ἐπὶ γαῖαν, ἐτεκμήραντο ἄνακτα·
τῆμος ὅτ᾽ ἀστρολόγοισιν ὁμοῦ πέσε μήδεα τέχνης,
ἀστρολόγων τὸν ἄνακτα σὺν οὐρανίοισι σεβόντων.
ἀλλ᾽ οἱ μὲν περόωεν ἑὴν ὁδόν, ἥνπερ ἔταξε　　　　65
Χριστὸς ἄναξ, πυρόεντες, ἀείδρομοι, ἀστυφέλικτοι,
ἀπλανέες τε πλάνοι τε παλίμποροι, ὡς ἐνέπουσιν,
εἴτε τις ἄτροφός ἐστι πυρὸς φύσις, εἴτε τι σῶμα,
πέμπτον ὃ δὴ καλέουσι, περίδρομον οἶμον ἔχοντες·
ἡμεῖς δ᾽ ἡμετέρην ὁδὸν ἄνιμεν. ἐς λογικὴν γὰρ　　　70
σπεύδομεν, οὐρανίην τε φύσιν καὶ δέσμιον αἴης.

438Α　**ϛ΄. Περὶ λογικῶν φύσεων**

Οἵη δ᾽ ὑετίοιο κατ᾽ ἠέρος εὐδιόωντος
439Α　ἀντομένη νεφέεσσιν ἀποκρούστοις περιωγαῖς
ἀκτὶς ἠελίοιο πολύχροον ἶριν ἑλίσσει,
ἀμφὶ δέ μιν πάντη σελαγίζεται ἐγγύθεν αἰθὴρ
κύκλοισιν πυκινοῖσι καὶ ἔκτοθι λυομένοισι·　　　　5
τοίη καὶ φαέων πέλεται φύσις, ἀκροτάτοιο
φωτὸς ἀποστίλβοντος ἀεὶ νόας, ἥσσονας αὐγάς.
ἤτοι ὁ μὲν πηγὴ φαέων, φάος οὔτ᾽ ὀνομαστὸν
οὔθ᾽ ἑλετόν, φεῦγόν τε νόου τάχος ἐγγὺς ἰόντος,
αἰὲν ὑπεκπροθέων πάντων φρένας, ὥς κε πόθοισι　10
τεινώμεσθα πρὸς ὕψος ἀεὶ νέον, οἱ δέ τε φῶτα
δεύτερα ἐκ Τριάδος βασιλήιον εὖχος ἐχούσης,
ἄγγελοι αἰγλήεντες, ἀειδέες, οἵ ῥα θόωκον

---

61 ἠέρος] ἤρεος VlCo　　　65 περόωμεν Bill.　　　67 prius τε om.
MaN　　　παλίμποροι ΠΝL] παλίμπορον CMaVa　　68 ἄτροφος ΠCVa²ˢᵛΝᵞᵖL:
ἄτροπος MaNVa　　ἔστι ΠLVa²ᵘᵛ] εἰσι Ω　　69 οἶμον] οἷον L　　70 ἄνιμεν
SVa²Νᵞᵖ] ἄνομεν CuVlCoMb, ἄννομεν CMaVa, ἴομεν NL　　　ἐς] εἰς edd.
71 δέσμιοι S　　περὶ προνοίας λόγος ε΄ CuVl, subscriptionem omittunt ceteri
　6 tit. περὶ λογικῶν φύσεων MaVa, περὶ προνοίας N, περὶ λογικῶν φύσεων δι᾽ ἐπῶν
C, περὶ τῶν λογικῶν οὐσιῶν λόγος ϛ΄ CuVlCo, περὶ λογικῶν οὐσιῶν SMb, περὶ νοερῶν
οὐσιῶν λόγος ϛ΄ Bill., Ζ΄ Περὶ νοερῶν οὐσιῶν Caill.　　　　2 ἀντομένην SMb
5 ἔκτοθι ΩL] ἔκτοθε Π　　δυομένοισι L　　　7 αὐγὰς ΩL] αὐγαῖς Π
10 ὑπεκπροθέον Vl²　　11 τεινώμεσθα CuS²MbCNVaL, τεινώμεθα VlCoSMa

26

learnt in advance, men whose lives were given over to concern with the stars. They observed this star alone out of the many they kept watching, a star newly shining, coursing through the air from the east till it reached the country of the Hebrews and they judged it to betoken a king. It was at this very time that the cleverness of the astrologers' craft came crashing down, when astrologers joined heavenly beings in worshipping the King. But the stars pursue their own path which Christ the King has assigned to them, the fiery stars, constant in motion, immovably placed, fixed, wandering or, as they put it, retrograding, whether their nature is the self-nourishing one of fire or whether there is what is called a 'fifth body', stars following a circular course. We shall take our upward path. For we are hastening towards a rational and heavenly nature, albeit one now bound to earth.

6. On Rational Natures

EVEN as a sunbeam, travelling through rain-heavy, calm air, encountering clouds in its refracted, revolving movements, produces the many-coloured rainbow curve; everywhere around, the upper air gleams brightly with many circles dissolving towards the edges; such is the nature of lights also, the highest light always shining brightly upon minds which are lesser beams. There is one who is the source of lights, a light inexpressible, eluding capture, fleeing the speed of a pursuing mind whenever it approaches, for ever outstripping the minds of all, that we may be drawn by desires to a height which is ever new. There are others who are second lights after the Trinity which holds the royal pride of precedence, shining angels without visible

ἀμφὶ μέγαν βεβαῶτες, ἐπεὶ νόες εἰσὶν ἐλαφροί,
440A   πῦρ καὶ πνεύματα θεῖα δι᾿ ἠέρος ὦκα θέοντες   15
ἐσσυμένως μεγάλῃσιν ὑποδρήσσουσιν ἐφετμαῖς,
ἁπλοῖ τε νοεροί τε, διαυγέες, οὔτ᾿ ἀπὸ σαρκῶν
ἐρχόμενοι (σάρκες γὰρ ἐπεὶ πάγεν αὖθις ὀλοῦνται),
οὔτ᾿ ἐπὶ σάρκας ἰόντες, ὅπερ δ᾿ ἐγένοντο μένοντες.
ἤθελον εἰ καὶ πάμπαν ἀτειρέες· ἀλλ᾿ ἄνεχ᾿ ἵππον   20
καὶ μάλα θερμὸν ἐόντα, νόου ψαλίοισιν ἐέργων.
καί ῥ᾿ οἱ μὲν μεγάλοιο παραστάται εἰσὶ Θεοῖο,
οἱ δ᾿ ἄρα κόσμον ἅπαντα ἑαῖς κρατέουσιν ἀρωγαῖς,
ἄλλην ἄλλος ἔχοντες ἐπιστασίην παρ᾿ ἄνακτος,
ἄνδρας τε πτόλιάς τε καὶ ἔθνεα πάνθ᾿ ὁρόωντες,   25
καὶ λογικῶν θυέων ἐπιΐστορες ἡμερίοισι.
θυμέ, τί καὶ ῥέξεις; τρομέει λόγος οὐρανίοισι
441A   κάλλεσιν ἐμβεβαώς, ἀχλὺς δέ μοι ἀντεβόλησεν,
οὐδ᾿ ἔχω ἢ προτέρω θεῖναι λόγον ἢ ἀναδῦναι.
ὡς δ᾿ ὅτε τρηχαλέῳ ποταμῷ περάων τις ὁδίτης   30
ἐξαπίνης ἀνέπαλτο καὶ ἴσχεται ἱέμενός περ,
πολλὰ δέ οἱ κραδίη πορφύρεται ἀμφὶ ῥεέθρῳ·
χρειὼ θάρσος ἔπηξε, φόβος δ᾿ ἐπέδησεν ἐρωήν·
πολλάκι ταρσὸν ἄειρεν ἐφ᾿ ὕδατι, πολλάκι δ᾿ αὖτε
χάσσατο, μαρναμένων δέ, φόβον νίκησεν ἀνάγκη,   35
ὣς καὶ ἐμοὶ Θεότητος ἀειδέος ἆσσον ἰόντι,
τάρβος μὲν καθαροῖο παραστάτας ὑψιμέδοντος
θεῖναι ὑπ᾿ ἀμπλακίῃ, φωτὸς κεκορημένον εἶδος,
μή πως καὶ πλεόνεσσιν ὁδὸν κακίης στορέσαιμι,
τάρβος δ᾿ ἄτροπον ἐσθλὸν ἐμοῖς ἐπέεσσι χαράξαι,   40
442A   μέσφ᾿ ὅτε καὶ σκολιόν τιν᾿ ὁρῶ κακίης μεδέοντα.
οὔτε γὰρ ἦν ἀγαθοῖο, κακοῦ φύσιν ἄμμι φυτεῦσαι,
ἠὲ μόθον προφέρειν καὶ ἔχθεα οἷσι φίλοισιν,
οὔτε μὲν ἀντιθόωκον ἀναστῆναι κακότητα
ὕστατον, ἢ καὶ ἄναρχον ἔχειν φύσιν ὥσπερ ἄνακτα.   45
ὧδέ μοι ἀσχαλόωντι Θεὸς νόον ἔμβαλε τοῖον.
πρώτη μὲν Θεότητος ἁγνὴ φύσις ἄτροπος αἰεί,
ἀνθ᾿ ἑνὸς οὔ ποτε πολλά. τί γὰρ Θεότητος ἄρειον

---

15 πνεύματα] πνεῦμα L   18 ἐρχόμενοι ΠΝVa²ˢᵛ] ἀρχόμενοι CMaVaN²L
αὖθις] αὖτις L   20 εἰ καὶ] εἰπεῖν edd.   30 περάων Π] πελάων ΩL
33 ἔπειξε VaN, corr. N²   36 ἆσσον Ω] ἐγγὺς ΠL   39 πως] πω edd.
στορέσωμεν L   41 τιν᾿] θ᾿ Vl, τε Co   44 μὲν ΠCVa] μὴν MaN, τιν᾿ L
47 πρῶτον Caill.

28

form, moving around the mighty throne, as they are nimble intelligences. As fire and divine spirits they run swiftly through the air, eagerly obeying God's great behests, being simple, intellectual, radiant, emanating not from flesh (for flesh when once compacted is afterwards destroyed), nor again coming into relationship with flesh, but rather remaining in their original state. I might have wished them also quite unyielding. But restrain the horse, for all its impetuosity, checking it with the curb of the mind. Some are attendants of the mighty God, while others use their powers to maintain the whole world, holding from the sovereign's hand varying offices, overseeing men, cities, and all nations, acquainted with the sacrifices reasonable for mortals to make.

My heart, I ask what you will do now. Reason trembles to enter upon the beauties of the heavenly world. A mist has come upon me. I do not know whether to advance my speaking or to withdraw. I am like a traveller attempting to cross a raging stream who is suddenly borne upwards by the current and is held fast for all his eagerness to cross. His heart is in a great swirl because of the current. Necessity stiffens his courage, while fear constrains his urge to go on. Often he raises his foot upon the water and as often he falls back. With emotions in conflict, necessity overcomes fear. This is my case, as I come closer to the Godhead which lies beyond visible form. I fear to ascribe sin to the attendants of the pure one who rules on high, them who are a form of being sated with light, in case I should somehow pave a way to evil for still more beings. I am also afraid to set down in my account the idea of changeless good, as long as I see a crooked being holding sway in the realm of evil. For it was not the way of a good being to plant in us the nature of evil and to produce strife and hatred in creatures he loves. Nor would he later establish evil upon a rival throne nor allow it an eternal nature, as if it were sovereign. Such was the thought God planted firmly in my distressed mind.

The primary pure nature of Godhead is always unchangeable; there are never many realities in place of one. For what state is superior to

εἰς ὃ μετακλίνοιτο; τὸ δὲ πλέον ὄντος ἄλυξις.
δεύτερον ἀκροτάτοιο φάους μεγάλοι θεράποντες,   50
τόσσον πρωτοτύποιο καλοῦ πέλας ὀσσάτιόν περ
αἰθὴρ ἠελίοιο. τὸ δὲ τρίτον ἠέρες ἡμεῖς.

443ᴀ   εἰς πᾶν ἄτροπός ἐστι Θεοῦ φύσις· ἐς κακίην δὲ
δύστροπος ἀγγελική, καὶ τὸ τρίτον εὔτροπος ἡμεῖς,
ὅσσον τῆλε Θεοῖο, τόσον κακίῃ πελάοντες.   55
τοὔνεκεν ὁ πρώτιστος Ἑωσφόρος ὑψόσ᾽ ἀερθεὶς
(ἢ γὰρ δὴ μεγάλοιο Θεοῦ βασιληΐδα τιμὴν
ἤλπετο, κῦδος ἔχων περιώσιον) ὤλεσεν αἴγλην,
καὶ πέσεν ἐνθάδ᾽ ἄτιμος, ὅλον σκότος ἀντὶ Θεοῖο·
καὶ κοῦφός περ ἐὼν χθαμαλὴν ἐπὶ γαῖαν ὄλισθεν,   60
ἔνθεν ἀπεχθαίρει πινυτόφρονας, οὐρανίης δὲ
εἴργει πάντας ὁδοῖο, χολούμενος ἦν διὰ λώβην.
οὐδ᾽ ἐθέλει θεότητος, ὅθεν πέσεν, ἆσσον ἱκέσθαι
πλάσμα Θεοῦ· ξυνὴν γὰρ ἔχειν ἐπόθησε βροτοῖσιν
ἀμπλακίην σκοτίην τε· τὸ καὶ βάλεν ἐκ παραδείσου   65
444ᴀ   κύδεος ἱμείροντας ὁ βάσκανος ἰσοθέοιο.
ὣς ἄρ᾽ ὅγ᾽ οὐρανίης ἐξ ἄντυγος ἦλθεν ἀερθείς·
ἀλλ᾽ οὐ μοῦνος ὄλισθεν, ἐπεὶ δέ μιν ὤλεσεν ὕβρις,
κάππεσε σὺν πλεόνεσσιν, ὅσους κακίην ἐδίδαξεν
(ὡς στρατὸν ἐκ βασιλῆος ἀπορρήξας τις ἀλιτρός),   70
βασκανίῃ τε χοροῖο θεόφρονος ὑψιμέδοντος,
καὶ πλεόνεσσι κακοῖσιν ἔχων πόθον ἐμβασιλεύειν.
ἔνθεν ἄρ᾽ ἐβλάστησαν ἐπιχθόνιοι κακότητες,
δαίμονες ἀνδροφόνοιο κακοῦ βασιλῆος ὀπηδοί,
ἀδρανέα, σκιόεντα, δυσαντέα φάσματα νυκτός,   75
ψεῦσταί θ᾽ ὑβρισταί τε, διδάσκαλοι ἀμπλακιάων,
πλάγκται, ζωροπόται, φιλομειδέες, ἐγρεσίκωμοι,
χρησμολόγοι, λοξοί, φιλοδήριες, αἱματόεντες,
Ταρτάρεοι, μυχόεντες, ἀναιδέες, ἀρχιγόητες,
445ᴀ   ἐρχόμενοι καλέουσιν, ἀπεχθαίρουσι δ᾽ ἄγοντες·   80
νύξ, φάος, ὧς κεν ἕλωσιν, ἢ ἀμφαδὸν ἢ λοχόωντες.
τοίη μὲν κείνων στρατιή, τοῖος δέ τε ἀρχός,

50 μεγάλου L   51 τόσσων L   53 πᾶν ΩL] πάντ᾽ ΠΝ²   ἐς CΩL] εἰς Π
55 τόσσον CoS   κακίης edd.   65 τὸ καὶ βάλεν CMaNSMbL] τῷ καὶ βάλεν
CuVlCoS²Va, τῷ ἔκβαλεν Caill.   67 ὅγ᾽ om. L   69 ἐξεδίδαξεν
CMaVa   77 φιλομειδέες CuSMb] φιλομηδέες VlCo, φιλομειδεῖς CMaN,
φιλομηδεῖς Va, φολομηδέες ex φολομειδέες L   ἐγρεσίκωμοι ΠC] εὐρεσίκωμοι
MaNVaL, ἐγερσίκωμοι S²   80 ἄγοντες ΠΜaN] ἄγοντας CVa item NL
82 δέ τε ΠL] δὲ καὶ Ω

Godhead into which it might change? Anything added would be a departure from absolute being. Second come the great servants of the highest light, as close to the original good as the other is to the sun. We human beings are the third rank, the air. The nature of God is changeless in relation to all. Angelic nature is hard to change towards evil, whereas we who occupy third place are easily susceptible to change, in as much as our distance from God brings us close to evil. Thus it was that first of all Lucifer, raised on high (for he aspired to the royal honour of the mighty God, though already granted outstanding glory), lost his radiant splendour and fell to dishonour in this world, becoming total darkness, rather than God. Although of light composition, he yet slipped to this lower earth, from where he displays hatred against the wise and, fired by anger at his own ruin, tries to turn all others from the path which leads to heaven. He has no wish that the beings fashioned by God should approach the place from which he fell. He conceived a desire to share with mortals the darkness of his sin. Therefore, the envious one cast out of paradise also the beings who sought glory equal to God's.

Thus did Lucifer, originally exalted, descend from the vault of heaven. But he did not slip alone when his pride ruined him. In his crash he brought down the many companions he had schooled in evil (like some wicked man detaching an army from allegiance to the Emperor), through envy of the godly host which serves the God who rules on high, possessed by desire to lord it over a great number of evil beings. This is the origin of the evils which sprang up on this earth, demons, associates of the evil king who slays humanity, feeble, shadowy phantom shapes of the night, portending evil, liars, insolent wretches, teachers of error, deceivers, hard drinkers, lovers of foolish laughter, rousers of revelry, soothsayers, dealers in ambiguity, contentious, murderous, hellish beings skulking in dark corners, shameless, sorcerers, coming on summons, yet full of hatred for those they lead off. They take the forms of darkness or light at will, acting openly or lying in wait.

Such is their army, such their leader. Christ did not by any act of

31

Χριστὸς δ᾽ οὔτε μιν ἔσχεν ἀϊστώσας ἰότητι
ἢ καὶ κόσμον ἔτευξεν ὅλον· καὶ τόνδ᾽ ἂν ὄλεσσεν
αἶψ᾽ ἐθέλων (χαλεπὴ δὲ Θεοῦ κοτέοντος ἄλυξις)   85
οὐδὲ μὲν οὐδ᾽ ἀνέηκεν ἐλεύθερον ἐχθρὸν ἐμεῖο,
ἀλλὰ μέσον μεθέηκεν ὁμῶς ἀγαθῶν τε κακῶν τε,
δῶκε δ᾽ ἐπ᾽ ἀλλήλοισι κακὸν μόθον, ὡς ὁ μὲν αἰνὸν
αἶσχος ἔχῃ καὶ τῇδε, χερείονί περ πτολεμίζων,
οἱ δ᾽ ἀρετῇ μογέοντες ἑὸν κλέος αἰὲν ἔχωσιν,   90
ὡς χρυσὸς χοάνοισι καθαιρόμενοι βιότοιο
446ᴀ   ἢ τάχα κεν μετέπειτα δίκας τίσειεν ἀτειρής,
ὕλης δαπτομένης, ὅτε ἔμπυρός ἐστιν ἄμειψις,
πολλὰ πάροιθεν ἑοῖσιν ἐνὶ δρηστῆρσι δαμασθεὶς
τειρομένοις· τὸ γάρ ἐστι κακῶν γεννήτορι τίσις.   95
ταῦτα μὲν ἀγγελικῆς αἴγλης πέρι Πνεῦμ᾽ ἐδίδαξε
πρώτης θ᾽ ὑστατίης τε. μέτρον δέ τε κἀνθάδ᾽ ἀνεῦρον,
μέτρον δ᾽ αὖ Θεός ἐστιν· ὅσον πελάει τις ἄνακτι,
τοσσάτιον φάος ἐστίν, ὅσον φάος, εὖχος ὁμοῖον.

ζ΄. Περὶ ψυχῆς

Ψυχὴ δ᾽ ἐστὶν ἄημα Θεοῦ, καὶ μίξιν ἀνέτλη
οὐρανίη χθονίοιο, φάος σπήλυγγι καλυφθέν,
447ᴀ   ἀλλ᾽ ἔμπης θείη τε καὶ ἄφθιτος. οὐ γὰρ ἔοικεν
εἰκόνα τὴν μεγάλοιο Θεοῦ λύεσθαι ἀκόσμως,
ἑρπηστῆρσιν ὁμοῖα βοτοῖσί τε ἀφραδέεσσιν,   5
εἰ καί μιν θνητήν γε βιήσατο θεῖναι ἁμαρτάς.
οὔτε πυρὸς μαλεροῖο πέλει φύσις· οὐ γὰρ ἐοικὸς
δάπτον δαπτομένοιο πέλειν κέαρ· οὔτ᾽ ἀποπνεύστου
ἠέρος, ἢ πνευστοῖο καὶ οὔ ποτε ἱσταμένοιο·
οὐδὲ μὲν αἱματόεσσα χύσις διὰ σάρκα θέουσα·   10

87 με μέσον θέηκεν SMb (ἔθηκεν S)   89 τῆσδε L   πτολεμίζων CMaN]
πολεμίζων ΠVaL   93 δ᾽ ἁπτομένης C   ὅ τ᾽ ἔμπυρος L   95 κακῶν]
κακοῦ Co in ras., κακὸν L   97 ἀνεῦρον ΩL] ἀνεῦρε Π   98 ὅσον ΠCL]
ὅσσον MaNVa   περὶ τῶν νοερῶν οὐσιῶν καὶ ἀγγελικῶν λόγος ϛ΄ CuVl, τῶν et
λόγος ϛ΄ add. Cu², subscriptionem omittunt ceteri
    7 tit. περὶ ψυχῆς MaN (deest Va) SMb, περὶ ψυχῆς δι᾽ ἐπῶν C, περὶ ψυχῆς λόγος ζ΄
CuVlCo, Η΄ Περὶ ψυχῆς Caill.   5 ἑρπυστῆρσιν edd.   6 γε ΠNL] τε CN²ᵘᵛ,
τ᾽ ἐβιήσατο Ma   8 ἀπὸ πνευστοῦ NSMb

will hold him in destruction, that will by which he had also created the whole world. Had he willed it, he could have annihilated Lucifer immediately (for it is hard to escape the anger of God). Yet it is not that he left my enemy in total freedom. Rather did he dismiss him to a midpoint between good and evil men. He provoked a dreadful struggle between Lucifer and humanity, that he might incur further awful shame, inasmuch as he was warring against a weaker opponent, whereas his human adversaries, striving through the exercise of goodness, might gain their everlasting glory, being purified like gold in the melting-pots of life. Perhaps also might Lucifer, for all his stubborn resistance, hereafter pay his penalty, his substance consumed, when there is requital by fire, though indeed he was to a great degree subdued before in the persons of his harried minions. These truths the Spirit has taught me concerning the radiance of angels, whether in first or later state. I have discovered even in this world a standard, and that standard, moreover, is God. The closer a man comes to the King, the more he is light and represents a corresponding glory.

7. On the Soul

THE soul is a breath of God and, for all its heavenly form, it has endured mingling with that which is earthly, light hidden in a cave, yet divine and immortal. For it is not right for the image of the mighty God to be dissolved in an unbecoming way, as happens with reptiles and senseless beasts, though sin has tried its hardest to render this image mortal. Nor is the soul's nature that of raging fire. For it is not plausible to suppose that that which consumes should be the core of what is consumed. Nor is its nature that of air exhaled or breathed in, for ever unstable. Nor again is the soul a flow of blood coursing through the flesh, nor yet the harmony of bodily parts coming together

ἀλλ' οὐδ' ἁρμονίη τῶν σώματος εἰς ἓν ἰόντων.
οὐ γὰρ ἴη σαρκῶν τε καὶ εἴδεος ἀθανάτοιο
ἔστι φύσις. τί δὲ πλεῖον ἀρειοτέροισι κακίστων,
οὓς κρᾶσις ἠὲ κακοὺς τεκτήνατο ἠὲ φερίστους;
πῶς δ' οὐ καὶ ἀλόγοισι λόγου φύσις; ἁρμονίη γὰρ   15
448A   ἡ σαρκῶν βροτέων καὶ εἴδεός ἐστ' ἀλόγοισιν,
εὐκραέες δ' ἄρα πάντες ἀρείονες, ὡς ὅ γε μῦθος.
κεῖνοι μὲν δὴ τοῖα· τὸ δ' αἴτιον, ὧν ἀπεόντων
ψυχὴ σῶμα λέλοιπε, κέαρ τάδε μυθήσαντο.
φορβῇ δ' οὔ ποτέ σοι κέαρ ἔπλετο, ἧς δίχα θνητὸν   20
ζώειν πάμπαν ἄπιστον, ἐπεὶ σθένος ἐστὶν ἐδητύς.
οἶδα δὲ καὶ λόγον ἄλλον, ὃν οὔ ποτε δέξομ' ἔγωγε,
οὐδὲ γὰρ αὖ ξυνή τις ἐμοὶ καὶ πᾶσι μεριστὴ
ψυχὴ πλαζομένη τε δι' ἠέρος. ὧδ' ἂν ὁμοίη
πᾶσι πέλοι πνευστή τε καὶ ἔκπνοος· ἐν δ' ἄρα πᾶσι   25
πάντες, ὅσοι ζώουσι μεταπνείοντες, ἔκειντο
ἡ δὲ καὶ ἠέρος ἐστὶ χυτὴ φύσις ἄλλοτ' ἐν ἄλλοις.
449A   εἰ δὲ μένει, τί μὲν ἔσχε, τί δ' ἐν σπλάγχνοισι τεκούσης
ζωὸν ἔτ', εἰ κείνη με προέσπασεν ἐκτὸς ἐόντα;
εἰ δὲ πλειοτέρων τεκέων σύ γε μητέρα θείης,   30
ψυχαῖς δαπτομένῃσιν ἔτι πλεόνεσσι γέρηρας.
οὐ πινυτῶν ὅδε μῦθος, ἐτώσια παίγνια βίβλων,
οἵ καὶ σώματα πολλὰ βίοις προτέροισιν ὁμοῖα
ἐσθλοῖς ἠδὲ κακοῖς ψυχῇ δόσαν αἰὲν ἀμείβειν,
ἢ τιμὴν ἀρετῆς ἢ ἀμπλακίης τινὰ ποινήν·   35
εἵμασιν ὥς τινα φῶτα μετενδύοντες ἀκόσμως
ἠὲ μετεκδύοντες, ἐτώσια μοχθίζοντες,
Ἰξίονος κύκλον τιν' ἀλιτροτάτοιο φέροντες,
θῆρα, φυτόν, βροτόν, ὄρνιν, ὄφιν, κύνα, ἰχθὺν ἔτευξαν.
πολλάκι καὶ δὶς ἕκαστον, ἐπὴν τὸ δὲ κύκλος ἀνώγῃ.   40
450A   μέχρι τίνος; θηρὸς δὲ σοφοῦ λόγον οὔποτ' ὄπωπα,
οὐδὲ θάμνον λαλέουσαν. ἀεὶ λακέρυζα κορώνη,
αἰεὶ δ' ἰχθὺς ἄναυδος ὑγρὴν διανήχεται ἅλμην.
εἰ δὲ καὶ ὑστατίη ψυχῆς τίσις, ὡς ἐνέπουσι

---

16 τε καὶ ex codice Paris. gr. 991 corr. Caill.   ἀλόγοιο L Syr   19 τάδε
μυθήσαντο–20 κέαρ om. C   23 αὖ Ω] ἂν ΠL   24 ὡς δ' ἂν L
25 πέλοι Π] πέλει CMa, πέλε NL   27 εἰ δὲ N   28 μένη L μὲν Π] μιν
ΩL   30 θείης] θήσεις L   36 μετενδύοντες] κατενδύοντες edd.
37 μοχίζοντες L   38 κύκλον τιν' Ω] τινα κύκλον L Cosmas, κύκλοισιν Π
40 ἀνώγει L   42 οὐ θάμνον L   44 ψυχῆς] ψυχῇ L

34

to form a unity. For flesh does not have the same nature as an immortal form. But, we may ask, what raises the better above the worse, if it is only the process of mixing which has pieced together evil and superior people? Why do not irrational beasts also have rational nature? For the harmony which belongs to mortal flesh and form is present no less in irrational creatures. According to this account, those of good temperament make up all who are superior.

Such are the versions these people produce. They reason that what departs when life leaves the body is soul. Never was your soul a fodder without which it is incredible that a human being could live at all, as food is the source of his strength. I know of yet another account, though again not one I shall ever accept myself. For I could not believe in some common soul separated into parts for me and everyone else, a soul which wanders restlessly through the air. It would thus have to be the same for everyone, breathed in and out. All who live by the process of breathing would be present in all the others. It is the nature of air to flow at different times from one to another. But if the soul is permanent, what has it occupied, what is it that was already alive in my mother's womb, if she drew me in from outside? If you suppose a mother to have several children, the reward you give her is more souls in process of destruction. This is the fantasy of foolish men, the kind of trifling found in books. These people allot to the soul the fate of a constantly changing succession of bodies to correspond with their former lives, whether good or bad, either as a reward for virtue or as some form of punishment for wrong-doing. It was as if in an undignified way they were changing a man's clothes, exerting themselves pointlessly in putting them on and taking them off. Dragging in some wheel like the arch-sinner Ixion's, they have concocted tales about a wild beast, a plant, a mortal, a bird, a snake, a dog, and a fish. Often each state comes round twice, when the cycle requires it. How long can this go on? I have never heard the discourse of a wise beast nor listened to a bush talking. For ever the crow does nothing but caw and always in silence the fish swims through the flowing sea. But if there is a final punishment for the soul, as this view asserts, this circular

κεῖνοι, τῶν ὅδ᾽ ἐλιγμὸς ἐτώσιος. εἰ μὲν ἀσάρκου,   45
θαῦμα μέγ᾽. εἰ δ᾽ ἅμα σαρκί, τίν᾽ ἐκ πλεόνων πυρὶ δώσεις;
καὶ τόδε θαῦμα μέγιστον· ἐπεὶ πλεόνεσσιν ἔδησας
σώμασι καὶ πλεόνων με δαήμονα θήκατο δεσμός,
πῶς τόδε μοῦνον ἄλυξεν ἐμὴν φρένα, τίς με πάροιθεν
εἶχε δορή, τίς ἔπειτα, πόσοις θάνον; οὐ γὰρ ἐπλούτει   50
ψυχαῖς, ὡς θυλάκοισι, δέτης ἐμός. ἦ ἄρα μακρῆς
καὶ τόδ᾽ ἄλης, λήθην με παθεῖν προτέρης βιότητος.

451A   ἡμέτερον δ᾽ ἀΐοις ψυχῆς πέρι μῦθον ἄριστον,
ἔνθεν ἑλὼν, τέρψιν δὲ μικρὴν ἀναμίξομεν οἴμῃ.
ἣν ποτ᾽ ἔην ὅτε κόσμον ἐπήξατο Νοῦ Λόγος αἰπύς,   55
ἑσπόμενος μεγάλοιο νόῳ Πατρός, οὐ πρὶν ἐόντα.
εἶπεν ὅδ᾽, ἐκτετέλεστο ὅσον θέλεν. ὡς δὲ τὰ πάντα
κόσμος ἔην, γαίη τε καὶ οὐρανὸς ἠδὲ θάλασσα,
δίζετο καὶ σοφίης ἐπιίστορα μητρὸς ἁπάντων,
καὶ χθονίων βασιλῆα θεουδέα, καὶ τόδ᾽ ἔειπεν·   60
"ἤδη μὲν καθαροὶ καὶ ἀείζωοι θεράποντες
οὐρανὸν εὐρὺν ἔχουσιν ἁγνοὶ νόες, ἄγγελοι ἐσθλοί,
ὑμνοπόλοι μέλποντες ἐμὸν κλέος οὔποτε λῆγον·
γαῖα δ᾽ ἔτι ζώοισιν ἀγάλλεται ἀφραδέεσσι.
ξυνὸν δ᾽ ἀμφοτέρωθεν ἐμοὶ γένος εὔαδε πῆξαι   65
452A   θνητῶν τ᾽ ἀθανάτων τε νοήμονα φῶτα μεσηγύ,
τερπόμενόν τ᾽ ἔργοισιν ἐμοῖς καὶ ἐχέφρονα μύστην
οὐρανίων, γαίης τε μέγα κράτος, ἄγγελον ἄλλον
ἐκ χθονός, ὑμνητῆρα ἐμῶν μενέων τε νόου τε."
ὡς ἄρ᾽ ἔφη, καὶ μοῖραν ἑλὼν νεοπηγέος αἴης,   70
χείρεσιν ἀθανάτῃσιν ἐμὴν ἐστήσατο μορφήν,
τῇ δ᾽ ἄρ᾽ ἑῆς ζωῆς μοιρήσατο. ἐν γὰρ ἔηκε
πνεῦμα, τὸ δὴ θεότητος ἀειδέος ἐστὶν ἀπορρώξ.
ἐκ δὲ χοὸς πνοιῆς τε πάγην βροτὸς ἀθανάτοιο
εἰκών· ἦ γὰρ ἄνασσα νόου φύσις ἀμφοτέροισι.   75
τοὔνεκα καὶ βιότων τὸν μὲν στέργω διὰ γαῖαν,
τοῦ δ᾽ ἔρον ἐν στήθεσσιν ἔχω θείαν διὰ μοίρην.

45 ὅδ᾽ ἐλιγμὸς ΩL] ὅδ᾽ ἐλεγμὸς Π (ὁ διελεγμὸς S)   47 τόδε] τότε edd.
49 τόδε] τάδε L   51 μακρῆς ΠL] μακρᾶς Ω   53 ἡμέτερος L   ἀΐοις ΠL]
ἀΐοι τε Ω   ἄριστε L   55 ποτ᾽ ἔην Ω] ποτε ἦν ΠL   56 νόῳ πατρὸς ΠL]
πατρὸς νόῳ Ω   58 οὐρανὸς] οὐρανοὶ MaN^mg   60 τόδ᾽ ἔειπεν ΩL] τόδε
εἶπεν Π   64 δέ τοι MaN   65 ξυνὸν ex ξυνὸς L   67 τ᾽ ΠL] om. Ω
μύστην ex μῦθον L   71 χείρεσσιν L   76 βιότων ΩL] βίοτον Π
77 μοίρην ΩL] μοῖραν Π

motion of souls becomes pointless. Punishment of a soul devoid of flesh would be a great surprise. But if the soul is punished along with the flesh, then which of the several manifestations will you assign to the flames? Now this would be the most surprising point. Since you have bound me to a considerable number of bodies and this binding has given me awareness of a great many, why is it that the one thing that escapes my mind is consciousness of the skin in which I was previously contained, which comes next, in how many bodies have I died? For the power which binds me would seem not to have such a wealth of souls as of bags to put them in. It is surely a great aberration to suppose that I undergo forgetfulness of a previous life.

Now I want you, picking up at this point, to hear my excellent account of the soul, and I shall mix a little enjoyment with my poem. There was a point in time when the lofty Word of Mind, following the intention of the mighty Father, framed the structure of the world which before did not exist. He spoke, and his whole will was accomplished. When everything, earth, heaven, and sea, cohered to form the world, he sought a being to be acquainted with wisdom, mother of all that is, to be also a godlike ruler of earthly affairs, speaking these words: 'Already pure and eternal servants inhabit the broad heaven, holy minds, singing hymns they celebrate my unending glory. But earth as yet rejoices in nothing more than senseless creatures. It is my will to compact from both sides a race partaking alike of things mortal and immortal, a man endowed with a mind set between the two worlds, taking pleasure in my works, an intelligent initiate of the heavenly realm, a great power upon earth, another kind of angel coming from earth, to sing the praise of my mighty purposes and my Mind.' With these words he took a portion of the new-formed earth and established with his immortal hands my shape, bestowing upon it a share in his own life. He infused Spirit, which is a fragment of the Godhead without form. From dust and breath was formed the mortal image of the immortal. For it is the nature of mind to rule over both parts. Thus I have affection for one of the ways of life because of my earthly component, while I have in my heart a longing for the other life through the divine part in me.

ἥδε μὲν ἀρχεγόνοιο βροτοῦ δέσις. αὐτὰρ ἔπειτα
453A σῶμα μὲν ἐκ σαρκῶν, ψυχὴ δ᾽ ἐπιμίσγετ᾽ ἀΐστως,
ἔκτοθεν εἰσπίπτουσα πλάσει χόος. οἶδεν ὁ μίξας   80
πῶς πρῶτόν τ᾽ ἔπνευσε, καὶ εἰκόνα δήσατο γαίῃ
εἰ μὴ τόνδε λόγον τις, ἐμοῖς ἐπέεσσιν ἀρήγων,
θήσει θαρσαλέως τε, καὶ ἑσπόμενος πλεόνεσσιν·
ὡς καὶ σῶμα τὸ πρῶτον ἀπὸ χθονὸς ἄμμι κερασθὲν
ὕστερον ἀνδρομέη ῥύσις ἔπλετο, οὐδ᾽ ἀπολήγει   85
ἄλλοτε ἄλλον ἔχουσα βροτὸν πλαστῆς ἀπὸ ῥίζης·
καὶ ψυχή, πνευσθεῖσα Θεοῦ πάρα, κεῖθεν ἔπειτα
ἀνδρομέοισι τύποισι συνέρχεται ἀρτιγένεθλος,
σπέρματος ἐκ πρώτοιο μεριζομένη πλεόνεσσι,
θνητοῖς ἐν μελέεσσιν ἀεὶ μένον εἶδος ἔχουσα.   90
τοὔνεκεν ἡγεσίην νοερὴν λάχεν. ὡς δ᾽ ἐνὶ τυτθοῖς
πνεῦμα μέγα στεινόν τε καὶ ἔκτροπον ἴαχεν αὐλοῖς,
454A καὶ μάλα ἴδριος ἀνδρός, ἐπὴν δ᾽ ἐς χεῖρας ἴκωνται
εὐρύποροι, τημόσδε τελειοτέρην χέον ἠχήν,
ὣς ἥγ᾽ ἀδρανέεσσιν ἐν ἄψεσιν ἀδρανέουσα,   95
πηγνυμένοις συνέλαμψε, νόον δέ τε πάντ᾽ ἀνέφηνεν.
αὐτὰρ ἐπειδὴ τεῦξε νέον βροτὸν ἄφθιτος Υἱός,
ὄφρα κε κῦδος ἔχῃσι νέον καὶ γαῖαν ἀμείψας
ἤμασιν ὑστατίοισι Θεῷ Θεὸς ἔνθεν ὁδεύσῃ,
οὔτε μιν οὔτ᾽ ἀνέηκεν ἐλεύθερον, οὔτε τι πάμπαν   100
δήσατο· θεὶς δὲ νόμον τε φύσει καὶ ἐσθλὰ χαράξας
ἐν κραδίῃ, γυάλοισιν ἀειθαλέος παραδείσου
θῆκέ μιν ἀμφιτάλαντον, ὅπῃ ῥέψειε δοκεύων,
γυμνὸν ἄτερ κακίης τε καὶ εἴδεος ἀμφιθέτοιο.
ζωὴ δ᾽ οὐρανίη πέλεται παράδεισος ἔμοιγε.   105
τοῦ ῥά μιν ἐντὸς ἔθηκε λόγων δρηστῆρα γεωργόν.
455A οἷου μιν δ᾽ ἀπέεργε τελειοτέροιο φυτοῖο,
ἐσθλοῦ τ᾽ ἠδὲ κακοῖο διάκρισιν ἐντὸς ἔχοντος
τὴν τελέην. τελέη γὰρ ἀεξομένοισιν ἀρείων,
ἀλλ᾽ οὐκ ἀρχομένοισιν, ἐπεὶ τόσον ἐστὶ βαρεῖα   110
ὅσσον νηπιάχοισι τελειοτέρη τις ἐδωδή.
ἀλλ᾽ ἐπεὶ οὖν φθονεροῖο παλαίσμασιν ἀνδροφόνοιο,

---

78 δέσις] φύσις L   81 πρῶτόν τ᾽ Π] τὸ πρῶτον ΩL   83 θαρσαλέος Bill.
88 ἀρτιγένεθλος ΠL] αὐτογένεθλος Ω   91 νοερὴν] ἱερὴν L ἐνὶ ΠL] ἐν ΜαΝ,
δ᾽ ἐνὶ ex δὲ C   93 καὶ μάλα ΠL] χ᾽ ὢ μάλα Ω   εἰς S   96 ἐνέφηνεν
Bill.   97 τεῦξε νέον Ω] τεῦξεν ἐὸν ΠLN²   98 κε ΠL] καὶ Ω ἔχῃσιν ἐὸν
L   107 δ᾽ ἀπέεργε Ω] ἀπέεργε ΠL   112 παλαίσμασιν] κακόφρονος L

This is how the parts were bound together in the original mortal. But thereafter body comes directly from flesh, while the soul is mingled in an unseen way, falling from outside into the form originally moulded from dust. It is he that mingled the elements who knows how first he imparted breath and bound the image to earth, unless some one, seeking to assist my exposition, should boldly propose a view which he has derived from many others. This claims that, as the body first mixed for us from earth later became the means by which human life flows on, constantly producing a succession of mortals from the source originally formed, so also soul, breathed in by God, is thenceforward joined to human forms as a newborn entity, being distributed to many recipients from the first origin, maintaining a continuing form while enclosed in human frames. In this way it has been granted intellectual sovereignty. Just as a powerful breath sounds pinched and out of tune on a small flute, however skilled the player may be, yet when an instrument of wide bore comes into his hands it then pours out a more acceptable sound, in the same way the soul is weak when housed in weak limbs. When they achieve strength, the soul shines along with them and displays the whole intellect.

But when the eternal Son created mortal man as a new creature, in order that he might have a new glory and, exchanging earth, might in the last days travel hence as God to God, he did not send him out entirely free nor yet did he totally bind him. Placing law in his nature, writing good injunctions in his heart, the Son set man in the vales of an ever-flowering paradise, waiting to see how this being who wavered in the balance might incline, one who was naked and devoid of evil and deceptive appearance. The life of heaven is, I think, paradise. Here the Son set him as a labouring farmer to perform divine commands. He forbade him only the one more perfect tree which contained perfect discrimination between good and evil. For perfect judgement is truly valuable to those who are growing up, but not to those who are merely at the start of their lives. It would be harmful in the way in which more adult food is indigestible to infants. But when through the tricks of his murderous, envious

θηλυτέροιο λόγοιο παραιφασίῃσι πιθήσας,
γεύσατο μὲν καρποῖο προώριος ἡδυβόροιο,
δερματίνους δὲ χιτῶνας ἐφέσσατο σάρκα βαρεῖαν   115
νεκροφόρος (θανάτῳ γὰρ ἁμαρτάδα Χριστὸς ἔκερσεν),
ἦλθε μὲν ἄλσεος ἐκτὸς ἐπὶ χθόνα τῆς γένος ἦεν,
καὶ ζωὴν πολύμοχθον ἐδέξατο. τῷ δ᾽ ἄρ᾽ ἔθηκε
ζῆλον ἑὸν πυρόεντα φυτῷ κληῖδ᾽ ἐριτίμῳ,
456A   μή τις Ἀδάμ, ὁ πρόσθε, προώριος ἐντὸς ἵκηται   120
πρὶν πτόρθου γλυκεροῖο φυγεῖν δαπτρεῖαν ἐδωδήν,
καὶ ζωῆς πελάσειε φυτῷ κακός· ὡς δ᾽ ὑπ᾽ ἀήταις
χειμερίοις παλίνορσος ἁλίπλοος ἦλθεν ὀπίσσω,
αὖθις δ᾽ ἠὲ πνοιῇσιν ἐλαφροτέρῃσι πετάσσας
ἱστίον ἢ ἐρέτῃσι μόγῳ πλόον αὖθις ἄνυσσεν,   125
ὡς ἡμεῖς μεγάλοιο Θεοῦ ἀπὸ τῆλε πεσόντες,
ἔμπαλιν οὐκ ἀμογητὶ φίλον πλόον ἐκπερόωμεν.
τοίη πρωτογόνοιο νεόσπορος ἤλυθεν ἄτη
δειλοῖσιν μερόπεσσιν, ὅθεν στάχυς ἐβλάστησε.

ηʹ. Περὶ Διαθηκῶν καὶ Ἐπιφανείας Χριστοῦ

Δεῦρ᾽ ἄγε καὶ δισσοῖο νόμου λόγον ἐξερέεινε,
457A   ὅς τε παλαιότερος καὶ ὃς νέος ἐξεφαάνθη,
πρῶτα μὲν Ἑβραίοισιν, ἐπεὶ Θεὸν ὑψιμέδοντα
πρῶτοι καὶ νώσαντο, ἔπειτα δὲ πείρασιν αἴης.
οὐ γὰρ μαρναμένοισι Θεὸς βροτὸν ἡγεμονεύει   5
δόγμασιν, ὥς τις ἄϊδρις ἐών—Λόγος ἴδρις ἁπάντων—
οὐδὲ παλιμβούλοισιν, ὃ καὶ θνητοῖσιν ὄνειδος.
ἀλλ᾽ ὅδ᾽ ἐμῆς λόγος ἐστὶ Θεοῦ φιλέοντος ἀρωγῆς.

115 δὲ ΠL] τε Ω   116 ἔκερσεν] ἐκέρασσεν L, ἔκορσεν edd., ἔκερσεν S² ex emend.   120 ὁ πρόσθε] ὡς πρόσθε con. Bill.   121 φυγεῖν] φαγεῖν Bill.   δαπτρίαν CuVlS², δάπτραν SMb   123 ὀπίσω MaS   124 ἠὲ] ἢ L   πετάσσας CuVlCMaN²L] πετάσας NSMb   125 πλόον ΠL] πλέον Ω   αὖτις L   126 ἥμες] καὶ ἡμεῖς MaN   πεσόντες] πλέοντες Cu, codex Sirletanus   περὶ ψυχῆς λόγος εʹ CuVl, subscriptionem omittunt ceteri
8 tit. περὶ διαθηκῶν καὶ ἐπιφανείας Χριστοῦ λόγος ηʹ CuVl, περὶ διαθηκῶν MaNVaSMb, περὶ διαθηκῶν δι᾽ ἐπῶν C, Θʹ Περὶ Διαθηκῶν καὶ Ἐπιφανείας Χριστοῦ Caill., inscriptionem om. L   4 νώσαντο CMaNL] γνώσαντο ΠVa   μετέπειτα L   γαίης L   5 βροτῶν L   8 δ᾽ ἐμῆς Ω] γ᾽ ἐμῆς L, δ᾽ ἐμῆος CuVl, δ᾽ ἐμὸς S, γ᾽ ἐμὸς Mb

enemy and trusting in the beguilements of a woman's advice, he tasted prematurely the sweet-flavoured fruit and clothed his now heavy flesh in coats of skin, becoming his own corpse-bearer (for Christ cut short the course of sin by death), he emerged from the grove on to the earth from which he had sprung and received a life of heavy toil. For him Christ set up his fiery anger to bar him from the precious tree, in case any Adam (I mean the first Adam) should prematurely enter and, before coming to avoid the destructive food of the sweet branch, might approach the tree of life in a state of evil. As a seafarer, driven backwards by wintry squalls, returns to port, having again spread his sail to gentler breezes, or has completed his voyage by laborious rowing, so we who have fallen far from the mighty God complete our own return voyage only with some effort. Such is the woe newly sprung from our first parent which has come upon wretched mortals and from this source has sprouted the crop of evil.

8. On the Testaments and the Coming of Christ

COME then, enquire into the reason for the two Laws, the one older, the other revealed in its newness. At first law was for the Hebrews, as they were the first to recognize the God who rules on high, and later it extended to the ends of the earth. For God does not govern mortal man by decrees which are at variance, as if he did not know what he was doing, since the Word knows everything, nor does he rule by decrees betraying second thoughts which is a reproach even to mortals. But this is a loving God's way of helping me.

λυσσήεις ὅτε πρῶτον Ἀδὰμ βάλεν ἐκ παραδείσου,
κλέψας ἀνδροφόνοιο φυτοῦ δηλήμονι καρπῷ,   10
ὡς στρατὸν ἡγητῆρος ὀλωλότος ἔγχεϊ τύπτων,
δίζετο καὶ τεκέεσσι κακὸν καὶ κῆρα φυτεῦσαι,
ῥήξας δ᾽ οὐρανίοιο Θεοῦ κλεψίφρονι βουλῇ,
τρέψατο ὄσσε βροτοῖο πρὸς οὐρανὸν ἀστερόεντα,
458A κάλλεσι παμφανόωσι τεθηλότα, πρός τε θανόντων   15
μορφάς, ἃς ἐτύπωσε πόθος καὶ μῦθος ἔτισε,
πιστὸς ἐν οὐ ξείνοισι κακοῖς, ψεύστης ἀνέλεγκτος,
αἰὲν ἐπερχομένοισιν ἀεξόμενος λυκάβασιν.
Ἑβραίων ἱερῶν ὀλοὸν γένος οὐχ ὑποφήταις
εἴκον ὀδυρομένοισι, λιταζομένοισιν, ἄνακτος   20
μῆνιν ἀεὶ προφέρουσι, πάρος γε μὲν ὄλλυον αὐτούς.
οὐδὲ μὲν οὐ βασιλῆες ἐτάρβεον, ἀλλ᾽ ἄρα καὶ τῶν
οἱ πλέονες κακίους, οὐδ᾽ ἄλσεα πάμπαν ἔλειπον,
οὐδ᾽ ὀρέων κορυφὰς καὶ δαίμονας αἱματόεντας.
τοὔνεκα καὶ μεγάλοιο Θεοῦ ζηλήμονα μῆνιν   25
εἴρυσαν, ἐκ δ᾽ ἐτίναχθεν. ὁ δ᾽ ἀντεισῆλθον ἔγωγε
459A ἀτραπιτόν, ζήλοιο ποδηγεσίῃ σφίσιν ἕλκων,
πίστιν ἐς εὐσεβέα Χριστοῦ παλίνορσα φέρεσθαι,
ὀψὲ μεταστρεφθεῖσιν, ἐπὴν κορέσωνται ἀνίης,
βασκανίῃ λαοῖο νεήλυδος, ᾧ διάμειφθεν.   30
ἀλλὰ τὰ μὲν μετόπισθεν, οἱ δ᾽ ὡς νόμον εἶχον ἄτιμον,
ὑστάτιον τοιῆσδε βροτῶν γένος ἔμμορε τιμῆς,
νεύμασιν ἀθανάτοιο Πατρὸς καὶ ἔργμασι Παιδός·
Χριστὸς ὅσον βροτέῳ ἐνὶ σώματι κάτθετο μοίρης
οὐρανίης, λεύσσων κακίης ὕπο θυμοβόροιο   35
δαπτόμενον σκολιόν τε βροτῶν μεδέοντα δράκοντα,
ὥς κεν ἀναστήσειεν ἐὸν λάχος, οὐκ ἔτι νοῦσον
ἄλλοισιν ἐφέηκεν ἀρηγόσιν (οὐ γὰρ ἐπαρκὲς
τοῖς μεγάλοις παθέεσσι μικρὸν ἄκος), ἀλλὰ κενώσας
ὃν κλέος ἀθανάτοιο Θεοῦ Πατρὸς Υἱὸς ἀμήτωρ   40
460A αὐτὸς καὶ δίχα πατρὸς ἐμοὶ ξένος υἱὸς ἐφάνθη·
οὐ ξένος, ἐξ ἐμέθεν γὰρ ὅδ᾽ ἄμβροτος ἦλθε βροτωθεὶς

---

11 ἔγχει] αἴσχει S, ἔσχει Mb   14 τρέψατο ΠVa²] τρέψαστ᾽ L, τρέψας C,
τρέψατ᾽ N², στρέψατ᾽ MaVaN   17 ξένοισι Cu   19 ἱερὸν Cu, δ᾽ ἱερῶν Va
21 ὤλυον CuMb, ὤλλυον VISL, ὄλλυον Mb²   23 ἔλειπον ΠVa²] ἔλιπον Ω
26 δὲ τίναχθεν S edd.   post v. 30 dist. περὶ ἐπιφανείας Χριστοῦ δι᾽ ἐπῶν C, περὶ
ἐπιφανείας Χριστοῦ dist. NVa²ᵐᵍ   31 μετόπισθ᾽ Caill.   34 ὅσον] δ᾽ ὅσσον
Ma, ὅσσον N   βροτέων edd.   35 λεύσσων] λεύσων CMaVa, corr. Va²

42

When his madly raging enemy first drove Adam from paradise, cheating him by the destructive fruit of the tree which brought death to the human race, he acted as one who attempts to strike an army when its general has been killed by a spear, seeking to plant in Adam's descendants also evil and death. By violently dividing them from the God of heaven through his scheme to mislead their minds he turned the eyes of mortal beings to the starry heaven, rich in radiant objects of beauty, and directed them to the shapes of dead men to which their desire had given visible form and which fable had come to worship, a fable to be trusted only to bring evil on his own kind, a lying tale not likely to be refuted, growing in potency with the passing years. The race of holy Hebrews came to ruin by not submitting to prophets who lamented their fall, besought them to repent, and never ceased to proclaim the anger of the divine King. Indeed, they actually killed prophets. Not even their kings feared God, most of them worse than their people, refusing to abandon the groves and mountain tops and the demons demanding blood. Therefore they attracted the fierce anger of the mighty God and were displaced. As a Gentile I entered in their place on the path, drawing them on to feel jealousy, that they might be brought back and might come to accept the holy faith in Christ, at last reversing their course, when they had had their fill of distress, by experiencing envy of a newcomer people for which they had been exchanged.

But this belongs to a later time. When the Hebrews came to hold their Law in dishonour, the whole human race at last gained its share in this great honour, by the will of the eternal Father and the deeds of the Son. Christ, seeing that whatever heavenly portion he had deposited in the human body was being devoured by the evil which consumes the soul and seeing the crooked dragon ruling over human beings, in order to raise up his own possession, no longer left the care of human disease to other physicians. For it was insufficient to supply a trifling cure to major ills. Rather did he empty himself of the glory which he shares with the everlasting God, his Father, and as Son without a divine mother he was revealed to us, a strange kind of son born without a human father. Yet he was no stranger, since it was because of me that this immortal one came in mortal form, born through his

43

παρθενικῆς διὰ μητρός, ὅλον μ᾽ ὅλος ὄφρα σαώσῃ·
καὶ γὰρ ὅλος πέπτωκεν Ἀδὰμ διὰ γεῦσιν ἀλιτρήν.
τοὔνεκεν ἀνδρομέοισι καὶ οὐ βροτέοισι νόμοισι,   45
σεμνοῖς ἐν σπλάγχνοισιν ἀπειρογάμοιο γυναικὸς
σαρκωθεὶς (ὢ θάμβος ἀφαυροτάτοισιν ἄπιστον)
ἦλθε Θεὸς θνητός τε, φύσεις δύο εἰς ἓν ἀγείρας,
τὴν μὲν κευθομένην, τὴν δ᾽ ἀμφαδίην μερόπεσσιν,
ὧν Θεὸς ἡ μὲν ἔην, ἡ δ᾽ ὕστατον ἄμμιν ἐτύχθη.   50
εἷς Θεὸς ἀμφοτέρωθεν, ἐπεὶ θεότητι κερασθεὶς
καὶ βροτὸς ἐκ θεότητος ἄναξ καὶ Χριστὸς ὑπέστη·
ὣς κεν Ἀδὰμ νέος ἄλλος ἐπιχθονίοισι φαανθεὶς
τὸν πάρος ἐξακέσαιτο, πετάσματι δ᾽ ἀμφικαλυφθεὶς
461Α (οὐ γὰρ ἔην χωρητὸς ἐμοῖς παθέεσσι πελάσσαι),   55
καὶ πινυτὸν δοκέοντα ὄφιν σφήλειεν ἀέλπτως,
ὡς μὲν Ἀδὰμ πελάσοντα, Θεῷ δέ τε ἀντιάσοντα,
τῷ πέρι κάρτος ἔμελλεν ἑῆς ἄξειν κακότητος,
τρηχείην περὶ πέτραν ἀλίκτυπον ὥς τε θάλασσα.
ὡς ἐφάνη, γαίη δὲ καὶ οὐρανὸς ἀμφὶ γενέθλῃ   60
σείετο. οὐρανίη μὲν ὕμνους κατέπεμπε χορείη,
ἀστὴρ δ᾽ ἀντολίηθε Μάγοις ὁδὸν ἡγεμόνευε,
δωροφόροις λάτρισι νεηγενέος βασιλῆος.
οὗτος ἐμοῦ Χριστοῖο νέης λόγος ἐστὶ γενέθλης.
αἶσχος δ᾽ οὐδὲν ἔπεστι, ἐπεὶ μόνον αἶσχος ἁμαρτάς·   65
τῷ δ᾽ οὐκ αἶσχος ἔπεστιν, ἐπεὶ Λόγος αὐτὸν ἔπηξεν.
462Α οὐδὲ ῥύσει βροτέῃ βροτὸς ἔπλετο, ἐκ δ᾽ ἄρα σαρκός,
τὴν Πνεῦμ᾽ ἥγνισε πρόσθεν, ἀνυμφέα μητέρα κεδνήν,
αὐτοπαγὴς βροτὸς ἦλθε, καθήρατο δ᾽ εἵνεκ᾽ ἐμεῖο.
καὶ γὰρ πάνθ᾽ ὑπέδεκτο, νόμῳ θρεπτήρια τίνων,   70
ἢ καὶ χαζομένῳ πεμπτήρια, ὥσπερ ὀΐω.
αὐτὰρ ἐπεὶ μεγάλοιο φάους ἐριλαμπέϊ λύχνῳ
κηρυχθεὶς προθέοντι γόνου, προθέοντι δὲ μύθου,
Χριστὸν ἐμὸν βοόωντι Θεὸν μεσάτῃ ἐν ἐρήμῳ,
ἐξεφάνη, λαῶν μὲν ἔβη μέσος ὅς τ᾽ ἀπὸ τῆλε,   75
ὅς τε πέλας (ξυνὸς γὰρ ἐπ᾽ ἀμφοτέροις ἀκρόγωνος

44 γεύσιν] βρῶσιν NVa   48 φύσις edd.   50 ἄμμιν ΩL] ἡμῖν Π (ἡρμῖν
Mb)   55 πελάσσαι ΠC²N] πελάσαι CMaVaL   57 πελάσοντα ... ἀντι-
άσοντα Π] πελάσαντα ... ἀντιάσαντα ΩL   59 ἀλίκτυπον ΠL] ἀλίκτυπος Ω
θάλασσαν L   60 γαίη ΩL] γαία Π   δὲ] τε Caill.   γενέθλην VaL
61 οὐρανίη ... χορείη Bill.   κατέπεμπε Π] κατέπεμψε ΩL   64 ἐμοῦ ΩL] ἐμοὶ
Π   70 τίνων Π] τείνων ΩL   73 γόνου ... μύθου ΠL] γόνῳ ... μύθῳ Ω,
μόρῳ N^{mgγρ}   75 τῆλε CMaNL] τηλοῦ ΠVa

44

virgin mother, that in his wholeness he might save me wholly. For the whole of Adam had fallen through the sinful tasting of the fruit. For this reason, following laws at once human and alien to mortal men, he took flesh in the holy womb of a woman who had no knowledge of marriage (a miracle incredible to feeblest minds) and came as both God and mortal, bringing together into one entity two natures, the one concealed, the other obvious to human beings. The one nature was God, the other formed at the last for us. He is one God on both sides, since imbued with Godhead and as a mortal, it was out of Godhead that he existed as King and Christ. This came about that a new and different Adam appearing to the inhabitants of earth might heal the former Adam, being hidden by a veil (for because of my ills I was unable to approach), and that, against all expectations, he might overthrow the seemingly wise serpent. This creature, approaching, as he thought, Adam, but encountering also God, was planning to deploy his evil around him, as the sea surges round some jagged wave-beaten rock. When Christ appeared, earth and heaven were shaken because of his birth. A heavenly choir sent down hymns of praise, while a star from the east guided the Magi on their way, Magi bringing gifts to worship the new-born King. Here is my teaching about the novel birth of Christ. There is no shame involved, since sin alone is shameful. To him no shame attaches, as the Word formed him. Nor was he mortal with a mortal's transience, but came from flesh which the Spirit had previously made holy, that of a noble mother, unwedded, and as a self-formed mortal he came and underwent purification for my sake. For he undertook all obligations, paying to the Law a due return for his nurture, indeed, as I see it, a parting gift to the Law as it withdraws from the scene. But when he had been heralded by the brightly shining lamp of great light, the lamp which preceded him at his birth and preceded him in his teaching, proclaiming Christ my God in the midst of the wilderness, then was he fully revealed and went as intermediary to those peoples who were afar and those who were near, being a cornerstone joining both. He bestowed on mortals the twofold

λᾶας ἔην), δισσὸν δὲ καθάρσιον ὤπασε θνητοῖς
πνεύματος ἀενάοιο, τό μοι προτέρην ἐκάθηρε
σαρκογενῆ κακίην, καὶ αἵματος ἡμετέροιο.

463A   καὶ γὰρ ἐμόν, τὸ Χριστὸς ἐμὸς Θεὸς ἐξεκένωσε   80
ῥύσιον ἀρχεγόνων παθέων κόσμοιό τ᾽ ἄποινον.
εἰ μὲν δὴ μὴ τρεπτὸς ἔην βροτός, ἀλλ᾽ ἀδάμαστος,
οἵης καὶ μεγάλοιο Θεοῦ χρήϊζον ἐφετμῆς,
ἤ μ᾽ ἐκόμει τ᾽ ἐσάω τε καὶ ἐς μέγα κῦδος ἄεξε.
νῦν δ᾽ οὐ γάρ με θεὸν τεῦξεν Θεός, ἀλλά μ᾽ ἔπηξεν   85
ἀμφιρεπῆ κλιτόν τε, τὸ καὶ πλεόνεσσιν ἐρείδει,
τῶν ἓν καὶ λοετροῖο βροτοῖς χάρις. ὡς γὰρ ὄλεθρον
Ἑβραίων ποτὲ παῖδες ὑπέκφυγον αἵματι χριστῷ,
τὸ φλιὰς ἐκάθηρεν, ὅτ᾽ ὤλετο πρωτογένεθλος
Αἰγύπτου γενεὴ νυκτὶ μιῇ, ὣς καὶ ἔμοιγε   90
464A   σφρηγὶς ἀλεξικάκοιο Θεοῦ τόδε, νηπιάχοις μὲν
σφρηγίς, ἀεξομένοισι δ᾽ ἄκος καὶ σφρηγὶς ἀρίστη,
Χριστοῦ φωτοδόταο θεόρρυτος, ὥς κεν ἀλύξας
βένθος ἄχους καὶ βαιὸν ἀπ᾽ ἄχθεος αὐχέν᾽ ἀνασχὼν
πρὸς ζωὴν παλίνορσον ἄγω πόδα. καὶ γὰρ ὁδίτης   95
ἀμπνεύσας καμάτοιο, νεόσσυτα γούνατ᾽ ἀείρει.
ξυνὸς μὲν πάντεσσιν ἀήρ, ξυνὴ δέ τε γαῖα,
ξυνὸς δ᾽ οὐρανὸς εὐρύς, ἅ θ᾽ ὥρια κύκλος ἑλίσσει·
ξυνὸν δ᾽ ἀνθρώποισι σαόμβροτον ἔπλετο λουτρόν.

77 θνητοῖς] βροτοῖς Va, corr. Va²   78 ἀενάοιο CVlCuLVa²] ἀεννάοιο MaNVa,
ἐννάοιο SMb   post v. 81 dist. περὶ βαπτίσματος δι᾽ ἐπῶν C, περὶ βαπτίσματος
VaᵐᵍN, περὶ τοῦ θείου βαπτίσματος Ma²   83 χρήϊζεν L   84 ἐσάωσε edd.
86 πλεόνεσσι μ᾽ L   87 τῶν Ω] ὧν ΠL   88 χριστῷ Π Vaʸᵖ] ἀμνοῦ ΩL
89 φλιὰς] φλοιὰς Bill.   96 ἀείρει Ω (ἀείρεις C) L] ἐγείρει ΠVa²   97 δέ γε
γαῖα Bill.   98 ἄθ᾽ CuVlMa²Va] ἄτ᾽ CMaNL, ἅμα SMb   ὥρια κύκλος ἑλίσσει]
τ᾽ ἡελίῳ σελήνῃ τε SMbVaᵐᵍ   99 σαόβροτον edd.   περὶ ἐπιφανείας
Χριστοῦ Ἰησοῦ λόγος η΄ CuVl, subscriptionem omittunt ceteri

cleansing of the everlasting Spirit who purged for me the former evil born of flesh and made pure my human blood. For mine is the blood Christ my Lord poured out, a ransom for primal ills, a recompense for the world. If I had not been a mutable, mortal man, but of inflexible purpose, all I should have needed was the command of the great God to be caring for me, saving me, and exalting me to great honour.

But as it is, God did not create me a god, but formed me prone to incline either way, an unstable being, and for this reason he supports me by many means, one being the grace of baptism given to mortal men. For just as once the Hebrews escaped destruction by the anointing blood which purified their doorposts, at a time when a whole generation of first-born children in Egypt died in a single night, so what corresponds for me is the seal of the God who wards off evil, a seal indeed for infants, but for those who are coming to maturity a cure and, flowing from God, the finest seal of Christ the giver of light, so that, avoiding the depth of grief and raising my neck a little from its burden, I may walk the way of return to life. For I am like a traveller who regains breath after his exertions and picks up his step anew. Common to all is air and common the earth, common too is the broad heaven and the seasons which the circle of the years brings round in its course. Common to all mankind is the baptism which gives salvation to mortals.

COMMENTARY

Introduction

I. THE TITLE ΑΠΟΡΡΗΤΑ/ARCANA

It must be conceded that there is an ambiguous, not to say arbitrary, element in this title. It is that which was given by Billius to designate the eight hexameter poems appearing in the Maurist–Migne numbering as Carmm. I. 1 (= *Poemata Dogmatica*) 1–5, 7–9 (M. 37. 397A–429A, 438A–464A).[1] It is convenient to refer to the poems by this title, but only in a conventional way. Nicetas signified by Ἀπόρρητα a wider selection of poems, nor is there any reason to take the title back to Gregory himself.[2] Though the restriction to these poems is no more than useful, Ἀπόρρητα is a fitting title. For fundamental Christian truths are, in Greg.'s view, ultimately 'ineffable', only to be adumbrated in words, however elevated their intention.

II. CONTENT AND STRUCTURE

(a) Outline

Arc. *1: On First Principles*

1–24   *Introduction* to the eight poems as a whole.
        Not even angels may fully proclaim the Godhead. Yet the poet may humbly beg the Holy Spirit's inspiration in his task.

25–39   *Godhead*
        There is one eternal God, Father, Son, and Spirit.
        Heretics are warned to depart.

Arc. *2: On the Son*

1–56   *The reciprocal relation of Father and Son*

1–4   The poet must defend the Son, man's Saviour, against detractors.

5–39   The Father is above all. The Son is his image and glory, begotten outside time and without division of the Godhead.

---

[1] See further D. A. Sykes, 'The *Poemata Arcana* of St. Gregory Nazianzen', in *JTS*, NS 21 (1970), 32–42; I no longer hold that the 60 lines given in L are integral.

[2] Cf. F. Lefherz, *Studien zu Gregor von Nazianz* (Bonn, 1957), 177ff.

40–56   To lower the status of the Son to that of a creature is a dis-
service to the Father's Godhead. A creature-Son could not
effect man's salvation.

57–83   *The Incarnation*
The Son took a body without losing his Godhead. He was
God and man, bearing flesh, yet outside the body, victim and
priest. He died to raise the dead. Honour the human form the
more for his having taken it.

Arc. *3*: *On the Spirit*

1–9   Do not hesitate to honour the Spirit as God, distinguished
from the Son, but of equal honour.

10–23   In not explicitly stating the divinity of the Spirit the Scriptures
accommodate to the weakness of human understanding,
which had still to be convinced of the Son's divinity.

24–36   The Spirit, like the Father and the Son, has been revealed in
progressive stages.

37–53   The three Persons are undivided in Godhead, though distin-
guishable.

54–70   To say that the Son and the Spirit hold second place to the
Father does not imply division. Analogies like 'source, spring,
and river' are dismissed.

71–93   'Monas' and 'Trias' are not conflicting terms. In 'Trias' there
is no suggestion of tritheism.

Arc. *4*: *On the Universe*

1–23   False views of creation must be countered. The One God
created in an absolute sense: he did not use pre-existent
matter.

24–54   Manichaean views are to be totally rejected. God precedes
darkness and is its master. Man is composed of soul and body,
but is not a battle-ground of Manichaean light and darkness.
God is without beginning. Darkness has a beginning, for it is
merely absence of light. Evil is not an eternal principle but
springs from specific denial of good, through Satan in the fall.

55–74   Religious writers agree that the world was formed com-
paratively late in time by the Logos of God. Before the
creation of the world the Trinity was occupied in self-
contemplation and in contemplating the forms of the world to

be created. 'Past', 'present', and 'future' are eternally present to God: time makes no division.

75–92 The creation of angels and human beings. The divine Mind willed to create two orders of intelligent beings, angels and men. But to prevent them from overreaching themselves and seeking equality with God, they are kept at appropriate distances from the divine glory. Man, being of earth mixed with divinity, is farther away.

93–100 There are two created worlds, one heavenly, to which deified man may rise, the other mortal. But both alike are of divine creation.

Arc. 5: On Providence

1–52 It was Mind, not chance, which founded the world and set it on its course. (Examples follow the Cosmological Argument.) The founder of the world is the one who maintains it and continues to guide it. The claims of astrology are refuted. God controls the harmonious order of the universe and it will take many forms not yet revealed. God provides for freedom, not astral determination, which would obliterate moral distinctions.

53–71 The star seen by the Magi is quite different from the stars of the astrologers. This was a completely new star, unforeseen by astrology. Christ has allotted ways for both stars and men to follow. But they are independent of each other.

Arc. 6: On Rational Natures

1–26 As with the rainbow, so with rational beings: the degree of 'illumination' depends on closeness to the source of light, God. Angelic beings are closest, beings uncompounded with flesh, and they are assigned functions of authority over men and nations.

27–46 The mind hesitates to approach in contemplation pure Godhead and fears to suggest the fallibility of angelic beings. Yet Lucifer fell and it is he who is responsible for evil in men.

47–55 There are three grades: God, angels, and human beings. God is one and unchangeable. Angels suffer change, but only with difficulty. Man is very much subject to change.

56–66 When Lucifer fell, he had to be despatched far from the divine light. Sinking to earth, he shows hatred of man in seeking to prevent his rise to heaven. In his envy he drove him out of Paradise.

67–81 Lucifer brought with him in his fall other angels, and thus a great host of evils entered the world.

82–95 Christ did not destroy Lucifer outright, as he might have done. The devil has a place in the process of refining men. He may be punished through the defeat of his minions and in his own person.

96–99 This is the Spirit's teaching. Nearness to the divine light is the true standard of judgement.

Arc. 7: *On the Soul*

1–17 The soul is the breath of God and immortal. It is not to be equated with fire, air or blood, nor is it simply a bodily harmony.

18–31 The soul is not merely that which gives life to the body. The individual soul is not part of some common soul.

32–52 The doctrine of transmigration is rejected in all its forms. In which of the supposed successive bodily states would final punishment take place?

53–77 The true teaching about man is that he was formed by the Logos of the newly created earth and the spirit of God. He is the image of God, at the mid-point between heavenly beings and the animals, a being which loves the earthly state and is yet drawn to the heavenly.

78–96 Human bodies reproduce by natural processes, but souls are joined to bodies in a mysterious way, unless there is truth in the view many hold, that souls are transmitted from parent to child in a way similar to physical characteristics. It is true that a soul's activity may be affected by the state or quality of the body to which it is joined.

97–129 Adam was created to progress to divinity. He was not given absolute freedom nor yet was he completely restricted. In paradise he was forbidden only the tree reserved for his maturity. After the fall he became subject to death and was driven out, Paradise being sealed off to prevent later generations from entering upon an eternity of sin. Man is to return to Paradise, like a sailor to port after a stormy voyage.

Arc. *8: On the Testaments and the Coming of Christ*

1–8   The Old Covenant for the Jews and the New for the whole world are not at variance: both show God's care.

9–30   As a consequence of the sin of Adam, all kinds of false worship came into the world through the devil, with many forms of idolatry. Israel, too, defects, paying no heed to prophets and led by kings in apostasy. God's anger calls in the Gentiles to provoke the Hebrews to jealousy and repentance.

31–59 (But this anticipates.) Because the Hebrews dishonoured the Law the Incarnation was necessary. For Christ saw that the divine element in man was being destroyed. In his Incarnation he was completely human that he might completely save man, uniting divine and human natures, one hidden, one visible. The new Adam foiled the serpent.

60–71 Heaven and earth proclaimed the birth of Christ, a birth in no way shameful, being the work of the Word through the Spirit. Christ pays the Law a parting gift as it leaves, its work over.

72–96 The redemptive work of Christ was heralded by John the Baptist. Christ is the stone which joins Jew and Gentile. He brought twofold cleansing through baptism and the shedding of his blood, human blood shed to deliver man from ancient sin. As man was made mutable, he needs baptism as a means of grace, baptism which corresponds to the 'seal' of the Exodus.

97–99 Like the natural gifts of creation, baptism is common to all.

(b) Structure

What we call these poems is less important than recognizing that they fall into a clearly distinguishable group. This is Keydell's contention,[3] though he surely went too far in treating them as a single poem, rather that what Werhahn called 'eine Gedichtgruppe'.[4] While it is true that particular poems may give fairly complete treatments of individual subjects, there is to be found a coherently developing pattern of interrelated themes which build up in sequence. Poems on, say, 'The Soul' or 'The Son', in a sense detachable, fit also into a wider pattern.

[3] 'Ein dogmatisches Lehrgedicht Gregors von Nazianz', *BZ* 44 (1951), 315–21.
[4] *Stud. Patr.* 7 (= 'Dubia und Spuria bei Gregor von Nazianz', TU, 92; Berlin, 1966), 337–47 at 338.

I tried to show previously[5] how Greg. develops his ideas about human nature and the person and work of Christ. Though the early poems are primarily concerned with the Three Persons of the Trinity, the contrasts which they draw with divinity give clear indications of the writer's understanding of key characteristics of the human state: dependence, inability to comprehend fully, composite nature, need for redemption. The fourth poem gives man a place below the angels, in the fifth he is left poised between earth and heaven, while the next poem again sets him in third place below God and angels. When, therefore, we come to *Arc.* 7, a more formal approach through theories of the soul, we already have a background of thought which prepares us for the final introduction of Adam as a figure in history. Similarly, Greg. sets out his teaching on the person and work of Christ. The second poem is the formal treatment of the Son. But all the others are needed to complete our understanding. We are taken beyond the eternal relationship with the Father by considering his revelatory role as Logos, his place within the Trinity, his function in creation and providential ordering of the world. Again, we are prepared, this time for the incarnation and for exploration of the Lord's humanity, in a context of the developing theme of the human condition.

The poems then remain eight and distinct, yet by interrelating ideas in an allusive way Greg. is able to produce a more complex pattern, not that of a highly integrated structure but a more discursive assemblage of themes, as he comes at them from different directions.

This claim to integrity of the *Arcana* is broken by the Maurist–Migne insertion of the iambic poem 1. 1. 6 (M. 37. 430A–438A) between *Arc.* 5 and 6, for no better reason than similarity of subject-matter. Caillau, in 1840, was going against his better judgement (cf. n. reprinted in M. 37. 429A f.)

The unity of the poems would be broken in a different way if we were to the follow the suggestion of E. Dubedout.[6] He wanted to separate the 'theological' poems, *Arc.* 1–3, 6, and 8, from the 'philosophical', 7 and 9. He claimed that the latter were aimed at a wider audience, appealing rather to the pagans than being addressed to the heretics of the 'theological' verse. But this distinction is of doubtful value. Each category contains themes which belong to the other. Such a dichotomy would not have seemed natural to Greg. and his

---

[5] 'The *Poemata Arcana*', 34.
[6] *De D. Gregorii Nazianzeni carminibus* (Paris, 1901), 38 ff.

contemporaries. For the subjects of the 'philosophical' poems, though they approached from the side of pagan philosophy are, without exception, directly relevant to Christian theology. Moreover, the answers to the 'philosophical' questions are frequently in direct theological terms, as in *Arc.* 4, where it is the doctrine of the Fall which is invoked to account for the origin of evil (vv. 46–50). Greg. shows the close connection in his mind between philosophy and theology in *carm.* 1. 2. 10. 181 ff. (M. 37. 693 A f.), asking how people can be called σοφοί who do not recognize God, τὸ πάντων αἴτιον πρῶτον καλῶν (v. 184). He advances the claims on the philosopher's attention of the theologian's view on the worlds of ὁρώμενα and νοούμενα on providence, astrology, and mythology. Greg. would have ascribed to that conjoining of *divina* and *humana* which is found in various Stoic definitions of philosophy and would have given both a specifically Christian content. For the Stoics cf. e.g. Aët. *Plac.* 1. proem. 2 (*Dox.* 273. 11): θείων τε καὶ ἀνθρωπίνων ἐπιστήμη. Cic. *Tusc.* 4. 26. 57: 'rerum divinarum et humanarum scientiam cognitionemque quae cuiusque rei causa sit.' Greg.'s words in *or.* 30. 20 (p. 139. 13–14, M. 36. 129A) are close to Origen's in *Cels.* 3. 72 (p. 263. 25–6, M. 11. 1013C). It is precisely this interrelation of *divina* and *humana* which is found in the *Arcana*, interwoven in such a way as to make separation pointless.

III. PLACE IN LITERARY HISTORY

The question has several times been asked: 'What made Greg. turn to the writing of verse?' The question has been directed not so much to the elegiac and to some of the personal verse which, for all its repetitions, contains elements of spontaneity, as to the bulk of the personal poems and the corpus of theological and moral writings which make up books 1 and 2 in the Maurist order. Why, in particular, did he write the *Poemata Dogmatica* of which the *Arcana* form a part? Greg. himself gives a general answer to the question of his taking to verse composition. In *carm.* 2. 1. 33. 39 ff. (M. 37. 1331 A ff.) he explains his purposes: to benefit from the discipline verse imposes, to provide a τερπνὸν . . . φάρμακον for young readers, to rival pagan poets, to gain personal solace. We may further question whether there was any Christian tradition into which poems of this kind might be fitted.[7]

---

[7] Cf. 'The *Poemata Arcana*'.

There are of course hymns and straightforward versifications of scripture and Greg. shows how tedious mnemonic verse can be in his *carmm*. 1. 1. 13–27. There turns out to be little of significance in earlier Christian Greek verse, examples found in Irenaeus, Clement of Alexandria, and Methodius offering little parallel.[8] Yet, while there is no Christian tradition, there are superficial examples of influence on Greg. in the hexameter verse of the *Oracula Sibyllina*; but they are no more than verbal reminiscences and the same may be said for *metaphrases in Psalmos*, questionably attributed to Apollinarius.[9] There is no sign of real influence.

Yet while stressing the antiquity of the didactic tradition in which Gregory stands, we should not forget its continuance down to Greg.'s time. He should not be thought of as an antiquarian who was seized by an eccentric notion of writing 'Homeric' hexameters. Surely a misleading impression is given by what Brooks Otis has written of Greg. as a poet: 'In one sense he is mainly imitative, like the Renaissance or English public school Grecians, showing a clever mastery of a meter and diction to which he was not really native.'[10] There is undeniably a strong imitative element in Greg.'s verse but it is imitation of a kind long accepted as appropriate to this kind of verse. If one is going to write didactic, this is the way to do it. Whether within his chosen style Nazianzen writes well or badly is another issue. He may be a good poet, he may be a bad one. The examination of the question demands a detailed study in itself, a study which cannot be taken up at this point. But we cannot begin to form a literary estimate of Greg.'s didactic verse unless we accept it for what it is, a form of contemporary verse, and not a purely academic pastime. Of course the world of didactic is a somewhat esoteric one. The man who could follow Greg.'s orations might have to make some cultural adjustments if he was to feel at home with the *Arcana* and their like. But there is a clear link between the Greek of the reasonably well-educated church attender in Constantinople and the language of the didactic poems. The second is fundamentally the same language as the first. To compare Greek verses written by Italian- or English-speaking scholars is quite unhelpful. It is one thing to compose verses in a dead language but quite another to write for a select segment of one's contemporaries in a carefully stylized genre, using language which is accepted as a

---

[8] Refs. 'The *Poemata Arcana*', p. 38.
[9] For discussions of authorship see ibid. 39 n. 8.
[10] 'The Throne and the Mountain', *Classical Journal*, 56 (1961), 146–65 at 160.

form of their own tongue. A degree of dependence on the past is part of the didactic tradition. In drawing vocabulary, forms, and direct reminiscences from his predecessors, both remote and comparatively recent, Gregory is doing no more than showing that he understood the conventions of his chosen form.[11]

It is in the well-established line of Greek didactic verse that we may hope to find a relevant tradition. This was a genre which went back to Hesiod and extends to the second and third centuries AD in the works of Oppian and Ps.-Manetho. The range of acceptable content was very wide indeed: mythology, moral teaching, cosmology (in the Ionian philosophers of the sixth and fifth centuries BC), astrology, even hunting and fishing. All that Greg. needed to do was to appropriate the tradition and extend it to include specifically Christian tenets and interpretations of standard philosophical views. By this form of adaptation Greg. may be thought at once traditional and original.

Nor is it necessarily helpful to invoke prose models of invective and sermon when considering the *Arcana*.[12] Werhahn showed the clear influence of diatribe on the Σύγκρισις βίων,[13] where there is ample evidence from content and the method of presentation. But polemic as such was always at home in didactic verse and there is no need to look for a shadowy prose model. Again, the contention of Keydell[14] that there is direct dependence of large sections of the *Arcana* on the structure of the *Theological Orations*[15] is overstated. A detailed side-by-side comparison shows no more than is to be expected when similar subjects are being discussed. This in no way inhibits the verse from finding its own development.

IV. LITERARY CHARACTERISTICS

(a) Language

The poems are written in the accepted style of didactic, with epic vocabulary and grammar diversified by expressions drawn from other

---

[11] This paragraph has been reprinted from 'The *Poemata Arcana*', 40. Cf. further D. A. Sykes, 'Gregory Nazianzen as Didactic Poet', *Stud. Patr.* 16/2 (= TU 129; Berlin, 1985), 433–7.

[12] As done by R. Keydell, 'Die literarhistorische Stellung der Gedichte Gregors von Nazianz', *Atti dell'VIII Congresso internazionale di studi bizantini* (Rome, 1953), i. 134–43.

[13] *Gregorii Nazianzeni Σύγκρισις βίων* (Wiesbaden, 1953), 75 ff.

[14] See above, n. 4.

[15] M. 36. 12 ff.; ed. A. J. Mason (Cambridge, 1899), J. Barbel (Düsseldorf, 1963), P. Gallay with M. Jourjon (Paris, 1978), and F. W. Norris (Leiden, 1991).

INTRODUCTION

sources. Adaptation of epic meanings and the incorporation of expressions from totally different sources is central to didactic tradition.

Most of Greg.'s use of epic language is in the straightforward didactic line of quarrying for words not necessarily intended to recall their original provenance and not infrequently occurring in a quite different sense. (Examples of remoulding are noted in the commentary.) Epic language frequently provides the basic, unobtrusive pattern against which key ideas are made to stand out in words with a different origin.

Much of the interwoven language is drawn from other styles of Greek verse, as was normal didactic practice. As Aristotle had said, heroic verse appears able to assimilate with ease rare words and metaphors (*Po.* 1459^{b}34 ff.). It is not surprising that Greg. draws on tragedy. The elevation of moral tone and the concern for divine–human relationship would have a natural appeal. The reminiscences of Pindar convey a similar feeling. Again, traces of Callimachus carry with them a certain air of elevation.[16] Other didactic poets may influence the variegated style and there are similarities with poems in *Anthologia Graeca*.[17]

The style of the *Arcana* is further diversified by the inclusion of words which might appear to have a more natural habitat in prose. To find contrasted εἴδεα with ὕλη might seem to take us into the prose world of Aristotle, despite the epic ending of εἴδεα.[18] Yet it was good didactic practice to allow 'prose' words as technical terms of direct communication, in preference to cumbersome 'poetic' periphrases. When, for instance, Empedocles wanted to talk about a membrane he introduced into his verse the prose word μῆνιγξ.[19] A major source for Greg. is naturally the vocabulary of LXX and NT. Though derived from prose, many of these biblical words must have conveyed something of the elevation of language traditionally coming from poets.

Greg. himself seems responsible for certain new coinages, for some of which he is the only known authority. They are quite a marked feature of the poems.[20]

---

[16] Cf. e.g. *Arc.* 7. 123.
[17] There is a good survey of literary influences on Greg. in B. Wyss, *RAC*, xii (1983), 835–59, verse being considered at 839 ff.
[18] *Arc.* 4. 3.
[19] Fr. 84; *DK* i. 342.
[20] The opening words of *Arc.* 1. 34, κοσμοθέτης νωμεύς, are both coinages.

(b) Grammar

Accidence

The eclectic nature of the vocabulary is in some degree reflected in the accidence. Homeric forms are found side by side with those of later times, as is the case in earlier didactic writers.

Syntax

The feature of Greg.'s syntax which has attracted most attention is his use of the optative, in particular through the work of Sister R. de L. Henry.[21] She shows that this is a distinctive feature in his writing, in both prose and verse, reflecting developments of the literary side of a spoken language, rather than mere adhesion to earlier models. It is, however, notable that in the *Arcana* the majority of optatives are in line with epic patterns. This must surely be intentional, perhaps as an indication that Greg. thought this conformity marked the grand style of epic to which he aspired.

(c) Metre

As I have suggested,[22] one of the ways in which Greg. maintains a place in a developing, rather than a static, form of didactic verse is in his use of metre. While generally following Homeric quantities, he allows himself the kind of variation which later writers of epic verse thought acceptable, similar to those found, e.g., in the *Orphic Hymns*.[23] Sometimes, one suspects, he simply makes errors,[24] though there may have been a view that epic convention sanctioned quite arbitrary changes, as in Martial, *Epigr.* 9. 11. 15. In another way, however, it is clear that Greg. was not arbitrary, but following developing trends. The hexameter was not a static form. Later writers introduced variations, for example in allowing hiatus, and Greg.'s practice may be paralleled in Quintus and Apollinarius Metaphrastes.[25] Similarly, in caesura and diaeresis he follows later practices, as he does in his

---

[21] *The Late Greek Optative and its Use in the Writings of Gregory of Nazianzus* (Washington, 1943).

[22] 'The *Poemata Arcana* of St. Gregory Nazianzen: Some Literary Questions', *BZ* 72 (1979), 6–15 at 14–15.

[23] Cf. A. Wifstrand, *Von Kallimachos zu Nonnos* (Lund, 1933), for a full account of development.

[24] *Arc.* 1. 5, 5. 7.

[25] Cf. W. Quandt, *Orphei Hymni* (Berlin, 1955), 41*.

INTRODUCTION

placing of long monosyllables.[26] However, the most obvious technical change came in later writers in the proportion of dactyls and spondees in a line and here it may be claimed that Greg. has a recognizable place in a changing tradition. In Homer and Hesiod the proportion was $2\frac{1}{2}$: 1 dactyl to spondee. In Quintus it is $4\frac{1}{2}$: 1, in Nonnus $5\frac{1}{2}$: 1. The *Arcana* show the same proportion as Davids discovered in his examination of Greg.,[27] 5 : 1, some indication of awareness of literary movement.

(*d*) *Word-order*

Once again, we find that in framing word-patterns within a line Greg. shows an awareness of literary tradition.[28] A simple pattern is the chiastic

ἦν θύος, ἀρχιερεὺς δὲ· θυηπόλος, ἀλλὰ Θεός περ   (*Arc.* 2. 75),

where two syllables and four are balanced by four syllables and two: θύος ἀρχιερεὺς θυηπόλος Θεός. Variants occur, as in Nonnus,[29] in these lines:

```
    a   (c)      b            b            a
ἄχθος ἄγειν κραδίῃσιν ἀφαυροτάτοισιν ἄπιστον   (Arc. 3. 18)
    a        b      b    (c)       a
οἴης καὶ μεγάλοιο Θεοῦ χρήϊζον ἐφετμῆς   (Arc. 8. 83)
```

In a third example Gregory reinforces the *b* element:

```
    a       b        b          b        a
δαίμονες ἀνδροφόνοιο κακοῦ βασιλῆος ὀπηδοί   (Arc. 6. 74).
```

More often he adopts the simpler 'frame' pattern, e.g.:

```
    a                              a
ἐλπωρήν τ᾽ ἀγαθοῖσιν ἐς ὕστερον ἀντιόωσαν   (Arc. 5. 48).[30]
```

More characteristic of Gregory however is the pattern *aabb*, as in

```
    a        a    (c)      b       b
δερματίνους δὲ χιτῶνας ἐφέσσατο σάρκα βαρεῖαν   (Arc. 7. 115).[31]
```

[26] Cf. 'Some Literary Questions', 15.
[27] H. L. Davids, *De Gnomologieën van Sint Gregorius van Nazianze* (Amsterdam, 1940), 143 ff.   [28] 'Some Literary Questions', 11 ff.
[29] e.g. *D.* 15. 39. Cf. Wifstrand, *Von Kallimachos zu Nonnos*, 133 ff.
[30] Cf. *Arc.* 5. 64, 6. 66 and, for a variant, 7. 128.
[31] Cf. *Arc.* 1. 2, 4. 63, 4. 65, 8. 10, 8. 63.

62

Again, an alternating pattern is found in *Arc.* 2. 61

$$a \qquad b \qquad a \qquad b$$
ἰητὴρ δυσόδμοισιν ἐπικύψας παθέεσσιν

However, while clearly able to fit into an accepted style, Greg. is sparing in its uses, being equally capable of employing such devices as enjambement where they suit his subject-matter better.

(e) Imagery

I have suggested[32] that, whereas Greg. can be tasteless and tedious[33] elsewhere in his verse, the imagery of the *Arcana* is generally controlled and pointed. Similes in extended form, following some way behind Homer,[34] are quite frequent. Of the examples I chose, one or two may suffice here. Greg. draws on nature in the picture of a dangerous river crossing as an image of hazards of attempting to penetrate divine mysteries,[35] while human life is drawn in when the disaster experienced by the human race at the Fall is likened to the confusion of an army with the loss of its general.[36] Metaphors are less frequent[37] but, as in the words φάος σπήλυγγι καλυφθέν,[38] they may be striking. Here we have a summary of the relationship of body and soul which the rest of the poem fills out.

V. PLACE IN GREGORY'S LIFE AND THOUGHT[39]

The *Arcana*, I hope to show, may be placed early in the last decade of Greg.'s life, at the end of his brushes with activity within the structures

---

[32] 'Some Literary Questions', 7 ff.

[33] A justifiable contention of M. Pellegrino, *La poesia di S. Gregorio Nazianzeno* (Milan, 1932), 52 ff.

[34] Cf. V. A. Frangeskou, 'Gregory Nazianzen's Usage of the Homeric Simile', Ἑλληνικά (Thessaloniki), 36 (1985), 12–26.   [35] *Arc.* 6. 30 ff.

[36] *Arc.* 8. 11.   [37] 'Some Literary Questions', 10.   [38] *Arc.* 7. 2.

[39] Greg.'s own account, *De vita sua, carm.* 2. 1. 11 (M. 37. 1029A ff.) has been admirably edited by C. Jungck (Heidelberg, 1974). Full discussion of his life and work is found in C. Ullmann, *Gregorios von Nazianz, der Theologe* (Gotha, 1866); A. Benoît, *Saint Grégoire de Nazianze* (Marseille, 1876); P. Gallay, *La Vie de saint Grégoire de Nazianze* (Lyon, 1943); and J. Plagnieux, *Saint Grégoire de Nazianze Théologien* (Paris, 1951). Among shorter versions may be mentioned J. Mossay, *TRE* xiv. 164–73, and B. Wyss in *RAC* xii. 794–869 (both with full bibliographies); H. von Campenhausen, ET *The Fathers of the Greek Church* (London, 1963); R. Ruether, *Gregory of Nazianzus* (Oxford, 1969); F. Trisoglio, *San Gregorio di Nazianzo = Rivista lasalliana*, 40/1–4 (1973); R. P. C. Hanson, *The Search for the Christian Doctrine of God* (Edinburgh, 1988), 699 ff.; and F. W. Norris, *Faith Gives Fullness to Reasoning: The Five Theological Orations of Gregory Nazianzen* (Leiden, 1991).

of public church life. Born in 329 or 330, son of the elder Gregory, Bishop of Nazianzus, he benefited from an extended education, at home in Cappadocia at Caesarea, before going on to rhetorical education at Caesarea in Palestine. Following a period in Alexandria he reached Athens, at the age of about twenty, for a ten-year period of rhetoric and philosophy, a time notable for his association in personal friendship and intellectual debate with Basil and for the teaching he received from Prohaeresius, who was a Christian, and Himerius, who was not. Basil was the first to leave, around 356, to set up a monastic life, while Greg. delayed his return to Cappadocia by three years, undecided whether to follow a career of rhetoric or to turn to a life of asceticism and contemplation. What came initially was neither. In 361 his father felt that he needed his son's help and ordained him as a rather unwilling priest in the day-to-day ministry of his see. Basil, however, now Bishop of Caesarea, also believed that he needed his friend's help and persuaded him to be consecrated Bishop of Sasima, by Greg.'s account a wretched collection of hovels not worth calling a village,[40] in support of an episcopal dispute in which Basil was engaged. Greg. expressed his disappointment and disillusion by never visiting the place. He sought a solitary life for a time, before again giving way to persuasion, this time to return to Nazianzus to work with his father. Further pressure was put to him following the death of the elder Gregory in 374. He resisted and again chose seclusion, this time in Seleucia. The pattern of his life, however, was to be changed when it seemed possible that the Arian hold upon Constantinople might be broken following the death of the Emperor Valens. Greg. took on the modest task of preaching the Nicene faith in the tiny Anastasia but soon began to attract wide attention. The five Theological Orations[41] in 380 quickly became a talking point and an encouragement to Nicenes reviving with the support of the Emperor Theodosius. That revival was greatly assisted by his action in expelling Arians from the churches of Constantinople and summoning a Council to settle the doctrinal affairs of the church at large. Almost at once the Council recognized Greg.'s place in the Nicene cause by declaring him true Bishop of Constantinople, rather than Maximus, who had played a dubious power game there for several years. As if this were not prominence enough for a supposedly retiring man, on the death of Meletius he was appointed president of the Council, only to resign in an

[40] *Carm.* 2. 1. 11. 439 ff. (M. 37. 1059A ff.); *or.* 9–11 (M. 35. 817A ff.).
[41] See above, n. 15.

64

atmosphere of controversy and acrimony. He did not at once abandon episcopal activity, returning to Nazianzus until a regular successor could be found, none too soon for Greg.'s tired sensibilities. From 383 he lived in retirement till his death in 389 or 390.

This brief outline has referred only in passing to Greg.'s work as a writer. The orations with which we have to deal concern specifically controversial areas of doctrine (like the Theological Orations) but also high points in the church year, such as Epiphany or Easter, or they celebrate the lives of contemporaries like Athanasius or Basil. Others again refer to occasions in his career. In *or.* 2, for instance, he allows defence of his conduct in moving in and out of office to develop into a full treatment of the duties of priesthood.[42] Less creditably he attacked the Emperor Julian after his death.[43] Throughout most of this writing Greg. employs a widely allusive style and one which shows awareness of accepted literary standards.[44] His letters equally demonstrate an awareness of style which qualify them for publication.[45] They are not, however, set-pieces, but engage correspondents in a personal way, revealing many of the writer's interests and preoccupations, while individually approaching each reader. A small number fall outside the personal category, using the form to present the substance of doctrinal debate.[46] Finally, there is the verse, diverse in content and variously judged, largely emerging in the years of retirement.[47] Some consideration has been given above to the didactic genre into which the *Arcana* fit. But much of Greg.'s verse is rather different.

It is true that the remaining poems which are grouped as *Dogmatica*[48] contain, alongside tedious versified catalogues, several treatments of specifically theological subjects, like an iambic poem parallel in subject to *Arc.* 5[49] and one directed at Apollinarius.[50] There is in the hymns, however, a more personal element which is found extensively elsewhere, in, for instance, the series grouped as *De*

---

[42] M. 35. 408A ff.; ed. J. Bernardi (*SC* 247; Paris, 1978).

[43] *Orr.* 4–5 (M. 35. 532A ff.); ed. J. Bernardi (*SC* 309; Paris, 1983).

[44] Cf. D. A. Sykes, 'Gregory Nazianzen as Didactic Poet', 433 ff.; id. 'The Bible and Greek Classics in Gregory Nazianzen's Verse', *Stud. Patr.* 17/3 (1982), pp. 1127–30.

[45] M. 37. 21A ff.; ed. P. Gallay in Budé edn. (Paris, 1964–7) and GCS 53 (Berlin, 1969).

[46] *Epp.* 101–2 (M. 37. 176A ff.); ed. P. Gallay with M. Jourjon (SC 208; Paris, 1974).

[47] M. 37. 197A ff., 38. 11A ff. Cf. M. Geerard, *Clavis Patrum Graecorum*, ii (Turnhout, 1974, nos. 3101–25; Wyss, *RAC* xii (1983), 808 ff. Studies of Greg.'s verse include M. Pellegrino, *La poesia di S. Gregorio Nazianzeno*, R. Keydell, 'Die literarhistorische Stellung der Gedichte Gregors von Nazianz', F. Trisoglio, *San Gregorio di Nazianzo*, ch. 14.

[48] M. 37. 397A–522A.

[49] 1. 1. 6 (430A ff.).

[50] 1. 1. 10 (464A ff.).

seipso.[51] While some aim at relative objectivity in giving an account of parts of Greg.'s life, notably in the long poems *De vita sua*[52] and *De seipso et de episcopis*,[53] others express feelings of fervour, aspiration, or despondency.[54] Much of the remaining verse fits into the pattern of the more objective treatment. The *Poemata Moralia*[55] cover a range of standard subjects like σωφροσύνη[56] and ἀρετή[57] or analyse the evils of anger,[58] while others look at the place of virginity in the life of the church[59] and, outstandingly in *Comparatio vitarum*,[60] the 'life of the world' and 'the life of the Spirit'. The *Poemata quae spectant ad alios*[61] include pieces written in the character of others, like sons putting their viewpoint to their fathers. Finally ascribed to Greg. are a number of epigrams and epitaphs which cover the conventional range of such verse while revealing something of his personality.[62]

Much of this verse production is hard to date and is often ascribed in a general way to the last decade of Greg.'s life. Can we be more specific with the *Arcana*? I have argued that a reasonable approximation is possible.[63] T. Sinko[64] placed them after 380 and this is an acceptable starting point if it is agreed that 1. 14–15, on how the Logos 'drove from our assembly very evil men with hearts set against God', refer to the action of Theodosius in expelling the Arians from the episcopal church of Constantinople in order to install Greg. under military protection (27 Nov. 380). A similar idea is found in *Carm*. ii. 1. 11. 1305 ff. (M. 37. 1119A ff.), where Christ is held to be the direct participant in the conquest of heresy which made Greg. bishop. I further suggested that it would be unwise to put much weight as evidence on the forthright declaration of the Holy Spirit's divinity. Greg. may well have been cautious about expressing this conviction as explicitly in a sermon before the spring of 380, but a poem could well have enunciated a view he had held privately as early as 372–3.[65] Again, anti-Manichaean legislation in the early 380s might have affected the

---

[51] M. 37. 969A–1452A.   [52] 2. 1. 11 (M. 37. 1029A ff.).   [53] 2. 1. 12 (1166A ff.).

[54] Examples are 2. 1. 22 (1281A f.), 2. 1. 38 (1325A ff.); 2. 1. 45 (1353A ff.).

[55] *Carm*. 1. 2 (M. 37. 521A–968A. Cf. D. A. Sykes, 'Gregory Nazianzen, Poet of the Moral Life', *Stud. Patr*. 22 (1989), 69–73.

[56] 1. 2. 6 (643A ff.).   [57] 1. 2. 9 (667A ff.), 10 (680A ff.).

[58] 1. 2. 25 (813A ff.).   [59] 1. 2. 1–7 (521A ff.).

[60] 1. 2. 8 (649A ff.). It is well edited by H. M. Werhahn.

[61] *Carm*. 2. 2 (1451A–1600A). Cf. D. A. Sykes, 'Reflections on Gregory Nazianzen's *poemata quae spectant ad alios*'. *Stud. Patr*. 18/3 (1989), 551–6.

[62] M. 38. 11A–130A.   [63] 'The *Poemata Arcana*', 36 ff.

[64] 'Chronologia poezji św. Grzegorza z Nazjanzu', *Sprawozdania z Czynności i Posiedzeń Polskiej Akademii Umiejętności w Krakowie*, 48/5 (1947), 147–56 at 151.

[65] *Ep*. 58 (M. 37. 116C f.).

fourth poem, but earlier laws may be cited.[66] It is perhaps Greg.'s approach to Apollinarius which allows closer approximation. Between 379 and 382 he moved from characterizing his difference from Apollinarius as ζυγομαχίαν ἀδελφικήν[67] to the hostility of *Ep*. 101 (M. 37. 176 A ff.). The theology of the *Arcana* offers no encouragement to Apollinarian views, but it is Eunomius, not Apollinarius, who is attacked in the second poem. (Cf. the introduction to that poem.) There is a clear contrast between the language of *Arc*. 2 and the precise anti-Apollinarian polemic of *Carm*. 1. 1. 10. 464A ff., with its expressions like ἥμισυς βροτός and ἡ σὰρξ ἄνους.[68] This gives reason for suggesting that the *Arcana* might have been written in 381 or early 382, before Greg. found it necessary to attack Apollinarius in hard-hitting precise terms.

VI. THE THOUGHT OF THE POEMS

A primary question in Greg.'s mind, one which runs through the poems, concerns the status of his *knowledge*. How is he to have confidence in the truth of the teachings he is putting forward? He has no doubt that there is a fundamental difference between divine and human knowledge, a gulf which separates the infinite great Mind, the 'uncontainable', from human comprehension. Even if angels know more, they too are subject to limits. Knowledge of the Godhead exists only internally, within the complete and ever-present contemplation of the Three Persons. Human knowledge, by contrast, exists within a created mind and is derivative, limited, and subject to error. These natural features are subject to further erosion through the effects of the fall of Adam when the deceptions of Lucifer and his minions proliferate. Yet there is a strong positive strain. Human beings are distinct from God by their created status, but the purpose of that creation is beings who may share divine rationality, cognate if far from equal in wisdom, made in an image which is marred by the fall but not destroyed. The possibility of knowledge of God is God's choice and the intention is never rescinded that men and women should grow up

---

[66] e.g. *Cod. Theod.* 16. 5. 3 (372).

[67] *Or*. 22. 13 (M. 35. 1145A). The *SC* ed. (no. 270; Paris, 1980) by J. Mossay with G. Lafontaine questions (pp. 201 ff.) the ascription to 379, arguing that the oration could be as late as 381. This, however, would still place the 'brotherly internal strife' before Greg.'s marked hardening of attitude.

[68] *Carm*. 1. 1. 10. 35, 47 (M. 37. 468A).

into understanding of the divine. The means of reaching this know-
ledge are of God's choosing, stages of revelation accommodated to
human understanding. Real knowledge may be imparted through the
law and the prophets. Supremely it comes in the Incarnation, yet in
such a way that there remain stages of comprehension to develop in
the life of the Church. Only when the Son's divinity is fully recognized
can Christians think seriously of the Godhead of the Spirit. Greg.
believes that a degree of true knowledge is possible because God wills
it and thus what is designedly limited is still to be highly valued. There
is always the element of hazard, as the human mind is prone to error,
whether it be from pagan thought, heretical distortion, or acqui-
escence in false analogy. The Spirit however works truly within the
Church to give correct understanding to those who meet the condi-
tions of humility and purification and what unfolds is authentic. It is
this conviction which allows Greg. to feel assurance for the genuine-
ness of his teaching. Ultimate knowledge is not granted to the human
mind, but the measure of truth is none the less real.[69]

When therefore Greg. propounds his doctrines of *Godhead* he
writes with commitment and belief in his insight. Yet he is careful to
distinguish what is true for human understanding from the ultimate
truth comprehensible to the divine Persons alone. The Trinity exists
in indivisible unity. The Persons may be expressed as 'three lights',
but not three Gods, for that is to misunderstand a true distinctness.
The unity is one of equality in rule, understanding, power, and will,
being infinite, unoriginate, a stable harmony in which each Person is
God. This is a harmony of purpose which leaves no place for chance
and no place for rival power, the ultimate standard by which all else is
judged. Essential to the goodness of God is the creation of upper and
lower worlds, for this is a sharing designed to bring happiness and
fulfilment through the unbroken manifestation of providential care.
All that has come from nothing depends upon the creator. The Trinity
has chosen modes of revelation in human history to take human minds
to the limits of their powers of comprehension and Greg. is prepared
to offer analogy and to seek confirmation of Trinity in the revealed
practice of threefold Baptism.[70]

In writing specifically of the *Father* Greg. stresses that he is utterly
without beginning, eternal Mind, the 'root', the original of whom the

[69] Among the main passages are 1. 1–24, 3. 10–23, 5. 1–33, 6. 27–46, 7. 55–77, 100–4, 8.
72–84.
[70] Teaching on the subject infiltrates the whole sequence, as will be seen from II(*a*).

Son is the image, while the Father remains 'timeless beginning'. In the economy of revelation his Godhead is the first to be recognized. In the Incarnation he remains unaffected in any corporeal sense as would result from human generation. Father and Son share in equal honour, while only within Godhead is the relationship understood.[71]

Over the eight poems Greg. is careful to build up a cumulative teaching on the person and work of the *Son*.[72] A fourfold division may be imposed for summary review: essential being within the Godhead, activity before the Incarnation, the Incarnation itself, and the work of redemption. The Incarnation is given careful preparation in the presentation of the timeless relationship of Father and Son. He is alone Son, the Word, the Image, unique, equal, timeless, the Father's understanding, sprung from the Father, dependent, yet not subordinate. He is sprung from the Father as everlasting light without division from the unoriginate root, united in generation quite unlike human generation, united in nature and manifest in a way known only to Father and Son. Greg. is no less eager to show the activity of God the Son beyond the Godhead. He is central to the foundation and providential government of the universe. In the fullness of Godhead he takes part in creation from nothing, assigning paths to the stars, and having a precise function in revelation. He it is who enunciates the divine purpose in proceeding from the creation of the world of heavenly beings to the creation of human beings who can participate on earth in the divine purpose. Yet it is part of that divine purpose that an understanding of the Son's Godhead should come as second phase of revelation to the human mind. The Son's relation to man, as distinct from a full knowledge of the Son, is emphasized in the account of the Fall. The Son had placed human beings in paradise and on their expulsion showed care for their ultimate return. Greg.'s teaching on the Incarnation takes up the relationship to the Father and to humanity. The human birth in no way divides the Son from his Father, as he does not emerge as a creature. While emptying himself of the glory he shares with the Father, the Son retains the essential Godhead which gives him the power to act as the supreme physician. Mortal characteristics do not diminish Godhead, rather are they glorified by it. The birth of Christ involves no shame, no sinking into mortal transience, for he is Word self-formed of flesh made holy by the Spirit, undergoing purification solely on man's behalf and fulfilling human obligations. Heaven and earth witness to the glory of the Birth. Greg. tries

---

[71] Cf. especially 1. 25–39, 2. 5 ff.   [72] Cf. 'The *Poemata Arcana*', 34.

hard to hold together in unity the two natures, presented as they are in 'double column' contrasts at some length. The sharing of human weakness and dependence is balanced by the divine strength and governance: it is the High Priest who offers himself as sacrifice, the one who penetrates the world of the dead, who raises from the dead. The one Person is revealed in two natures, yet the revelation may come with equal force to the human observer who finds it difficult to go beyond the surface characteristics which he shares to the full power of divinity which may remain concealed. But the reality remains of 'one God on two sides' and this is central to Greg.'s understanding of the atoning purpose of the Incarnation. Only the full power of Godhead could be adequate and only the full participation in the whole Adam could have meaning. Throughout the range of images that conviction recurs. There is equipoise of natures in the physician who heals the whole Adam, in the overthrow of the serpent in which God is encountered in place of the supposed Adam, in divine cleansing through human blood, in the language of ransom and recompense. Victory is won, but not the defeat of Lucifer through an arbitrary exercise of divine power from which the human nature would be excluded. It is the whole Christ, God from eternity, fully revealed in the economy of revelation as the corner-stone to join Israel and Gentiles.[73]

Into this same economy of revelation comes the *Spirit*, later in recognition by human minds but equal in essence within the indivisible Godhead, uncreated, self-determined, acknowledged in his divinity by the heavenly choir. He is to be distinguished from the Son in a way at which analogy may hint, as Greg. suggests that of Adam, Eve, and Seth. Though hesitation was understandable in Christian past, that time is over. The acceptance of Christ's divinity makes possible the emergence of further truth: the Spirit need no longer remain 'half-hidden' but must be proclaimed as God. The evidence of Scripture converges on this point, as does the threefold formula of baptism. The functions of the Spirit become clear: to reveal God in unity and Trinity, to infuse divine life in human beings through knowledge and purification, especially through the cleansing of baptism. In contrast to these habitual manifestations of life-giving power is the specific and unrepeatable action within the Incarnation pattern, where the Spirit makes pure the body of the Virgin who is to give birth to Christ. Again it is he who brings purity to the human blood of Christ poured in

[73] Again II(*a*) will show the development.

sacrifice. Every function coheres with divine being, to the point where the Spirit may be said to bring deification in baptism.[74]

Great as is Greg.'s concern for deepening an understanding of the nature of the divine Being, he finds an inevitable correlative in a doctrine of *creation*. For in positive terms it derives directly from his conception of Godhead. God alone enjoys absolute existence, but his will in creation gives value to what he has made, yet without affecting his irreducible separateness. Creation involves Godhead through will and the generous love of sharing existence, but always remains outside, above. All creation is the result of timeless contemplation in which everything which in human terms would fall into categories of past, present, and future is constantly present to the divine Mind. The Three exist eternally and bring into existence two worlds. The first is more closely cognate with their being, an immaterial world 'above', stable and harmonious (or at least relatively so), consisting of spiritual beings, angelic, a 'second light' after the Trinity. The second world below is later in creation and, involving as it does matter and existing within time, is subject to change. It comes out of nothing and is dependent on its divine creator both for its origin and for its continued existence. All this Greg. finds it necessary to state in opposition to views of a very different kind. A fundamentally irreconcilable approach attributes the world we see to causeless chance. A dualism on Manichaean lines which assigns matter to negativity and evil is no more acceptable. Nor will Greg. give any credence to a creator who shares existence with forms and matter; his creator is absolute. The forms of the world to be created exist in his mind and he brings things into being by simultaneous combination with matter produced from nothing, all planned and cohering. Nor again has Greg. anything but incredulity for the notion that the world itself is eternally existent. Its being depends on benevolent action outside itself, expressed through the divine will.[75]

A major interest of the poems is the creation and history of *humanity*.[76] We find discussion of theory, the nature of man over against God and angels, activity within the temporal processes of history and the final destiny of human beings. Central to Greg.'s understanding is God's purpose in creating man, a clear link with the exposition of

---

[74] Main passages, apart from *Arc.* 3 itself, are 1. 25–39, 6. 96–9, 8. 60–71.

[75] Though *Arc.* 4 ostensibly contains the central discussion, the building-up of ideas is constant in, e.g., 5. 1–15, 34–44, 6. 8 ff., 7. 53 ff.

[76] Cf. 'The *Poemata Arcana*', 33–4.

intent in the creation of the angelic world. Man is placed in the physical world to share its physicality, while granted a share in divine being through genuine participation in the image of God. The affinity with God gives man the ultimate purpose of travelling to God. He is represented as possessing an intellectual nature, the human soul being a breath of God, enjoying freedom from determinism, as befits a fragment of Godhead, infused with divine Spirit, potentially an initiate of heaven, on earth meant to resemble God in exercising rule. Greg. opposes traditional views of the soul as composed of fire, air, or blood, or as being a harmony of physical parts, together with any approach to transmigration, because he believes that none of these contains the truth of God's direct creation. His mortal qualities, though contrasting him with God, are not dishonourable but are appropriate for Christ's acceptance in the incarnate state. Yet this strong affirmation of affinity is balanced by an equally strong awareness of man's difference from God. The human soul is not in essence divine: the whole human being is created and thus dependent, subject to change. His mutability is a concomitant of his composite nature. It makes him unstable, subject to dissolution. He may not be bound in determinism, but he is still not totally free. He is not free from passions and his longing for the divine, real though it is, may be thwarted by his ignorance and tendency towards the purely earthly. Man may be called 'another kind of angel', but the adjective is no less important than the noun. For he is set in contrast with the simple essence of angels and, for his own good, kept at a greater distance from the divine. Within history the human being exercises false choice in the Fall and becomes subject to sin and death. Forfeiting his place in paradise, he must contend with the temptations to evil put in his way by the prior fall of Lucifer and his comrades. The history of Israel shows a particularly poignant failure, in resistance to law and prophets. The Incarnation is the supreme acknowledgement of the worth of the whole human person, Christ coming as God to a state which does not demean him, as it is part of divine creation itself.

In redemptive purpose is to be found final and complete affirmation of the unchanging intent of human creation. Human life continues in history and Greg. concentrates on life in the church which, while not exempted from the fundamental human state, is the primary locus of divine insight and activity, in true teaching and sacrament.[77]

[77] Notable passages *Arc.* 7 *passim*, 2. 40 ff., 4. 32 ff., 75 ff., 6. 52 ff. *Arc.* 8 sets man in history.

The question of *evil* is a recurring one, considered both in its theoretical aspects and through the consequences of its occurrence within the created order. Evil has no existence in its own right within any dualistic system. Rather is it to be thought of in one traditional way as the absence of good. Nor can evil be attributed to such an agency as astral influence. It is something which occurs when created beings, in either world, who are created good, reject the fullness of their creation. First Lucifer in the heavenly world loses through his insolent choice the goodness of light, punished by banishment. Yet his evil choice does not set him up on a rival throne. In the earthly Fall human beings are deceived into evil and their successors come more and more into the power of demonic fraud. Yet what is evil is the breaking of divine commandments, not the nature of the men and women who infringe. Their composition may make them mutable, unstable. But that does not make composition bad. The rust on the iron does not produce fundamental change. The damage to humanity is not total. As God's goodness, goodness remains to be taken up in final redemption, in cleansing and cure.[78]

This then is one way of setting out the main ideas of the poems. As the commentary should show, some of this thinking would be regarded by Greg. as direct exposition of biblical material as developed in a traditional way in the Church. At other times he makes clear his polemical intentions, whether directing himself against what he takes to be heretical interpretations within the church or attacking notions which he identifies as anti-Christian in pagan writers.

VII. SOURCES AND AFFINITIES

Greg. clearly writes in an acceptably allusive way; in line after line it becomes clear how much he owed to other writers, verbally and in thought-forms, while attempting to shape his verse with some degree of originality. Literary allusions, it has already been observed, frequently stop short at the verbal level and are not necessarily expected to carry over the original ambience.

The *Scriptures* clearly form a primary area of reference. Generally in the *Arcana* Scripture is used in a narrative or illustrative way, rather than for the purposes of detailed argument: contrast, for instance,

---

[78] Much, of course, overlaps with the teaching on humanity. *Arc.* 4 raises questions of theory, while 5 tackles the fall of angels and men.

Or. 29. 17 (pp. 99 f., M. 36. 96B ff.), with its detailed exegetical polemics. We do find the Magi story being defended against astrological interpretation in 5. 53 ff. and events in the life of Christ support the proposition ἦν βροτός, ἀλλὰ Θεός in 2. 62. Scripture is appealed to for the threefold baptismal saying (3. 47). Again, it is the Bible which supplies the central argument on the nature of the soul, infused by God (*Arc.* 7) and the fundamental view of creation in *Arc.* 4, while the analogy of Adam, Eve, and Seth is used to support an interpretation of Trinitarian relationships (3. 37 ff.). Typological use of the Bible is restricted and standard, as in the correspondence of the blood sprinkled in the Exodus story with the blood of Christ (8. 87 ff.), while allegory is little used, though the 'coats of skin' instance in 7. 115–16 has significance. Greg.'s overall understanding of Scripture is one in which inspiration is assured but only gradually making itself felt through accommodation to human understanding in progressive providentially appointed stages. Sometimes he works into his pattern blocks of biblical material, like the Adam passage which follows theories of the soul (7. 97 ff.). But equally he infiltrates language drawn from LXX or NT in a glancing way, similar to his use of classical expressions, without invoking an original context.[79]

A reading of these poems will quickly reveal indebtedness to, or at least parallels with, a number of *patristic* writers. The commentary refers frequently to Irenaeus, Clement, and Origen, for instance. But the *Arcana* show also something of Greg.'s independence. As early as 358 he had joined with Basil in producing the *Philocalia*, a selection of Origen which reveals as much by what it omits as by what it includes. Similarly in these poems alongside a degree of dependence will be found instances of divergence or modification. Among his contemporaries we find that passages from Athanasius cited in the commentary invariably support Greg.'s position and those of his Cappadocian colleagues usually do. To Basil's views he shows deference (cf. e.g. the introduction to *Arc.* 4), while his relationship to Gregory of Nyssa may be more ambivalent. (Cf. n. on 4. 82–90.)

When it comes to *Greek philosophy*, Greg.'s knowledge as shown in these poems is fairly wide-ranging, though the scope of the work does not allow very profound discussion. Presocratics and Epicureans make their appearance to be refuted. The Cynic influence, prominent in other parts of Greg.'s writings,[80] is not noticeable here. Aristotle is

[79] Cf. D. A. Sykes, 'The Bible and Greek Classics in Gregory Nazianzen's Verse', *Stud. Patr.* 17/3 (1982), 1127–30.   [80] Cf. above, n. 13.

perhaps more a source for other people's views (cf. especially the commentary on *Arc.* 7) than a philosopher who is treated in his own right in the poems. But the value of Aristotelian logic was not lost on Greg. As J. Focken showed,[81] a number of the arguments used may be reduced to basic logical forms; he points out (p. 4) that even Platonists who would acknowledge little debt to Aristotle's metaphysics make good use of his logic. Traditional syllogisms and enthymemes occur with some frequency and it may be claimed that these forms contribute something to economy of argument and clarity of structure. It is, however, on Plato and later Platonists that most stress must fall.[82] Reminiscences abound, starting with the opening lines of the first poem, which recall *Phaedo* and *Phaedrus*. However, reminiscence does not carry with it acceptance of the thought of an original passage. Where parallels are cited from Plato or Plotinus they are to seen as having passed through Greg.'s mind with varying degrees of acceptance or set out for complete rejection. Levels of influence must be assessed in individual instances, rather than assumed in some general way. At times Greg. will make clear his profound differences, as when he will have nothing to do with independent eternal Forms and pre-existent matter in *Arc.* 4 or with any with any form of metempsychosis in 7. At other times he uses language which has parallels in Platonic thought but gives it specifically Christian content. The purification which must precede any genuine knowledge of God is directly linked with baptism (3. 47). That God is ultimately unknowable is certainly a view which Greg. would share with Platonists, but his expression of it is distinctively Christian.[83] The creation of 'upper' and 'lower' worlds naturally recalls νοητός and αἰσθητός, but they are to be placed within a Christian concept of creation (*Arc.* 4). When we examine the language which Greg. applies to Godhead we may find expressions which may be paralleled in Platonic usage but which need to be interpreted within the pattern of Greg.'s development of Trinitarian

---

[81] *De Gregorii Nazianzeni orationum et carminum dogmaticorum argumentandi ratione* (Diss. Nuremberg, 1912).

[82] The influence is set out clearly in C. Moreschini, 'Il platonismo cristiano di Gregorio Nazianzeno', *Annali della Scuola Norm. Sup. di Pisa*, 3rd ser., 4/4 (1974), 1347–92. Earlier discussions include J. Dräseke, 'Neuplatonisches in des Gregorius von Nazianz Trinitätslehre', *BZ* 15 (1906), 141–60; C. Gronau, *De Basilio Gregorio Nazianzeno Nyssenoque Platonis imitatoribus* (Göttingen, 1908); R. Gottwald, *De Gregorio Nazianzeno Platonico* (Berlin, 1906); H. Pinault, *Le Platonisme de Saint Grégoire de Nazianze* (La Roche-sur-Yon, 1925); E. von Ivánka, *Hellenisches und christliches im frühbyzantinischen Geistesleben*, 43 ff.; *CHLGEMP* 438–47 (I. P. Sheldon-Williams).

[83] Cf. Moreschini, 'Platonismo', 1370 ff.

thinking.[84] Reference is constant, but so are adaptation and reworking. As for Stoics, it is possible to see some influence in the terminology of μίξις applied to man.[85] But much is in opposition, on cosmology and providence, for instance, and there is nothing to correspond to the kind of reminiscence which Werhahn found in his edition of Σύγκρισις βίων.[86]

VIII. TRANSLATIONS

The early editions have been dealt with in Professor Moreschini's introduction; otherwise only A. B. Caillau's edition of 1840, reprinted by Migne, need be noticed. It remains only to mention a small number of translations. In English J. A. McGuckin has translated *Arc.* 2 in *Saint Gregory Nazianzen: Selected Poems* (Oxford, 1986), 1–5. The French translation of P. Gallay gives extracts from all but *Arc.* 8, some 139 lines in all, in *Poèmes et lettres choisies*, reprinted by E. Devolder, *Saint Grégoire de Nazianze: Textes choisies* (Namur, 1960), 66 ff. In Italian a translation of *Arc.* 2 was made by R. Cantarella in *Poeti bizantini* (Milan, 1958), ii. 56–7 and F. Corsaro translated 6 and 7 in *MSLC* 5 (1955), 1–42. Recently we have all the poems in a version by C. Moreschini in *Gregorio Nazianzeno: i cinque discorsi teologici* (Rome, 1986), 231–52, 258–73, with footnotes.

---

[84] Moreschini, 'Platonismo', 1382 ff.
[85] Cf. F. X. Portmann, *Die göttliche Paidagogia bei Gregor von Nazianz* (Sankt Ottilien, 1954), 63 ff., 109 ff.
[86] Pp. 86–94.

1. On First Principles

Title and purpose

The varying titles given to this poem in the MSS indicate the doubt felt about its purpose. Caillau, in preferring Περὶ τοῦ Πατρός, sees in it the first of a group of three poems dealing respectively with Father, Son, and Holy Spirit. But the content shows little more concern with the Father than with the other two Persons. The title is an attempt to fit the first three poems into too neat a pattern. The title Περὶ ἀρχῶν favoured in this edn. shows an awareness that the poem has a more general function. For the purpose is two-fold. Vv. 1–24 form an introduction to the *Arcana* as a whole, while vv. 25–39 lead into a discussion of the Trinity (cf. Va). The notion of 'First Principles', if correct, would certainly be influenced by Origen's work.

This poem is fully discussed in a recent article by C. Nardi: 'Note al *Primo Carme Teologico* di Gregorio Nazianzeno', *Prometheus*, 16 (1990), 155–74. Cf. also R. Keydell, *BZ* 44 (1951), 318.

1–24. *The Conditions for Knowledge of God*

Notable discussions of Gregory's teaching on the nature and extent of human knowledge of God and of the means of attaining it are to be found in H. Pinault, *Le Platonisme de saint Grégoire de Nazianze*, chs. 3 ff., J. Plagnieux, *Saint Grégoire de Nazianze théologien*, 81–113; V. Lossky, *The Vision of God* (London, 1963), ch. 4 on the Cappadocians (pp. 67–70 on Gregory); R. Williams, *The Wound of Knowledge* (London, 1979), 64–6, A. Louth, *The Origins of the Christian Mystical Tradition: From Plato to Denys* (Oxford, 1981), for the whole background of thought; and Moreschini, 'Platonismo', esp. 1370 ff. See also I. P. Sheldon-Williams, in 'The Cappadocians', *CHLGEMP*, ch. 29 (pp. 438–47 on Nazianzen).

1–5. *The gulf between man and God*

Gregory begins by stressing the negative side of the relationship between God and man. (Cf. Plagnieux, 279–80.) Complete knowledge of God is impossible for man, however intense his intellectual strivings. For all his knowledge of God man is dependent upon God. The futility of human wisdom in pursuit of divine knowledge is a subject treated in *or.* 28. 21 (p. 52. 11 ff., M. 36. 53A) where a figure parallel to those found in the present passage occurs: καὶ οἷον ὀργάνῳ μικρῷ μεγάλα δημιουργοῦμεν, κ.τ.λ. See further M. Schubach, *De b. patris Gregorii Nazianzeni Theologi carminibus commentatio patrologica*, (Koblenz, 1871), 18; Portmann, *Die göttliche Paidagogia bei Gregor von Nazianz*, 60–1). As in the passage from *or*. 28, Greg. may have Eunomius in mind, Eunomius with his claims to precise knowledge of God (see *Arc*. 2. 32b–35 n.).

Nardi 156–7 points to the poetic tradition, in both Greek and Latin writers, of perplexity and feelings of insufficiency in the face of great subjects.

1. **οἶδα μὲν**: this is the reading accepted by the majority of editors and it is supported by Nicetas. The μὲν is to be taken as an instance of μέν inceptive (cf. J. D. Denniston, *The Greek Particles*, 2nd edn. (Oxford, 1954), 382–4), a usage found in both oratory and verse. Denniston notes that five of the seven extant plays of Aeschylus begin in this way, and we should have a suitable introduction to a poem opening a sequence if this were the correct reading. But οἶδα-μεν, the reading of Hoeschel, found also in the scholion he prints on p. 9, is not implausible. A number of Greg.'s poems begin with similar asyndeton, e.g. *carmm*. 1. 1. 10. 1 (M. 37. 464A), 1. 1. 12. 1 (472A), 1. 2. 1. 1 (521C). Yet Greg. may equally well be cited for μέν inceptive, as *Arc*. 5. 1 shows. It could also be argued that there is here genuine μέν . . . δέ opposition. The 'nevertheless' element (ἔμπης) could support this.

σχεδίη here looks to the flimsy nature of a raft, as in H. *Od*. 5. 33 and elsewhere. In later poetic use it comes to mean any kind of craft. In Pl. *Phd*. 85 D 1 Simmias compares the best available teaching to a raft on which to brave the hazardous voyage of human life: ὥσπερ ἐπὶ σχεδίας κινδυνεύσοντα.

2. Here the bird's wing is the symbol of fragility and weakness. Elsewhere Gregory uses the Platonic imagery (cf. *Phdr*. 246B-C) of the winged soul soaring towards heaven; cf. e.g. *carmm*. 1. 2. 1. 6 (M. 37. 522C), 1. 2. 9. 26–7 (669A), 2. 1. 23. 13–14 (1283A). Nardi compares Anacreon fr. 52 E Diehl for the figure of feeble wings attempting to reach Olympus (p. 158).

Any attempt to reach heaven without divine aid might well suggest to Gregory the foolish pride of Icarus. (Cf. *RE* ix/1. 985 ff., ii 1994 ff.)

ἀστερόεντα: for the Homeric reminiscence cf. Introd.

3. θεότητ' ἀναφαίνειν: the words are picked up in 36 below. Though no human mind can adequately proclaim Godhead, the Holy Spirit may inspire such proclamation. Human reason is transcended.

4. The notion of the limitation of angels is picked up in *Arc*. 3. 92–3. A full discussion of angelic faculties is reserved for *Arc*. 6.

5. ὅρους: Nicetas glosses: αὐτῆς τῆς σοφίας τὰ ἔσχατα. The angels cannot grasp the bounds of Godhead because Godhead is boundless. Billius (cf. Introd.) in his verse tr. gives 'dogmata' and in his n. writes: 'doctrinae divinae per certa capita traditionem'. This understanding is followed by Caillau's 'decreta' (mistranslated 'décrets' by Gallay, *Poèmes et lettres choisies*, 126). Though Nicetas' interpretation is quite possible, the balance of judgement inclines towards a tr. like 'decreta' which forms a good parallel to οἴακα.

οἴακα: for the quantity cf. Introd. IV (*c*). As a figure of government οἴαξ occurs, e.g. in A. *Th*. 3, *Ag*. 802. The use of the word for divine government may be parallelled in Anaxandrides Comicus (iv BC), fr. 4. 4 Kassel–Austin, where δαίμων is the subject of the sentence. Heraclitus uses οἰακίζειν for the power controlling the universe (fr. 64; DK i. 165), with κυβερνᾶν in a similar sense in fr. 41 (DK i. 160); cf. Greg.'s κυβερνᾷ in *Arc*. 5. 34. Nardi 160 compares πάντων οἴηκα in Orphica, *H*. 58. 8, 87. 1. The astrological use of the word is not without significance when one considers that the poem in which Greg. develops the idea of divine government (*Arc*. 5) has a strong interest in refuting astrology. Greg.'s contemporary, Paulus Alexandrinus, for instance, talks of οἴαξ in describing the ascendant governing a child's nativity (ch. 24, p. 54. 1–2 Boer, cf. p. xxiii. 29–30). The metaphor is amplified in *carm*. 1. 1. 6. 112 (M. 37. 438A) and in 1. 2. 25. 535 (M. 37. 850A). M. Gigante in his edn. of Eugenius Panormitanus, *Versus iambici* (Palermo, 1964), 200 cites this with other passages of Greg. as an influence upon xxii. 42. (See further *PGL* s.vv. οἴαξ and οἰακίζω.)

The opening lines express Christian diffidence about the unaided power of the human mind but also may reflect passages such as Pl. *Tim*. 28C2–5, where it is set out that discovery of the maker and father of the universe is difficult, exposition to human beings impossible. Cf. Gregory's ref. in *or*. 28. 4 (p. 26. 12 ff.). The influence of hermetic literature on such passages as this is studied by J. Pépin, 'Grégoire de Nazianze, lecteur de la littérature hermétique', *VC* 36 (1982), 251–60. The pervading idea of the 'greatness' of

God is fully treated in M. Bissinger, *Das Adjektiv* μέγας *in der griechischen Dichtung* (Munich, 1966).

6-8a. *Humble approach to the divine mysteries*

Gregory makes his bold approach to writing of Godhead in the humble spirit of the widow making her offering (Matt. 12. 41-4, Luke 21. 1-4), at the same time alluding to classical examples like Eumaeus in H. *Od*. 14. 58 and Hecale (Call. *Hecale* frs. 33-9 Hollis). His humility opens him to divine inspiration as a poet.

8. ῥήξω λόγον: with their reminiscence of expressions like ῥῆξαι φωνήν or αὐδήν (cf. e.g. Hdt. 1. 85, E. *Supp*. 710), these words suggest breaking into speech after a silence, here the silence of hesitation and awe.

8b-15. *Only the pure may approach*

These lines introduce the more positive side of Greg.'s teaching on man's knowledge of God. Purity is a condition for knowledge of God, but it is not an unfulfillable one. For a degree of purity is possible for man and with it a corresponding degree of divine knowledge. The connection of purification and knowledge occurs at several points in Greg.'s writings, notably *carm*. 1. 2. 10. 972 ff. (M. 37. 750A f.), *or*. 20. 1 (M. 35. 1065B-1068A), 23. 11 (1161C), 45. 3 (M. 36. 625C f.) = 38. 7 (317B f.). A certain advance in purity must precede even the initial stages of knowledge of God. Only a man who has submitted to discipline of mind and body may be allowed to attempt to reach knowledge of God, *or*. 27. 3 (pp. 4 ff., M. 36. 13C-16B). The nature of this purification is discussed by Plagnieux 81-113, where it is shown that Greg. teaches a sequence κάθαρσις, θεωρία, θεολογία. When man is purified from the distractions of the sensible world, he may approach the contemplation of God γυμνῷ . . . τῷ νῷ, *carm*. 1. 2. 10. 81 (M. 37. 686A). But this does not involve abrogation of the body. Rather is the body itself involved in the purification, a contrast with Neo-Platonist teaching (cf. Plagnieux 94) and deserving of note; cf. *or*. 23. 3 (p. 4. 18-19, M. 36. 13D): . . . καὶ ψυχὴν καὶ σῶμα κεκαθαρμένων, ἢ καθαιρομένων, τὸ μετριώτατον (cf. vv. 9-10 below). Cf. further Pinault 114 ff., 145 ff. and the full discussion of C. Moreschini, 'Luce e purificazione nella dottrina di Gregorio Nazianzeno', *Augustinianum*, 13 (1973), 535-49.

Other aspects of the ideas of purity and purification are found in the

Arcana. They are associated with the work of Christ (cf. αἷμα . . . καθάρσιον *Arc*. 2. 1–2), baptism (*Arc*. 3. 47), the nature of angels (*Arc*. 7. 61 ff.). In *Arc*. 3. 70 right thinking is described as a 'pure sacrifice'.

9. For the hiatus cf. Introd. IV (*c*).

In warning off sinners, Gregory reproduces the words of Callimachus, *Ap*. 2 ὅστις ἀλιτρός. The pure whom he will allow to approach correspond to ἐσθλός in v. 9 of Callimachus. In Gregory, cf. *or*. 27. 3 (pp. 4–5, M. 36. 13 c f.).

10. βέβηλοι: the banishing of the 'profane' was a commonplace of ancient literature; cf. e.g. Vergil, *Aen*. 6. 628, Horace, *Carm*. 3. 1. 1. See further Nardi 162–3.

The language is reminiscent of *or*. 22. 6 (M. 35. 1137 C), where Greg. is lamenting the way in which the great Christian mysteries (ἀπόρρητα) are handed over to profane discussion and even decision, heretical or pagan; cf. *or*. 2. 79 (M. 35. 485 B), Plagnieux 116 ff.

11–13. Here the Christian 'pure' are placed in a biblical context, through the introduction of the comparison with *Moses* on Mount Sinai (Exod. 19. 12 ff.).

The figure of Moses plays an important part in the writings of both Nyssen and Nazianzen. For the former, see C. Nicosia, *MSLC* 6 (1956), 24 ff. In *or*. 28. 2 (pp. 22–3, M. 36. 28 A–29 A) Nazianzen identifies himself with Moses in a way similar to that found in the present passage, dismissing the impure and allowing access κατὰ τὴν ἀξίαν τῆς καθάρσεως (p. 22. 13, M. 28 A). Other instances which may be compared are *or*. 20. 2 (M. 35. 1068 A–B), 40. 45 (M. 36. 421 D–424 A), *carm*. 2. 1. 13. 116 ff. (M. 37. 1236 A f.). See also Greg. Nyss. *v.Mos*. (M. 44. 372 C). Moses is at once the symbol of approach to God, of the incomplete nature of human knowledge of God, *or*. 28. 3 (p. 24. 8 ff., M. 36. 29 A f.) and of the awareness of a call to a prophetic function (cf. 16 ff. n.).

θῆρες: cf. Exod. 13, 19, *or*. 45. 11 (M. 36. 637 C).

The parallel passage in *or*. 28. 2 (p. 22. 20 ff., M. 36. 28 B f.) might indicate that this, too, is a reference to Exod. 19. 13, an injunction to stoning. Yet the language is odd if stoning is meant. σκοπέλοισι suggests not stones one could throw (I can find no parallel for such a sense for either σκόπελος or 'scopulus'), but rather a towering rock. ῥηγνυμένοισιν might confirm the view that we have here a picture of the rending of great rocks, an intensification which makes it appear that the mountain is guarded supernaturally and which may well be derived from the quaking mountain of Exod. 19. 18 (Heb.). The allegorical interpretation of Nicetas, who glosses σκοπέλοισι as σφοδροτέροις ῥήμασιν, is derived from parallels in Greg.'s writings: *or.* 28. 2 (pp. 23. 7–8, M. 36. 28B) λίθοι γὰρ τοῖς θηριώδεσιν οἱ ἀληθεῖς λόγοι καὶ στερροί, and *or.* 40. 45 (M. 36. 424A) . . . λιθοβολούμενον τῷ λόγῳ τῆς ἀληθείας. A very similar line is *carm.* 2. 1. 13. 123 (M. 37. 1237A).

The idea of 'Christ as Illuminator' is well established in the writings of the Fathers; cf. H. E. W. Turner, *Patristic Doctrines of Redemption* (London, 1952), ch. 2. Here it is carried back into OT theophanies, following a patristic line of thought going back as far as Justin. The figure of Christ as giver of the New Law is strengthened by his representation as giver of the Old Law. Gregory follows Origen in seeing Sinai as a symbol of the holy man's approach to God, *princ.* 3. 1. 22 (pp. 239. 13–14, M. 11. 297C). For Origen's effect on Gregory's thought see C. Moreschini, 'Influenze di Origene su Gregorio di Nazianzo', *Atti e memorie dell'Accademia Toscana di scienze e lettere 'La Colombaria'*, 44 = NS 30 (1979), 35–57.

14. κεῖνοι μὲν δὴ τοῖα . . .: Caillau takes κεῖνοι as referring back to βέβηλοι v. 10, making the sentence express a wish: 'May they be treated similarly.' Billius, following Nicetas, understands the words as summary: 'That is how they (the Hebrews) acted.' The second is the better way. Even if a verb like πάθοιεν could be understood to give Caillau's 'sic fiat' (and this is doubtful), there would still be a break in the natural run of the thought. Greg. continues not with a wish but with a further statement: 'And it was thus that (in our time) the Logos . . .'. There is then a strong parallel between 14a and 14b–15. Not only did the Hebrews drive away the profane but we too have seen them driven from our company. Nardi cites a parallel expression οὗτοι μὲν δὴ ταῦτα in *or.* 28. 16 (p. 46. 4, M. 36. 47D).

14b–15. It is possible to take these lines as a general statement about the work of the Logos in the Church, preserving it by driving out heretics. ὦσε would then be a gnomic aorist; cf. W. W. Goodwin, *Syntax of the Moods and Tenses of the Greek Verb* (London, 1989), §§ 154–5; E. Schwyzer, rev. A. Debrunner, *Griechische Grammatik* (Munich, 1953), ii. 285–6. But I am inclined to see in ἡμετέροιο χοροῖο a more specific reference. On 27th November 380 (cf. Gallay, *La Vie de saint Grégoire de Nazianze*, 178), Theodosius had driven the Arian occupants from the episcopal church of Constantinople and had installed Greg. under military protection. In his account of how he became bishop, *carm*. 2. 1. 11. 130 ff. (M. 37. 1119A ff.), Greg. addresses Christ as the direct author of his triumph over heresy (v. 1323, 1120A). So here, he attributes to the Logos the expulsion of the Arians from 'our company'. We should read ὧς with Nardi.

θεημάχον: θεομάχος or its verse form θεημάχος is regularly applied to heretics (cf. *PGL* s.v.). This is the earliest occurrence of the form θεημάχος cited in the lexica, the others being from Nonnus, Proclus, and Agathias.

ἡμετέροιο χοροῖο recalls Ar. *Frogs* 345–71, but may also be equated with Plato's θείου χοροῦ in *Phdr*. 247A7. The Platonic motif of φθόνος found here could well be compared with hearts 'at war with God'; cf. Nardi 165–6.

16–24. *Proclamation under the influence of the Holy Spirit*

In claiming the inspiration of the Holy Spirit Gregory is placing himself in the literary tradition of a poet who in classical usage called upon the Muses, but as a Christian poet he goes beyond it. He claims that the authenticity of his teaching is based upon faithfulness to scripture and tradition, yet the whole tone of this section, with its interweaving of allusions to the Sinai revelation and the inspiration of Isaiah, indicates that he recognizes in his thought an element of a prophetic role in drawing out a fuller revelation. His open proclamation of the divinity of the Holy Spirit makes him feel that he is 'marked' (cf. v. 36) as the intermediary of revealed truth; cf. Plagnieux 113. See also 3. 36 n. and 90–3 n., together with *carm*. 2. 2. 7 (poem.) 179 (M. 37. 1565A).

16. αὐτὰρ ἐγὼν: these words, showing Gregory's awareness of individuality, recall parallels in Hes. *Op*. 10, Archilochus fr. 1. 1 West, Parmenides fr. 2. 1 (DK i. 23), Callimachus, fr. 112. 9 Pfeiffer, *Ap*. 71; cf. Nardi 166 n. 53.

προοίμιον: the introduction is to the whole sequence of the *Arcana*.

σελίδεσσι: σελίς is a word which Greg. successfully naturalizes in Epic verse (cf. *Arc*. 3. 10.). It is found in the LXX meaning leaves or columns of writing, Jer. 43. 23 (Heb. 36. 23), and elsewhere in a similar sense, mainly in the Palatine Anthology.

19. The parenthesis recalls Mark 13. 14 and for the use of ἐπισταμένοις cf. Archilochus fr. 1. 2 West. In Gregory, cf. *carm*. 1. 2. 10. 720 (M. 37. 732A). Also Eugenius Panormitanus 1. 16 (Gigante 167). The 'perceptive' are not recipients of any secret knowledge of a gnostic kind. Rather are they Christians within the traditional structures of the church who are amenable to the exposition of the faith as the true interpreter sets it out.

20. **νεόπηγα:** this is the only citation in the lexica of the form νεόπηξ. Cf. νεοπαγής and the two forms which Greg. uses elsewhere, νεοπηγής in *Arc*. 7. 70 and νεόπηκτος in *carm*. 1. 2. 1. 378 (M. 37. 550A).

21. This line represents the substance of Deut. 32. 1 and Isa. 1. 2. Both verses occur in passages which attack Israel's unfaithfulness, as Greg. attacks the unfaithfulness of some of his generation. It is not necessary to seek in the line refinements of meaning such as Billius (based on Nicetas) attempts to find. Because the earth is the home of what is sinful, he suggests that χθών may mean those on earth destined to eternal life, contrasted with οὐρανός, which means the spiritual beings. But the biblical connection of 'heaven and earth' is so strong (cf. e.g. Ps. 95 (Heb. 96). 11) that Greg. could surely balance them without intending any such contrast. The words simply mark the solemnity of the proclamation. Gregory makes a similar call in *or*. 4. 1 (M. 35. 532A).

22-5. Gregory points the contrast with pagan poets by calling not on the Muse, as, e.g., in Hom. *Od*. 1. 1, 10, Arat. *Phaen*. 16–18, but on the Holy Spirit. Not only does he hope that his mind will be inspired to express truth: the truth he is to utter will include an account of that same Spirit's nature.

23. The line has ancient and solemn ring, ἀτρέκεια occurring in Pi. *Fr*. 213. 4 and ἐρίβρομος going back to the Homeric Hymns, where it describes the god Dionysus. (*h. Bacch*. 26. 1). The claim to truth was the concomitant of invocation in Hes. *Th*. 28; cf. other refs. in Nardi 168. In wishing that his tongue may be a trumpet, Gregory suggests comparison with that accompaniment of revelation in Exod. 19. 16, 19. The trumpet appears prominently in the context of purification in a parallel passage in *or*. 28. 2 (p. 22. 16 ff., M. 36. 28B). Cf. also Gr. Nyss. *v.Mos*. M. 44. 373 ff.

24. While the opening of the poem shows the gulf between God and man, this line alludes to the other side of the question, the kinship of God and man. Man's creation is described in *Arc*. 4. 91–2 χθονὸς ἐκγενόμεσθα | μιχθείσης θεότητι. The language of 'mingling' is reinforced by its use in passages dealing with the Incarnation, e.g. Θεοῦ σοι τοῦ μεμιγμένου *carmm*. 1. 1. 10. 12 (M. 37. 466A), 1. 1. 11. 7–8 (471A). A passage which holds together the ideas of kinship with

God through both Creation and Incarnation is *carm*. 1. 1. 10. 56 ff. (M. 37. 469A), esp. v. 59: τῷ συγγενεῖ μιγεῖσα ἡ Θεοῦ φύσις (cf. Pinault 151 ff.). Similar language of 'mixture' is found in Nyssen, *or. catech*. 5 (p. 23. 3-4, M. 45. 21C): ἀναγκαῖον ἦν ἐγκραθῆναί τι τῇ ἀνθρωπίνῃ φύσει συγγενὲς πρὸς τὸ θεῖον, ὡς ἂν διὰ τοῦ καταλλήλου πρὸς τὸ οἰκεῖον τὴν ἔφεσιν ἔχοι.

Elsewhere he expresses the same idea through words like μετέχειν and μετουσία; cf. R. Leys, *L'Image de Dieu chez saint Grégoire de Nysse* (Brussels, 1951), 47-51 ('Parenté'). It is this kinship of God and man which underlies and gives meaning to the μιγέντες of the present passage. Because man is so 'mingled' with God in his very constitution and because the Logos 'mingled' with human nature in the Incarnation, man, through purification and contemplation, may find in his earthly life a foretaste of the heavenly, ἐπειδὰν τὸ θεοειδὲς τοῦτο καὶ θεῖον, λέγω δὲ τὸν ἡμέτερον νοῦν τε καὶ λόγον, τῷ οἰκείῳ προσμίξῃ, καὶ ἡ εἰκὼν ἀνέλθῃ πρὸς τὸ ἀρχέτυπον, οὗ νῦν ἔχει τὴν ἔφεσιν, *or*. 28. 17 (p. 47. 17 ff., 36. 48C). Though man may 'mingle' with the whole Godhead, the experience on earth is an incomplete one, to be contrasted with that of the heavenly life where there is an entire 'mingling' with the whole Godhead: [Τριάδος] ὅλης ὅλῳ νοῖ μιγνυμένης, *or*. 16. 9 (M. 35. 945C). See further *carmm*. 1. 2. 10. 59 ff. (M. 37. 685A f.), 2. 1. 85. 13 ff. (1432A) and n. on *Arc*. 7. 1, 79.

Yet we may see that Greg. believes in the reality of man's union with God in contemplation while still on earth, by considering the opening of *or*. 20 or lines from the poem *De rebus suis*. He may enjoy communion with God ἔξω σαρκὸς καὶ κόσμου, untrammelled by the world of sense, *or*. 20. 1 (M. 35. 1065A ff.). Greg. describes his own awareness of this communion when he writes:

> ἐξ οὗ γὰρ πρώτιστον ἀποτμήξας βιότοιο
> ψυχὴν οὐρανίοισι νοήμασι μίξα φαεινοῖς,
> καί με φέρων νόος αἰπὺς ἀπόπροθι σαρκὸς ἔθηκεν,
> ἔνθεν ἀναστήσας, σκηνῆς δέ με κρύψε μυχοῖσιν
> οὐρανίης.

(*carm*. 2. 1. 1. 194 ff., M. 37. 984A f.)

It is something of this experience that Greg. desires for his readers.

25-35a. *Summary teaching on the Trinity*

These lines offer an outline of Trinitarian doctrine which is filled out in the following two poems, in particular, with cross-references elsewhere in the *Arcana*. Greg.'s teaching on the Trinity is recognized as one of the most important parts of his work, involving him in lengthy debates and numerous shorter references throughout his writings. Of secondary works, reference may be made to J. Hergenröther, *Die Lehre von der göttlichen Dreieinigkeit nach dem hl. Gregor von Nazianz, dem Theologen* (Regensburg, 1850); K. Holl, *Amphilochius von Ikonium in seinem Verhältnis zu den großen Kappadoziern* (Tübingen, 1904), 158–78; J. Dräseke, *BZ* 15 (1906), 141–60; Pinault, *Le Platonisme de saint Grégoire de Nazianze* 209–33; F. W. Green, 'The Later Development of the Doctrine of the Trinity' in A. E. J. Rawlinson (ed.), *Essays on the Trinity and the Incarnation* (London, 1928), 241 ff., esp. 280 ff.; Plagnieux 246 ff., 301–2, 441 ff.; G. L. Prestige, *God in Patristic Thought* (London, 1952), esp. 225, 234, 254, 260 ff., 291 ff.; J. N. D. Kelly, *Early Christian Doctrines* (London, 1972), 252, 264 ff.; P. Gerlitz, *Außerchristliche Einflüsse auf die Entwicklung des christlichen Trinitätsdogmas* (Leiden, 1963), 212–13; M. F. Wiles, *The Making of Christian Doctrine* (Cambridge, 1977), 124–46; E. Bellini, 'Il dogma trinitario nel primi discorsi di Gregorio Nazianzeno', *Augustinianum*, 13 (1973), 525–34.

In writing on the Trinity Gregory is attempting not merely an outline intellectual exposition. Belief in the Trinity is central to his whole devotional life and is a powerful emotional adhesion. Cf. F. Trisoglio, 'La poesia della Trinità nell'opera letteraria di S. Gregorio di Nazianzo', in *Forma futuri; Studi in onore di M. Pellegrino* (Turin, 1975), 712–40.

25. εἰς Θεός: these are words to which Greg. is to recur in *Arc*. 3. 75, 76, 4. 3, 39. Cf. also 1. 1. 6. 20 (431A). The expression has a well-established place in pre-Christian Greek philosophy, opening the famous couplet of Xenophanes (fr. 23, DK i. 135):

εἰς θεὸς ἔν τε θεοῖσι καὶ ἀνθρώποισι μέγιστος,
οὔ τι δέμας θνητοῖσιν ὁμοίιος οὐδὲ νόημα.

The precise level of monotheistic thought to be found in these lines has been debated through the centuries; cf. Arist. *Metaph.* 986[b]24 and, of modern discussions, e.g., E. Zeller, rev. W. Nestle, *Die Philosophie der Griechen*, i (Leipzig, 1919), 646 ff.; W. Jaeger, *Theology of the Early Greek Philosophers* (Oxford, 1947), 38 ff., G. S. Kirk, J. E. Raven and M. Schofield, *The Presocratic Philosophers*, 2nd edn. (Cambridge, 1983), 169 ff., W. K. C. Guthrie, *A History of Greek Philosophy*, i (Cambridge, 1964), 374 ff., J. Barnes, *The Presocratic*

Philosophers (London, 1982), i. 89 ff. Certainly Clement of Alexandria saw here a genuine intimation of monotheism, quoting the lines with approval, *str*. 5. 109. (GCS 2 (1960) 391. 16 f., M. 9. 165 B). The *Oracula Sibyllina* provide other examples, as in 3. 11 (p. 47).

Christian use of the words may be traced back to 1 Cor. 8. 6 (cf. Herm. *mand*. 1. 1) and in the accusative case became a common feature of the first clause of Eastern creeds (cf. J. N. D. Kelly, *Early Christian Creeds* (London, 1977), 195).

Greg.'s tendency to emphasize the oneness of God against the suspicion of teaching virtual tritheism is discussed by Holl 173 ff. That Greg. was sensitive to criticism on this score may be seen from *or*. 31. 13–14 (pp. 161 ff., M. 36. 148 B–149 A), where he defends himself against what he regards as a long-dead charge. He takes as the key-sentence of his reply the words ἡμῖν εἷς Θεός, ὅτι μία θεότης c. 14 (p. 162, M. 13. 148 D). They might serve equally well as the starting point of Greg.'s exposition in the *Arcana*.

The repetition of εἷς Θεός of the Son (v. 29) and ἓν Πνεῦμα (v. 35) follows the pattern of creeds like those of Caesarea and Jerusalem (*Symb. Caes.* ap. Eus. *ep. Caes*. 3 (Opitz 3. 439 ff., M. 20. 1537 B f.); *Symb. Hier*. (M. 33. 533 A) and probably shows that Greg. is anxious to maintain an anti-Sabellian emphasis by showing clearly the distinctness of the Three Persons of the One Godhead; cf. T. H. Bindley, rev. F. W. Green, *The Oecumenical Documents of the Faith* (London, 1950), 29. Attacks on the Sabellian position occur with some frequency in Greg., often paired with denunciations of the Arian view. Cf. e.g. *carm*. 2. 1. 11. 1176–7 (M. 37. 1109 A); *orr*. 2. 37–8 (M. 35. 444 C–445 C); 18. 16 (1005 A); 21. 13 (1096 B–C); 32. 16 (M. 36. 233 D). Looked at from another point of view, εἷς Θεός could be taken as stressing the unity of the Godhead in opposition to the Arians; cf. Ath. *Ar*. 3. 4 (M. 26. 329 A).

ἄναρχος, ἀναίτιος: ἄναρχος is applied to the Father, as here, in *carm*. 1. 2. 10. 988 (M. 37. 751 A), where the Three Persons are designated Ἄναρχον, Ἀρχή, Πνεῦμα. The parallel titles of the following line are ἀναίτιον, γεννητόν, ἐκπορεύσιμον. The bearing of the word ἄναρχος on the relationship of the Father and the Son is discussed in *Arc*. 2. 19 ff. For the use of negative epithets, cf. *Arc*. 3. 41–2.

οὐ περίγραπτος: the meaning is not quite the same as that found in *or*. 28. 7 (p. 31. 14, M. 36. 33 B). In that passage Greg. is arguing that God has no physical location in space, no σῶμα. (Cf. *Arc*. 2. 37 n.). Here the issue is the rather more subtle notion of time as a quasi-physical restriction. Divine freedom from the bonds of time is an idea which is picked up in the *Arcana*, particularly in 4. 67 ff.

Nardi 170–1 traces the idea of God's freedom from all constriction, in Christian writers back to Origen, and in the works of Philo and Plotinus. Cf. Moreschini, 'Il platonismo', 1376.

27. ἀπείριτος here may be thought to continue the idea of God's timeless quality, as ἄπειρος does in *or.* 38. 7 (M. 36. 317B): μήτε ἀρξάμενον, μήτε παυσόμενον, οἷόν τι πέλαγος οὐσίας ἄπειρον καὶ ἀόριστον, cf. also c. 8 (320A-C).

28. μουνογενοῦς: cf. John 1. 18. In *or.* 30. 20 (pp. 139. 2–3, M. 36. 128D f.) Greg. explains his understanding of μονογενής as relating to the unique manner of Christ's Sonship (cf. μονοτρόπως, 129A).

28–9. οὔ τι πεπονθὼς ... Νόος: in writing these words Greg. had in mind the Arians and Eunomians. Arians had claimed that the Incarnation meant that the Father was παθητός, *Symb. Ant.* (345), 7 (p. 253. 16–17, M. 26. 732C) and the orthodox had maintained the counter position, asserting that the generation of the Son was free from πάθος; cf. e.g. Ath. *Ar.* 1. 28 (M. 26. 69A ff.). Basil took up the argument in his polemic against Eunomius, *Eun.* 2. 23 (G. 1. 258D, M. 29. 621B), while Greg. himself alludes to the question in *or.* 29. 4 (p. 77. 13 ff., M. 36. 77C), cf. c. 2 (p. 75. 9 ff., 76B): ὁ μὲν γεννήτωρ καὶ προβολεύς, λέγω δὲ ἀπαθῶς, καὶ ἀχρόνως, καὶ ἀσωμάτως. Cf. further *Arc.* 2. 15, *or.* 30. 20, p. 139. 4 (M. 36. 129A), with Mason's n. Gregory will also have in his mind the patripassian position taken up by earlier Modalistic Monarchians. (Cf. Kelly, *Doctrines*, 119–26). He is constantly aware of his need to hold a stance between the Arian and the Sabellian positions; cf. e.g. *or.* 2. 37 (M. 35. 444B f.) Here both heresies may be attacked on the same issue; cf. 25 n.

On Sabellianism and the related views of Marcellus of Ancyra cf. notes on *Arc*, 3. 60, 64, 69, 72, and 85.

29. Νόος: cf. *Arc.* 5. 2 n. Here the emphasis on God as transcendent Mind distances him from physical involvement.

εἷς Θεὸς ἄλλος: Greg, refers to this Trinitarian formulation ἄλλος καὶ ἄλλος in *ep.* 101 (M. 37. 180A-B) to distinguish it from his use of ἄλλο καὶ ἄλλο in Christological debate: λέγω δὲ ἄλλο καὶ ἄλλο, ἔμπαλιν ἢ ἐπὶ τῆς Τριάδος ἔχει. ἐκεῖ μὲν γὰρ ἄλλος καὶ ἄλλος, ἵνα μὴ τὰς ἓν γὰρ τρία καὶ ταὐτὸν τῇ θεότητι. Cf. *or.* 37. 2 (M. 36. 284C f.).

30. οὐκ ἄλλος: here ἄλλος corresponds to ἀλλότριος or ἀνόμοιος, words which mark the Arian and Eunomian position; cf. Ar. *Th. fr.*

COMMENTARY ON *ARC*. 1. 30–1

10 (M. 26. 24A); Bas. *Eun*. 1. 16 (G. i. 228C, M. 29. 548C). Greg. uses θεὸν ἄλλον in *or*. 31. 10 (p. 157. 2, M. 36. 144B) in the sense which we find here, 'another kind of God'. (Cf. also G. Müller, *Lexicon Athanasium* (Berlin, 1944–52), s.v. ἄλλος II. 2. for this sense in Athanasius.)

31. **σφϱηγὶς κινυμένη πατϱώϊος:** a number of parallels exist in Greg. for the application to the Logos of the title σφραγίς (in verse σφρηγίς). It is closely linked with εἰκών, as found in *Arc*. 2. 8, in the line εἰκὼν ἀθανάτοιο Πατρὸς καὶ σφρηγὶς ἀνάρχου, *carm*. 2. 1. 38. 7 (M. 37. 1326A). Cf. σφράγισμ᾽ ἀνάρχου, *carm*. ii. 1. 14. 41 (M. 37. 1248A), in a Trinitarian context. In *or*. 29. 17 (p. 99. 13 ff., M. 36. 96C) the sequence χαρακτήρ, εἰκών, σφραγίς occurs, with John 6. 27 explicitly quoted as warrant for σφραγίς, and *or*. 30. 20 (p. 139. 19 ff., 36. 129B) links the word directly, through εἰκών, with the ὁμοούσιος concept.

For the application of the title σφραγίς to the Logos we may begin with Philo. In his teaching on creation he identifies the Logos with the archetypal idea which, without change, itself the exact impression of God, is impressed upon the universe and upon the human soul. Philo writes: εἰ δὲ τὸ μέρος εἰκὼν εἰκόνος [δῆλον ὅτι] καὶ τὸ ὅλον εἶδος, σύμπας οὗτος ὁ αἰσθητὸς κόσμος, εἰ μείζων τῆς ἀνθρωπίνης ἐστίν, μίμημα θείας εἰκόνος, δῆλον ὅτι καὶ ἡ ἀρχέτυπος σφραγίς, ὅν φαμεν νοητὸν εἶναι κόσμον, αὐτὸς ἂν εἴη [τὸ παράδειγμα, ἀρχέτυπος ἰδέα τῶν ἰδεῶν] ὁ θεοῦ λόγος (*opif. mund*. 6. 25, i. 5 M.= i. 6 C.–W.), cf. *migr. Abr*. 18. 103, i. 452 M.; 2. 279 f. C.–W.); *somn*. 2. 6. 45. (i. 665 M.; 3. 248 C.–W.); *fug. inv*. 2. 12 (1. 547–8 M.; 3. 99 C.–W.). There is a full discussion of these and other passages in F. J. Dölger, *Sphragis* (Paderborn, 1911–12), 65 ff. See also G. Kittel and G. Friedrich, *TWNT* vii. 939 ff.; G. W. H. Lampe, *The Seal of the Spirit* (London, 1951), 16–17, 250; J. Ysebaert, *Greek Baptismal Terminology* (Nijmegen, 1962), 420. Philo thinks of the σφραγίς in a twofold relationship, receiving and transmitting exact likeness. Greg.'s intention here is to concentrate on the reception of the likeness by the Son, as Basil does in *Spir*. 15 (G. 3. 11E–12A, M. 32. 92A). Where Cyril of Alexandria later develops both the active and the passive sides of Philo's thought, with a personal Logos for Philo's more impersonal, showing that the σφραγίς imprint of the Father is, in turn, imprinted upon humanity (cf. Lampe p. 251), Greg. is content to confine the figure to the passive sense.

κινυμένη 'living', a sense which resembles Ath. *hom. in Mt*. 11. 27

(M. 25. 217B): σφραγὶς γάρ ἐστιν ἰσότυπος ἐν αὐτῷ δεικνὺς τὸν πάτερα, λόγος ζῶν. There is a close parallel in the passage of John Monachus quoted by Lampe (loc. cit.). Wisdom is described as ἡ ζῶσα σφραγίς, a term which is balanced by ὁ ἀπαράλλακτος τοῦ Πατρὸς εἰκών and ὁ ἀκριβὴς χαρακτήρ, *Hymn. Chrys.* 8 (M. 96. 1384).

In contrast may be quoted *or*. 38. 13 (M. 36. 325 B) = 45. 9 (633 C) where the Son is called ἡ μὴ κινουμένη σφραγίς. Here Greg. is thinking of a different aspect of κινέω, denying movement equated with change.

The form κινυμένη is to be preferred to that printed by Billius, Caillau, and Migne, κιννυμένη (cf. app. crit.). There is no attestation of κίννυμαι beyond certain MSS of this passage. *PGL* marks the double ν form '[*]' and suggests that it might be admissible *metri gratia* for κινυμένη. But metre is in no way served by the double ν. The first syllable of κίννυμαι, as of κινέω and all its by-forms and derivatives, is always long without any doubling of the ν. Nor, surely, is there any reason for *PGL*'s gloss 'stamp?'.

32. **ἰσοφέριστος**: this passage and *Arc*. 4. 65 are the only occurrences of the word recorded in the lexica. For equality of the Persons of the Trinity, cf. *Arc*. 3. 41b n.

33. **μίμνῃ ... ὅλον** taken together guard against any diminution of the Father's authority. Godhead is not a physical substance which would be decreased by giving an equal share. Whether the adverbial ὅλον or the adjectival ὅλος is read, the sense remains the same.

34. **κοσμοθέτης**: a formation of Greg.'s, on the analogy of νομοθέτης. νωμεύς also appears to be a coinage of Greg.'s, cf. *carm*. 2. 2 (poem.), 3. 4 (M. 37. 1480A). It is unlikely to be equivalent to νομεύς, as Sophocles suggested. νομεύς would make little sense here without a defining genitive, such as Plato's ἀγαθῶν (*Leg*. 931D). The word is best taken as a nautical figure, following an established use of νωμάω (LSJ s.v. II, literal and metaphorical usages), and agreeing with Greg.'s own use of the verb in *carmm*. 1. 2. 25. 535–6 (M. 37. 850A), 2. 1. 1. 573 (1013A). (Cf. also, for the sense, v. 5 above.) Caillau's tr. 'gubernator' is exact. A similar coinage of Greg.'s, νωμητής, is found in *carm*. 2. 1. 38. 11 (M. 37. 1326A). The idea of νωμεύς anticipates the discussion in *Arc*. 5, as κοσμοθέτης is amplified in *Arc*. 7. 55 ff.

νόημα has here its early meaning of 'mind', as in H. *Od*. 20. 346 and in the fr. of Xenophanes quoted above, 25 n. Cf. *Arc*. 4. 68, where νόημα and νοῦς are distinguished. The language corresponds to the δύναμις and σοφία of 1 Cor. 1. 24.

35a. *Arc*. 3 is an extended commentary on these words.

35b–39. *The heretical are warned off*

Though Greg. here condemns those who deny the divinity of the Holy Spirit, his condemnation is modified. They are clearly not beyond help who acknowledge the divinity of the Father and the Son. The asperity of ἔρρετε is softened by ἡμιφαεῖς. Half light is still light and a lamp does not cease to be a lamp when it is hidden away in a dark corner. In *or*. 31. 24 (p. 175. 14, M. 36. 160c) there is a similar reference to τοὺς ἐξ ἡμισείας εὐγνώμονας, contrasted with out-and-out Eunomians. In several places Greg. claims to hold a tolerant attitude towards certain unorthodox views. While rigorously opposed to all brands of Arianism and Sabellianism, he is prepared to allow the adherents of more recent aberrations time to correct their opinions. We may, e.g., find a parallel to the present passage in *or*. 41. 8 (M. 36. 440B), where Greg. is trying to win over people who hold the same inadequate estimate of the Holy Spirit's divinity as those who are addressed here. Cf. intro. to *Arc*. 3.

Gregory's attitude to heresy has been surveyed by F. Trisoglio, 'La figura dell'eretico in Gregorio di Nazianzo', *Augustinianum*, 25 (1985), 793–832.

36. ἐτύπωσεν: when the Holy Spirit has 'left his mark' upon him the believer appreciates his divinity, being, in some sense, a 'copy'. *PGL* gives the tr. 'appoint'.

37. Cf. the metaphorical use of βένθος in Paulus Silentarius, *AP* 5. 273: βένθεϊ τῆς κραδίης.

38. ἡμιφαεῖς: apart from this passage, lexical attestation of ἡμιφαής is slight. It appears as a disputed reading in *AP* 7. 478 (Leonidas, 3rd c. BC). The Teubner editor, H. Stadtmüller, accepted the reading ἡμιφαεῖ λάρνακι, as does H. Beckby (Munich, 1957). But R. P. Waltz (Budé edn., Paris, 1928) reads ἡμιφαγεῖ, while LSJ suggests ἡμιχανεῖ.

φθονεροί: the personal motive of φθόνος in contention among Christians is put forward as early as Phil. 1. 15. The idea of ill-will has already been found in vv. 14b–15. Callimachus may well be in mind: in *Ap*. 105–13 Φθόνος is set in opposition to the poet's inspiration (cf. Nardi, 'Note', 165–6).

αὐτοδίδακτοι: the implied contrast is with θεοδίδακτοι. The word has thus a different slant from the meaning found in Homer and Aeschylus. In H. *Od*. 22. 347 the word has a commendable sense. The poet who is αὐτοδίδακτος is marked off from the 'school-poets' by a spontaneity which derives from divine inspiration (cf. n. in W. B. Stanford's edn.). In A. *Ag*. 992 αὐτοδίδακτος . . . θυμός points to a spontaneous apprehension of the moral law on the part of the chorus (cf. nn. in the edns. of E. Fraenkel, and J. D. Denniston and D. Page). But here the point is not spontaneity but wilful refusal to learn from those who have a right to teach.

2. On the Son

Title and purpose

The MSS agree that the subject is the Son. Vv. 1–56 concern the relationship of the Father and the Son, while 57–83 introduce the Incarnation and the Work of Christ. But the purpose of the poem must be further examined. R. Cantarella in *Poeti bizantini*, ii (Milan, 1948), 55, in writing an introduction to his tr. of the poem, asserted that the aim was to defend the humanity of Christ against the Apollinarians and referred to vv. 3–4 and 34–5 as evidence. This is, surely, to misunderstand the text. As the notes on these passages try to show, the issue concerns Eunomius. Vv. 3–4 defend the divinity of Christ against Eunomius, not his humanity against Apollinarius. Again, vv. 34–5 treat a Trinitarian question, the unity of the divine nature, not a Christological one. They certainly contain no vindication of Christ's humanity. (Cf. Introd. IV.)

Discussion of Greg.'s *Christology* will be found in Ullmann, *Gregorius von Nazianz*, 276–88; A. J. Mason, *Five Orations of Gregory of Nazianzus* (Cambridge, 1899), pp. xvi ff.; Holl, *Amphilochius von Ikonium*, 178–96; E. Weigl, *Christologie vom Tode des Athanasius bis zum Ausbruch des nestorianischen Streites* (Munich, 1925), 53–79; L. Stephan, *Die Soteriologie des hl. Gregor von Nazianz* (Vienna, 1938); E. Mersch, *Le Corps mystique du Christ* (Paris, 1951), i. 441 ff.; R. V. Sellers, *Two Ancient Christologies* (London, 1940), 65–79; Kelly, *Doctrines*, 297–8; H. A. Wolfson, *The Philosophy of the Church Fathers*, i (Cambridge, Mass., 1964), 370–1, 396–7, 421–2, 424; A. Grillmeier, *Christ in Christian Tradition* i (London, 1975), 367 ff.; H. Althaus, *Die Heilslehre des heiligen Gregor von Nazianz* (Münster, 1972); D. F. Winslow, *The Dynamics of Salvation: A Study in Gregory of Nazianzus* (Cambridge, Mass., 1979); A. S. Ellverson, *The Dual Nature of Man: A Study in the Theological Anthropology of Gregory of Nazianzus* (Stockholm, 1981). For studies dealing with specific questions, see J. Quasten, *Patrology*, iii (Utrecht, Antwerp, and Westminster, Md., 1960), 252–3.

Studies of Greg.'s Christology tend, not unnaturally, to concentrate on his answer to Apollonarius. As Holl 184 observed, drawing a contrast with the defence of orthodox Christology which Greg. put forward against Eunomius, 'Viel schwieriger, aber auch viel fruchtbarer war die Polemik gegen Apollinaris.' But here, as in the *Theological Orations*, concerned as we are with the defence against Eunomius in the period before Greg.'s Christological thinking was shaped by anti-Apollinarian formulation, we find that the thought may profitably be compared with that of Basil (cf. Grillmeier 367 ff.). In particular might be quoted Grillmeier's words on p. 367: 'Basil's christology is more concerned to distinguish the divine and human characteristics in Christ than to stress the unity of the person (in the language of *communicatio idiomatum*).' We may ask whether this is true of vv. 62 ff. of the present poem. Certainly there is clear distinction within the balanced lines between the manifestations of βροτός and θεός. But, when we look at the overall pattern and purpose, we may conclude that the overriding intention is to demonstrate the unity of the Person rather than the diversity of the natures. The earlier part of the poem opposes the degradation of the Son to the rank of a creature, heretical doctrine which at least obviates the need to stress the reality of the human experience. What is aimed at in the half-lines which detail this experience is the presentation of a belief in the continuity of the Person of the divine Logos and the Person who undergoes the vicissitudes of human life. A parallel for this development of thought is in *or.* 29. 19–20 (pp. 102. 7 ff., M. 36. 100A ff.) where, as here, the balanced μὲν/ἀλλὰ clauses are animated by the proposition: ὃ μὲν ἦν, διέμεινεν· ὃ δὲ οὐκ ἦν, προσέλαβεν (c. 19). See Sellers 73 ff.

It will be seen that the Christology of vv. 62 ff. offers no explanation: the contrasting statements are held in dramatic tension by sharp juxtaposition. Even more compressed and paradoxical language is found elsewhere in Greg., e.g. *carm.* 1. 1. 6. 77 (M. 37. 435A) ὅσην περ ἡμεῖς, τοῖς Θεοῦ παθήμασιν, *or.* 30. 1 (p. 108. 10, M. 36. 104D) Θεῷ παθητῷ. More examples are cited by Stephan 17–18 and by Holl 179–80.

The *structure* of the poem is described by J. Focken as 'forma orationis iudicialis' (*De Greg. . . . ratione*, 53). Up to a point this is an acceptable way of characterizing a poem in which the author accepts advocacy for particular views of Godhead and defends them against his opponents. But the implications which Focken draws are to be disputed. The poem need not be dismissed as a poem, in the way in which Focken tends to dismiss it, merely because it answers to some of the formal characteristics of a prose speech.

1–4. *Introduction*

The soteriological note is heard at the start of the poem. What is to follow is not a mere abstract debate on the relationship of the First and

Second Persons of the Trinity: it is an attempt to show that this rela-
tionship enables man to make sense of the Incarnation (vv. 57 ff.) and
Redemption (vv. 75 ff.).

1. πρώτιστον indicates the first major theme of the sequence of
poems, *Arc.* 1 being treated as a proem to the whole. For αἷμα cf.
below, v. 76 n.

2. παθέων: by Christ's πάθη (v. 48), 'sufferings', man is saved from his
πάθη, 'passions'. The NT associations of πάθος in the second sense
are, for the most part, with sexual passions, as will be seen from
Rom. 1. 26, 1 Thess. 4. 5, Col. 3. 5. In its wider sense, πάθος included
all which might distract the soul from approach to God, as e.g. in
Aristotle's association of πάθη with pleasure and grief (*EN* 1105ᵇ21),
and it is the more general meaning which may be seen here.

2b ff. These lines recur to a theme found in the opening lines of *Arc.*
1. If the angels are aligned with men in the imperfect nature of their
understanding of Godhead, then, despite their inferior position,
men may assist the angels in their task of combating false doctrine.
The masc. οὐράνιοι = 'angels' is found in *Arc.* 3. 6, as well as in *Arc.*
1. 4. In this understanding I follow Billius, who diverges from
Nicetas by not accepting that δόγμασι or the like should be under-
stood, against F. Combefis (cit. Caillau), who follows Nicetas.

3. γλώσσης: if any specific tongue is meant, it will be that of
Eunomius; cf. 32 ff. below.

4. With αὐτοφονῆος or αὐτοφόνοιο (see app. crit.) two meanings are
possible. The word might have the sense 'murdering its own kin'
which is found in A. *Ag.* 1091, constituting a charge of causing
serious harm to fellow Christians by false teaching. If it is taken to
mean 'suicidal' (cf. Cantarella, together with Billius and Caillau), it
implies that false teaching, whether by its internal inconsistency or
through the providence of God, contains within itself the seeds of
its own destruction.

5-39. *The relationship of the Father and the Son within the undivided
Godhead*

5-8. These lines contain two related problems: the subject of ἔχει
and the reading in v. 6. Caillau takes the Father to be the continuing
subject. In support of this one might cite *Arc.* 5. 2 as parallel: νοῦς
μέγας, ἐντὸς ἅπαντα φέρων, καὶ παντὸς ὕπερθεν. This meaning
however is arrived at only by replacing the better attested ἀπήορος

with ὑπέρτερον οὐδέν. Caillau, declining Billius' 'a magno pendetque Parente', does not look for a meaning for ἀπήορος but turns to ὑπέρτερον. His difficulty is understandable. There are few examples of ἀπήορος listed in the lexica and the word with a following genitive occurs with a meaning quite the opposite of Billius'. The meaning 'hanging on high, far distant' occurs in Aratus 396 and 975 of stars, while Pindar uses the word with a following genitive to mean 'aloof from' (*P.* 8. 86). Gregory provides a parallel to Aratus in *carm.* 1. 2. 2. 627 (M. 37. 627A). Nicetas, on the other hand, suggests that the expression matches ὁ πατρὸς/ἐκπεφυώς. Gregory is certainly capable of reinterpreting an uncommon word. Though most of the occurrences of the corresponding verb ἀπαίρω or ἀπαείρω favour the meaning of separation, C. Moreschini has pointed to a passage in Damascius, *De princ.* i. 74 Ruelle (i. 111. 17 Westerink): πάντα οὖν αὐτοῦ ἀπηώρηται (from ἀπαιωροῦμαι, 'I am suspended'). Here is a sense of dependence which would support that interpretation of the present passage. The reading of LCVa² ἀπήορος οὐδέν is perhaps possible. With the disappearance of οἶδεν we would have to supply ἐστι twice, in both vv. 6 and 7. For the reading ἀπήορον οὐδέν cf. Introd., pp. xiii–xiv; it looks like assimilation to οὐδέν. It is clear that ἀπήορος, *difficilior lectio*, should be read.

There is no difficulty in making the Son subject of ἔχει. Similar language of 'containing' is found, e.g., in Ath. *inc.* 42. 6 (M. 25. 172A).

7. ἄχρονος refers to the Eternal Generation of the Son, as set forth in *or.* 29. 9 (pp. 85 ff., M. 36. 84D ff.). Questions of 'before' and 'after', whether or not there was a time 'before' the generation of the Son, are quite pointless. οὗτος γὰρ περὶ τῶν χρόνῳ διαιρετῶν ὁ λόγος (p. 87. 5–6, 85C). See further Hergenröther 138. Freedom from the restrictions of time is an essential attribute of divinity in Greg., as will be seen in vv. 18 ff. below. It is the freedom of the Logos from these restrictions which at once sets him apart from man and, at the same time, enables him to come to man's assistance.

8. εἰκὼν ἀρχετύποιο: the intention of this expression is similar to that of σφρηγίς in *Arc.* 1. 31, where see n. εἰκών, as a title of Christ, has a long history in Christian writing, beginning with 2 Cor. 4. 4. and Col. 1. 15 (cf. Wisd. 7. 26), and taken up by generations of the Fathers. Greg. uses the word to stress the complete likeness of the Son to the Father in *orr.* 29. 17 (p. 99. 13 ff., M. 36. 96C), 30. 20 (p. 139. 20–140. 3, 129B), 38. 13 (325B) = 45. 9 (633C). ἀρχέτυπος is not

a biblical word. It occurs in Philo and finds considerable currency in the Fathers. (Cf. *PGL* s.v. 4.c for the use as correlative of εἰκών.)

It is to be noted that the same εἰκών–ἀρχέτυπος language comes to Greg. when he is writing about the return of the human soul to God, in the passage quoted in the n. on *Arc*. 1. 24. This identification in language may be taken as an indication of the reality for Greg. of the identification of man and God through deification. (See *Arc*. 4. 95 n.)

φύσις . . . ἴση: for φύσις as the ground of unity for the Persons of the Trinity see nn. on *Arc*. 3. 41, 71.

9–10. The epic κλέος is made to answer to all the uses of the biblical δόξα, strengthening the εἰκών language in the same way as δόξα does in, e.g., Origen, *Jo*. 13. 25 (p. 249. 30, M. 14. 444A). For the statement that the Son *is* the glory of the Father, cf. Cyr. *ador*. 11 (1. 402A). Something of the light imagery which is found with δόξα may perhaps be attached to κλέος, if ἐκ δὲ φαάνθη and ἐξεφαάνθη are taken to retain something of their Epic meaning. The passive of ἐκφαίνω appears in H. *Il*. 19. 17 (ἐξεφαάνθη), for instance, of eyes shining like lightning. This meaning is brought out in Caillau's 'resplenduit' (cf. Cantarella's 'risplende'). But the element of 'manifestation' or 'revelation' in the word must not be ignored, as F. Scheidweiler noted in *BZ* 49 (1956), 345, when he suggested the tr. 'er kam aus Licht' or 'wurde gezeugt', a meaning which may also be paralleled in Homer (e.g. *Il*. 13. 278). The lines then mean that the generation of the Son is a secret known only to the Father and the Son. This use of the verb is thus in line with the meaning of the noun ἔκφανσις which, in Christian writers, specialises in references to the revelation of the Godhead. *Or*. 31. 9 (p. 155. 14, M. 36. 141C) provides a good example in Greg., and Mason's n. sums up no less for the verb than for the noun: '"Εκφανσις does not mean their manifestation to *us*, but their eternal issuing forth from the First Source.' (Greg. is here speaking of both the Son and the Holy Spirit.) In calling the Son 'great' Gregory links him in equality with the 'greatness' of the Godhead in *Arc*. 1. 5 and with μεγάλοιο Πατρός in v. 5.

11–19a. *The difference between God and man*

Verse 11 takes us back to the opening theme of *Arc*. 1. The gulf which separates man from God is now seen as difference of γενέθλη. 'Birth' (cf. *Hymn. Is*. 36 for this meaning) is a human term, not to be applied by analogy to the Godhead (vv. 13–14).

14. ῥύσιν ... τομὴν: Greg. regards these words as countering Eunomius, resembling as they do *or*. 29. 8 (p. 84. 11–13, M. 36. 84c): κατάβαλέ σου τὰς ῥεύσεις, καὶ τὰ διαιρέσεις, καὶ τὰς τομάς, καὶ τὸ ὡς περὶ σώματος διανοεῖσθαι τῆς ἀσωμάτου φύσεως· There he is arguing against Eunomius that, as even the processes of human generation are only imperfectly understood, it is futile to claim anything approaching a full understanding of divine generation. For even if one could master the complexity of the way in which a human being comes into existence, this could still mean that there was a complete disjunction from 'begetting' in the divine sense. As Norris points out in his note (pp. 140–1): 'The leaders of later Arianism would not accept this description of their positions. They know that the incorporeal is not embodied'. He suggests however that a popular understanding of the Neo-Arian position might have fallen into 'the corporeal trap'. For the 'flux' associated with the human condition, cf. *Arc*. 8. 67.

κακοαισχής appears to be a coinage of Greg.'s.

ἔγωγε: as often, ἐγώ = 'man' (cf. e.g. *Arc*. 4. 32).

15. ἀπαθής: cf. *Arc*. 1. 28–9 n.; above, v. 2 n.

δετός: the lexical treatment is not extensive. LSJ list only Opp. *C*. 4. 289, of hands 'that may be bound'. Soph. and *PGL* mention only the present passage, translating respectively 'bound' and 'that may be bound'. Other expressions in the poems fill out the sense. In *Arc*. 5. 71 men are described as δέσμιοι αἴης while in 7. 78 Adam's creation is called ἀρχεγόνοιο βροτοῦ δέσις. Cf. also 7. 81. Man, unlike the angels, is not ἁπλοῦς: he is a composite being in whom the divine image is bound to the earthly element, in whom body and soul are bound together and who may thus be described as δετός. *PGL*, by following the tr. in LSJ, gives a different impression. To call man one 'that may be bound' is to think not of his essential nature but of a state to which he may (or, presumably, may not) be called.

16. God's freedom from passion is linked with his being incorporeal, cf. *or*. 28. 10 (p. 37. 1, M. 36. 37c); for ἀσώματος below, v. 37 n. No other passage is cited in the lexica for ἄπηκτος in the meaning 'not compacted, simple'. The sense may be taken to be close to that given to ἁπλοῦς. Man is πηκτός, a composite of parts, while God is simple in essence.

17. γεννήσιες: this Ep. form in -ιες (cf. D. B. Monro, *A Grammar of the Homeric Dialect*, §94. 2, p. 80, Chantraine, *Grammaire homérique* (Paris, 1958), i, §93, pp. 216–17) is affected by Greg. in *carm*. 2. 1. 16. 40 (M. 37. 1257A), *al.*, being found also in Ps.-Manetho 3. 472, 1.(5). 219, and in *or. Sib*. 11. 2, *al.*

18–27. *God, man, and time*

A sign of man's subject status is his subservience to time: he exists in a world of 'before' and 'after' where he has no control over time's passage. Time, as Basil writes, is the natural environment of the created being, as eternity is of the Godhead; cf. *Hex*. 1. 5 (G. 1. 5E ff., M. 29. 13B-C), *Eun*. 1. 21 (i. 23C ff., M. 29. 560B). For the timelessness of God, cf. v. 7 above, together with *Arc*. 4. 76 ff.

19. ἀνάρχου: as in *Arc*. 1. 31 ἄναρχος is applied to the Father. If ἀνάρχου were read, it could be taken either with the Son (cf. v. 21) or, as Dr L. R. Wickham has suggested, construed with θεότητος. Cf. the use in a temporal sense in *or*. 39. 12 (M. 36. 384B), with p. 175 n. 2 Moreschini–Gallay.

Gregory shows in *or*. 29. 3 (pp. 76–7, M. 36. 77A–B) that he is aware of the anomaly of using such temporal language as ἦμος ... τῆμος to describe the extra-temporal relationships of the Godhead, but he holds that such language must be admitted, as there is no other open to us.

21. ἄχρονον ἀρχήν: ἀρχή is here used to mean 'principle', as in Or. *Jo*. 1. 17 (p. 22. 10, M. 14. 53A): ἀρχὴ υἱοῦ ὁ Πατήρ, and Ath. *Ar*. 1. 14 (M. 26. 41A): ὁ Πατὴρ ἀρχὴ τοῦ υἱοῦ καὶ γεννήτωρ. Important for Greg.'s understanding of ἀρχή is *or*. 20. 7 (M. 35. 1073A). Writing about the Trinity, he says that unity will be preserved if the Son and the Spirit are referred to one cause: εἰς ἕν αἴτιον καὶ Υἱοῦ καὶ Πνεύματος ἀναφερομένων. The passage goes on to equate αἴτιον with ἀρχή, and ἀρχή in this sense is reserved for the Father: ὁ δὲ Υἱός, ἐὰν μὲν ὡς αἴτιον τὸν Πατέρα λαμβάνῃς, οὐκ ἄναρχος· ἀρχὴ γὰρ Υἱοῦ Πατὴρ ὡς αἴτιος (v.l. αἴτιον). The Son has the Father as divine principle. Yet (according to the variant in v. 19) he is ἄναρχος as having no beginning in time.

22. Elsewhere Gregory shows himself wary of the use of figurative language to represent Divine realities (cf. n. on *Arc*. 3. 60–1). Here, too, he limits the application of the figure (v. 23), while allowing it some illustrative value. The point of the figure is to emphasize continuity of substance without temporal priority. In *or*. 31. 32 ff. (pp. 187. 10 ff., 36. 169B ff.) he discusses the shortcomings of the analogy of sun, ray, and light, fearing an interpretation which would introduce composition into the uncompounded nature and would deny the identity of the Second and Third Persons.

23–7. *The Father and the Son are indivisible*

23. εἴδη is used here to mean 'images', 'figures'. All figurative language fails to reach (cf. κάτω) God.

24. Picks up the argument from 21. The Father's priority in time would sever him in the equality of divine rule from the Son.

26–7. Θεοῖο refers to God the Son. (Cf. v. 18 above). θέλησις carries the argument a stage farther. If the Father is prior to the Son, he may be thought to have willed the Son's existence, a view which Greg. attacks in the course of his anti-Eunomian polemic in *or*. 29. 6 (pp. 80 ff., M. 36. 80c ff.). The brief reference to θέλησις in the present passage is preferable to the extended treatment in the oration. Here it is maintained simply that to say that the Father 'willed' the existence of the Son means that the Son was not always in existence (cf. n. on v. 7 above). In the oration there is an attempt to score a point by suggesting that the Eunomian position implies that θέλησις is some sort of mother within the Godhead, an elaboration which succeeds only in obscuring the issue. (See further Mason's n. on p. 80. 11, Hergenröther, p. 147, and Norris p. 139, where he refers to Greg.'s 'gamesmanship'.

For a full discussion, see E. P. Meijering, 'The Doctrine of the Will and of the Trinity in the Orations of Gregory of Nazianzus', *Nederlands Theologisch Tijdschrift*, 27 (1973), 224–34, reprinted in id., *God Being History* (Amsterdam, 1975), 103–13.

τμῆξις is *hapax leg*. Elsewhere Greg. uses forms from the τέμνω root, e.g., τῇ γε οὐσίᾳ μὴ τέμνεσθαι, *or*. 29. 2 (p. 75. 6–7, M. 36. 76B) and τομή, *orr*. 27. 6 (p. 10. 2, M. 36. 17C) and 29. 8 (p. 84. 12, 84C).

28–39. *The true meaning of 'generation'*

28. Billius claimed to have detected an early corruption in this line in the repeated γενέτης. He held that the sense required a line like ὡς

COMMENTARY ON *ARC*. 2. 28–32

Θεός, ὡς κόσμου γενέτης μέγας κτλ. But more than that, he held that his restoration was supported by Nicetas. This is not so. Nicetas' paraphrase begins: μέγας μὲν ὁ Θεός and continues with an unnecessary description of the way in which God's greatness is sung by the twofold worlds, αἰσθητός and νοητός. (This is a favourite theme with Nicetas who is here merely recapitulating his comment on κοσμοθέτης in *Arc*. 1. 34.) The connection of γενέτης with the Son is made quite clear: ὅτι πατήρ ἐστιν ἀεὶ υἱοῦ μεγάλου ὑπερουσίου καὶ ὁμοουσίου συνανάρχου καὶ συναϊδίου (fo. 22). γενέτης was used in Classical Greek with either an active or a passive sense, 'father' or 'son', according to context (cf. e.g. Jebb's note on S. *OT* 470). Greg. maintains the active meaning. When Christ is called γενέτης in *carm*. 2. 2. 3. 4 (M. 37. 1480A) it is in the expression πάντων γενέτης.

29. ἀφορμὴν, 'starting point', 'origin', is a synonym for αἰτίαν or ἀρχὴν.

31–2. Such greatness of the Father is inevitably shared by the Son.

γέννημα is a word of varying theological fortune. Its use by the Eunomians inclined Basil at one stage to reject it as a term for the Son, *Eun*. 2. 7 (G. 1. 243A; M. 29. 584C). Previously the word had been identified with κτίσμα in Arian circles, with Athanasius coming in as its orthodox defender; cf. e.g. *Ar*. 1. 31 (M. 26. 76C). Athanasius represented the prevailing tendency in refusing to abandon the word to heretical subordinationism, a tendency found in Greg. in *or*. 29. 10 (p. 88. 2, M. 36. 88A). He distinguishes 'uncreated' and 'created' on the one hand from 'unbegotten' and 'begotten' on the other, on the grounds that the second pair imply identity of nature: αὕτη γὰρ φύσις γεννήματος, ταὐτὸν εἶναι τῷ γεγεννηκότι κατὰ τὴν φύσιν.

σεπτῷ: Cf. *Arc*. 3. 41–2.

ῥίζαν continues the notion of unity, guarding alike against separation and subordination. Cf. *Arc*. 3. 58.

32b–35. *The general understanding of the lines*

F. Scheidweiler, 'Zu den Gedichten Gregors von Nazianz bei Cantarella und Soyter', *BZ* 49 (1956), 345–8, found no sense in the punctuation and translations offered by Caillau and by Cantarella. The latter's translation he described as 'unverständliches Gerede' (p. 345). The solution he saw was to repunctuate:

ἡ δ᾽ ἀγένητος

Φωνή· γέννησίς τε Πατρὸς ἄπο, οὐ θεότητος

ἔπλετο· εἴδεα δισσά τις ἔπλασεν, ἀμφὶ δ᾽ ἐκείνην

ἀμφότερ᾽ ἐκτὸς ἐόντα· φύσις δ᾽ ἀκέαστος ἔμοιγε.

In this interpretation, ἡ δ᾽ ἀγένητος Φωνή is a statement that the Logos is unbegotten. The passage continues as an assertion that the Logos proceeds from the Father and not from a Godhead underlying both Father and Logos and goes on: ' . . . so daß beide, Vater und Sohn, als deren Arten (εἴδεα), wie jemand dies erdichtete, anzusehen wären und sich, was jene (die θεότης) angeht, außerhalb ihrer befänden.' Now as anti-Eunomian theology (cf. below) this clearly makes sense. Scheidweiler does not mention Eunomius explicitly, but his understanding of these lines points to him. (As we have seen from the introduction to this poem, Cantarella does not appear to have any convincing understanding of the purpose of the lines, referring inappropriately to Apollinarius.) There are, however, objections to the suggestions put forward by Scheidweiler.

(i) Is it natural to write Φωνή with a capital and make it equivalent to Λόγος? To change from the precise Λόγος to the non-technical Φωνή would be confusing, unlikely to be understood.

(ii) Even if Φωνή were understood as = Λόγος, could ἡ δ᾽ ἀγένητος Φωνή mean 'The Logos is ingenerate'? Φωνή is in the attributive, not the predicative, position and the words would mean 'the ingenerate Logos'. The sense is thus incomplete if we follow the punctuation of placing a colon after Φωνή.

We may, therefore, ask whether Caillau's translation may not have more to be said for it than Scheidweiler supposed. The view that φωνή means 'vox, vocabulum, verbum', that is, 'term' or 'expression', is held by Stephanus when he cites Greg. as an authority (*Thes*. s.v. φωνή, 1191 D). The instances given in *PGL* (5) include Origen, Basil, and Nyssen. This fits well with Caillau's tr. 'voces . . . ingenitus et generatio'. The meaning is made clearer if the sentence is read without punctuation from ἡ δ᾽ ἀγένητος to δισσά, and continues after the parenthesis τίς ἔπλασεν from ἀμφὶ to ἐόντα: 'The expressions "ingenerate" and "generation from the Father" do not constitute two different forms of Godhead (who invented that notion?) but both are externals around Godhead.' Here ἀμφὶ has a similar sense to περὶ in *or*. 42. 15 (M. 36. 476) of that which is merely concomitant.

The argument of the lines thus runs: 'To be ἀγένητος is not the prerogative of one form of the Godhead (i.e. the Father) nor does being γεννητός exclude the Son from Godhead. The Son, too, is ἀγένητος, "uncreated".' The Arians had tried to equate ἀγένητος and ἀγέννητος and thus to deny to the Son the title ἀγένητος, as being γεννητός; cf. Ath. *syn.* 16 (p. 244. 12, M. 26. 709C). Greg. would hold that the Son was at once γεννητός and ἀγένητος, as the former referred solely to his relationship with the Father while the latter spoke of his essential Godhead in unity with the Father. This is in line with Greg.'s argument in *or.* 25. 16 (M. 35. 1221B), where he contrasts the distinctive characteristics of the Three Persons with their common element (κοινόν). ἀγεννησία, γέννησις, and ἔκπεμψις are the distinguishing marks, but in common the Three Persons have τὸ μὴ γενονέναι and ἡ θεότης. In other words, ἀγένητος is applicable to all Three.

The specifically anti-Eunomian tone becomes clear in the words εἴδεα δισσά, reinforced by ἐκτός. Eunomius, as Greg. argues in *or.* 29. 11 ff. (pp. 88 ff., M. 36. 88B ff.), confuses οὐσία with ἰδιότης. ἀγένητος describes θεότης, the οὐσία of Father and Son alike. γέννησις is not the οὐσία of the Son, but his specific characteristic. εἶδος here comes very close to meaning οὐσία, as it does in Arist. *Metaph.* 1032^{b}1. Eunomius elevates to the level of οὐσίαι characteristic distinguishing marks which are 'outside' the essence of Godhead. As Hoeschel's scholiast observes of γέννησις and ἀγεννησία: οὐ θεότητός εἰσι σημαντικαί (p. 17 of his edn.). The εἴδεα δισσά of this passage makes a similar point to the expression φύσεις θεῶν ὁμωνύμων in *or.* 39. 12 (M. 36. 348C). In both cases Greg. is dealing with the attempt to make distinctions of essence within the Godhead while still wishing to assert that, in some sense, the Son shared in divinity through his generation. The meaning of ὁμώνυμος is well brought out in *or.* 29. 13–14 (pp. 92 ff., M. 36. 89C ff.), especially p. 93. 4 ff. (92A-B). The effect of the argument is to apply the term 'God' equivocally in different senses. Now this is exactly what is implied by δισσά, which means both 'twofold' and 'ambiguous'. Cf. *Arc.* 8. 5 n. (Cf. also *or.* 41. 9, M. 36. 441C.)

Eunomius

Much of the Cappadocian Fathers' time was taken up with Eunomius and his followers, with what they taught or were believed to teach. Basil wrote three books *Contra Eunomium* (G. 1. 207 ff., M. 29. 497 ff.;

SC 299 and 305.) Nyssen wrote extended works in defence of Basil's position (*Opera*, ed. Jaeger, 1. 2; M. 45. 244 ff.), while Nazianzen devoted a large part of the *Theological Orations* to attempting to controvert what he took to be the position of Eunomius (M. 36. 12A ff.) Cf. Mason's edn. and for a full discussion Norris. Texts of Eunomius are found in Vaggione and SC 305. The discussion in the present poem is comparatively slight. Full studies of Eunomius and his opponents are found in T. A. Kopecek, *A History of Neo-Arianism* (Cambridge, Mass., 1979); M. Simonetti, *La crisi ariana nel quarto secolo* (Rome, 1975); and Hanson, *Search*.

32b. ἀγένητος: the single ν form is guaranteed by metre. The confusion with the form in double ν, frequent in MSS, does not arise.

37. ἄσαϱκος: it is true that there is here no real case to answer: no one asserted that God was σάρξ. The Stoics held that both God and the soul were material, corporeal. This teaching was based on the view that only corporeal things could either act or be acted upon. πᾶν γὰρ τὸ ὁρῶν ἢ καὶ ποιοῦν σῶμα· . . . ἔτι πᾶν τὸ κινούμενον σῶμά ἐστι (*Placit.* 4. 20. 2; Diels, *Dox.* 410; *SVF* 2. 387; cf. Plu. *comm. notit.* 30. 2, 1073E). But σάρξ was another matter. This is why Greg. can dismiss as absurd the association of σάρξ with the Father, while finding it necessary to argue that he is ἀσώματος, *or.* 28. 7 (pp. 31–2, M. 36. 33B-C). (It is questionable whether in that particular context such an argument was called for. As Mason pointed out (p. 31. 9 n.), it was unlikely that Eunomius maintained any such position. But the point still remains that the corporeity of God could be taken seriously, whereas the idea that he was flesh could not).

39. For εὖχος used of a person cf. *AP* 7. 27. 1 (Antip. Sid., 2 c. BC). The collocation of υἱός and ἄξιος may suggest a side-reference to Luke 15. 19, 21. This is he who is eternally worthy to be called the Son of his Father.

40–56. *The Father's divinity is not safeguarded by lowering the status of the Son*

40. ἐπίηϱα: the sense 'trying to find favour' is unaffected, whether we read ἐπίηρα or ἐπὶ ἦρα (cf. H. *Il.* 1. 572, 578, *Od.* 3. 164, S. *OT* 1094, etc.). In *carmm.* 2. 1. 17. 60 (M. 37. 1266A) and 2. 2 (poem.) 1. 12 (1453A) he takes ἦρα as fem. sg. with an adjective in agreement.

41. δέος here means 'awe', 'godly fear'. Classical and LXX usages regularly indicate straightforward fear induced by physical danger. In Heb. 12. 28 our present sense is found.

πραπίδεσσι χαράσσων: cf. *carm*. 2. 1. 13. 212 (M. 37. 1244A).

42. Rather than Caillau's 'generationem' we should render τὴν μὲν as 'divinity'. It is the θεότης of Christ which is denied.

κτίσματα: κτίσμα suggests an attack upon a basic tenet of Arianism. Arius had held that the Son was a κτίσμα or ποίημα; cf. Ath. *Dion.* 21 (p. 62. 13–14, M. 25. 512B) and κτιστόν in the anathemata of the Nicene Creed (*Symb. Nic.* (325), Opitz 3. 52. 3; M. 20. 1540C). But, despite the modifications in the theology of Eunomius, which encouraged him to call the Son in some sense 'God', it appears that he still retained the 'creature' language, *apol*. 17 (M. 30. 852C f.). Greg. attributes to him this term κτίσμα in *or*. 29. 4 (p. 77. 15, M. 36. 77C), asking how it can be squared with Θεός.

44. The underlying argument is: if Christ is created, he is not God; if not God, he is not the Son of God; therefore the Father is not Father and his divinity is impaired. (Cf. *or*. 40. 43, M. 36. 420B ff.) Behind this reasoning there lies the understanding of the word 'Father' in Christian theology and, in particular, in the creeds. An earlier tendency to associate the Fatherhood of God with his function as Creator was giving way to a close connection between the Fatherhood of God and the Sonship of Christ. (Cf. Kelly, *Creeds*, 132 ff., esp. 134: 'As early as the middle of the fourth century St Cyril of Jerusalem was explaining, in his discussion of the creed, that FATHER properly belonged to God in virtue of His relation to the Son, the very word suggesting the idea of a son to the mind', citing Cyr. H. *cat*. 7. 4 (M. 33. 608 f.).)

ἐτύχθη: τεύχειν is used of divine creation in Pi. fr. 141 Maehler, quoted by Clem. Al. *Str*. 5 (GCS 2 (1960), 413. 16, M. 9. 142); cf. Did. Alex. *Trin*. 3. 1 (M. 39. 784A). But frequently in Classical usage the word denotes manufacture and ἐτύχθη may be here used in this way, as derogatory to the Eunomian position.

45–6. There is here a side-glance at the Arian ἦν ποτε ὅτε οὐκ ἦν; cf. the first anathema of the Nicene Creed (*Symb. Nic.* (325), Opitz 3. 52. 2; M. 20. 1540). The argument, still directed against Eunomius, is that no difference in degree can alter a difference in kind. If the Son were created, he would remain a creature even if he attained to an exalted and permanent place in the Father's plans. To call him 'God' would not change his original status.

ποτ᾽ ἔην, λυτὸν: this reading is preferable to Caillau's αὐτῶν, which is awkward and difficult to translate convincingly. It is not at all obvious that αὐτῶν may be taken as κτισμάτων, which is what his tr. suggests. On the other hand, λυτόν (found in Pl. and Arist.) carries the argument further with its sense of 'capable of being dissolved (again into nothing)'. The equation of the composite with that which is resolvable into parts and destructible, in contrast with the simplicity and indestructibility of that which is self-constituted, is found, e.g., in Proclus, *Elements*, 40 ff.

46. The subjunctive μένῃ for Caillau's optative represents a stylistic variation, not a change of meaning.

47–50 introduce soteriological objections. How could man come to deification through the sufferings of one who was no different from himself? The idea of the deification of man is dealt with in *Arc*. 4. 95–6 n.

49–50. The 'bounds' are those of the created being (cf. above, v. 15 n.).

ὁμόδουλον: a similar anti-Arian expression is found in *or*. 25. 17 (M. 35. 1221 C f.): οὐ γὰρ Θεός, εἰ γέγονε, μὴ Θεῷ συνηγορῶν διακενῆς, Θεὸν ἀνέλῃς, ὁμόδουλον ποιῶν τὸ ὁμόθεον, ὃ καὶ σὲ τῆς δουλείας ἐλευθεροῖ, ἂν γνησίως ὁμολογῇς δεσποτείαν. Cf. also Gr. Nyss. *or. cat.* 39 (p. 159. 2–3, M. 45. 101 A).

50. ἀντὶ Θεοῖο: this gives a stronger meaning than ἀντιθεοῖο (*recte* ἀντιθέοιο), found in L. A state of slavery might be called 'hostile to God', cf. *or*. 20. 6 (M. 35. 1072 B), but the contrast between being a slave and actually being God is more forceful.

51–3. The Father might have created the Son as the instrument for the further creation of man. That Christ would thus be little more than a means to an end is brought out by the analogy of the smith. He makes the hammer not for its own sake but because he needs it to make a wagon.

51. ἔπειτα, 'at a later point in time', picks up v. 45.

ὄργανον appears with some frequency in Arian discussions of the nature of the Logos, the emphasis, as Athanasius brought out, being on coming into existence out of nothing; cf. Ath. *decr*. 23. (p. 19. 29, M. 25. 457 B).

53. The reading followed by Caillau, Θεός, allows the assumption that Greg. is following the argument he is attacking by using Ἀρχεγόνοιο in a diminished sense, consonant with ὄργανον. The word ἀρχέγονος is applied to Adam in *Arc*. 3. 37, 7. 78. Greg. would be saying that his opponents' argument made the Logos, as the first creature, the 'author' or 'producer' of a cart. If, however, we follow the better attested Θεοῦ, Greg. is inserting his own belief that the Logos is, in reality, the divine author of creation.

55–77. *The Incarnation does not impair the Godhead of Christ*

57. ὑπεδέξατο: an appropriate meaning here is that found in the 4th c. AD in *POxy.* 67. 11, 'to submit to'.

παθέεσσιν: cf. above, vv. 2 n., 48 n. If ἀρήγων is taken here in a strong sense of deliverance, we have an allusion to a common notion that Christ's Passion achieves for man the state of ἀπάθεια, freedom from sinful emotion, a concomitant of deification. (Not infrequently we find this idea combined with that of the suffering of the impassible Word: cf. e.g. *or.* 30. 5 (p. 115. 8–9, M. 36. 109B): σεσωσμένοι τοῖς τοῦ ἀπαθοῦς πάθεσιν). Two passages from Athanasius well illustrate this play on the senses of πάθος: τὸ γὰρ πάθος αὐτοῦ, ἡμῶν ἀπάθειά ἐστι, *inc. et c. Ar.* 5 (M. 26. 992A); αὐτὸς γὰρ ἐνηνθρώπησεν, ἵνα ἡμεῖς θεοποιηθῶμεν . . . τοὺς δὲ πάσχοντας ἀνθρώπους, δι᾽ οὓς καὶ ταῦτα ὑπέμεινεν, ἐν τῇ ἑαυτοῦ ἀπαθείᾳ ἐτήρει καὶ διέσωζε, *inc.* 54. 3 (M. 25. 192B f.).

58. Cf. below, v. 64.

59. Greg. is bringing out what he takes to be a possible implication of the view that the Incarnation set limits upon the Godhead, that it involved Christ in sin. The argument might run: if Godhead alone is sinless, limitation of Godhead means limitation of sinlessness, i.e. the possibility of sin.

60. ἀπέξεσε: ἀποξέω graphically describes the supposed renunciation of Godhead as 'stripping, scraping off', a metaphorical use like that of Alciphron 3. 2: ἀπέξεσας τὴν αἰδῶ τοῦ προσώπου. Elsewhere Greg. uses the word in its common sense of 'polish': *carm.* 2. 1. 11. 1524 (M. 37. 1135A); *orr.* 40. 22 (M. 36. 389A), 43. 64 (581A). ἀπέξεσε is contrasted with κένωσας, *Arc.* 8. 39, where see n. To strip off Godhead is quite different from 'emptying' it of κλέος, a divine form of manifestation.

61. On the structure of the line cf. *Intro.* IV (d).

ἰητὴρ: common in Homer in a literal sense, the word is established in Classical Greek in a figurative sense also. Heracles in S. *Tr.* 1209 speaks of ἰητῆρα τῶν . . . κακῶν. The absolute use of the word occurs in Pi. *P.* 4. 270 (= 'deliverer'), but the idea of healing is not lost. So here, the deliverance from πάθη is seen as the healing of a disease. In Christian literature the cognates ἴασις and ἰάομαι are to be found in figurative use at an early date. The verb occurs, e.g., in Hermas, *vis*. 1. 1. 9 of the healing of sins (cf. 1. 3. 1). But of course the idea may be carried back much farther. When the writer of 1 Pet. says of Christ in 2. 24 οὗ τῷ μώλωπι ἰάθητε, he is attributing to him the healing functions of Isa. 53. 5, the healing not precisely of sins but of a sinful people. ἴασις, too, is found in Hermas of the forgiveness of sins (*mand*. 4. 1. 11, *sim*. 7. 4), and it is of interest to trace the figurative sense back to Sir. 28. 3 (καὶ παρὰ κυρίου ζητεῖ ἴασιν) and to find it in late Plato (*Leg*. 9. 862c). A good parallel is Philo, *Leg. All*. 2. 20. 79. (1. 80 M., 1. 96. 5 C.–W.) ἴασις τοῦ πάθους. As for ἰατρός, of which ἰητήρ is an archaic equivalent, we find it applied to Christ in a similar sense to that considered here: Ign. *Eph*. 7. 2 (Bihlmeyer, p. 84. 25 ff.; M. 5. 649b f.); cf. also Grillmeier, *Christ in Christian Tradition*, 87–8. A large number of examples of this figurative use of ἰατρός and its cognates has been collected in J. Dziech, *De Gregorio Nazianzeno diatribae quae dicitur alumno* (Poznán, 1925), 207 ff. As well as listing passages from Greg. to show that it was a well-used figure by him, Dziech quoted extensively from other Fathers and from pagan writers.

ἐπικύψας: perhaps ἐπικύπτω deserves mention in *PGL*, as LSJ provide no example in the sense 'condescend'.

62–77. These lines are an extended illustration of the opening words ἦν βροτός, ἀλλὰ Θεός.

63. πλάστης: the connection between the Second Person of the Trinity and the creation of man is treated specifically in *Arc*. 7. 57–77.

σαρκοφόρος well illustrates the way in which words take their colouring from the thought of those who use them. To Apollinarius θεὸς σαρκοφόρος (fr. 109, Lietzmann 233) is an expression which supports a one-nature Christology, a view which sees Christ as composed to form a unity of impassible divinity and passible humanity (fr. 6, Lietzmann 206–7; cf. Kelly, *Doctrines*, 291–2). Greg., on the other hand, without denying the unity of the Person of Christ (cf. the section *Christology* in the introduction to the poem), sees in σαρκοφόρος a way of drawing a distinction between the divine and the human natures.

Among Gregory's predecessors in the use of the term in the sense 'incarnate' are Ignatius and Clem. Alex.; Ath. in *inc. et c. Ar*. 8 (M. 26. 996c) speaks of θεὸς σαρκοφόρος.

σώματος ἐκτός: the work of the Logos in the universe, his providential government (*Arc.* 5. 35), cannot be interrupted by the Incarnation. The Word continues to exercise his functions 'outside the body'. Greg. is thus saying something akin to what we find in a well-known place in Athanasius, *inc.* 17. 1 (M. 25. 125A): οὐ γὰρ δὴ περικεκλεισμένος ἦν ἐν τῷ σώματι· οὐδὲ ἐν σώματι μὲν ἦν, ἀλλαχόσε δὲ οὐκ ἦν κτλ.

64. παρθενικῆς: for Greg.'s teaching on the Virgin, see *or.* 38. 13 (M. 36. 325B f.) = 43. 62 (M. 36. 576C ff.), *ep.* 101 (M. 37. 177C ff.). Cf. also *orr.* 45. 9 (M. 36. 633D), 29. 4 (p. 78. 11–12, M. 36. 80A), *carmm.* 1. 1. 10. 49 (M. 37. 468A), 2. 2. 7. 172 (M. 37. 1564A), together with G. Söll, 'Die Mariologie der Kappadozier im Lichte der Dogmengeschichte', *ThQ* 131 (1951), 288–319. References to the Virgin carry comparatively little weight in Greg.'s anti-Eunomian writings (the *or.* 29. 4 passage mentioned is little more than a side-glance). It is not until Greg. is engaged against Apollinarius (cf. *ep.* 101) that he puts stress in his Christology on the place of Mary.

περίγραφος is not at variance with οὐ . . . περικεκλεισμένος in the sentence of Athanasius quoted on v. 63. Greg. is affirming the voluntary self-limitation of Christ in the Incarnation (cf. Sellers, *Two Ancient Christologies*, 71), while Ath. loc. cit. is denying his essential restriction κατ' οὐσίαν. Greg.'s equivalent of the latter is ἀμέτρητος (for which cf. Cyr. *Jo.* 1. 3 (4. 22A), applied to Christ).

65–6. Cf. Luke 2. 7, Matt. 2. 2, 9–11 and *Arc.* 5. 53 ff., 8. 60 ff.

δωροφόροι: cf. P. *Pi.* 5. 86. The noun δωροφορία is used by Isid. Pel. *epp.* 1. 18 (M. 78. 193B) of the Magi; cf. Cyr. *Ps.* 8: 1 (M. 69. 757A).

67. ἀγῶνα: Origen refers to the Temptation as πρὸς τὸν διάβολον ἀγῶνα τοῦ Κυρίου, *Jo.* 10. 1 (p. 171. 15, M. 14. 308A).

ὑπέρσχεθε: the choice lies between this otherwise unattested form and the regular Homeric ὑπερέσχεθε (Cu) which, however, does not here scan. The former is the more likely: Greg. might well have taken it for a Homeric form. But a line with an extra syllable, whatever his other metrical shortcomings may be, is not what one would expect of Greg.

68. Cf. Matt. 4. 1–11, Luke 4. 1–13. (Mark 1. 12–13 does not have the threefold form).

69. Cf. Mark 6. 30–44, 8. 1–10, Matt. 14. 13–21, 15. 32–39, Luke 9. 10–17, John 6. 1–14.

ἄμειψε: the Gospel narrative (John 2. 1–11) uses no word to describe Christ's action, saying merely that the water 'had become' (γεγενημένον) wine. ἀμείβω is a regular Classical word for effecting a change, being, for instance, Euripides' word for the change of Dionysus into mortal form (*Ba.* 4).

70–1. Cf. Mark 1. 9–11, Matt. 3. 13–17, Luke 3. 21–2. He who underwent baptism, described in *Arc.* 3. 47 as κάθαρσις, is himself the giver of purification.

72. Cf. Mark 4. 35–41, Matt. 8. 23–7, Luke 8. 22–5.

73. πάρετος = 'palsied' is found in *Ap* 5. 54 (Diosc.). *PGL* s.v. 1, points out the connection of the word with Matt. 9. 2 in Mac. Mgn. *apocr.* 2. 8 (p. 10. 5).

75. The structure of the line is discussed in Introd. III (*d*). The θύος/ Θεός play may be compared with ὁ θεὸς θυόμενος in CTrull. *or. imp.* (H. 3. 1652 D), AD 692.

ἀρχιερεύς: cf. Heb. 2. 17, 3. 1, 5. 10, 6. 20, 7. 26, 8. 1, 9. 11. Here ἀρχιερεὺς directs attention to the divine function of Christ: it is as the divine Son that he is able to carry out the office of High Priest. *Or.* 30. 16 (p. 134. 5, M. 36. 124 D) lists ἀρχιεροσύνη with προσφορά as words concerned with τὸ πάσχον, i.e., the human side of Christ, and a similar view is set out in Cyr. *Heb.* 2. 17 (M. 74. 965 C–D): αὐτὸς γέγονεν ἀρχιερεὺς κατὰ τὸ ἀνθρώπινον. Cf. Thdt. *eran.* 2. (4. 92, M. 83. 128–9): ... ἥτις (*sc.* ἀρχιεροσύνη) ἀνθρώποις μᾶλλον ἢ Θεῷ προσήκει: cf. *PGL* s.v.

76. The question to whom Christ's blood is offered is raised in *carm.* 1. 1. 10. 65–72 (M. 37. 470A), where the answer given is that it is an ἀντάλλαγμα to God. Christ is here said to have made a votive offering to God. This is the meaning which ἀνέθηκε would have had in Classical Greek and *PGL* shows that the sense continued. The verb is used of devoting someone or something to God's service: God is to use the offering. This form of expression in this line points to the human side of Christ, who, *qua* man, accomplishes nothing by the offering of his blood until the Father has accepted and used the offering in the purification of man. But looked at from the divine side, Christ, *qua* God, may be said by his sacrifice to have purified the whole world.

Elsewhere Gregory is careful to guard against possible misinterpretation of this language. In *or.* 45. 22 (M. 36. 653B) he rejects the idea of the transactional payment of a ransom either to the devil or to the Father. The Father however accepts an offering which he had not demanded. Yet because of the complete involvement of the Three Persons in the οἰκονομία, the Father himself shares in the very sacrifice which he accepts. (Cf. Winslow, ch. 5.)

77. M. Guignet remarks on a similar image in *or*. 43. 64 (M. 36. 581 A): '. . . le péché, notion abstraite, devient une sorte d'être immonde dont Jésus s'est chargé pour le clouer avec lui sur la croix' (*S. Grégoire de Nazianze et la rhétorique* (Paris, 1911), 138).

78–83. *Conclusion*

The life, death, and resurrection of Christ all point to his divine and human natures.

The strict pattern of contrasting half-lines is now broken. The second part of v. 78 depicts Christ's action as man, corresponding to the whole of v. 79, his action as God. The internal contrast is taken up again in v. 80, for the last time in the poem.

78–9. For the Descent into Hades cf. *or*. 29. 20 (p. 106. 2 ff., M. 36. 101 B-C) and *carm*. 1. 1. 33. 8–9, M. 37. 514A (if it is genuine; cf. Werhahn, 'Dubia und Spuria unter den Gedichten Gregors von Nazianz', 342–3).

ἐμίχθη: it is no casual encounter that is implied by this verb. Christ did not 'mingle' with the dead as, in English, observers 'mingle' with a crowd. He became one of them. (For the force of μίγνυμι cf. *Arc*. 1. 24 n.)

Note that the text does not specify which of the dead were raised by Christ and the possibility, which is supported by *carm*. 1. 1. 35. 8–9 (M. 37. 517A)

> . . . εἰς ὅ κε πάντας
> Ταρταρέων μογέοντας ὑφ' αἵματι λύσατο δεσμῶν,

is that he intended to indicate that all the dead were released. But the authenticity of this poem is questioned (cf. Werhahn, loc. cit.). Moreover, the weight of tradition known to Greg. points to the view that Christ's Descent released the Old Testament saints and prophets, not that it signified the redemption of mankind in general. This latter view emerges in Rufinus (*comm. in symb. apost.* 16–17 (M. *PL*. 21. 354 ff.)) and is developed in later Latin writers. But it is the first understanding which is found from Irenaeus (*haer*. 1. 25. 2, M. 7. 689A f.; 4. 42. 4. 1058B f.) to Chrysostom (*in Matt. hom.* 36. 3, M. 57. 416 f.) and it is this which justifies Caillau's addition of 'multos' to 'antea mortuos'. Additional references from Clem. Alex., Origen, Eusebius, Cyril of Jerusalem, and Epiphanius are given in J. N. D.

Kelly, *Rufinus: A Commentary on the Apostles' Creed* (Westminster, Md., and London, 1955), 128–9, cf. p. 121 and id., *Creeds*, 378 ff.

80. Caillau's ἐκεῖνα cannot stand; the suggested κἀκεῖνα saves the metre but does little for the sense. The well-attested εἰ κεῖνα gives clear sense.

πλοῦτος: cf. 2. *Cor.* 8. 9, where 'rich' refers to the pre-existent Christ. For ἀσάρκου we may cite *or.* 38. 2 (M. 36. 313B) as parallel: ὁ ἄσαρκος σαρκοῦται.

81. The imperatival infinitive may be thought to give a stronger sense than the deferential optative.

82. The preferred reading κείνη . . . τεύχει makes an assertion of truth: Godhead exalts the earthly form. Caillau's κείνην . . . τεύχειν exhorts the reader to acknowledge this.

ἐρικυδέα: In Homer the word is often associated with the glorious qualities of gods. (Cf. e.g. *Il.* 14. 327.)

82–3. μορφήν . . . μορφώσατο: though a stronger form than Phil. 2. 7, μορφήν . . . λαβών, the cognate adds little to the sense. (Contrast this with the words found in the poem of disputed authenticity referred to in n. on vv. 78–9 above, *carm.* 1. 1. 35. 7 (M. 37. 517A), where ἑκὼν ἠλλάξατο μορφήν, also used of the Incarnation, introduces the element of change.) Cf. μορφὴν ἀνδρομέην in 1. 1. 11. 6 (M. 37. 471A).

ἄφθιτος Υἱός: the closing words are a summary affirmation of the central thought of the poem. Strong as is the emphasis on the humanity of Christ, it is his divinity which has been attacked and which calls for defence.

ἄφθιτος, applied to divine persons as early as the Homeric Hymns and Hesiod (*h.Merc.* 326, *Th.* 389, 397), came to be almost a stock term in the Sibylline Oracles; cf. ἄφθιτος θεός, *orac. Sib.* 5. 298, 12. 132, *al.* Apollinarius Metaphrastes also takes it up, e.g. in *met. Ps.* (p. 42. 2 Ludwig; M. 33. 1336D). Much of the importance of the word in this line lies in its correspondence with the prose ἄφθαρτος which formed a point of dissension in the controversy with Eunomius. He demanded that ἄφθαρτος in its absolute sense be reserved for the Father alone, maintaining that ἀφθαρσία cannot be shared by the Son, *apol.* 28 (M. 30. 868A; Vaggione p. 74. 9–10). Basil and Nyssen both assailed this view. (Major passages are conveniently collected in *PGL* s.vv. ἄφθαρτος B. 3 and ἀφθαρσία A.) This poem throughout is adding its impetus to that anti-Eunomian thrust. It may also be said that ἄφθιτος Υἱός maintains a theological emphasis which is found from *Diognetus* onwards: that the Son, immortal, incorruptible, while present in mortal, corruptible flesh, retains his ἀφθαρσία untouched; cf. *Diogn.* 9. 2 at one end of the time-scale and Leo Mag. *ep.* 35 (p. 41. 17, M. *PL* 54. 808c ff.) at the other. The exigencies of polemic should not figure too largely in our assessment.

3. On the Spirit

Title and purpose

The MSS' title περὶ (τοῦ ἁγίου) Πνεύματος accurately describes the contents of vv. 1–36. The remainder of the poem, as one might expect, concerns itself with the relationships within the Trinity of the Three Persons, pointing to conclusions which were implicit in the first two poems but which may now be drawn explicitly, the divinity of the Holy Spirit being established.

Greg.'s teaching on the *Holy Spirit* is discussed in books referred to for his Trinitarian thinking (cf. *Arc.* 1. 25–35a introduction). Additional treatment, referring more specifically to the Holy Spirit apart from the Trinitarian question, will be found in T. Schermann, *Die Gottheit des Heiligen Geistes nach den griechischen Vätern des vierten Jahrhunderts* (Freiburg i. B., 1901), 145–67; P. Galtier, *Le Saint-Esprit en nous d'après les Pères grecs* (Rome, 1946), 175–80.

Within Greg.'s works particular attention may be given to these passages dealing with the Holy Spirit: *carm.* 2. 1. 14. 33 ff. (M. 37. 1247A f.); *orr* 2. 38 (M. 35. 445C), 20. 10–11 (1077A ff.), 21. 33 (1121C ff.); 31 *passim* (pp. 145–90; M. 36. 133B–172B), 41 *passim* (428A–452C); *ep.* 102 (M. 37. 193B ff.).

Something of Greg.'s teaching on the Holy Spirit has already emerged in *Arc.* 1 (see notes on *Arc.* 1. 16–24, 35 ff.). Greg. clearly took very seriously his role as defender of the full divinity of the Spirit. He does not think of himself as an innovator but rather as one who is privileged to make explicit teaching about the Holy Spirit which had been implicit in Christian doctrine from the start. He follows closely on the heels of Basil (cf. Galtier 175), but claims that in so doing he is loyal not only to a personal friend but to the intention of the Creed of Nicaea itself (*ep.* 102, M. 37. 193C). Basil's circumspection on the subject of the divinity of the Holy Spirit has been often remarked.

Thus, while Greg. continues the work of Basil, he also goes beyond it. The arguments of the *De Spiritu Sancto* make sense only on the assumption that the Spirit is God, but this belief is not explicitly stated. We may compare *ep.* 236. 6, where τὸ θεῖον, rather than the reading of one codex (Harl.) τὸν Θεόν is surely correct. Gregory discusses Basil's diffidence in a passage of a speech in his praise, *or.* 43. 69 (M. 36. 589A ff.), maintaining that his friend held a full doctrine of the divinity of the Spirit, while, to avoid the risk of being deposed by heretics, allowing himself to come to an arrangement in the matter of overt expression (ἑαυτῷ μὲν τὴν οἰκονομίαν ἐπέτρεψεν, 589Α). For Basil's position, see Quasten, *Patrology*, iii. 231–3, with the bibliography there, and Galtier 135 ff. (Cf. also Holl, *Amphilochius von Ikonium*, 158 ff.)

The opponents of the acceptance of the Holy Spirit's full divinity who are attacked by Greg. are the Pneumatomachians or Macedonians (cf. Kelly, *Doctrines*, 259–60; Quasten, *Patrology*, iii. 259, bibliography to Nyssen's *Sermo de Spiritu Sancto adversus Pneumatomachos Macedonianos*) and Eunomius (cf. *Arc*. 2. 32b–35 n.). The former were the object of the clauses on the Holy Spirit in the Creed of Constantinople (cf. Kelly, *Creeds*, 339–40, 342–4), while the latter, having rejected the divinity of the Son, was scarcely likely to be more favourable towards that of the Spirit. Eunomius is a thoroughgoing heretic who is contrasted with the half-orthodox (*or*. 31. 24: 175. 14, M. 36. 160c). Cf. *Arc*. 1. 35b–39 n. Greg. clearly makes a distinction between him and the more moderate of the Pneumatomachi who, as he remarks in *or*. 41. 8 (M. 36. 440b ff.), comes very close to acceptance of the fully orthodox position. The tone of the oration is conciliatory, more conciliatory than that of, say, *Arc*. 1. 35b–39 where there is a note of asperity as well as encouragement in Greg.'s approach to the ἡμιφαεῖς. In addressing his congregation Greg. concentrates on the soundness of his hearers' beliefs on the First and Second Persons, regretting their failure to take the next step of professing faith in the Holy Spirit, but expressing confidence that they will, once the issues are clearly explained to them. *Arc*. 3, on the other hand, is much closer in spirit to the polemic of *or*. 31 where Eunomius, rather than progressive Pneumatomachi, is the target. (Cf., for instance, vv. 37 ff. which contain the arguments used against Eunomius in cc. 10 f. of *or*. 31).

1–9. *The Holy Spirit is to be worshipped as God*

1. θυμέ, τί δηθύνεις;: Keydell, 'Ein dogmatisches Lehrgedicht', 315, compares the opening words with those of Call. *H*. 4. 1–2:

> τὴν ἱερήν, ὦ θυμέ, τίνα χρόνον ἢ πότ' ἀείσεις
> Δῆλον, Ἀπόλλωνος κουροτρόφον;

But, apart from the occurrence of θυμέ, the resemblance is not very marked. Callimachus is not expressing awe or reluctance as Greg. is in τί δηθύνεις; Closer parallels for the rhetorical figure of hesitation in the face of a great theme will be found in K. Thraede,

'Untersuchungen zum Ursprung und zur Geschichte der christlichen Poesie II', *JAC* 5 (1962), 128-31 ('Schwierigkeitsäußerungen'), where examples are given from Latin poetry.

There is, however, a very close verbal parallel in Apollinarius Metaphrastes. Four times in his metrical version of the Psalms he asks θυμέ, τί δηθύνεις; In his versions of *met*. *Ps.* 41. 6 (p. 87. 11 Ludwich; M. 33. 1369D), 41. 12 (p. 87. 27, M. 33. 1372A), 42. 5 (p. 88. 12, M. 33. 1372B) he renders the LXX ἵνα τί περίλυπος εἶ, ἡ ψυχή, καὶ ἵνα τί συνταράσσεις με; as θυμέ τί δηθύνεις; τί δέ μοι νόον ἔνδον ὀρίνεις; In *met*. *Ps.* 114. 7 (p. 241. 13, M. 33. 1489B) θυμέ, τί δηθύνεις μετὰ σὴν ἀνάπαυσιν ἱκέσθαι; represents ἐπίστρεψον, ἡ ψυχή μου, εἰς τὴν ἀνάπαυσίν σου in LXX. It is, however, one thing to detect a verbal correspondence and another to determine its significance. We may dismiss the possibility that the two writers independently hit on this expression, involving as it does the unusual word δηθύνω. Three possibilities remain: (*a*) that Greg. borrowed the words from Apoll.; (*b*) that Apoll. borrowed the words from Greg.; (*c*) that both borrowed from a third source.

Of an earlier source I have been able to find no trace. Should such a source emerge, the whole question would have to be reopened. But, in the meantime, we may consider (*a*) and (*b*). We cannot here set out upon an examination of the complex questions of ascription and dating which are inseparable from any consideration of this version of the Psalms. Most critical scholarship regards as doubtful the attribution of the *metaphrases* to Apollinarius of Laodicea. Some scholars have no hesitation in dissociating him from this work, others (in recent years F. Scheidweiler, *BZ* 49 (1956), 336-44) are prepared to defend his authorship (see Quasten, *Patrology*, iii. 380-1, and Introd., III. 58.) In favour of the view that Greg. provides the original which has been imitated by a later writer it should be observed that *Arc*. 3. 1 is the only one of the passages quoted where the words have any real point. δηθύνω means 'I delay, hesitate' and this is precisely the meaning called for in the present passage. But δηθύνεις does not provide an obvious paraphrase of ἵνα τί περίλυπος εἶ; It may, therefore, be suggested that in the *metaphrases* θυμέ τί δυθήνεις; is quoted as a formula and, unless some other source is proved, a formula derived from Greg.

2. For φύσις as the ground of unity within the Godhead cf. n. on v. 41 below.

3. ὅ μοι Θεός: the manuscript text is supported both by Nicetas (ὅτι μοι Θεὸς οὗτος) and by the anonymous scholiast quoted in Hoeschel (p. 23: ὅπερ ἐμοι Θεός ἐστι). The traditional ὁμοίθεον of the editions is an incorrect formation found nowhere else (*PGL* s.v.), and not to be justified as a metrical adjustment of ὁμόθεον. Certainly, ὁμόθεον would give splendid sense here, claiming identity of Godhead for the Holy Spirit as it is claimed for the Son in *or.* 25. 17 (M. 35. 1224A). But can the words be taken as equivalent? There is no justification for Caillau's 'pariter Deo' or Gallay's 'Dieu également'. *PGL* is surely right in holding that the meaning cannot be pushed beyond 'like God', and such a meaning falls below the level of doctrinal demand made in the poem. In his speech in honour of Athanasius, Greg. had shown his awareness that, in Christological formulation, ὅμοιος language is a 'bait to catch simple souls' (*or.* 21. 22, M. 35. 1108A). (He was talking about *Symb.CP* (360), ap. Ath. *syn.* 30.) It is scarcely likely, therefore, that he should allow himself to slip into such language, with its obvious theological escape-clause, when he is trying to commend the full divinity of the Holy Spirit in precisely the same way as he was upholding that of the Son in the oration. Nor, it may be remarked, is Greg. so metrically inept as to be forced into using a word of dubious theological import merely because he could think of no other way of keeping his hexameter right. Hence only ὅ μοι Θεός, which states Greg.'s belief succinctly, can be considered the correct text. (Note that the following ᾧ Θεὸν ἔγνων, together with Θεὸν in the corresponding position in the next line, would make it easy to explain by assimilation a change from ὅ μοι Θεός to ὁμοίθεον.)

The words ᾧ Θεὸν ἔγνων emphasize Gregory's belief in the directness of his inspiration to proclaim true doctrine. Cf. *Arc.* 1. 16–24 n.

4. Caillau's text which reads ὅς in both halves of the line should be retained against suggestions in his note of reading καὶ ὅ or, with Billius, καὶ ὡς. The masc. relative is easily assimilated to the following Θεός in the first part of the line and may well be preserved for balance in the second, in preference to the grammatically correct ὅ. To read ὡς would be to preserve the same sense but in a weakened form: the effect of baptism would be that man should become not God, but 'as' God.

The real difficulty in the line is the meaning of ἔναντα. Caillau tr. 'manifeste' and Gallay follows him with his 'clairement'. (Billius does not translate at all.) But lexical investigation fails to provide any direct evidence for such a meaning: ἔναντα means 'opposite'. The only way, apart from guessing, by which one could arrive at a meaning 'clearly, openly' for ἔναντα would involve some very dubious equations. Nicetas glosses ἔναντα by ἄντικρυς, without, however, making clear the way in which he understood that word. For ἄντικρυς may mean either 'opposite' or 'openly' (cf. LSJ s.v.). But it is semantically unsound to assume that the virtual equivalence of the two words in the sense 'opposite' makes it possible to carry over to ἔναντα the ἄντικρυς meaning 'openly'. It remains, therefore, to ask whether the passage will yield good sense if ἔναντα is taken in the attested sense 'opposite'. Now the run of the line might suggest that ἔναντα and ἐνθάδε are contrasted. If ἐνθάδε is taken as 'in this world' (a regular usage from Pindar on: cf. LSJ s.v.), ἔναντα might perhaps mean 'on the opposite side', i.e. 'in heaven'. I can find no instance of ἔναντα in this precise sense, but it appears a reasonable extension of the normal meaning, especially when ἐνθάδε is there to point the contrast. The Holy Spirit is God in heaven, the world of eternal verity, and he is God in the physical world, where, through baptism, he deifies believers. Greg.'s belief in the deification effected by the Holy Spirit in baptism is stated in *or*. 31. 28 (p. 181. 11–12, M. 36. 165A); cf. also Hipp.† *theoph*. 8. (p. 262. 4 ff., M. 10. 860A), together with Lampe, *The Seal of the Spirit*, 144. Greg.'s teaching on deification in general is discussed in *Arc*. 4. 95–6 n., where references to other passages will be found. Another possibility might be to take ἔναντα in the sense of ἔναντι and supply τοῦ Θεοῦ to give 'in the presence of God.' This I find difficult.

5. **πανσθενής** is not found before Patristic times, when it comes into use to denote aspects of divine power. *PGL* cites no other instance of the application of the word to the Holy Spirit. But there may be an indirect connection in Clem. *str*. 7. 7 (p. 33. 18 ff., M. 9. 464B). For close on his reference to τῇ πανσθενεῖ δυνάμει Clement goes on: πνευματικὸς εἶναι σπουδάσας διὰ τῆς ἀορίστου ἀγάπης ἥνωται τῷ πνεύματι. It is suggested in the edn. of F. J. A. Hort and J. E. B. Mayor, *Clement of Alexandria: Miscellanies, Book VII* (London and New York, 1902), 226 that it is 'best to take πνεύματι here of the Holy Spirit, rather than to translate "in his spirit".' ('His' refers to the true gnostic.) If this is so, there is association of πανσθενής with the Spirit, if not application of the word to him. In *carm*. 2. 1. 38. 10, M. 37. 1326A πανσθενές is addressed to Christ.

αἰολόδωρον: the only other example of the word cited in the lexica is from the 6th c. BC philosopher Epimenides, who applied it to the Eumenides (fr. 19, DK 1. 36). Whether Greg. knew this passage or other instances unknown to us or whether he believed that he was coining a new compound as, apparently, he coined αἰολόδερμος in *carm.* 1. 2. 15. 11 (M. 37. 766A), it is impossible to tell. The word admirably renders the idea of the gifts of the Spirit in 1 Cor. 12. 1 ff. and Heb. 2. 4. The variant ὀλβιόδωρον, reported by Caillau (it occurs in Vat. gr. 482, fo. 83), is found also in LΩ. It is not difficult to account for the appearance of this reading in MSS. It represents assimilation to the text of *carm.* 2. 1. 38. 9–10 (M. 37. 1326A):

> αἰῶνος πείρημα, μεγακλεές, ὀλβιόδωρε,
> ὑψίθρον’, οὐράνιε, πανσθενές, ἆσθμα νόου . . .

ὀλβιόδωρος itself is not a common word, being found in most MSS at E. *Hipp.* 749 and *AP* 11. 69 (Paulus Silentarius, 6th c. AD). ὕμνημα first appears in this passage. It is possible that ἀγνῆς . . . χορείης may include in its meaning ‘*casti . . . chori* (virginum)’, as Caillau suggests, but more probable that the words have reference to the heavenly choir, as do similar words in *Arc.* 8. 61. Perhaps Is. 6 may be in mind.

6. φερέσβιον: the word goes back to the Homeric Hymns and to Hesiod, where it describes the life-giving forces of the earth (*h. Ap.* 341, *h. Cer.* 450, *h. Hom.* 30. 9; Hes. *Th.* 693), and it is applied to various gods by Empedocles 6. 2 (*PPF*, p. 108; DK i. 312), A. *Fr.* 300. 7, Antipho 1; cf. also Ps.-Arist. *Mu.* 391ᵇ13. Here we may suppose that it does duty for the Constantinopolitan ζωοποιόν, *Symb. Nic.-CP* (*ACO* 2. 1. 2. p. 80. 12; H. 2. 288B), a word excluded by its metrical intransigence. But, metrical considerations apart, it is in Greg.’s style to find words with pagan religious associations and to naturalize them in Christian use; cf. Introd., IV (*a*). This is a good example. As Dr A. Meredith has suggested to me, this is a very apt word to set out the range of the Holy Spirit’s gifts of physical and spiritual life, leading to eternal life.

ὑψιθόωκον is an expression of the equality of the Holy Spirit with the other Persons of the Godhead. Again, we find a coinage of Gregory’s, used also in *carm.* 1. 2. 9. 148 (M. 37. 679A). It corresponds to ὑψίθρονος, which Pindar had applied to the gods (*N.* 4. 65, *I.* 6(5). 16) and which Gregory himself uses several times of Christ, e.g. *carm.* 2. 1. 38. 10 (M. 37. 1326A, above, v. 5 n.), and also of human rulers, *carm*. 2. 1. 32. 34 (M. 37. 1303A), *ep*. 154 (M. 37. 206C, GCS p. 113. 5).

7. Again, a technical term of the Nicaeno-Constantinopolitan Creed is excluded by metre, for ἐκπορευόμενον cannot be fitted into a hexameter: see *Symb. Nic.-CP* (*ACO* 2. 1. 2, p. 80. 13; H. 2. 288B). Greg., who elsewhere emphasizes the distinction between the Son and Spirit by contrasting γέννησις and ἐκπόρευσις, *or*. 31. 8 (p. 154. 10 ff., M. 36. 141A f.), cf. 39. 12 (M. 36. 348B), is here content to use non-technical language, writing Πατρόθεν ἐρχό-μενον. Indeed, anyone who saw these words out of context might well associate them not with the Spirit but with the Son, recalling as they do the expression used of Jesus in John 3. 2b. He is said to have 'come from' God (ἔρχεσθαι ἀπὸ is used). In this poem, the difference between the way in which the Son 'comes from' the Father and the way in which the Spirit 'comes from' him is made clear not by distinctions in the verb but in the discussions of vv. 37 ff.

αὐτοκέλευστον: the tone of the word is different from that found when it is used by Classical authors (cf. LSJ s.v.) and once in Nonnus, *par.Jo*. 19. 5 (M. 43. 901A), where it indicates a certain arrogation of authority. Here it has very much the sense of 'self-determined' which is associated with αὐτοκίνητος; cf. Gr. Nyss. *or. cat*. 2 (p. 15. 7, M. 45. 17C). It is in this meaning that αὐτοκέλευστος is found in other places in Nonnus: *par.Jo*. 5. 15 (M. 43. 788A), 18. 4 (889B). Cf. v. 42 n. below.

8. Aware of the open nature of ἐρχόμενον, Greg. guards against any confusion of the First and Second Persons by asserting the unique-ness of the relationship of the Son to the Father. It is this precise question, why the Spirit is not a second Son, which produces the anti-Eunomian distinction of γέννησις and ἐκπόρευσις mentioned in the previous note; cf. *or*. 31. 7–8 (pp. 153 ff., M. 36. 140C ff.), and below, v. 34 n.

9. ὁμόδοξον: in *or*. 42. 16 (M. 36. 476C) Greg. asserts his right to walk a middle path between Sabellians and Arians, beginning his summary of faith by claiming that the Three Persons are ὁμοούσιά τε καὶ ὁμόδοξα, and thus cutting away the Arian subordination. So here, the equality of the Persons is guarded. Cf. also the adverb ὁμο-δόξως in *or*. 31. 14 (p. 163. 8, M. 36. 149A) with a similar intent.

ἀειδέος: the emphasis may be not only on the stock idea that Godhead is 'invisible' but also that it is above all notions of form.

Cf. Gr.Nyss. *Eun*. 1 (1. 89. 11, M. 45. 321 A) and citations in *PGL* s.v. ἀνείδεος.

10–23. *Scripture accommodates to human weakness in treating the Spirit's divinity*

The alleged silence of Scripture about the divinity of the Holy Spirit is treated at length in *or*. 31. 21–30 (pp. 171–86, M. 36. 156 C–169 A), where Eunomius is addressed as the opponent to be confuted. There, as here, Greg. devotes himself to showing that the Holy Spirit is no ξένον θεὸν καὶ ἄγραφον, *or*. 31. 1 (p. 145. 6, M. 36. 133 B). The contrast between what he is in his eternal being and the way in which he is manifested to men is fundamental and confusion must be avoided. In introducing the subject in *or*. 31. 21, Greg. claims no originality but says that he realizes that others have treated it before (p. 171. 1 ff., M. 36. 156 C), principally, no doubt, thinking of Athanasius *Ad Serapionem* and Basil, *De spiritu sancto*; cf. J. Barbel, *Gregor von Nazianz: Die fünf theologischen Reden* (Düsseldorf, 1963), 225 n. 36.

10. 'Inspired Law' means OT Scripture in general; see *PGL* s.v. νόμος C 8 b. iii. For σελίδεσσι cf. *Arc*. 1. 16 n.

12 ff. The many evidences of the Spirit's divinity which Greg. claims may be deduced from Scripture are enumerated in *or*. 31. 29 (pp. 182 ff., M. 36. 165 A ff.). Here he confines himself to naming the conditions which make it possible to appreciate Scripture's indirect attestation. These are: (*a*) readiness of the human will; (*b*) personal reception of the Spirit; (*c*) mental clarity. These lines, by concentrating attention on the human side of the apprehension of divine truth, balance the emphasis on divine initiative found in the following lines and in lines like *Arc*. 1. 36.

M. Kertsch, *Bildersprache bei Gregor von Nazianz* (Graz, 1978), 12–13, sees in v. 12 a reference to the figure of the road or river which divides only to come together again further down; cf. *or*. 31. 1 (p. 145. 7 ff., M. 36. 133 B).

14. εἴρυσεν: the figure may be a Christianized version of H. *Il*. 8. 21, where ἐρύω depicts the drawing down of Zeus from heaven (cf. οὐρανίοιο v. 11).

15–16. Cf. the note on *Arc*. 1. 1–5.

γυμνὴν ... φωνὴν: similar language is found in *or*. 43. 68 (M. 36. 588 A). Basil, Greg. says, had been unable to give plain, unequivocal expression to the belief 'the Spirit is God', because of the personal dangers involved (γυμνῆς τῆς περὶ τοῦ Πνεύματος φωνῆς).

ἐραννῆς: is there here an echo of Neoplatonic thought? τὸ ἐραννόν is found in Anon. *in Parm.* 2. 30 as the Beatific Vision. Such an association would add another facet to the notion of the beauty of the Godhead.

16b–23 correspond, in short form, to the argument of *or.* 31. 26 (pp. 178–9, M. 36. 161 C ff.). There three successive stages are spoken of: the OT, the NT, and the present age. In the first the Father was clearly revealed, the Son more faintly. The second made clear the Son but merely gave glimpses (p. 178. 6, 161 C: ὑπέδειξε) of the Spirit's divinity. In the third stage, the Spirit dwells with men, giving clearer demonstration of his divinity. Then follows an expanded parallel to our present passage: οὐ γὰρ ἦν ἀσφαλές, μήπω τῆς τοῦ Πατρὸς θεότητος ὁμολογηθείσης, τὸν Υἱὸν ἐκδήλως κηρύττεσθαι· μηδὲ τῆς τοῦ Υἱοῦ παραδεχθείσης, τὸ Πνεῦμα τὸ Ἅγιον ... ἐπιφορτίζεσθαι. Cf. ἐπιφορτίζεσθαι with ἄχθος (v. 18).

Greg. is here adumbrating the view that the development of the doctrine of the Holy Spirit shows an accommodation on the part of God to the weakness of human understanding and that such has been the divine method from the start of revelation. Though it is primarily the evidence of Scripture which is under discussion, it is clear that the era of the Son's revelation, beginning in the NT, extended to Greg.'s own day, through slow assimilation. This is why the third stage has taken so long in finding recognition.

H. E. W. Turner, in *The Pattern of Christian Truth* (London, 1954), 266–7, refers to this argument in *or.* 31 in terms which have relevance for the present passage also. After mentioning similar treatment of the subject in Tertullian, Basil and Epiphanius, he outlines Greg.'s version and concludes; 'Such caution harmonises well with the theological nervousness which St. Gregory displays in dealing with the Pneumatomachi.' But is this quite fair to Greg.? The chapter to which specific reference is made (p. 267 n. 1), *or.* 31. 26, is part of a forthright attack upon Eunomius and contributes to an unequivocal affirmation of the divinity of the Holy Spirit. Far from exhibiting 'nervousness', Greg. is quite aggressive. His argument for the delayed manifestation of the full divinity of the Holy Spirit in no way plays down Scriptural evidence (c. 29 is full of it), but simply takes account of the historical fact that, while the status of the Son was a matter of dispute, the Church had given little thought to the explicit development of that evidence into a doctrine of the Spirit's divinity. Greg.'s clear distinction between the essence of the Holy Spirit and the mode of His manifestation allows him a consistent, not to say uncompromising, position.

18. ἄχθος ... ἄπιστον, meaning 'burden of belief they could not face', recalls John 16. 12.

19. ἀρχομένοισι: catechumens may here be meant, as the word is used in Or. *Cels.* 3. 51 (p. 247. 9, M. 11. 988A), with the Church of earlier times likened to a catechumenate. Or the reference may be less technical, simply to any beginners or novices (cf. Caillau's tr. 'tironibus'). Theodoret used the words οἱ ἀρχόμενοι to denote 'the ignorant' in a fairly general way, contrasted with οἱ τετελειωμένοι, *Cant.* 3. 9–10 (S. 2. 87, M. 81. 125A). Some such general sense may be all that is needed here; cf. also *Arc.* 7. 109–10 n.

20–3. The imagery of mental illumination may be found in Classical authors (e.g., E. *IT* 1026), but the sense is greatly filled out by Christian writers to whom God is not merely the source of illumination but light itself. In this passage light and fire are not simply metaphors: God may be identified with both (cf. 32 below). Cf. Moreschini, 'Luce'. The idea of God's *accommodation* to human capacity is one with which Greg. would have been familiar in his reading of Origen. The Alexandrian, for instance, has passages similar to those before us. In *Cels.* 6. 67 (M. 11. 1400C; GCS 2. 137. 18 ff.) he writes: ἔμψυχον δὲ τυγχάνον τὸ ἀληθινὸν φῶς ἐπίσταται, τίνι μὲν δεικτέον ἔσται τὰς μαρμαρυγὰς τίνι δὲ φῶς, οὐ παριστάντος αὐτοῦ τὴν λαμπρότητα ἑαυτοῦ διὰ τὴν ἔτι ἐνυπάρχουσαν ἀσθένειαν τοῖς ὀφθαλμοῖς ἐκείνου. *Pr.* 1. 2. 7 (M. 11. 136A; GCS 5. 37. 14 ff.) may also be compared: 'Qui splendor fragilibus se et infirmis mortalium oculis placidius et lenius offerens et paulatim velut edocens et adsuescens claritatem luminis pati ... capaces eos efficit ad suscipiendam gloriam lucis'. (On the idea of accommodation in general, cf. Turner, *The Pattern of Christian Truth*, 258 ff.).

Kertsch, *Bildersprache*, 205–6 cites parallels in Gregory and points to Philo, *Quod deus sit immutabilis* (i. 284 M. = ii. 74 C.–W.).

21. ἀπληστοτέροιο: 'excessive', a meaning which may be compared with that found in *or.* 21. 23 (M. 35. 1108B), 'immoderate'.

22. πυριθαλπέας: cf. LSJ for the meaning 'heated in the fire'. Here, it may be suspected, the word means more than 'ardentes' (the Caillau tr.), perhaps 'cherishing with warm (beams)'. Cf. LSJ s.v. θάλπω, III. 2.

23. γλυκεροῖο φάους: this looks like a reminiscence of H. *Od.* 16. 23, where the words γλυκερὸν φάος are addressed to Telemachus.

24–36. *The stages of revelation*

24. προφαίνων continues the idea of light, for the word has a basic sense of 'bring to light, manifest'.

25. κλέος: cf. *Arc.* 2. 9 n.

26. The weight of the line falls on the first two words. In *or.* 31. 26 (p. 178. 5, M. 36. 161C) it is ἀμυδρότερον which points the contrast with the revelation of the full divinity of the Father. Here Greg. specifies those to whom the Son's Godhead was revealed, albeit 'rather obscurely'. The 'wise' would include Moses who received the Law from Christ and prophets who foretold his coming.

A similar theme is taken up in the lines from L published by B. Wyss, vv. 34 ff. (cf. Textual Introd., p. xii).

28. αἰγλήεντος: this is Homer's word for Olympus (*Il.* 1. 532, *Od.* 20. 103). The noun αἴγλη came into Christian use to describe, e.g., Christ's divine nature (cf. *PGL* s.v.). For Greg.'s use of adjective and noun cf. *Arc.* 6. 13 and 4. 64.

ὑπήστραψεν: Caillau's tr. 'splendide promulgavit'. But this does not fit the context which calls for a limited manifestation of the Holy Spirit in the second stage of revelation. LSJ gives only one reference for ὑπαστράπτω, to Philostratus, *VA* 2. 24, tr. 'flash or gleam by reflection'. Soph. cites that passage, together with the present one of Gregory, tr. simply 'gleam'. What is needed is something like 'began to show gleams of' or 'showed half-hidden gleams of', as *PGL* sees by offering 'illuminate only a little, reveal only partially'. Parallel senses are found in ὑπολάμπω v. 29 and ὑποδείκνυμι (*or.* 31. 26, p. 178. 6, M. 36. 161C).

29. ὑπέλαμψε: for the meaning 'began to shine' cf. e.g. Hdt. 1. 190.

30–1. The limits of the second stage of revelation are here fixed: from the Incarnation to Pentecost. But there is clearly a certain overlap between the second and the third stages, in that the full recognition of the Son's deity takes place during the third stage and with it goes the gradual recognition of that Spirit, announced for those who could comprehend it—the λαμπρότεροι of *or.* 31. 26. (p. 179. 1, M. 36. 164A)—in the teaching of Jesus, spectacularly proclaimed at Pentecost and slowly assimilated into the understanding of the Church over the centuries.

γλώσσῃσι: cf. Acts 2. 3.

σῆμα: the use of the word to depict a sign from heaven goes back to Homer (e.g. *Il.* 13. 244) and recurs in Pindar (*P.* 4. 199) and (?) Aeschylus (*Pr.* 498).

ἐκ χθονὸς ἆλτο represents Luke's ἐπήρθη (Acts 1. 9). Greg.'s is a vivid expression, associated as it is with vigorous action in Homer (e.g. *Il.* 6. 103, of leaping from a chariot).

32. Behind the first part of the line lie passages like Deut. 4. 24, 9. 3, Heb. 12. 29. On the third passage J. Moffatt observes, *ICC, Hebrews* (Edinburgh, 1924), 223: 'There is no allusion to fire as purifying; ... it is (the) punitive aspect of God which is emphasised here, the divine ζῆλος.' This is how Greg. understands the symbolism of fire here. The avenging is one of the two kinds of fire of which Greg. writes in *or.* 40. 36 (M. 36. 412A). But whereas in the oration Greg. contrasts the avenging with the purifying fire, here the distinction is between punishment and illumination. It is the former contrast which is regularly found from Clem. Alex. onwards. He sets τὸ φρόνιμον πῦρ, the fire which purifies sinful souls, over against τὸ παμφάγον καὶ βάναυσον, *str.* 7. 6 (p. 27. 5 ff., M. 9. 449B); cf. Hort and Mayor's edn., pp. 250–1 n. Here the stress falls heavily on the purifying, over against the purely punitive, fire and this is true in a number of places in Origen, e.g. *princ.* 2. 10. 4 ff. (pp. 177 ff., M. 11. 236C ff.), *Cels.* 4. 13 (pp. 282–3, M. 11. 1041D ff.), 5. 14–16 (pp. 15 ff., M. 11. 1201A ff.). The idea that the two elements in fire to be distinguished are the punitive and the illuminating is found in Basil, *hex.* 6. 3 (G. 1. 52A f., M. 29. 121C f.) Taking the Burning Bush (Exod. 3. 2) as his model, Basil holds that burning and light are inseparable, in human terms, but that God can hold one element of the complex phenomenon fire in suspense (σχολάζουσαν): in a similar way God can separate in the final recompense the natural elements of fire, καὶ τὸ μὲν φῶς, εἰς ἀπόλαυσιν τοῖς δικαίοις, τὸ δὲ τῆς καύσεως ὀδυνηρόν, τοῖς κολαζομένοις ἀποταχθήσεσθαι (52A f., 121D).

John Climacus mentions Greg. in a passage on the heavenly fire, glancing at the teaching of *or.* 40. 36 and rendering the thought of the present line: τὸ αὐτὸ γὰρ πῦρ καταναλίσκον (Deut. 4. 24, etc.) καὶ φωτίζον φῶς ὀνομάζεται, *scal.* 28 (M. 88. 1137C).

34. Cf. above, v. 8 n. Greg. presents an objection in similar language to his assertion that the Spirit is God and ὁμοούσιον in *or.* 31. 10 (p. 156. 11 ff., M. 36. 144A f.). In the following chapter he gives the example of Adam, Eve and Seth.

36. κἀνθάδ': 'at this point also'. Greg. writes as one who can claim some measure of inspiration for the doctrine he teaches, corresponding to the consistency of his proclamation of the Holy Spirit's divinity and, thus, of the true unity of the Godhead. (Cf. *Arc*. 1. 16–24 n.)

37–43. *Distinction without division in the Godhead*

37–9 uses the analogy of Eve and Seth to show that different modes of origin are compatible with consubstantiality. The same argument is set out in *or*. 31. 11 (pp. 158–9, M. 36. 144D ff.) and *or*. 39. 12 (M. 36. 348C). Eve and Seth, though coming into being in different ways, are both alike human and consubstantial with Adam. So the Son and the Spirit, bearing the differences of γέννησις and ἐκπόρευσις, are both alike divine and consubstantial with the Father.

37. ἀρχεγόνοιο: the word is applied again to Adam in *Arc*. 7. 78, *carm*. 1. 1. 18. 3 (M. 37. 481A).

38. ἡμίτομος: Eve was composed of two elements, 'half' being the rib 'cut' from Adam and half the flesh created by God around it (Gen. 2. 21–2). Cf. τμῆμα, applied to Eve in *or*. 31. 11 (p. 158. 8, M. 36. 144D).

41. πρόσθε φέρων τόδ' ἔνερθεν: Billius and Caillau agree in their understanding of these words, tr. respectively 'Celsius inferiusve locans' and 'Aut supra statuens aut infra', and in this they are followed by Gallay who writes 'en mettant l'un avant ou au-dessus de l'autre' (p. 129; repr. Devolder 68). Dishonour is brought upon the Godhead by introducing the distinctions of 'higher' and 'lower'. But there are difficulties in this view—which requires correcting τόδ' to τὸ δ', cf. Denniston, *Greek Particles*, 166. An assumed contrast between πρόσθε and ἔνερθεν has forced a disjunction upon this half-line where none exists. Now the basic meaning of πρόσθε (the poetic form of πρόσθεν) is 'in front, before' (of space or time). Only in a secondary sense does it denote priority of rank. Is it not, therefore, possible to take the words simply as: 'adducing this (thing = analogy) from below'? Greg. is thus warning his reader of the dangers of analogy (cf. vv. 54–70 below). To apply slavishly to the Trinity the analogy of Adam, Eve, and Seth would clearly dishonour it. Adam, for instance, is anterior to Eve and both are anterior to Seth. Such temporal distinctions are meaningless and totally misleading if applied to the Godhead. The following lines support this interpretation, stressing precisely those attributes of the divine nature which distinguish God from man, the only epithet which might favour the 'higher–lower' distinction being ὁμόσεπτον (v. 42); ἴη φύσις, of course, as we shall see, implies the denial of such a distinction.

41b. ἴη φύσις: the words recur in v. 71 below; cf. also v. 73. In Greg.'s terms the ground of unity of the Three Persons, that which they have in common, may be expressed as φύσις, οὐσία, or θεότης, to be distinguished from the principles of differentiation, ἰδιότητες. It is φύσις which takes the weight of Greg.'s answer to all heresies in *or*. 33. 16 (M. 36. 236A), where μία θεότης is amplified as: μίαν φύσιν ἐν τρισὶν ἰδιότησιν. The peroration of *or*. 26 shows a similar pattern: μία φύσις, τρεῖς ἰδιότητες, εἷς Θεός, ὁ ἐπὶ πάντων, καὶ διὰ πάντων, καὶ ἐν πᾶσιν, 19 (M. 35. 1252C); cf. Eph. 4. 6. Cf. also *or*. 32. 21 (M. 36. 197C), *carm*. 2. 1. 12. 310–11 (M. 37. 1188A). The unity of the Persons thus depends entirely upon the very content of the word 'God', upon the unvarying divine activity which φύσις denotes. (On this, see Prestige, *God in Patristic Thought*, 234–5. Cf. further Barbel, *Fünf theol. Reden*, 292 ff.)

ἄμετρον: the use of negative terms like ἄμετρον and ἄκτιστον, ἄχρονον in the following line, together with ἄναρχος, ἀναίτιος (*Arc*. 1. 25), ἀπείριτος (27), ἄπηκτος, ἀσώματος (*Arc*. 2. 16), ἀκέαστος, ἄναρχος, ἀδήριτος (*Arc*. 4. 39), places Greg. in a tradition which goes back to Plato and continues into the Middle Ages, a tradition which finds it so difficult to make meaningful positive statements about the Being of God that it concentrates on negatives as giving a kind of approximation. But, just as Plato has a place for positive affirmation when he speaks (*Rep*. 508E) of the Form of the Good (though it was left to later Platonists to make the identification with God), so Greg. finds positive affirmation possible in his attempt at definition: Θεὸς μέν ἐστιν οὐσία, πρῶτον καλόν, *carm*. 1. 2. 34. 1 (M. 37. 945A). See further Gottwald, *De Gregorio Nazianzeno Platonico*, 19, Gerlitz, *Außerchristliche Einflüsse*, 176–7; Moreschini, 'Platonismo', 1374 ff.

42. ἄκτιστον ἄχρονον: to describe Godhead thus in general terms was straightforward enough. But Greg.'s anti-Eunomian intention is that the epithets be applied individually to the Son and the Spirit.

ἐλεύθερον: again, the word is to be specifically applied to the Second and Third Persons. In particular, the freedom of the Spirit had been a point of dispute between Basil and his opponents in *De spiritu sancto*, where Basil had resisted their attempt to apply ἐλεύθερος to the Spirit as indicating an intermediary state between that of master and servant, *Spir.* 51. (G. 3. 42E ff., M. 32. 160C ff.). Here Greg. is maintaining the fullest possible meaning of 'free' (cf. n. on v. 7 above), with divine freedom tacitly contrasted with man's conditional freedom as it is described in *Arc.* 7. 100-1.

ἐσθλόν: classical and poetic, ἐσθλός may be taken to carry all the senses of the Biblical ἀγαθός as it is applied to God (cf. Arndt–Gingrich s.v. ἀγαθός).

ὁμόσεπτον: apparently a *hapax legomenon.* The reader's attention is again drawn to the status of the Holy Spirit, as is the case with ὁμόδοξον in v. 9. The intention of the word is similar to that of the expression in the Niceno-Constantinopolitan Creed (*ACO* 2. 1. 2. p. 80; H. 2. 288): τὸ σὺν Πατρὶ καὶ Υἱῷ συνπροσκυνούμενον καὶ συνδοξαζόμενον.

43. **ἀμαρύγμασι:** ἀμάρυγμα deserves a mention in *PGL*, as LSJ offer no metaphorical use which corresponds to this application to the Trinity. A similar line is found in *carm.* 2. 2 (poem.), 4. 88 (M. 37. 1512A): ἓν φάος ἐν τρισσοῖς ἀμαρύγμασιν ἰσοθέοισι. This helps to make clear the imagery of the present passage. The picture is not one of three separate lights, but rather of three 'gleaming facets' as one might see light from a jewel (cf. Tryph. 71). The figure is not to be pressed too far: the facets of a gem merely reflect and do not produce light.

κόσμον ἑλίσσων: cf. *carmm.* 2. 1. 42. 19 (M. 37. 1345A) and 2. 2 (poem.), 3. 5 (M. 37. 1480A) for similar words, with Christ or the Logos as subject. ἑλίσσω is something of a favourite word with Greg. in his verse; cf. e.g. *carmm.* 1. 2. 1. 71 (M. 37. 527A), 1. 2. 14. 15 (756A), 2. 1. 11. 1945 (1165A). In the *Arcana* it recurs in 4. 16. Caillau's tr. in the present passage is 'gubernans', a version presumably based on examples like E. *IT* 1145 (εἱλίσσων θιάσους) or Stratt. 66. 5 (ἑλίσσειν χορούς). But it should be noted that the fundamental sense 'turning, whirling, about' is not lost (being indeed present in Euripides and Strattis): it is in making the dancers or the bands of women 'move round' that the subject 'leads' them. The same is true here, where a suggested tr. is 'keeping the universe in its whirling course'.

44-53. *The evidence from baptism*

Arc. 8. 87-99 offers the other major reference to baptism in the *Arcana*.

44-5. Rom. 6. 4, together with Col. 2. 12, provides the NT idea of dying and rising with Christ in baptism.

νέος: cf. Col. 3. 10.

ἐγείρομαι: cf. συνηγέρθητε, Col. 2. 12.

παλίσσυτος is a forceful, not to say violent, word as used e.g. by Sophocles in *OT* 192. Here it is appropriate to describe the swift action of baptism which rushes a man back from death to life.

ἐς φάος: the words have a twofold meaning, contrasting the darkness of death with the light of life, but equally glancing at the concept of baptism as enlightenment. For the second idea, a common one, reference may be made, e.g., to Clem. *paed.* 1. 6 (p. 105. 20, M. 8. 281 A), G. Nyss. *or.cat.* 32 (p. 122. 12, M. 45. 84A), Bas. *hom.* 13. 1 (2. 113E, M. 31. 424C) and in Nazianzen himself, *or.* 40. 1 (M. 36. 360C) *al.* (Cf. Ysebaert, *Greek Baptismal Terminology*, 158 ff.; C. Moreschini, 'Luce'.

46. φαεσφόρον ἐξανέτειλεν is a reminiscence of 2 Pet. 1. 19, καὶ φωσφόρος ἀνατείλη ἐν ταῖς καρδίαις ὑμῶν, perhaps combined with a memory of Ps. 111 (112 Heb.) 4: 8 ἐξανέτειλεν ἐν σκότει φῶς τοῖς εὐθέσι. But φαεσφόρον must be taken in a way different from any possible for φωσφόρος in 2 Pet; see e.g. C. Bigg, *ICC* (Edinburgh, 1901), 269; J. E. B. Mayor (London, 1907), 110; H. Windisch, *HNT* 15 (1951), 90, for discussion of possibilities. For there the word denotes a divine, here it has a human, subject. Greg. speaks of himself as a 'bearer of light' in a derivative way: he is one who has been enlightened by baptism. The word is thus in Greg.'s reinterpretation analogous with Χριστοφόρος and θεοφόρος, Ign. *Eph.* 9. 2 (Bihlmeyer, p. 85. 14–15, M. 5. 652B).

47. The connection of baptism with purification is a common one. Cf. references in *PGL* s.v. κάθαρσις A. 1. Greg.'s use of the idea may be exemplified in passages like *carm.* 1. 2. 34. 200 (M. 37. 960A), *orr.* 38. 16 (M. 36. 329B), 40. 8 (368A).

οὐ ψεύσομαι: this is an emphatic statement, contrasting the writer's loyalty to his baptismal profession not simply with the implied infidelity of all who deny the Spirit's divinity but with the actual betrayal of his baptism practised by Eunomius. The charges against him are given by Sozomen, *h.e.* 6. 26 (M. 67. 1361C): φάσι δέ τινες, πρῶτον τοῦτον Εὐνόμιον τολμῆσαι εἰσηγήσασθαι ἐν μιᾷ καταδύσει χρῆναι ἐπιτελεῖν τὴν θείαν βάπτισιν ... Socrates writes of the Eunomians: τὸ βάπτισμα παρεχάραξαν. οὐ γὰρ εἰς τὴν Τριάδα ἀλλ᾿ εἰς τὸν τοῦ Χριστοῦ βαπτίζουσι θάνατον, *h.e.* 5. 24

(M. 67. 649A), while Didymus Alexandrinus, writing at much the same time as Greg. (Quasten, *Patrology*, iii. 87–8, dates his *De Trinitate* as 'composed between 381 and 392'), asserts: οἱ δὲ Εὐμονιανοὶ μέν, διὰ τὸ μίαν κατάδυσιν ποιεῖσθαι, λέγοντες μόνον εἰς τὸν θάνατον τοῦ Κυρίου βαπτίζεσθαι, *Trin*. 2. 15 (M. 39. 720A). Cf. Philostorgius, *h.e*. 10. 4 (GCS 127. 12–16, M. 65. 585B). A rather different account, however, is given by Nyssen in one of the treatises which Jerome reports that he and Nazianzen heard read out during the period of the Council of Constantinople, *de vir. ill*. 128 (M. *PL* 23. 713B). In the second of his works *Adversus Eunomium* he quickly comes to the baptismal command of Matt. 28. 10, claiming that the orthodox make no subtraction from, addition to, or alteration in the faith which was handed down to them from the Apostles. Anyone who substitutes in that baptismal formula words of his own is πατὴρ ψεύδους. Nyssen goes on to specify forms of heretical tampering such as speaking not of the Son but of ἔργον καὶ κτίσμα καὶ ποίημα and of the Spirit as κτίσμα κτίσματος καὶ ἔργον ἔργου, *Eun*. 2 (M. 45. 468B ff., Jaeger 1. 363. Cf. Epiphanius *Haer*. 76. 54 (GCS 414. 3 ff., M. 42. 637B), where it is stated that the Eunomians baptize into the names of the Son and the Holy Spirit, but that they are explicitly designated κεκτισμένος and κτισθέν.) But whatever the precise terms of the Eunomian baptismal formula, it is clear that its abuse by such a πατὴρ ψεύδους might well provoke in Greg. the response οὐ ψεύσομαι. Cf. *orr*. 33. 17 (M. 36. 236A ff.), 34. 11 (252B).

48. διατμήξαιμι: for Greg.'s horror at any 'division' of the Godhead cf. *Arc*. 2. 25 ff. n., together with v. 35 of the same poem and v. 84 below.

49. The aposiopesis may be intended to recall Matt. 26. 24 καλὸν ἦν αὐτῷ κτλ. The construction is Homeric, as *Od*. 20. 331 shows; cf. Monro, *Homeric Grammar*, § 324, p. 295. It continued in Attic use as one of a group of expressions denoting 'fitness, suitability' and the like which dispensed with ἄν; cf. Goodwin, *Moods and Tenses*, §§ 416, 433.

50. χαρίσματος ἠὲ λοετρῶν is best taken as a hendiadys, expressing the assurance of the gracious gift which issues from baptism.

51–4. Caillau in his note shows some doubt about the text they print in v. 51, wondering whether to read ὅλος or ὅλη for ὅλον. But an understanding of the relationship between vv. 51–2a and 52b–3 makes the printed text quite defensible. The argument is: If God cleansed man in his entirety, man should worship God in his entirety. (The cleansing of baptism means that man is made God.) If man worships only part of the Godhead in baptism, only part of divinity is bestowed on him in baptism.

52. Billius' reading τὸ δ᾽ ἄνισον is found in Cu. With this text τὸ ἄνισον would be equivalent to τὴν ἀνισότητα, ἀνισότης being a word which Greg. employs in *or*. 29. 14 (p. 95. 5, M. 36. 93A) to denote alleged inequality within the Godhead. The meaning would then emerge as: 'May whatever mortal is a sinner keep inequality (in the Godhead) . . . (i.e., this is a doctrine fit only for sinners).' But the printed text also gives good sense, with τὸ ἴσον = 'a just recompense'. In either case the optative can be defended as good Homeric Greek.

ὅστις ἀλιτρός is an echo of *Arc*. 1. 9 (where see n.). Here the words are in the Callimachean position as the concluding feet of the verse.

53. Greg. is suggesting that his opponent has adopted an absurd position. He is not considering the possibility of any partial deification but claiming that division of Godhead amounts to its negation and that the gift of deification in the name of a divided God is illusory.

γέρας here has its simplest sense of 'gift', 'privilege'.

54–70. *There is no inferior grade within the Godhead*

54–9 raise the question 'What is meant by saying that the Son and the Spirit hold "second place"?'

55. ἐν θείοισι λόγοις: John 14. 28, e.g., was regularly cited by those who preached the inferior status of the Son, while the 'sending' of the Spirit was held to imply his lower status.

55–6: θειοφόροισιν / ἀνδράσιν: *PGL* cites only this passage and *Arc*. 4. 94 for the θειο-form. This is not surprising. For how often were theological writers under Greg.'s constraint of avoiding a tribrach? For the interpretation of the word in this context *PGL* offers two suggestions: that the word refers to the writers of Scripture, 'or perh. of theologians'. The first alternative would provide a doublet to the preceding words: the second would take cognisance of the use of the actual word δεύτερος by theological writers of note. The second is the more pointed interpretation, as δεύτερος itself, as distinct from passages which were held to imply its meaning, is not used in Scripture in this connection. If Greg. were thinking of

Fathers who had called the Son δεύτερος, he might begin with Justin. In 1 *Apol*. 13. 3 (M. 6. 348A) he writes of the Son and the Holy Spirit as ἐν δευτέρᾳ χώρᾳ and ἐν τρίτῃ τάξει respectively. These words may be cleared of the suggestion of subordinationism—cf. the edn. of A. W. F. Blunt (Cambridge, 1911), pp. xxii–xxiii, but the same cannot be said of Origen, who, in *princ*. 1. 3. 5 (p. 56. 3, M. 11. 150B) and *Cels*. 5. 39 (p. 43. 22, M. 11. 1244B), makes a subordinationist position clear by his use of δεύτερος. (For other references cf. GCS 5. 55 n.) But if Greg. is indeed thinking of earlier writers, it is not with the intention of defending or even explaining their position. He simply asserts as a principle that no interpretation is acceptable which gives to the Son and the Holy Spirit the kind of 'second place' which divides the Godhead. The implication is that the writings alluded to are amenable to this understanding, but there is no attempt to prove this. On subordinationism, v. Prestige, *God in Patristic Thought*, ch. 7 and index refs.

57. σοφίης βαθυκόλπου: the adjective, literally applied in descriptions of divine or human female figures in Classical authors, is once found metaphorically in Pindar, of the 'deep-bosomed earth' (*P*. 9. 101). A shift in meaning towards a simple sense 'deep', in which the -κολπος element is passed over, is found in Nonnus (*D*. 12. 327, cf. 40. 534, 21. 94). Greg. may be thought to have anticipated Nonnus. Yet, despite the association of Wisdom with the Son—e.g. *or*. 30. 2 (pp. 109 ff., M. 36. 105A ff.)—*carm*. 1. 2. 1. 81 (M. 37. 528A) shows that Wisdom may still be a personified female figure. This may have influenced the choice of adjective here.

58. In Pl. *Rep*. 511c f. occurs the expression ἐπ' ἀρχὴν ἀνελθόντες, meaning 'going up to, back to, a first principle'. We have very much the same sense here. Wisdom goes back to an eternal source, without dividing the Godhead.

ῥίζαν refers to the Father. Of him it is said in *Arc*. 2. 5: οὐδὲν ἔην μεγάλοιο Πατρὸς πάρος. To the bare ἄναρχος by which the Father is designated in *Arc*. 1. 25 ῥίζα adds an image but no new thought. Greg. is striving after the same truth in *or*. 28. 13 (p. 43. 7, M. 36. 44A) in calling the Father ἡ πρώτη αἰτία and in *or*. 29. 3 (p. 77. 8, M. 36. 77B) when he speaks of him as τὸ αἴτιον. But in all these expressions Greg. is trying to avoid the suggestion of inferiority of the Son and the Spirit which, as Cyril reported him, Eunomius held to be inherent in the use of αἴτιος and similar words: δεύτερος ἔσται τοῦ πατρὸς ὁ υἱός, αἴτιον αὐτὸν ἔχων, *thes*. 9 (5¹. 68c). This sums up precisely what this section of the poem is concerned to deny. The language of ῥίζα relating to Father and Son goes back to Or. fr. 69 *in Jo.* (p. 538. 8). Cf. *Arc.* 2. 31.

59. πολύσεπτον: this is the only example recorded in the lexica in which the word, uncommon in any case, has the sense 'worshipped as plural'. It recurs in v. 73.

60. Greg. talks of the relationship of μονάς and τριάς in *or.* 29. 2 (pp. 74 ff., M. 36. 76A f.). Cf. especially: διὰ τοῦτο μονὰς ἀπ᾽ ἀρχῆς εἰς δυάδα κινηθεῖσα, μέχρι τριάδος ἔστη (p. 75. 7 f., 76B), where διὰ τοῦτο follows the assertion that, though the Persons differ in number, they are not divided in essence. The present passage minimizes any inadvertent suggestion of Sabellianism which might be suspected in the oration. For, despite Barbel's attempt to remove the suspicion by different punctuation (*Fünf theol. Reden*, 13. n. 8), the substance of Mason's n. on the passage still stands, with its assertion that the language is perilously close to Sabellianism. (For the subsequent history of the influence of this section in *or.* 29, cf. J. Dräseke, *BZ* 15 (1906), 143 ff.) Cf. 71–93 n.

61–70 deal with, indeed dispense with, certain *Trinitarian analogies*. It is possible that Greg.'s use of ῥίζαν in v. 58 suggested to him the wisdom of guarding against the misuse of analogy. For if ῥίζα were thought to indicate a threefold figure like Tertullian's celebrated 'radix—frutex—fructus', *adv.Prax.* 8 (M. *PL* 2. 186D ff.; CSEL 47. 238. 19 ff.), objections would come to mind. He does not, however, discuss the use of ῥίζα, but switches his attention to countering possible errors which might spring from the parallel figure, in Tert. 'fons—flumen—rivus', in Greg. πόρος—πηγή—ποταμός. A similar rejection of analogy is found in *or.* 31. 31 ff. (p. 186. 10 ff., M. 36. 169A ff.), where Greg. dismisses the images of mouth—spring—river, sun—ray—light, and the reflection of sunlight upon a wall. But Greg. is prepared, on occasion, to allow himself some use of analogy. His likening of the Three Persons to three suns joined together and sharing one light, a figure produced in passing in *or.* 31. 14 (p. 163. 3 f., M. 36. 149A), must be accounted careless. (Cf. v. 71 below.) On the credit side is the analogy of νοῦς—λόγος—πνεῦμα, *orr.* 12. 1 (M. 35. 844B), 23. 11 (1161C f.) which, though only partly developed in Greg., has affinities with the mental analogy put forward by Augustine in *De Trin.* 15. 17 ff. (M. *PL* 42. 1069 ff.).

61–2. The basic figure of outflowing water applied to the Godhead may be traced back to John 7. 38–9, where the Holy Spirit's coming is predicted. Hippolytus indicates the relationship of Father and Logos by the figure of water flowing from a fountain, *Noët.* 11. (Nautin, p. 253, M. 10. 817c). Tertullian develops the threefold pattern in *adv.Prax.* 8 (M. *PL* 2. 1868 ff.; CSEL 47. 237. 19 ff.). In the Arian disputes considerable use was made of πηγή in putting forward the orthodox answer to Arius. Athanasius, for instance, defends Dionysius against a charge of Arianism by showing that the figure of the river flowing from the spring is a perfectly acceptable image of consubstantiality: τὸν λόγον εἶναι ὡς ποταμὸν ἀπὸ πηγῆς καὶ βλαστὸν ἀπὸ ῥίζης καὶ τέκνον ἀπὸ γονέως καὶ φῶς ἐκ φωτὸς καὶ ζωὴν ἐκ ζωῆς, *Dion.* 19 (p. 60. 15 ff., M. 25. 508β); the text of Dionysius' letter, with the πηγή illustration, is given in the previous paragraph, ibid. 18. (p. 60. 2, M. 25. 505c). Cf. *Ar.* 1. 19 (M. 26. 52a). Later Basil uses the idea in his contention against Eunomius, *Eun.* 2. 25 (1. 261e, M. 629β) as does Nyssen in his reply to a rather naïve tritheism, *tres dii* (M. 45. 128c); other references are collected in *PGL* s.v. πηγή B 6 a. Now there can be little doubt that Greg. would accept this much of the figure, the characterization of the relationship of the Father and the Son in terms of source and stream. Anyone who could use ῥίζα in this way (cf. v. 58 n.) could use πηγή. Greg.'s misgivings begin at the point where the attempt is made to extend the analogy to include the Holy Sprit, the point reached by Tertullian long before the Arian dispute. Greg.'s objections, as he gives them in *or.* 31. 31 (p. 186. 15–16, M. 36. 169a f.), are twofold. The instability of water as a medium might suggest a corresponding instability in the Godhead. The uniformity of water as a medium does not allow a sufficient distinction of Persons: ὀφθαλμὸς γὰρ καὶ πηγὴ καὶ ποταμὸς ἕν ἐστιν ἀριθμῷ, διαφόρως σχηματιζόμενα (p. 187. 8–9, 169β). 'The wheel is come full circle.' The analogy is accused, in the second criticism, of that very Sabellianism which Tertullian had intended it to combat. See E. Evans, *Tertullian's Treatise Against Praxeas* (London, 1948), 238, for discussion of Tertullian's use of this analogy and Augustine's criticism of it in *de fide et symbolo*, 17 (M. *PL* 40. 189–90 = CSEL 41. 18 ff.).

In detail the rejected analogy differs from Tertullian's. The latter's elements are the spring, the river, the irrigation canal, while Greg. places the spring in the middle, fed by the underground passage (πόρος) and leading to the river. A third variant is found in Athanasius, who writes: πάλιν τε τοῦ Πατρὸς ὄντος πηγῆς, τοῦ δὲ

Υἱοῦ ποταμοῦ λεγομένου, πίνειν λεγόμεθα τὸ Πνεῦμα, *ep.Serap.* 1. 19 (M. 26. 573D).

63. Tatian, in his desire to show that the Logos in issuing forth from the Father caused no diminution in the divine economy, used the figure of the torch which lights another and subsequent torches without loss of its own light, *orat.* 5 (Schwartz, p. 5. 27 ff., M. 6. 817A): ὥσπερ γὰρ ἀπὸ μιᾶς δᾳδὸς ἀνάπτεται μὲν πυρὰ πολλὰ, τῆς δὲ πρώτης δᾳδὸς διὰ τὴν ἔξαψιν τῶν πολλῶν δᾳδῶν οὐκ ἐλαττοῦται τὸ φῶς, οὕτω καὶ ὁ λόγος προελθὼν ἐκ τῆς τοῦ Πατρὸς δυνάμεως οὐκ ἄλογον πεποίηκε τὸν γεγεννηκότα. The same reasoning is taken up by Nyssen in a Trinitarian argument in favour of the equality of the Holy Spirit, when, using the same word as Nazianzen (λαμπάς), he wrote: εἰ δὲ κωλύει οὐδὲν πῦρ εἶναι τὴν τρίτην λαμπάδα, κἂν ἐκ προλαβούσης ἀναλάμψῃ φλογός, τίς ἡ σοφία τῶν διὰ ταῦτα τὴν τοῦ ἁγίου Πνεύματος ἀξίαν ἀθετεῖν ἀσεβῶς νομιζόντων, ἐπειδήπερ μετὰ Πατέρα καὶ Υἱὸν ἠριθμήθη παρὰ τῆς φωνῆς; *Maced.* 6 (M. 45. 1308B). This idea of transference without diminution is found in Numenius and Plotinus; cf. *CHLGEMP* 102-3 (P. Merlan).

The form of the analogy to which Greg. objects is referred to in *or.* 30. 6 (p. 117. 11 ff., M. 36. 112B). In a context which mentions Sabellians he rejects the image of a torch which is temporarily snatched from a pyre and then returned to it. This 'resolving back into the Father' (ἀναλυθέντος, 1. 12) reflects the language of Marcellus of Ancyra. Cf. *or.* 25. 16 (M. 35. 1221A).

πυρκαϊῆς: the visual effect is strengthened by this word, introducing the picture of mourners lighting torches from a funeral-pyre.

64. The teaching here attacked is related to that of the λόγος προφορικός and ἐνδιάθετος, an originally Stoic doctrine which the Apologists developed to explain the relationship of the pre-existent Christ to the Christ manifested in creation and revealed in history. (Cf. Prestige, *God in Patristic Thought*, ch. 6; Kelly, *Doctrines*, 95 ff.; Wolfson, *The Philosophy of the Church Fathers*, i. 192 ff.) But, though προϊών and ἔνδοθι bear a close resemblance to προφορικός and ἐνδιάθετος, the line refers to a specialized and individual interpretation, that of Marcellus of Ancyra (cf. Kelly, *Doctrines*, 240 ff.; id., *Creeds*, 102 ff., 108 ff.; Quasten, *Patrology*, iii. 197 ff.). Marcellus envisaged the Word's 'going forth' as an expansion of the Monad, without his becoming a second ὑπόστασις. His 'going forth' is thus subject to his 'remaining within' the Godhead: the δυάς signifies a temporary and reversible process. Eusebius supplies several parallels for the language of which Greg. complains. For Marcellus' understanding of 'going forth' cf. Μάρκελλος οὐ βούλεται μὲν ἀληθῶς τὸν υἱὸν ἐκ τοῦ πατρὸς γεγεννῆσθαι, ὡς υἱὸν ζῶντα καὶ ὑφεστῶτα, οἷα δὲ λόγον αὐτὸν σημαντικόν τινος ἢ προστακτικὸν προελθεῖν τοῦ θεοῦ φάσκει, *e. th.* 2. 8 (p. 106. 25 ff., M. 24. 913B). See also the following lines, which are quoted from Marcellus himself, fr. 36 (31 Rettb.) 190. 29 ff.). ἔνδοθι μίμνων may correspond to ἔνδον μένων in *Marcell.* 1. 1 (p. 4. 15, M. 24. 717B): λόγος, ἔνδον μένων ἐν ἡσυχάζοντι τῷ πατρὶ ἐνεργῶν δὲ ἐν τῷ τὴν κτίσιν δημιουργεῖν, ὁμοίως ἡμετέρῳ ἐν σιωπῶσιν μὲν ἡσυχάζοντι ἐν δὲ φθεγγομένοις ἐνεργοῦντι, unless we should read μέν ὤν: Eusebius goes on to argue that this view is insufficiently distinguished from Jewish belief. Cf. also: λόγον δέ φησιν (sc. Μάρκελλος) ἔνδον ὄντα ἐν τῷ θεῷ ποτὲ μὲν ἐνεργείᾳ δραστικῇ προιέναι, ποτὲ δὲ ἔνδον εἶναι ἐν αὐτῷ μὴ ἐνεργοῦντα, *e. th.* 3. 3 (p. 157. 4 ff., M. 24. 1001B).

65–7. These lines strongly recall *or.* 31. 32 (p. 188. 8 ff., M. 36. 169C): μαρμαρυγήν τινα ἡλιακὴν τοίχῳ προσαστράπτουσαν, καὶ περιτρέμουσαν ἐξ ὑδάτων κινήσεως, ἣν ἡ ἀκτὶς ὑπολαβοῦσα διὰ τοῦ ἐν μέσῳ ἀέρος, εἶτα σχεθεῖσα τῷ ἀντιτύπῳ, παλμὸς ἐγένετο καὶ παράδοξος. This analogy is introduced by 'I once heard a man suggest . . .', but there is no hint of his identity. The precise point of the analogy is scarcely more obvious than its author. Mason (p. 188. 8 n.) is disinclined to see a direct analogy of sunbeam, water, and wall, though this may seem likely at first sight. 'The point, however, appears to lie rather in the junction of unity with multiplicity (the number three being for the moment lost sight of) displayed in the vibrations of the sunbeam.' The passage before us is even less amenable to the discovery of direct correspondences. Greg. uses the figure merely to discredit abhorrent suggestions of flux and instability.

There is a full discussion of the background to the imagery of this passage in Kertsch, *Bildersprache*, 210–16. Perhaps we may single out as of particular interest the citations of Plu. *de facie in orbe lunae* 23, 936B–C and Bas. *hex.* 2. 7 (G. 1. 19B, M. 29. 45A f.). See also Trisoglio, 'La poesia della Trinità', 734.

66. περίτρομος: cf. Opp. *H.* 2. 309, together with περιτρέμουσαν in the passage from *or.* 31. The variant περίδρομος (cf. app. crit.) represents a scribal attempt to find a common word for the rare περίτρομος. (Oppian and the present passage are the only lexical citations.)

ἀστατέουσα: something of the flavour of this word may be caught from Plutarch's use of it to describe the ever-changing, unstable motion of the sea (*Crass*. 17). Here it admirably presents the fleeting glints of sunlight reflected on a wall. Cf. ἄστατος, v. 68.

67. For the structure of the line, see Introd., p. 62.

68. ἄστατος: what Greg. takes to be a suitable subject of ἄστατος is φορά, *carm*. 1. 1. 6. 9 (M. 37. 430A). Epicurus' application of the word to τύχη may be compared, *ep*. 3. 133 (p. 65 U.).

ῥέουσα: it is men who may be called a ῥοιῆς . . . γόνος, *carm*. 1. 2. 15. 43 (M. 37. 769A). Similar expressions are found in *carmm*. 1. 2. 9. 10 (M. 37. 668A), 1. 2. 14. 73 (M. 37. 761A), *or*. 14. 7 (M. 35. 865B f.). Cf. H. M. Werhahn, Σύγκρισις βίων (Wiesbaden, 1953), 95.

69. πάλιν συνιοῦσα: again, language attributed to Marcellus seems to be in Greg.'s mind. συνιέναι here would correspond to Marcellus' συστέλλεσθαι, the verb which Eusebius uses when he is reporting his opponent's teaching of the 'contraction' which is correlative with the 'expansion' (πλατύνεσθαι) of the Monad into Dyad and Triad, *e. th*. 2. 6 (p. 103. 22, M. 24. 908A), 2. 9 (p. 108. 34, 917A).

τὸ ἔμπεδον: ἔμπεδος is a word which would carry with it a range of association for the well-read. Homer finds here a word to delineate what is reliable (e.g. *Il*. 6. 352), events that are certain to take place (e.g. *Od*. 8. 30), or things that are everlasting (*Il*. 8. 521), and later writers pick up these meanings. ἔμπεδος, therefore, is at the other pole from human experience in Greg.'s thought, as he shows in the couplet *carm*. 1. 2. 14. 27 f., M. 37. 757A:

> ἔμπεδον οὐδέν· ἔγωγε ῥόος θολεροῦ ποταμοῖο
> αἰὲν ἐπερχόμενος, ἑσταὼς οὐδὲν ἔχων.

Cf. Werhahn, loc. cit.

70. The idea is similar to the biblical view of spiritual sacrifice. If righteousness in general may be thought of as a sacrifice, as in Ps. 4. 6 (4. 5 Heb.), the extension to right thinking is an easy one.

71–93. *The relationship of 'Monad' and 'Triad'*

Greg. has already, in v. 60, juxtaposed *Monad* and *Triad* in a compressed, epigrammatic way. He must now try to make good his right to use both terms.

71. When this line is compared with vv. 41 and 43, it will be seen that there is a change of emphasis. ἴη φύσις is still the ground of unity, but the separateness of the Three is stressed in a way which may be thought unhelpful: the three lights are like the three suns of *or*. 31. 14 (p. 163. 3–4, M. 36. 149A), on which cf. vv. 61–70 n. There is no hint of how they are related, in causal terms. Is one light the source of the others? If so, why is the torch analogy rejected (63)? The impression given there is that the whole figure is unacceptable, not merely the suggestion of return to a single source. Cf. Norris 198–9.

ἐστήρικται: this is, like ἔμπεδον (v. 69), an evocative word. Cf. Empedocles fr. 27 (DK i. 324), Hes. *Th*. 779, Call. *Ap*. 23, A.R. 4. 816, Ps. 111 (112 Heb.). 8, Luke 16. 26 for a variety of ways in which stability, fixity, strength, are indicated. Of later writers, Ps.-Manetho is like Greg. in finding a place for the word in didactic verse 2(1). 3, 40 Koechly).

72–3. μονὰς νήριθμος: Marcellus may again be the target of these words or, more generally, the Sabellianism which he was taken to represent. In *e. th*. 2. 4 (p. 102. 24–5, M. 24. 905A) = fr. 71 = 62 Rettb. (p. 198. 22) Eusebius quotes Marcellus as speaking of μονὰς ... ἀδιαίρετος an expression to which Greg.'s words could well be taken as equivalent, and charges him with Sabellianism; cf. *e. th*. 3. 4 (p. 158. 14 f., M. 24. 1004B) = fr. 67 = 60 Rettb. (p. 198. 2). The poetic form νήριθμος is found in Theoc. 25. 57, Lyc. 415, meaning 'countless'.

The correlation of μονάς and τριάς is an important one for Greg. to maintain, as it had been for Athanasius; cf. *hom. in Mt*. 11. 27 (M. 25. 220A). In *or*. 29. 2 (p. 75. 7 ff.) Greg. includes the middle term δυάς. The terms are related directly to Father, Son, and Holy Spirit in language of incorporeal passionless begetting and of emission. For Greg. τριάς is a word of frequent occurrence and rich association. Where μονάς stresses the inoriginate and indivisible, τριάς at once reinforces the idea of absolute unity and gives scope for the development of notions of the divine relationships of the Three Persons. Cf. Norris on *or*. 29. 2, pp. 133–4 n.

πολύσεπτος: cf. v. 59 n.

ἀκέαστος: Greg., as always, is anxious to avoid the kind of division which makes the Second and Third Persons less God than the First. He is searching for a way of expressing distinction without division and subordination, walking the path between Sabellianism and Arianism, as he says in *or*. 34. 8 (M. 36. 249A), cf. 42. 16 (476C). The distinction is here made in terms of ἀριθμός, not, as more regularly in Greg. (cf. v. 41b n.) in terms of ἰδιότης. The use of ἀριθμός may be paralleled in *or.* 29. 2 (p. 75. 6, M. 36. 76B): ὥστε κἂν ἀριθμῷ διαφέρῃ, τῇ γε οὐσίᾳ μὴ τέμνεσθαι. Later Cyril was to distinguish in this way, e.g. in *thes.* 12 (5¹. 110A): ὁ πατὴρ καὶ ὁ υἱὸς ἐν μέν εἰσι κατὰ φύσιν, δύο δὲ ἐν ἀριθμῷ. The principle there applied to the Father and the Son could be extended to the Holy Spirit.

74. τρισάριθμα: the meaning 'thrice numbered', found in Orac. apud Luc. *Alex.* 11, is changed to 'three in number'.

75. In this line Greg. gives concise expression to the doctrine of co-inherence, the teaching that the whole of the Godhead is present in each Person. The history of this idea is traced in Prestige, *God in Patristic Thought*, 282 ff. (cf. xxxii–xxxiii). The stage at which we observe the doctrine in Greg. is a stage before the development of technical language like περιχώρησις. Rather do we find him writing in *or.* 31. 14 (p. 163. 2–3, M. 36. 149A): ἀλλὰ ἀμέριστος ἐν μεμερισμένοις . . . ἡ θεότης. (Cf. Hergenröther 44.)

76–80 state the converse. If the Three Persons may be discerned in any one, the consideration of the Three individually must not be thought of as damaging the essential unity of the Godhead. Again Greg. is following a narrow path in his argument, this time between excessive emphasis on the oneness of God and a stress on the Three which might be taken as tritheism. He begins by treating tritheism as simply a species of polytheism.

76. Cf. *Arc.* 1. 25. The divine nature is inexhaustibly rich, in that access to one Person inevitably opens up a full relationship with all Three.

79. μονοκρατίην ἐριλαμπέα: both words may be coinages of Greg.'s. The lexica record no other case of μονοκρατία, while ἐριλαμπής, apart from a recurrence in *Arc.* 8. 72, is mentioned only in the 5th-c. Proclus (*H.* 4. 13). μονοκρατίη stands for μοναρχία, the word Greg. uses in e.g. *orr.* 29. 2 (p. 75. 1, M. 36. 76A), 38. 8 (M. 36. 320B), 40. 41 (M. 36. 417B).

80. Similarly contemptuous language is used when Greg. is dismissing those who hold pagan polytheistic views in *carm.* 1. 1. 6. 5 (M. 37. 430A): he talks of a 'swarm' of gods. Here, quite adeptly, Greg. is using emotive language suitable to Christian disparagement of polytheism to forestall a suggestion of Christian aberration. LSJ cite θεῶν ἀγορά as a proverbial expression corresponding to 'Babel'.

81–3 develop the argument against polytheism in a form similar to that found in *or.* 29. 2 (p. 74. 15 ff., M. 36. 76A): without a single principle of authority divided rule must end in anarchy and self-destruction. A parallel argument, for a different purpose, is outlined in *or.* 28. 7 (pp. 31–2, M. 36. 33B f.) Anything which is composite has within it the possibility of internal strife and of dissolution: σύνθεσις γὰρ ἀρχὴ μάχης· μάχη δὲ διαστάσεως· ἡ δὲ λύσεως (p. 32. 1–2, 33C). This argument itself may be traced back to Pl. *Phd.* 78B f.

84–6. *The question of tritheism.* It will be noted that Greg. is here trying to turn an argument which had been used against him. For in *or.* 31. 13 (pp. 161. 4 ff., M. 36. 148B ff.) he says that he had been accused of tritheism; cf. Evag.Pont. *ep.* 8 ‡ Bas. (M. 32. 248C); Gr. Nyss. *tres dii*, *passim* (M. 45. 116 ff.), Kelly, *Doctrines*, 267 ff. In the present passage there is no attempt at explicit defence. Greg. has ridiculed in general terms the notion of Christian polytheism. He now tries to maintain that the real tritheists are those who have introduced the divisive elements which he lists in vv. 84–5.

84. χρόνος: cf. *Arc.* 2. 7 n., 4. 67 ff. n.

νόημα: Any Arian understanding of the creaturely ignorance of the Son, of his failure to comprehend the Father, would constitute such a division in νόημα.

85. κράτος: Arians diminished the power of the Son and the Spirit. In *Arc.* 1. 34 the Son is called Πατρὸς σθένος ἠδὲ νόημα.

θέλησις: again it is the Arians whom Greg. has in mind. Cf. the word of Arius quoted by Athanasius, *syn.* 15. 3 (Opitz 2. 243. 5, M. 26. 708B): ἡ σοφία σοφία ὑπῆρξε σοφοῦ θεοῦ θελήσει. Marcellus had strongly opposed the use of θέλησις or βούλησις because, as he said, to allow the Father's will as a condition of the Son's generation is to introduce priority in time and thus to favour Arianism: Eus. *Marcell.* 1. 4 (p. 19. 11 ff., M. 24. 753C f.) = *fr.* 34 = 29 Rettb. (p. 198. 15 ff.). For his pains he had directed against him a sentence in the *Ecthesis Macrostichos*: see *Symb.Ant.* (345) ap. Ath. *syn.* 26. VIII. (Opitz 2. 253. 22 ff., M. 26. 732C), as the framers of the creed did not accept the view that this terminology supported Arianism. Marcellus' objections were upheld by Athanasius, who, in *Ar.* 3. 62 (M. 26. 453A ff.), wrote against the use of θέλησις and βούλησις; cf. Kelly, *Creeds*, 276.

Greg. believed that it was possible to employ language of will, the Father willing the generation of the Son. He is the 'cause' of the Son, but only within an understanding of the coeternity of the Three Persons. The Son is thus caused by the eternal will of the

Father and is indivisibly united with and equal to him. Whether Greg. is successful in arguing this position has been disputed, notably by Meijering, 'The Doctrine of the will'.

86. There can be little doubt that Caillau gives the basic meaning of the line in his tr. 'Cum unusquisque nunquam secum ipse consentiat' (cf. Billius). But it is difficult to see how αὐτοῦ could be tr. 'secum'. The simple change to αὑτοῦ, however, would ease the difficulty. The genitive is to be taken closely with ἀδήριτον, on the analogy of α-privative adjectives like ἀκρατής.

ἀδήριτον has here the early, Homeric meaning 'without strife'. Later writers give it the sense 'unconquerable' (cf. A. *Pr*. 105) or 'undisputed' (cf. Plb. 1. 2. 3). The word recurs in *Arc*. 4. 29, where, contrary to earlier practice, it again has short ι.

87. In writing of 'my Trinity' Greg. means at once 'the Trinity in my way of understanding' and 'the Trinity of my personal devotion'. For the latter cf. Trisoglio, 'La poesia della Trinità'.

88. ἄρευστος: cf. *carm*. 2. 1. 11. 1176 (M. 36. 1109A) τῆς ἀρεύστου τριάδος, and v. 68 n.

90-3. Greg. is here claiming a quite definitive quality for his teaching, a feature for which *Arc*. 1. 16-24 and v. 36 above have prepared the way. Indeed, he appears to imply that he has reached the limits of knowledge possible to human beings, leaving open the question whether even angels know more of the Trinity. This is perhaps a fitting point at which to recall that behind the poet there lies the rhetorician and to remember H. von Campenhausen's warning not to take all Greg.'s rhetorical flourishes too seriously (*The Fathers of the Greek Church*, 184-5).

90. φαέεσσι is a play on the sense of φαέεσσι in v. 71 (cf. 78) above, here used in the Homeric sense of 'eyes' (cf. *Od*. 16. 15 etc.).

91. The imagery is drawn from biblical language of the Holy of Holies. ἐκ πτερύγων refers to the wings of the cherubim, as in Exod. 25. 19 (20), where they are described as part of the 'mercy-seat': ἔσονται οἱ χερουβεὶμ ἐκτείνοντες τὰς πτέρυγας ἐπάνωθεν, συσκιάζοντες ἐν ταῖς πτέρυξιν αὐτῶν ἐπὶ τοῦ ἱλαστηρίου. This verse deals with the tabernacle, but similar language is found in the description of Solomon's Temple in 3 Kgds. 8. 6-7: (the ark was carried in) εἰς τὰ ἅγια τῶν ἁγίων, ὑπὸ τὰς πτέρυγας τῶν χερουβείν, ὅτι τὰ χερουβεὶν διαπετασμένα ταῖς πτέρυξιν ἐπὶ τὸν τόπον τῆς κιβωτοῦ. Cf. ibid. 6. 26 (27), 1 Paral. 28. 18, 2 Paral. 3. 13, 5. 7 f.

πετάσματος: πέτασμα is here used in a sense different from any found in Classical Greek, where it signified something spread or spreading out, like a carpet or antennae. Nor again does it have the meaning 'flight' which Greg.'s contemporary, Didymus, gives it when he writes of τὰ τοῦ νοητοῦ ἀετοῦ πετάσματα, *Pr*. 30. 19 (M. 39. 1641 C). Here πέτασμα = καταπέτασμα as it does in *Or. Sib*. 8. 305 (GCS p. 161): ναοῦ δὲ σχισθῇ τὸ πέτασμα. Nicetas saw this and wrote καταπέτασμα in his paraphrase. In both Greg. and the Sibylline Oracle passage the word means the curtain which separated the Holy of Holies from the holy place or that which covered the entrance to the forecourt, the meaning of καταπέτασμα in biblical literature (cf. Arndt–Gingrich, s.v.). Greg. here intends πέτασμα to signify the veil of the innermost sanctuary as e.g. in Exod. 26. 31 ff., Lev. 21. 23, 24. 3 and in the NT καταπέτασμα does. Greg. uses καταπέτασμα in this sense in *or*. 28. 31 (p. 69. 19–20, M. 36. 72 A).

The reason for this preference for πέτασμα is not hard to determine: the initial tribrach of καταπέτασμα cannot be accommodated in a hexameter. For a recurrence of the former word see *Arc*. 8. 54, *carm*. 1. 1. 20. 34 (M. 37. 490 A).

The association of revelation with the mercy-seat and the cherubim is seen in Exod. 25. 21 (22). Greg. uses the same imagery in *or*. 28. 3 (p. 25. 1 ff., M. 36. 29 A).

92–3. For a similar suggestion of the limitations of angels cf. *Arc*. 1. 4. Angels are discussed at length in *Arc*. 6.

4. On the Universe

Title and purpose

The MSS agree on the title Περὶ Κόσμου or variants. Its subject is certainly 'God and the created order'. The first 23 lines assert *creatio ex nihilo* against all doctrines of pre-existent matter while vv. 24–54 use anti-Manichaean polemic as a means of introducing Greg.'s teaching on the creation of man and the place of evil in the created order. The poem goes on to set the Creation of the world in the pattern of eternity (vv. 55–74), leading to the creation of the two orders of angels and men (vv. 75–100).

R. Keydell, in *BZ* 44 (1951), 316, pointed to a certain similarity between vv. 1–23 and Bas. *Hex.* 2. 2 f. (G. 1. 13B ff., M. 29. 29C ff.) and between vv. 24–54 and Basil *Hex.* 2. 4 (G. 1. 15C ff., M. 29. 36B ff.), and compared vv. 55–100 with passages in Greg's *or.* 38. 9–10 (M. 36. 320C ff.) = 45. 5 (629A f.).

In presenting a *Christian cosmology*, *Arc.* 4 outlines an important aspect of Cappadocian theology. In 370 Basil had already written his striking homilies *In Hexaëmeron* (G. 1. 1A ff., M. 29. 4A ff.), linking philosophical argument and biblical exposition, a work which Nyssen followed with his *De hominis opificio* (Forbes 1. 102 ff., M. 44. 125 ff.) and *Apologia in Hexaëmeron* (Forbes 1. 4 ff., M. 44. 61 ff.). These were written shortly after Basil's death, the former early in 379 and the latter in the course of the same year (cf. J. Daniélou, 'La chronologie des œuvres de Grégoire de Nysse', *Stud. Patr.* 7 (= TU 92; Berlin, 1966), 159–69 at 162–3. Nyssen is at some pains to show that he thinks of Basil as his master and that his aim in writing his treatises is merely to clarify his brother's teaching (cf. the introduction to *hom. opif.*, Forbes 1. 102–6, M. 44. 125A f.). Nazianzen is no less impressed, as may be seen from his words in *or.* 43. 67 (M. 36. 585A): ὅταν τὴν Ἐξαήμερον αὐτοῦ μεταχειρίζωμαι, καὶ διὰ γλώσσης φέρω, μετὰ τοῦ κτίστου γίνομαι, καὶ γινώσκω κτίσεως λόγους, καὶ θαυμάζω τὸν κτίστην πλέον ἢ πρότερον, ὄψει μόνῃ διδασκάλῳ χρώμενος. Perhaps it is because he assumed the work of Basil and Nyssen that Nazianzen himself nowhere attempts a detailed study of Creation following the Genesis account. It is notable that Greg.'s references to Creation, scattered over his writings, are very much of a piece with what is before us in the present poem. He concerns himself with the theory of creation, the idea of the world as ... ῥευστῶν καὶ νοουμένων δέσις, *carm.* i. 2. 34. 2 (M. 37. 946A), for

143

instance, the argument from Creation to Creator, cf. 2. 2 (poem.). 7. 67 ff. (M. 37. 1156A), the relation of ὁ νοητὸς κόσμος to the visible material universe, *or*. 38. 10 (M. 36. 321A f.), the notion of the world as exhibiting harmony, *or*. 6. 15 (M. 35. 741B), the reason for Creation in the nature of God, *or*. 38. 9 (M. 36. 320C) = 45. 6 (629C), and like questions. But nowhere is there a sustained appeal to Genesis to substantiate propositions rationally stated. A good part of *or*. 28. 5 ff. (M. 36. 32B ff.; pp. 27 ff.) is taken up with questions similar to those raised in this poem. The commentary of Norris (pp. 110–31) will be found helpful at a number of points.

Of secondary literature relating to Greg.'s doctrine of creation the following should be consulted: G. Florovsky, 'The Idea of Creation in Christian Philosophy', *ECQ* 8/3 (1949), suppl. 53–77; A. H. Armstrong, 'Plotinus's Doctrine of the Infinite and its Significance for Christian Thought', *Downside Review*, 73/231 (1954–5), 47–58, esp. 56–7; E. Osborn, *The Beginning of Christian Philosophy* (Cambridge, 1981), ch. 5 'Cosmos and Creation'; J. F. Callahan, 'Greek Philosophy and the Cappadocian Cosmology', *DOP* 12 (1958), 29–57 (this deals specifically only with Basil and Nyssen but much of the paper has direct relevance for Nazianzen); Ullmann, *Gregorius von Nazianz der Theologe*, 341 ff.; Dubedout, *De D. Gregorii Nazianzeni carminibus*, 48 ff.; Gottwald, *De Gregorio Nazianzeno Platonico*, 16 ff.; Portmann, *Die göttliche Paidagogia bei Gregor von Nazianz*, 53 ff.; Ruether, *Gregory of Nazianzus*, 130 ff.; Moreschini, 'Platonismo', 1375, 1381.

1–23. *God created in an absolute sense, without pre-existent matter*

1. εἰ δ' ἄγε is a Homeric formula, used here to introduce a hortatory subjunctive (cf. P. Chantraine, *Grammaire homérique*, ii. §404, pp. 274–5), introducing a new poem as Homer uses the words to introduce a speech in *Il.* 6. 376.

3–4. The assertion of monotheism is related directly to the question of κτίσις: it had always been a strong part of the Church's answer to Gnostic teaching on creation, for instance. Here it is traditional forms of Greek philosophy with which Greg. is concerned to deal. His association of creation with the activity of the One God may be turned against Plato. The *Timaeus* discusses at some length the work of the δημιουργός in making the world (27C–40D5), but the intention is not monotheistic, as may be seen from 40D6–41D2. For here Plato mentions subsidiary gods who are to be intermediaries in the creation of the θνητά. Though the passage dwells on the derived and conditional nature of their divinity (41 B 1–6), they are still gods. For explicit attribution of the world to the creative activity of a number of gods we may look among Greg.'s contemporaries to the writings of Sallustius Philosophus. ('He was, roughly speaking, a Neo-Platonist': G. Murray, *Five Stages of Greek Religion* (Oxford, 1925), 219.) If one accepts the identification of this Sallustius with the friend of Julian, one may see in him a particularly pointed example of the kind of creation teaching which Greg. was concerned to counter; cf. Murray, loc. cit.: 'Sallustius then may be taken to represent in the most authoritative way the Pagan reaction of Julian's time, in its final struggle against Christianity.' Discussion of the identity of Sallustius is found in Praechter's article in *RE* iA. 1960–7. He hesitates over Preller's view that Sallustius Philosophus is the same as the friend of Julian who became prefect of the East in 361, but A. D. Nock regards the identification as probable (*Sallustius: Concerning the Gods and the Universe* (Cambridge, 1926), pp. ci ff.) and the latest editor, G. Rochefort, (*Saloustios: Des Dieux et du Monde* (Paris, 1960), Introd., pp. x ff.), agrees. But even if the writer of Περὶ Θεῶν καὶ κόσμου does not have official support and even if Greg. did not know his work (Nock finds little evidence that it was influential in its own day, op.cit. pp. ciii ff.), there is no doubt that it represents the kind of thinking about the nature of the universe which would have appealed to many of Greg.'s contemporaries (cf. Murray 219 ff.). There is thus point in contrasting with Greg.'s teaching a characteristic sentence or two from this treatise: τῶν δὲ Θεῶν οἱ μέν εἰσιν ἐγκόσμιοι, οἱ δὲ ὑπερκόσμιοι· ἐγκοσμίους δὲ λέγω αὐτοὺς τοὺς τὸν Κόσμον ποιοῦντας Θεούς· τῶν δὲ ὑπερκοσμίων οἱ μὲν οὐσίας ποιοῦσι Θεῶν, οἱ δὲ νοῦν, οἱ δὲ ψυχάς· (6. 1; Nock, p. 10. 28 ff.). Now these gods are secondary; above them is the One. But both the secondary gods and the One are quite different from the One God of Greg.'s Christian monotheism, the God who created a world out of nothing.

The πινντοί are Platonists in general with their eternal Forms and creation from pre-existent matter. Plato himself does not refer to ὕλη in the sense of 'matter', cf. A. E. Taylor, *A Commentary on Plato's 'Timaeus'* (Oxford, 1928), 493; but *Tim.* 30 A 1–6 uses language which is amenable to the interpretation of pre-existent matter:

βουληθεὶς γὰρ ὁ Θεὸς ἀγαθὰ μὲν πάντα, φλαῦρον δὲ μηδὲν εἶναι κατὰ
δύναμιν, οὕτω δὴ πᾶν ὅσον ἦν ὁρατὸν παραλαβὼν οὐχ ἡσυχίαν ἄγον ἀλλὰ
κινούμενον πλημμελῶς καὶ ἀτάκτως, εἰς τάξιν αὐτὰ ἤγαγεν ἐκ τῆς ἀταξίας,
ἡγησάμενος ἐκεῖνο τούτου πάντως ἄμεινον.

Cf. F. M. Cornford, *Plato's Cosmology: the 'Timaeus' of Plato* (London,
1937), 37, convincing in its opposition to Taylor, 79–80. Certainly
Plato was held by Athanasius, for example, to have maintained this
view; cf. *inc.* 2. 3 ff. (M. 25. 100A f.); *Ar.* 2. 22. (M. 26. 192B). In the
former passage, mentioning Plato by name, Ath. is concerned with
what would be weakness on God's part if he had to use pre-existent,
uncreated matter to make the universe. But Greg. sees in eternally
pre-existent Forms an additional, and, we may think, even more
fundamental restriction upon God's freedom of action. He would
be subject to the indignity not only of having to work with material
which he did not create but would be limited by the Forms in what
he could do with it.

Argument against the existence of pre-existent matter, coexistent
with God, is found several times in Origen. He attacks the idea in
princ. 1. 3. 3 (p. 50. 14 ff., M. 11. 147C ff.), 2. 1. 4 (p. 110. 7 ff., M. 11.
185B ff.), *Jo.* 1. 17 (p. 22. 14, M. 14. 53B), *comm. in Gen.* 1 (= Eus. *p.e.*
7. 20 (M. 21. 654D ff.), *hom. in Gen.* 14. 3 (p. 124. 6 ff., M. 12. 238A ff.).
Koetschau notes (GCS 5. 51) that sometimes Origen is thinking of
Gnostics as well as of Platonists.

We may contrast with the line of reasoning found here in Greg.
the argument of Aristotle against the coexistence of Forms and
formless matter. He held that forms could not produce things,
insisting that form and matter could not exist apart (*gen. et corr.* 2.
335^{b}9 ff.). But, whereas Greg. would see here a reason for believing
that God created a world, the forms of which were in his mind and
which had no other existence, a world in which form and matter
came together at the moment of Creation, Aristotle saw here an argu-
ment for the eternal existence of the world (see below, vv. 55–74).

συνάναρχα: Greg. uses the word here in a way similar to that
found in Cyr. *Juln.* 2 (6. 54A). Elsewhere he is cautious about giving
the word meaning in a trinitarian context, refraining from its
application even to the Son and the Holy Spirit, unless the term is
meticulously defined in a way which gives it the kind of temporal
reference which in no way questions the position of the Father as
absolute ἀρχή.

5–6. The attributes of the Platonists' Forms, their eternal, unchanging qualities, are, in Greg.'s terms, applicable only to Godhead. Forms of this kind are illusory. The only things which can in any way correspond to them are direct creations of the mind of God.

μορφώματα: the choice of μόρφωμα to denote a Form is significant: it is a word used by other authors—and by Greg. himself in *carm.* 2. 1. 12. 561 (M. 37. 1206A) to denote visible forms or shapes. Its use here seems rather contemptuous, as is that of οὐσία in v. 8.

7–15. Greg. is arguing for *creatio ex nihilo* by denying the possibility of form and matter as separate entities. God created objects in which form and matter were inseparably combined. This argument, as is seen in the n. on vv. 3–4 above, goes back to Aristotle. In *Metaph.* Z 3. 1028[b] f., to take another instance, he maintains in the course of a discussion on οὐσία that matter can have no separate existence, except by mental abstraction; cf. W. D. Ross's edn. (Oxford, 1924), ad loc. and pp. xciii f.

7–8. The expression ἀνείδεος ὕλη does not occur in Plato or Aristotle, but is found in a passage about Aristotle in the *Epitome* of Arius Didymus (Diels, *Doxo.* 448. 3–4): ἡ μὲν γὰρ (sc. ὕλη) ἀνείδεος, τὸ δὲ εἶδος ἀεί, καὶ ἡ μὲν οὐ σῶμα, σωματικὴ δέ, τὸ δὲ καθάπαξ ἀσώματον. (Cf. Aristotle's use of ἀειδής in *Cael.* 306[b]17). The words are found also in a passage in Damascius where he is writing about the *Parmenides* (Ruelle, ii. 425, p. 281. 13 ff.): τὸ μὴ μετέχον τῶν εἰδῶν ἡ ὕλη ἐστὶν ἡ ἀνείδεος . . . ὅλως δὲ περὶ οὐσιῶν ὁ λόγος, ἀλλ' οὐ περὶ σχέσεως καὶ μεταφορῶν, ἀλλὰ περὶ πάσης τῆς ἀνειδέου ὕλης. Cf. also the words in the parallel sections from Plutarch and Stobaeus at Diels 308, together with Sallustius 17. 6 (Nock, p. 32. 3 ff.).

Greg. is appealing to 'common sense' observation, rather than to metaphysical speculation. He considers only the side of the question which conflicts most directly with *creatio ex nihilo*.

Origen had made distinctions which were not to Greg.'s purpose when he spoke (*princ.* 2. 1. 4 (p. 109. 22, M. 11. 185A) of matter as 'that which underlies bodies' ('quae subiecta est corporibus'), following in the line of Plat. *Tim.* 51A. Much more germane to that purpose is the practical conclusion that matter is never actually found existing apart from qualities: 'Haec tamen materia quamvis, ut supra diximus, secundum suam propriam rationem sine qualitatibus sit, numquam tamen subsistere extra qualitates invenitur.'

(ibid. 110. 4 ff., 185 B). Cf. *princ.* 4. 4. 7 (p. 357. 29 ff., M. 11. 408 A f.), *Cels.* 3. 41 (p. 237. 10 ff., M. 11. 975 A f.), 4. 57 (p. 330. 7, 1124 A), *Jo.* 13. 61 (p. 293. 18 ff., M. 14. 516 C f.), together with Koetschau's n. in *GCS* 5. 109.

In the works of his fellow Cappadocians Greg. could look for similar denials of the severance of form and matter. But, again, Greg. goes only so far in his use of the idea. Basil adumbrates (*hex.* 1. 8 (G. 1. 8 E ff., M. 29. 21 A ff.)) and Nyssen developed (*hom.opif.* 24 (Forbes 1. 248 ff., M. 44. 212 D ff.) a notion which goes beyond Origen's Platonism in advancing the view that matter might consist entirely of qualitative differences in a state of pure potentiality and without any *substratum*; cf. H. von Balthasar, *Présence et Pensée* (Paris, 1942), 20 ff.; A. H. Armstrong, Plotinus' Doctrine', 54–5; id., 'The Theory of the Non-Existence of Matter in Plotinus and in the Cappadocians', *Stud. Patr.* 5 (= TU 80; Berlin, 1962). Nyssen here holds that the withdrawal of properties causes the dissolution of the whole notion (λόγος) of body and that it is their combined presence which produces material nature: a body cannot exist without such qualities as colour. Greg. makes no use of this more subtle reasoning, being content to limit himself to the straightforward denial of the existence of formless matter in the recognized sense.

There remains for consideration a view which is intermediate, lying between the doctrine of formless, pre-existent matter and that of the simultaneous creation of form and matter. This is the idea found in Tatian, *orat.* 12 (p. 12. 18 ff., M. 6. 829 C ff.), where two stages of Creation are envisaged. In the first God created formless matter which, in the second stage, he ordered to form the universe as we know it. Tatian could claim for this understanding of Creation the support of Wisd. 11. 17 (κτίσασα τὸν κόσμον ἐξ ἀμόρφου ὕλης) and could at the same time defend it against Greg. by taking seriously the questions of vv. 7–8 and answering 'God has'.

ἄϋλον μορφὴν: is μορφή to be taken as a synonym for εἶδος? The two are distinguished in Pl. *R.* 380 D, but as Ross points out (edn. of *Metaphysics*, ii. 165), in Aristotle 'μορφή is often identified with εἶδος and τί ἦν εἶναι, but means primarily sensible shape'. It may be suspected that εἶδος is here a virtual equivalent for μορφή (cf. μορφώματα in v. 5 above), but that it carries over some of the distinctive connotations of the former. It is easier to ridicule immaterial μορφή, which, though technically representing εἶδος, has the associations of tangible 'shape' and the suggestions of impermanency. Objections may be made to belief in immaterial εἶδος, but the words do not seem to contain the same internal contradiction as is present in immaterial μορφή.

στροφάλιγξι: the picture is of ideas 'whirling' in the mind as dust, smoke, or water might swirl (LSJ s.v. I). Cf. *carm.* 1. 2. 14. 15 (M. 37. 756A).

9. **ἄσωμος** is cited in *Etymologicum Magnum* 161. 140 but otherwise it is known only from this passage where it is metrically convenient.

10. **φύσις** may be taken as closely parallel in meaning to that found in *Arc.* 3. 2: 'its own inherent nature'. But equally it could mean 'the world of nature', the divinely established natural order.

11–15. The God who combined form and matter also created them. The argument is that, if one is prepared to admit a divine power which could make a universe out of mysteriously separate elements of form and matter, one may as well admit that this power also created them, presumably on the grounds that such a unifying act would call for such a high degree of control over form and matter as to make easy belief in their creation by this same power.

12–13. There are two related problems in these lines: the meaning of κόσμος and the choice of reading at the beginning of v. 13. Nicetas' paraphrase reads: τίς γὰρ ἂν καὶ εἴη κόσμος ἐν τῷ ἑστάναι καθόλου πάντα χωρὶς μὲν τὴν ὕλην, χωρὶς δὲ τὸ εἶδος; It is clear that if a reading is preferred which gives an active verb in v. 13, κόσμος will be best taken to mean 'order, ordering'. If a verb of intransitive or passive meaning is read, it will mean 'world'. The possibilities may be examined in this way:

(i) An *active* sense. If we take Caillau's ἕστακεν, we have an attested active verb. ἕστακα occurs in Cercidas (3rd c. BC) as the perf. act. indic. of ἵστημι. On this interpretation the lines would mean: 'What ordering established the universe, hitherto utterly fragmented?'

(ii) An *intransitive* sense. (*a*) This could be obtained by accepting Caillau's understanding of his reading ἕστακεν as = ἕστηκεν. (*b*) Read ἑστάμεν, the Ep. intr. perf. infin. (*c*) Read ἑστάναι, the regular intr. perf. infin. in most forms of Greek. The translation would thus be: (*a*) 'What world then stood, being in all ways utterly fragmented?' (*b*) and (*c*) 'What world (was this), to stand in all ways utterly fragmented?'

Several points should be noted. (1) There is no evidence that
ἕστᾰκα was ever used = ἕστηκα. (2) Though Cercidas may seem
tenuous evidence for ἕστακεν in an active sense, the form is found in
compounds in writings including Plato, LXX, and Sextus Empir-
icus. In his edition of Cercidas, J. U. Powell noted (*Collectanea
Alexandrina* (Oxford, 1925), 203): 'sed ἕστᾰκα et composita transitiva
sunt, velut τοὺς μὴ παρεστακότας τὰ πορεῖα *Tebt. Pap.* i. 5, l. 196';
better examples follow. But whether Greg. was as well informed as
Powell may be questioned. (3) ἐστάμεν is found four times in
Homer, all in the same position as here, first word in the line (*Il.* 4.
342, 12. 316, 15. 675, *Od.* 21. 261). (4) *Difficilior lectio* casts doubt on
ἐστάναι: it looks very much as if it appeared first as a gloss on the
epic form ἐστάμεν, especially as Nicetas uses it in his paraphrase.

The best choice appears to lie between (i) and (ii) (*b*). The first
avoids tautology, giving πάντα a meaning which is not simply a
doublet of διαμπερές. But the pleonasm πάντα διαμπερές is good
Homeric style (cf. *Il.* 16. 499). The second alternative gives Nicetas'
sense. I incline to the second.

ἄνδιχα πάντα: note the Homeric reminiscence. In *Il.* 18. 511 the
words concern the distribution of spoil at the sacking of a city.
Greg.'s habit of reusing expressions of this sort in a totally different
context is discussed in Introd.

14. **κεραστής:** like κτίστορα, the word is to be connected with
πάντων. Cf. the description of Zeus in Orph. fr. 297 as πάντων
κεραστής.

15. **κτίστορα:** κτίστωρ here = κτίστης, as in ὁ κτίστης ἁπάντων (Sir.
24. 8), ὁ πάντων κτίστης (4 Macc. 11. 5).

16–23. *God is more than a craftsman.* The distinction between the
human craftsman who has to work within the limits of the material
to hand and the divine Creator was one which had been developed
by Theophilus of Antioch in *Autol.* 2. 4 (p. 102, M. 6. 1052в f.).
Amongst other passages in the same vein may be mentioned Ps.-
Justin, *coh.Gr.* 22 (M. 6. 281в), Iren. *haer.* 2. 10. 2 (M. 7. 736в), Ath.
inc. 2. 3 ff. (M. 25. 100A ff.), *decr.* 11 (Opitz 2. 9. 33 ff., M. 25. 433с f.).

Kertsch, *Bildersprache*, 152 n. 4, points to the Stoic use of the
figure of the potter, comparing C. W. Müller, *Die Kurzdialoge der
Appendix Platonica* (Studia et testimonia antiqua 17, Munich, 1975),
303.

16. **ἐλίσσων:** see *Arc.* 3. 43 n.
18. Neither Billius nor Caillau is quite accurate, translating as if

φρενός were a dative. There is a difference between 'Grant to God more than would be appropriate to a human mind' and 'Grant to God something more than a human mind'.

φιλάναρχε: an advocate of the view that forms and matter are, like God, eternal is addressed, following the contention of συνάναρχα in v. 3. The word is not cited in LSJ; *PGL* gives only this passage and *or*. 23. 7 (M. 35. 1160A), there coupled with φιλαγέν-νητος in a Trinitarian discussion.

19. Inert, formless matter is purely a mental concept, whereas matter, as it was created by God, given individual structure by activating forms, is part of the recognizable world.

20. **νώσατο:** the act of divine will is stressed; cf. Florovsky, 'Idea of Creation', 58 ff. For the form cf. the ep. νοήσατο (H. *Il*. 10. 501) and the participle νωσάμενος (e.g. Theognis 1298).

τὰ . . . ἐνείδεα: no other example of τὸ ἐνεῖδος is recorded in the lexica.

γενέτειρα is not common in earlier literature. Pindar applied it to Hera (*N*. 7. 2) and Artemidorus Daldianus (2nd c. AD) to the earth. For a metaphorical use we may look to Plotinus 5. 8. 4, where we find ἀλήθεια . . . καὶ γενέτειρα καὶ τροφὸς καὶ οὐσία καὶ τροφή.

πολύπλοκος: perhaps Aristophanes' πολύπλοκον νόημα may have suggested the use (*Th*. 463).

21-3. Unlike a painter who needs an external object to copy, God was able to create from the model in his own mind.

ἐοικὸς . . . εἶδος means a plausible representation of the original. There is a play upon the two senses of εἶδος: the 'form' and the 'visible representation' (the second frequent in Homer).

24-54. *An attack on Manichaean views*

As useful for understanding the Manichaean position may be mentioned: F. C. Burkitt, *The Religion of the Manichees* (Cambridge, 1925); A. V. W. Jackson, *Researches in Manichaeism* (New York, 1932); H. J. Polotsky, 'Manichäismus', RE Suppl. vi (1935), 240-71; H. C. Puech, *Le Manichéisme, son fondateur, sa doctrine* (Paris, 1949); A. Adam, *Texte zum Manichäismus* (Berlin, 1954); G. Widengren, *Mani and Manichae-ism*, ET (London, 1965); S. C. Lieu, *Manichaeism in the Later Roman Empire and in Medieval China* (Manchester, 1985); H. Jonas, *The Gnostic Religion*, 2 edn. (Boston, 1963), ch. 9 and elsewhere. Cf. G. Bardy, 'Manichéisme', DTC 9 (1927), 1841-1895, and 1954-7 for Patristic references to Manichaeism; Quasten, *Patrology*, iii. 356 ff. gives full bibliography.

Part of the earlier argument of the poem applies to the Manichees, though it is only now that they are mentioned by name. For it was part of Manichaean teaching that there were two eternal elements, God and matter, neither of which was created. The word ἄναρχος (cf. v. 4 above) is applied by the Manichees to ὕλη, according to Macarius Aegyptius in *hom*. 16. 1 (M. 34. 613B), or whoever the real author may be (cf. Quasten, *Patrology*, iii. 162 ff.). In the Manichaean system these two elements might also be known as Light and Darkness or Truth and Falsehood. It is the Light–Darkness presentation which Greg. here selects for attack.

Nyssen introduces an anti-Manichaean polemic in a similar context in *hom.opif.* 23 (Forbes 1. 242 ff.; M. 44. 209B ff.), when he argues against the coeternity of matter with God, holding that the admission of δύο ἄναρχα καὶ ἀγέννητα plays directly into the hands of the Manichees (p. 246; 212B). Athanasius writes extensively on similar themes in *Contra Gentes* (M. 25. 4 ff.). In attacks which include in their objects Gnostics, Marcionites, Manichees, and followers of cosmic religion, he argues for a unitary control of the universe by the incorporeal God who is creator out of nothing and the sustainer who holds together in harmony elements which would otherwise be mutually destructive. It is he who has placed within his providential plan human beings who are designed by their image likeness to the Creator to discern by thoughtful observation of his works some pointers to the nature of the Father and the Word who shares the unity of divine government.

24–31 form a unit of argument (*argumentum ex remotione*, Focken, *De Greg. . . . ratione*, 38), designed to show that the two principles, God and evil Darkness, cannot coexist from all time. Cf. Bas. *hex*. 2. 4 ff. (G. 1. 15C ff., M. 29. 36B ff.) throughout this section.

24–5 Basil attacks the Manichees in *hex*. 2. 4 (G. 1. 15C., M. 29. 36B ff.) for taking the 'darkness' of Gen. 1. 2 not as a mere absence of light (cf. v. 43b below, with n.), but as a self-existent evil power. The same belief lies behind these lines and the subsequent ones. Cf. *carm*. 2. 1. 11. 1173 (M. 37. 1109A), where in ἀρχικῷ σκότῳ Greg. disputes the same point.

πάρος: here it is possible to tr. as 'before' in either a spatial or a temporal sense. The former would strengthen the picture of the rival throned before the divine light. But the second is the more likely when one recalls that Basil had tried to answer the question 'Is darkness older than light?' He seeks a solution in the suggestion that the darkness which was 'upon the face of the deep' was a withdrawal of original light caused by the shadow of heaven, *hex.* 2. 5 (G. 1. 17B ff., M. 29. 40C f.).

For the departure from the more usual postpositive prepositional use of πάρος cf. S. *OC* 418, E. *Andr.* 1112, 1208.

ἀντίθρονον: Greg. is the only writer recorded as using this word—*orr.* 21. 8 (M. 35. 1089B), 42. 22 (M. 36. 484B)—or the related ἀντιθόωκος of *Arc.* 6. 44.

25b–31. No form of coexistence is thinkable which sets up the positive principle of darkness or evil alongside God. If evil were allowed to oppose God, he would not be God. Neither would he be God if he permitted an 'arrangement' with evil. The possibility that God and evil are evenly matched is dismissed because there is no third power to end the deadlock. If there were a conflict, the stronger would win. But how could this conflict, once started, be calmly resolved?

Such is the structure of the argument. But the basis is found in v. 26 in the words οὐ γὰρ ἔοικεν. Greg. is assuming the omnipotence of the Christian God, not arguing for it, and he can thus advance from the starting point of what is fitting for that God. In a rather rhetorical manner Greg. is setting up positions which the Manichees did not need to hold in order to knock them down again. The impression of an exhaustive survey of all the possibilities is largely illusory. Though the Manichees did claim parity in some respects between the God of Light and the power of matter, darkness, or evil (e.g., both are eternal, uncreated), there is still a vital distinction. Darkness is not a god, not the brother of Light, as he is in ancient Iranian dualism, but, in violation of strict dualism, ultimately inferior. There is not in the Manichaean system the everlasting equipoise which Greg.'s τρίτος would have to resolve. The future triumph of Light, in Mani's system, would be caused not by any external intervention, but by the completion of a process which is already started—the separation of the particles of Light from the material prison in which, in the present age, they are held. A Manichee could reply to v. 28 that the victory would, indeed, go to the stronger, but the time is not yet. Cf. Burkitt 64; Polotsky, RE Suppl. vi. 245 ff.; Widengren 43 ff., and Lieu 5–24.

27. There is no reason for the change suggested by Caillau's n. from οὐ to ὄν. This would produce not a sentence but a group of words without a main verb. The text printed is amenable to Caillau's tr. 'Deus evanescit'; seeing a direct parallel with vv. 25–6 εἰ Θεὸς ἦεν, / οὐ σκότος, he understands ἦεν with σκότος. The meaning is thus: 'If darkness really existed, you do not know God (i.e., there is no God for you to know; 'Deus evanescit'). The same text may equally well be repunctuated to read: εἰ σκότος, οὐ Θεόν, οἶδας. This presents the same absolute choice in a different way: 'If you know (acknowledge) darkness, you do not know God.'

ἄκοσμον: there is a play on two senses of the word: e.g. *carm.* 2. 1. 13. 182–3 (M. 37. 1241 A). Agreement is 'unbecoming' (cf. οὐ ... ἔοικε v. 26). But such agreement with evil would be a denial of the order of the universe: the result would be a κόσμος ἄκοσμος. For the expression cf. *orac. Sib.* 7. 123; *AP.* 9. 323. 3 (Antip. Sid.); Nonnus *D.* 6. 371, *al.*

30–1. This surprising end to the conflict would come about only on the assumption of Greg.'s hypothetical mediator. Mani did not teach that the conflict would end without trace and be forgotten. In the final dispensation, the powers of darkness will not simply disappear. Though they will be 'confined within their own original domain' (Burkitt 64), incapable of returning to their attack upon the world of light, they will still remain in existence to represent the second principle; cf. Widengren 68–9. The form ἔγειρας (ep. aor.) is paralleled in H. *Od.* 15. 44.

32–50. *Opposition to Mani's views on the nature of Man and the Fall.*

The poem now changes direction. Instead of continuing to discuss cosmology, Greg. follows up the Manichaean teaching on the related subject of man's involvement in the created order. According to Mani, Adam came into being at the end of a complicated mythological process as a creature in whom the King of Darkness had imprisoned a number of light particles. The initiative in man's creation belongs to the King of Darkness: man is not created in the image of God, by God. Only in a secondary sense can man be thought of as created in God's image, inasmuch as he was made like the Divine Messenger who, in turn, had been created by the King of Light. Manichaean teaching did not concern itself with the nature of man in the terms in which Greg. would want to describe it. For him 'man' represents a recognizable unit, a composite being about whom statement can be made. Mani did not take the idea of 'man' seriously, regarding him, in Burkitt's words as 'essentially a fortuitous conglomeration', merely 'a particle of Light enclosed in an alien and irredeemable envelope' (p. 39).

32. **ψυχὴ καὶ δέμας:** Greg. here places himself in a long line of traditional writing on anthropology. As R. A. Norris Jr. writes, 'It is the initial commonplace of all Greek anthropology that man, as a living being (ζῷον), is a composite, being made up of two parts, a body and a soul', *Manhood and Christ: A Study in the Christology of Theodore of Mopsuestia* (Oxford, 1963), 21. Many examples might be cited from Greek philosophers to illustrate this δόξα, e.g., Pl. *Phd.* 70A *al.*, Plot. 1. 1. 3. In taking this as his starting point Greg. is attempting to place Manichaean teaching in the wrong, not only from the viewpoint of Christian theology, but equally of Greek philosophy.

It is important to limit the scope of Greg.'s statement of the bipartite nature of man. What is here intended is opposition to the Manichaean depreciation of the human body and the disappearance of man as an identifiable entity, not a contribution to the question whether man is best described in bipartite or tripartite terms. In the anti-Apollinarian polemic of *carm.* 1. 1. 10 Greg. adopts a threefold division of man: ψυχή, νοῦς, σῶμα (v. 3, M. 37. 465A). This need not be thought of as an inconsistency on Greg.'s part, but rather as a restatement of the nature of the non-bodily part of man to answer a different set of questions (cf. R. A. Norris 57 ff.). Greg.'s understanding of the question is discussed in Winslow, *Dynamics*, chs. 3–4; Althaus, *Heilslehre*, esp. 22–32, 51–60, 87–9, 96–100, and 207–10; Ruether, *Gregory*, 130–6; Ellverson, *The Dual Nature of Man*.

ἀπορρώξ: Billius' tr. clearly takes this as a Manichaean expression, no less part of their 'fiction' than the root of darkness. Certainly ἀπορρώξ looks an admirable word for a 'particle' of light in the Manichaean scheme. Caillau, on the other hand, leaves it open to us to accept the description of the soul as Greg.'s own and to take only words about the body as Manichaean. In favour of the second view is Greg.'s willingness to use ἀπορρώξ to characterize the Spirit breathed into man at his creation (*Arc.* 7. 73). But the combination of ἀπορρώξ with φωτὸς ἀπειρεσίοιο so much suggests the Manichaean terminology that it is difficult to believe that Greg. used it approvingly.

33. The Manichees spoke of the two primary elements as two 'roots' of Light and Darkness.

34. πολλὸν ἀπόπροθεν looks like meiosis for 'directly opposite'. Greg. is claiming that Manichaean teaching about soul and body makes them so completely antithetical that no such unity as man could be produced from them.

35. ξυνὴ φύσις: what is meant by this expression may be judged from the speech put into the mouth of the Logos in *Arc.* 7. The creation of man is envisaged thus:

> ξυνὸν δ' ἀμφοτέρωθεν ἐμοὶ γένος εὔαδε πῆξαι,
> θνητῶν τ' ἀθανάτων τε νοήμονα φῶτα μεσηγύ, κτλ.   (*Arc.* 7. 65–6)

Man is not a battle-ground but a meeting-ground. (Cf. the discussion in *Arc.* 7. 65 ff. n.) He has affinities both with the world of physical creation and with the heavenly world.

35b ff. Greg. is not denying the possibility of conflict between the elements of man's composition. The way in which, in a number of his poems—2. 1. 22 (M. 37. 1281 A f.) is a good example—he writes, at times almost despairingly, about the conflict which results from the 'binding' of the soul to the flesh, makes this quite clear. One may say that emotionally Greg. never came to terms with the intellectual position he maintained on the unity of body and soul. But he still upheld that position. Here he is disputing the Manichaean view of an unending (cf. ἔμπεδος) unrelenting struggle between the two elements, a struggle incapable of resolution. The stress falls upon πλεκτή. The elements of which man is formed are capable of being 'interwoven', an impossibility if they were basically inimical.

39b–54 return to the opening theme of the One God as the only ultimate principle. As evil is not a positive principle, the Fall must be explained as rejection of good.

39 picks up and amplifies the opening words of v. 3, claiming for God the title of 'Light' wrested from the Manichees.

ἀδήριτος: on the quantity of the ι and the possible meanings, cf. *Arc.* 3. 86 n. The most likely meaning here is 'beyond the reach of strife' (such as would arise from the Manichaean darkness).

40. ἁπλῶν: Greg. is better evidence for the application of ἁπλοῦς to angels than Ps.-Dionysius Areopagita, cited by *PGL* s.v. A. 2. a. The other passage mentioned there is of interest here, coming as it does from a context in which Evagrius Ponticus is discussing the applicability of the word to angels. An angel, he argues, is not simple in the way in which God is. For an angel is a compound of essence and holiness, as man is compound (ἐκ σώματος καὶ ψυχῆς συνεστώς),

ep. 2 (M. 32. 248B ff.). This argument is a curious one, but its object
is clear enough—to establish a distinction between God and the
angels. Greg. is no less well aware of the need to make this distinc-
tion. Elsewhere we shall see how he can draw a line which places
man with the angels on one side and God alone on the other (cf. *Arc*.
4. 89–92 n.). But here, Greg. is able to point an understandable con-
trast between God and the angels on the one side and man on the
other, by using the distinction of 'simple' and 'composite'. For
ἁπλοῦς of angels, cf. *Arc*. 6. 17.

πλεκτῶν: the word is now put in perspective. πλεκτὴ φύσις is a
step above the Manichaean view of man, but well below the status of
pure intelligence. Cf. v. 92.

ὑψιθεόντων: *PGL* cites this passage as the first appearance of the
word. Soph. cites also *carm*. 2. 2 (epigr.), 17. 1 (M. 38. 91A). Greg.'s
liking for ὑψι-compounds may be seen from the occurrence in *PGL*
of 9 of them to be found in his verse. Cf. v. 51 n.

41–3a. The 'dark' element in man was not there from the start, but
came as a negative quality.

42. ἑστηκυῖα: cf. Billius' n. 'Hoc est, vel per se existens natura, vel a
Deo procreata.'

περίγραφος: cf. *Arc*. 2. 64 n. 'Circumscribed' here indicates not
the limitations of darkness, but the supposition that it had by right a
fixed territory, as it were.

43b–6. Evil is not an eternal principle, as embodied in the Mani-
chaean darkness which was said to be in existence before the world.
It is to be traced to a point in history, the breaking of God's
command. Cf. *or*. 40. 45 (M. 36. 424A): πίστευε, μὴ οὐσίαν εἶναί τινα
τοῦ κακοῦ, μήτε βασιλείαν, ἢ ἄναρχον, ἢ παρ' ἑαυτῆς ὑποστᾶσαν, ἢ
παρὰ τοῦ Θεοῦ γενομένην, ἀλλ' ἡμέτερον ἔργον εἶναι τοῦτο καὶ τοῦ
πονηροῦ ... Gr. Nyss. argues for the same point in *or.cat*. 6 (p. 33.
4 ff., M. 45. 28C), as does Basil in *hex*. 2. 4–5 (G. 1. 16C ff., M. 29.
37C ff.).

The idea that darkness is no more than absence of light had a
long history in antiquity. Aristotle propounded it in *Col*. 791ᵇ2: τὸ
σκότος οὐ χρῶμα ἀλλὰ στέρησίς ἐστι φωτός. Cf. *An*. 418ᵇ18. A
number of later examples of the same thought were collected by
J. E. B. Mayor, *Journal of Philology*, 28/56 (1903), 289 ff., taking his
title from *Paradise Regained*, 4. 400: 'Privation mere of light and
absent day.' Mention may be made of a few instances. Synesius used
the idea without drawing from it any moral implication in *Calv*. 11

(T. 211. 18 ff., M. 66. 1188c): σκιὰ δὲ οὐδὲν ἕτερόν ἐστιν ἢ σκότος· ἑκατέρῳ γὰρ τῶν ὀνομάτων φωτὸς ἀπουσία σημαίνεται.

Augustine commonly refers to this view, e.g. *contra ep. Man.* 30. 33 (M. *PL* 42. 195; CSEL 25. 230. 21 ff.): 'quamquam tenebrae non sunt corporeae: totumque hoc nomen lucis absentia est; sicut nuditas carere vestitu . . .' and *de nat. boni contra Man.* 15 (M. *PL* 42. 556; CSEL 25. 861. 15–16). Here Augustine had the same anti-Manichaean reasons as Greg. for discounting the notion of darkness as a positive quality. Cf. further *conf.* 12. 3 (M. *PL* 32. 827; CSEL 33. 311. 19–20), *civ. Dei* 11. 10. 2 (M. *PL* 41. 326; CSEL 40/1. 527. 26 ff.; CCSL 48. 331. 60 ff.), *contra sec. Iul. resp. imperf. op.* 5. 44 (M. *PL* 45. 1480–1).

We may notice that Greg., in preparing the way for the introduction of the Fall, does not use his analogy in such abstract terms as became common. Plotinus, for example, defined evil in these terms: ὅλως δὲ τὸ κακὸν ἔλλειψιν τοῦ ἀγαθοῦ θετέον (3. 2. 5). Again, Augustine may be cited: 'cum omnino natura nulla sit malum, nomenque hoc non sit nisi privationis boni', *civ. Dei* 11. 22 (M. *PL* 41. 335; CSEL 40/1. 543. 15 f.; CCSL 48. p. 341. 22 f.); 'non est ergo malum nisi privatio boni', *contra advers. leg. et proph.* 1. 5. 7 (M. *PL* 42. 607); cf. further *conf.* 3. 7. 12 (M. *PL* 32. 688; CSEL 33. 53. 23 ff.), *enchir.* 11 (M. 40. 236). Sallustius shares this view, *De dis.* 12. 1 (Nock p. 22. 14 ff.). As the gods are good, evil is to be thought of as absence of good, as darkness is absence of light. Greg. does not follow out exactly the 'privatio' notion which would parallel the light–darkness analogy, but points not to the consideration of the essence of evil so much as to its appearance as a historical phenomenon. Basil treats the idea in *hex.* 2. 4 (G. 1. 16B–C, M. 29. 37C–D) and 5 (17D–18A, 41B).

45. ἄνω: not 'australes ad auras', (Billius), which would be κάτω, but 'north' (cf. Hdt. 1. 143. 2; Pl. *R.* 435E): 'the sun's course brings in the north the icy winter'; cf. Nicetas: ὁ ἥλιος πρὸς τὰς χειμερινὰς τὸν αὐτοῦ δρόμον ἀνελίσσων. There is a touch of artistry in the implication, rather than the outright assertion, that it is the disappearance of the sun on its winter journey which brings winter.

χεῖμα φρικτόν is exactly Ovid's 'hiems . . . horrida' (*M.* 15. 212).

46b–50. Lucifer's fall and subsequent hatred of mankind. Cf. *Arc.* 6. 56–99.

47. As Caillau's n. points out, ἧς ὑπεροπλίῃσι is a reminiscence of H. *Il.* 1. 205, where the words are spoken by Achilles against Agamemnon.

49. For Adam's 'tasting' of evil, cf. *Arc*. 7. 114. The metaphorical use of γεύομαι is common from Homer on, but it is particularly appropriate to Adam who 'tasted' (experienced) evil in tasting the forbidden fruit.

ἀνδροφόνοιο: cf. the application to the devil of ἀνθρωποκτόνος (John 8. 44).

θανάτου: cf. Matt. 16. 28, Mark 9. 1, Luke 9. 27, John 8. 52, Heb. 2. 9, *AP* 7. 662. 4 (Leonidas, 3rd c. BC).

51–4. *The nature of evil*. It is like rust on iron.

51. ὀψιγόνοιο: despite its acceptance by Billius and Dronke, the evidence for ὑψίγονος is not strong. The latter was mistaken in supposing this to be the reading of Cu (*S. Gregorii Nazianzeni Carmina Selecta* (Göttingen, 1848), 198). The only recorded instance of ὑψίγονος is Nonnus, *D*. 27. 98. Greg.'s predilection for compounds of ὑψι- might encourage its adoption and it makes good sense, in referring to Lucifer's part in the origin of evil. ὀψιγόνοιο on the other hand, by stressing the late appearance of evil, points to its secondary nature.

52. λώβη is well chosen, suggesting at once 'ruin' (cf. S. *Ant*. 792) and the spreading contagion of a disease like leprosy (cf. Galen 14. 757; Isid. Pel. *ep*. 1. 28 (M. 78. 200C), *al*.) Dr A. Meredith has drawn my attention to Plot. 4. 7. 10. 46, an image of the soul restored to purity through the removal of a massive accretion of rust.

Note the quantity of ι in ἰὸς. Elsewhere it is long.

κρατεροῖο: cf. Hes. *Th*. 864 σίδηρος . . . κρατερώτατός ἐστιν.

53–4. In contrast to inanimate iron, man has a responsibility for his ruined state.

αὐτοδάϊκτος = 'killing oneself' is found in *AP* 9. 293. 1 (Philippus, 1st c. AD) and in didactic verse in Oppian *H*. 2. 349.

κακίην ἐφύτευσα: similar expressions are in H. *Il*. 15. 134, *Od*. 5. 340. Cf. *Arc*. 8. 11–12 n.

φθονεροῖο: for the relationship of envy and pride in Lucifer's actions cf. *Arc*. 6. 56 ff. n.

παλαίσμασιν: the sense of 'tricks' may be illustrated from, e.g., Ar. *Ra*. 689.

ἦν = 'his' (the devil's) is quite Homeric. Cf. Monro, *Homeric Grammar*, §254, p. 220. 'Occasionally it (the possessive ἑός, ὅς) refers to a prominent word in the same sentence which is not grammatically the subject.' (He cites *Il*. 6. 500 and *Od*. 9. 369 as examples.) Cf. Chantraine, *Grammaire homérique*, i, §128, pp. 272–3.

55-74. *The world is not eternal, but created by the timeless God*

Greg. now takes up some of the problems treated in vv. 3 ff., looking at them in a different way. Both there and here we are faced with the possibility of something eternally existent alongside God. In the earlier passage we were asked to contemplate a stage at which form was imposed upon eternally existent matter: here we must consider the view that the world itself, in its union of form and matter, is eternal. The place which the idea of the eternity of the world holds in Greek thought is fully dealt with by J. Baudry, *Le Problème de l'origine et de l'éternité du monde* (Paris, 1931). Greg.'s two approaches to the question are the two which Baudry distinguished at the beginning of his study as fundamental to the whole debate (p. 6).

The notion of the eternity of the world in a developed form may be traced back to Aristotle, though there are indications of it in an earlier writer. Xenophanes appears to have held some doctrine of an ungenerated cosmos (cf. Guthrie, *History*, i. 380). Aristotle wrote in *Cael.* 296ᵃ33-4: ἡ δέ γε τοῦ κόσμου τάξις ἀΐδιος. He set his face against earlier Greek beliefs that the world had a beginning, arguing that it had neither a beginning nor an end. (Cf. Baudry 139 ff.) Aristotle's opinion gained ascendancy over many philosophers in the following centuries, not only among avowed Aristotelians, but also among some, like Crantor (*c.*335-*c.*275 BC), who tried to combine it with Platonic beliefs. Baudry shows how complete was the triumph of this notion of eternity of the world by the third century BC (p. 226).

This ascendancy was to be challenged in the following centuries. But much of the opposition stemmed from schools of thought which produced counter-arguments scarcely more acceptable to Christian cosmology than the notion they attempted to disprove. The Stoics denied the eternity of the world, but asserted the eternity of matter and the material nature of the god who formed it into a succession of worlds. Epicureans believed that the world had a birth and would be destroyed, but allied to this a mechanistic cosmology, a chance arrangement of uncreated atoms without any moving intelligence.

The Fathers generally took occasion to deny the eternity theory as being inconsistent with the Christian doctrine of creation (cf. Baudry 191). It continued as a point of dispute in the century following Greg.'s and later, as may be seen from the instances cited by P. de Labriolle, *La Réaction païenne* (Paris, 1950), 484 ff. In Greg.'s day we may again turn to Sallustius for an example of belief in the eternity of the cosmos.

In *De dis* 7. 1 (Nock, p. 12. 24 ff.) the argument is stated beginning: αὐτὸν δὲ τὸν Κόσμον ἄφθαρτόν τε καὶ ἀγέννητον εἶναι ἀνάγκη. The relationship between this eternal cosmos and the Cosmic Gods of the previous chapter (cf. v. 3 n. above) is not easy to determine, but it is clear that Sallustius intended both ideas to be taken seriously. (Cf. further c. 17 Nock, pp. 30. 6 ff.) Among Greg.'s immediate Christian predecessors it is Basil who treats the question most seriously. In *hex*. 1. 2–3 (G. 1. 2E ff., M. 29. 5C ff.) he reviews theories in rivalry with the Christian view, dealing specifically with the eternity of the world in c. 3 (3E ff.; 9A ff.). Basil argues that we have no evidence of any phenomena eternally existent without beginning. The circular movement of the heavenly bodies in no way proves that the circles did not begin at some point in space and time. A circle drawn on paper has no visible starting-point but, obviously, the man who drew it had to begin somewhere. Similarly, the universe had a starting-point, and, in accordance with the principle that things which have a beginning also come to an end, is due for ultimate destruction. Cf. S. Giet, SC 26 (Paris, 1949), 99–100. But, despite this argument, Basil grounds his case mainly on the authority of Scripture. Greg. bases his entirely on authority. If the world were eternal, 'inspired' writers would turn out to be mistaken.

In the following century the argument was taken up again. Proclus, for example, arguing for the eternity of the world, is opposed by Aeneas of Gaza. Cf. *CHLGEMP*, chs. 19 (A. C. Lloyd) and 31 (I. P. Sheldon-Williams).

55. κόσμε: in thus addressing the cosmos Greg. is not being entirely rhetorical. For where his vocative is pure apostrophe, others were accustomed to call upon the cosmos as a divine being. The association of eternity and divinity is an obvious one. The variety of beliefs compassed by this attribution of divinity to the cosmos need not here concern us (cf. A. J. Festugière, *La Révélation d'Hermès Trismégiste*, ii, *Le Dieu cosmique* (Paris, 1949), esp. 238 ff.). It is sufficient to notice that the divinity of the cosmos formed a significant part of many people's religious attitude. As Philo had claimed long before, there was a strong religious element in Aristotle's original affirmation of the eternity of the world, *de aet. mundi* 10 (2. 489 M., 6. 52 ff. C.-W. Cf. Baudry 104). When Sallustius writes of offering prayer directly to the cosmos, *De dis* 17. 10 (Nock, p. 32. 22 ff.), he is following up one aspect of the divinity theory, as others had done before him: Rochefort in his note on the passage (p. 51 n. 10), cites Manilius, *Astron*. 1. 523; Pliny, *HN* 2. 1; Porphyry fr. in Eus. *p.e.* 3. 9 (pp. 126 ff., M. 21. 184B ff.). See further A. H. Armstrong, 'The World of the Senses in Pagan and Christian Thought', *Downside Review*, 68/213 (1950), 305–23.

57. Χριστοφόροι: Χριστοφόρος is first found in Ignatius, *Eph*. 9. 2 (Bihlmeyer p. 85. 15; M. 5. 652B). For the meaning 'Christ-bearing' which it there has cf. J. B. Lightfoot, *The Apostolic Fathers*, II. ii (London, 1889), 21, 56 nn.. The word came into use as a title of respect for martyrs and prominent Christians: cf. Phileas ap. Eus. *h.e.* 8. 10. 3 (p. 760. 13; M. 20. 764B) of the Alexandrian Martyrs, Asterius Amasenus (M. 40. 348A) of St. Stephen, Ath. *inc*. 10. 5 (M. 25. 113C), *gent*. 5 (M. 25. 12C), in both places of St. Paul. In *Ar*. 3. 45 (M. 26. 417C), Ath. uses the word Χριστοφόροι (joined with φιλό-χριστοι) in a context which justifies Müller's gloss 'orthodoxi' (*Lexicon Athanasianum* s.v.). This may be the meaning here. Another possibility is that we are to see an analogy with θεοφόρος (*PGL* s.v. 4 b) = 'inspired': on a question such as this it would be appropriate that Greg. should invoke the authority of Scripture. Elsewhere Greg. applies the word to the human soul or a mouth uttering praise: *carm*. 1. 2. 38. 8 (M. 37. 967A) and 2. 2. 7. 313 (1575A).

See further, for the history of the word, F. J. Dölger, 'Christophorus als Ehrentitel für Märtyrer u. Gläubige im christlichen Altertum', *AC* 4 (1934), 73–80; A. Hermann, 'Christophorus', *RAC* ii (1954), 1241–50.

58. Cf. Pindar's Ὧραι . . . ἐλισσόμεναι (*O*. 4. 2 ff.). For ἐλίσσω see *Arc*. 3. 43 n.

59. For the work of the Logos in Creation cf. *Arc*. 7. 55 ff.

59b–62 accept the belief that Creation took place at a point fixed by God but ask what was the nature of divine contemplation and concern before the universe was in being. Origen had faced a similar issue in *De Principiis*. Following an attack upon those who imagined that they could reconcile the idea of a Maker of the universe with that of uncreated, coeternal matter, he continued: 'secundum hanc enim eorum rationem si ponamus verbi gratia materiam non fuisse, ut isti asserunt dicentes quia deus non potuerit aliquid facere, cum nihil esset, sine dubio futurus erat *otiosus*, materiam non habens ex qua posset operari, quam ei non sua provisione, sed fortuito sentiunt adfuisse' (*princ*. 2. 1. 4: p. 110. 17 ff., M. 11. 185C). This Origen dismisses as completely lacking in understanding of the nature and intelligence of the uncreated God (v. 63 n.). Considering where the argument appears in the present poem, one should notice that it is to the Manichees that Augustine attributes the question of God's activity before Creation:

> primum ergo librum Veteris Testamenti, qui inscribitur *Genesis*, sic solent Manichaei reprehendere. quod scriptum est, *In principio fecit Deus caelum et terram*, quaerunt, in quo principio; et dicunt: si in principio aliquo temporis fecit Deus caelum et terram, quid agebat antequam faceret caelum et terram? et quid ei subito placuit facere, quod numquam antea fecerat per tempora aeterna? his repondebimus, Deum in principio fecisse caelum et terram, non in principio temporis, sed in Christo, cum Verbum esset apud Patrem, per quod facta et in quo facta sunt omnia.
>
> (*de Gen. contra Manichaeos*, 1. 2. 3, M. *PL* 34. 174)

Proclus was later to ask why, according to his opponents' view of creation, God had waited so long 'in idleness' (*in Ti.* 88c).

60. κίνυτο: for the reasons for preferring this form to Caillau's κίν-νυτο, cf. *Arc.* 1. 34 n. Again, both L and Cu read the single ν form (as they do in v. 67 below). For the form κίνυτο see Monro, *Homeric Grammar*, § 17, p. 18; cf. Chantraine, i, §§ 132–42, pp. 382 ff.

61. ἄπρηκτος: 'idle', as 'otiosus' in Rufinus' Origen, quoted in vv. 59b-62 n.

ἀτέλεστος: there appears to be no lexical parallel for the sense which is required here. LSJ give passive senses like 'unaccomplished, uninitiated' (III and IV are irrelevant here). *PGL* and Soph. add Christian examples in the sense 'unbaptized', mostly taken from Greg.: cf. *orr.* 18. 31 (M. 35. 1024c); 40. 28 (M. 36. 400A); *carm.* 2. 1. 1. 324 (M. 37. 994A). But here the sense must be active = 'not accomplishing anything'. ἀτέλεστος here has the meaning found in ἀτελής (LSJ II Act.: 'Not bringing to an end, not accomplishing one's purpose, ineffectual').

63–6. *The Trinity's self-contemplation.* M. Pellegrino, with justice, points to these lines as showing a quality of verse which is rising towards poetry (*La poesia di S. Gregorio Nazianzeno*, 30: 'Versi grandi, fulgenti di luminosa bellezza, . . .'). A finer poet than Greg. was later to write, in prose, words of similar import. 'For all Eternity is at once in Him, both the empty durations before the World was made, and the full ones after' (Traherne, 'Centuries of Meditations', i. 44, ed. H. M. Margoliouth (Oxford, 1958), i. 22, ll. 6–8).

On the thought of these and the following lines cf. Florovsky, 'Idea of Creation', 60 ff.

63. αἰῶσιν κενεοῖσιν: they are 'empty', as devoid of temporal events. These ages are to be thought of as equivalent to the singular αἰών (= 'eternity') which Greg. defines in *carm.* 1. 2. 34. 14 (M. 37. 946A): αἰών, διάστημ᾽ ἀχρόνως ἀεὶ ῥέον and, at greater length, in *or.* 38. 8 (M. 36. 320A f.) = 45. 4 (628C): αἰὼν γάρ, οὔτε χρόνος οὔτε χρόνου τι μέρος· οὐδὲ γὰρ μετρητόν· ἀλλ᾽ ὅπερ ἡμῖν ὁ χρόνος, ἡλίου φορᾷ μετρούμενος, τοῦτο τοῖς ἀϊδίοις αἰών, τὸ συμπαρεκτεινόμενον τοῖς οὖσιν, οἷόν τι χρονικὸν κίνημα καὶ διάστημα.

But there is one other interpretation which must be considered. Schubach, *Commentatio*, 51, claimed to find here a refutation of Origen's teaching about the existence of other worlds before this one. Origen held that the Creator could never have been without a world over which to exercise his power. As we have seen, in vv. 59b–62 n., Origen will not have God idle and the form of activity prescribed is occupation with the concerns of a succession of worlds, as he writes in *princ.* 3. 5. 3 (pp. 272 ff., M. 11. 327B ff.). Dismissing the suggestion of 'otiosam ... et immobilem ... naturam Dei', he goes on: 'nos vero consequenter respondebimus observantes regulam pietatis et dicentes, quoniam non tunc primum cum visibilem istum mundum fecit Deus, coepit operari, sed sicut post corruptionem huius erit alius mundus, ita et antequam hic esset, fuisse alios credimus.' It must be said that κενεοῖσιν could well carry this meaning. But one wonders whether Greg. would have dealt with such a theory in this passing way if this had been in his mind.

64. κίνυτο: cf. v. 60 n. Taken with θηεύμενος it means 'active in contemplation of'. Greg. writes of divine self-contemplation in *or.* 40. 5 (M. 36. 364B): αὐτὸ (sc. φῶς) ἑαυτοῦ θεωρητικόν τε καὶ καταπληκτικόν, ὀλιγὰ τοῖς ἔξω χεόμενον.

65. τρισσοφαής is found in a Trinitarian context in Or. *exp. in Pr.* 16 (M. 17. 196B) and again applied to Godhead by Greg. in *carm.* 2. 1. 13. 214 (M. 37. 1244A).

67–74. *The content of the divine mind.* For these lines cf. Florovsky, 'Idea of Creation', 61 ff. Greg.'s idea of self-contemplation may be contrasted with that of Aristotle. The latter thinks of the divine mind as totally absorbed in itself: its whole knowledge is self-knowledge. For this, see *Metaph.* 1074^{b}15 ff., especially 1074^{b}33–5: αὐτὸν ἄρα νοεῖ, εἴπερ ἐστὶ τὸ κράτιστον, καὶ ἔστιν ἡ νόησις νοήσεως νόησις (cf. notes in Ross's edn., ii. 396 ff.). Greg., while wishing to preserve the mystery of contemplation within the Godhead, stresses the outflowing activity of God in Creation: see e.g. *or.* 38. 9 (M. 36. 320C) = 45. 5

(629A), ἐπεὶ δὲ οὐκ ἤρκει τῇ ἀγαθότητι τοῦτο, τὸ κινεῖσθαι μόνον τῇ ἑαυτῆς θεωρίᾳ, ἀλλ' ἔδει χεθῆναι τὸ ἀγαθὸν καὶ ὁδεῦσαι, ὡς πλείονα εἶναι τὰ εὐεργετούμενα (τοῦτο γὰρ τῆς ἄκρας ἦν ἀγαθότητος) κτλ. That passage goes on to describe how the heavenly powers were formed (cf. vv. 77 ff. below). The present passage concerns itself with another aspect of the divine activity, the way in which the mind of God looks from self-contemplation, not to active creation, but to regard the forms of the worlds to be created, the worlds of mind and matter.

To guard against any reappearance of coeternal Forms (cf. vv. 2 f. above), Greg. says that God 'established' them (v. 67). This view collides sharply with that of, say, *Timaeus*, where it is clear that the Demiurge does not bring the Forms into being, but merely uses them, taking them as he finds them; *Tim.* 29D–31A. Cf. Cornford's note in his edn., pp. 33 ff., esp. p. 41: 'The model, as strictly eternal, is independent of the Demiurge, whose function it is to be the cause, not of eternal Being, but only of order in the realm of Becoming. ... The Forms are always spoken of as existing eternally in their own right.' Nor is there the restriction upon God which Plotinus places upon his Divine Mind. Here, as A. H. Armstrong pointed out in *Downside Review*, 73/231 (1954–5), 51, the Mind is limited because the Forms which are its content are definite and fixed in number. Greg. accepts no such restriction. The Forms (here the Forms of the world are specified) are no more and no less than thought in the mind of God. Greg. is thus in line with an understanding of the Forms which had been developed by Albinus, who reinterpreted the Platonic Forms as thoughts of God, not self-existent beings (*Epitome* 9. 1–2). The relationship between these Forms and the created order is quite direct: in creating the worlds, the intelligible and the visible, God simply follows the thoughts in his mind. With Philo there had been an intermediary stage: the Forms, starting as thoughts in God's mind, achieve the status of real, created beings which form the intelligible world, which are situated within the Logos, and which form the model for the visible world. (Cf. references in Wolfson, *The Philosophy of the Church Fathers*, i. 258 n. 4; the whole chapter is valuable for its account of the Patristic interpretation of the Platonic Forms: ch. 13, 'The Logos and the Platonic Ideas', pp. 257–86.) For Greg., as will be seen from vv. 93 ff., the intelligible world is quite different. It is created, as the visible world is created, directly by God, while his thoughts remain his thoughts and do not take on any existence of their own. The heavenly world which is created is a world of beings, of angels who, as Greg. is forced to admit (cf. *Arc*. 6. 53 ff. n.), may make wrong choices, not a world of ideas.

It is not necessary to trace in full the development of the notion to understand Greg.'s allusion to it. For the way it is treated in Antiochus of Ascalon, Seneca, Philo, and Albinus cf. *CHLGEMP*, 53 ff., 66–7 (P. Merlan) and 142 ff. (H. Chadwick) together with A. N. M. Rich, 'The Platonic Ideas as Thoughts of God', *Mnemosyne*, 4th ser., 7 (1953), 123–33 and A. H. Armstrong, 'The Background of the Doctrine "That the Intelligibles are not outside the Intellect"', *Les Sources de Plotin* (Entietiens Hardt, 5; Vandœuvres-Geneva, 1960), 393–425.

I. P. Sheldon-Williams points to the more dynamic function of the Forms in the thought of Basil and Nyssen (*CHLGEMP*, 430).

67. κίνυτο: cf. v. 60 n.

68. κοσμογόνος: this is the first recorded use of the word, but cf. *Arc*. 5. 2 n.

69 provides the link with the following lines.

70–4. *The Forms exist in a timeless state in the mind of God.* On these lines Schubach observed (Commentatio, 52): '... responsum modo citatum quasi emendans pergit: πάντα Θεῷ προπάροιθεν ... κτλ.' What Greg. has spoken of up to v. 69 is Forms of the world which found expression at a point in time but which existed independently of time in the Divine Mind. Schubach meant by 'emendans' that Greg. implied in vv. 70–4 (he added that Greg. failed to draw the explicit conclusion) the view that God contemplated not the Forms of the universe but the universe itself from all eternity. As he says (p. 53): 'ex aeterno omnia creavit vel creat'. On this interpretation πάντα (v. 70) = 'the universe', as frequently. But why should there be any such implication? The natural sense of the lines makes them a continuation, not a correction, of what has preceded. 'All things' (πάντα) are 'before' God, not in the sense that they have been created by him 'ex aeterno', but because they are present in the mind of God precisely as the Forms of the world are present. The expression πάντα goes beyond the Forms in its inclusion of events taking place in time. (For the importance of the distinction between the 'idea' of the world and the world itself see Florovsky, 'Idea of Creation', 63.)

That Greg. was unlikely to have adumbrated such a view as

Schubach suggested may be further demonstrated from *or.* 38. 9–10 (M. 36. 320C ff.) = 45. 5–6 (629A ff.). Despite his proviso that temporal language has no meaning when applied to the actions of the eternal God—cf. *or.* 38. 7 (317B ff.) = 45. 3 (635C ff.)—Greg. easily slips into the use of temporal expressions. He thinks of stages of creation: it was only when the first order of creation (the world of thought) was well established that God formed the concept (ἐννοεῖ) of the material world (321A = 629C). This is far removed from creation 'ex aeterno'.

71–2. Time is a divisive factor, 'splitting' past, present, and future as an axe splits wood. To be subject to time is essentially a creaturely condition, as Greg. has stressed in *Arc.* 2. 18–27, 3. 84–6; cf. also Balthasar, *Présence et pensée* 4, 20. C. Moreschini in his tr. aptly compares Plot. 3. 7. A modern writer who is affected by the contrast between immortality and human bondage to time is Edwin Muir. One thinks of 'Variations on a Time Theme' (1934) which contains such lines: 'If there's no crack or chink, no escape from Time, . . . Imprisonment's for ever; we're the mock of Time . . .' (*Collected Poems* (London, 1960), 48.)

73. The language becomes suddenly more personal and more biblical, recalling the thought of Deut. 33. 27: ὑπὸ ἰσχὺν βραχιόνων ἀενάων.

75–92. *The Creation of angels and of men*

75–6. The travail figure is applied to the mind in Pl. *Tht.* 148E, *al.* In the present passage the auxiliary idea of pain or difficulty is absent.

Again temporal language appears (cf. 70–4 n.), with εἰς ὕστερον indicating a further stage. Elsewhere the phrase denotes progression in time or alteration in status (cf. e.g. S. *Ant.* 1194, Pl. *Ti.* 82b).

77. ἤθελε: this affirmation was seen by many of the Fathers as fundamental for the doctrine of Creation: God's will was the only cause of the created order. Origen demurred, but most held that God was not inevitably Creator. Ignatius had used the words: ἐν θελήματι τοῦ θελήσαντος τὰ πάντα ἃ ἔστιν, *Rom.* proem. (Bihlmeyer, p. 96. 20, M. 5. 685A). Clement, *str.* 7. 12 (p. 50. 4, M. 9. 496D), *prot.* 4 (p. 48. 18, M. 8. 164A). ψιλῷ τῷ βουλεύεσθαι δημιουργεῖ and Athanasius, *Ar.* 2. 2 (M. 26. 152A f.) are amongst those who take them up. Greg. here balances and corrects any suggestion of divine compulsion which

COMMENTARY ON *ARC*. 4. 77–81

might be thought to reside in the words from *or*. 38 (45) quoted in n. on vv. 67–74: ἔδει χεθῆναι τὸ ἀγαθὸν καὶ ὁδεῦσαι. For Greg.'s understanding cf. Meijering 'Doctrine of the Will'.

νοερὰν ... φύσιν places man in his primary alignment as a rational being who shares his faculty with the angels and with God himself. However much Greg. finds it necessary to point to the discontinuity of Creator and all created things, he never neglects the kinship of νοῦς which binds together God, angels, and men.

78. **ἔσοπτρα:** where ἔσοπτρον is used in a figurative sense it usually directs attention to the function of a mirror in presenting a secondary image of the original, whether this be a close correspondence (as e.g. *Lyr. Alex. Adesp.* 37. 26 Powell) or an inferior or distorted representation of the subject (as 1 Cor. 13. 12). But a mirror serves also to transmit light, as in the following passage, Aët. ii. 20. 12 (DK 44 A 19. i. 404. 4 ff.). Φιλόλαος ὁ Πυθαγόρειος ὑαλοειδῆ τὸν ἥλιον, δεχόμενον μὲν ἐν τῷ κόσμῳ πυρὸς τὴν ἀνταύγειαν, διηθοῦντα δὲ πρὸς ἡμᾶς τό τε φῶς καὶ τὴν ἀλέαν, ὥστε τρόπον τινὰ διττοὺς ἡλίους γίνεσθαι, τό τε ἐν οὐρανῷ πυρῶδες καὶ τὸ ἀπ' αὐτοῦ πυροειδὲς κατὰ τὸ ἐσοπτροειδές, εἰ μή τις καὶ τρίτον λέξει τὴν ἀπὸ τοῦ ἐνόπτρου καὶ ἀνάκλασιν διασπειρομένην πρὸς ἡμᾶς αὐγήν. Both representation and transmission appear to be present in ἔσοπτρα here.

79. **ὑποδρήστειραν:** no other instance of the fem. is recorded. The word here has the same cultic sense as ὑποδρηστήρ in *carm*. 2. 1. 16. 11 (M. 37. 1255A), where Greg. is describing a dream about the Anastasia church: οἱ δ' ἄρ' ὑποδρηστῆρες ἐν εἵμασι παμφανόωσιν ἔστασαν, ἀγγελικῆς εἰκόνες ἀγλαΐης.

80. **πλησιφαῆ:** elsewhere the word is used of the moon to mean 'with full light' (cf. LSJ and Soph. s.v., together with Plotinus' πλησίφωτος in 2. 3. 5). Greg.'s use of the word implies not a distinction of phases, but contrasts the permanent fullness of light enjoyed by the angels with the partial light experienced by human beings. Cf. *Arc*. 6. 38.

81. **πηγάζων:** there are two ideas here. The first is that of 'bounty'—cf. Philo *de opif. mundi* 45. 133 (M. 1. 31. 44; C.-W. i. 38. 7), *al.*—and the second that of 'source'. The first idea is picked up by ὀλβιόδωρον v. 82. God, as the source of divinity, graciously allows it to gush forth. The meaning is coloured by NT reminiscences, John 4. 14, Rev. 7. 17, 21. 6. We may note that Proclus, writing some time later than Greg., uses not dissimilar language: κατὰ δὲ τὴν ἐν ἑαυτῷ

168

'Ρέαν τριπλῆν πηγάζει (sc. Ζεὺς) ζωήν, νοεράν, ψυχικήν, σω-
ματικήν (*in Cra.* p. 52. 12–13). Cf. also *Arc.* 6. 8 n. Creation is
presented as showing at once God's power (ἀνάσσῃ) and his grace
(ὀλβιόδωρον), a contrast with the Manichaean doctrine of particles
of stolen light.

82. ὀλβιόδωρον. Cf. *Arc.* 3. 5 n.

83. The very essence of God's rule is beneficent, his generosity and
the φθόνος of Satan standing in contrast. Cf. Ath. *inc.* 3. 3 (M. 25.
191 B; *gent.* 41. 81 D). Augustine was to make much of the 'bonitas' of
God in creation. Cf. *Civ. Dei* 11. 24 (M. *PL* 41. 338; CSEL 40/1. 548.
4 ff.; CCSL 48. 343. 30 ff.), for instance: 'in eo vero quod dicitur: *vidit
Deus quia bonum est*, satis significatur, Deum nulla necessitudine,
nulla suae cuiusquam utilitatis indigentia, sed sola bonitate fecisse
quod factum est, id est quod bonum est.'

ὄλβον ὀπάζειν recalls a line of Hesiod where Hecate rewards her
suppliant: καί τέ οἱ ὄλβον ὀπάζει ἐπεὶ δύναμίς γε πάρεστιν (*Th.*
420). But, whereas for Hesiod ὄλβος means physical well-being or
wealth (cf. H. *Il.* 16. 596; *Sir.* 30. 15), Greg. writes of the blessing of
sharing something of the divine nature. Cf. also Ps.-Manetho 2 (1).
221: Ζεὺς ὄλβον ὀπάζει.

84–92. The purpose of the Logos in placing creation at some distance
from God is to prevent a desire for the impossible, the full posses-
sion of God's glory. Such desire can result only in the loss of the
light and glory which were granted to created beings. In other
words, the Logos intended to guard against precisely the case of
Satan, for the language used applies directly to him and, if ὀλέσσῃ is
right in v. 85, echoes v. 47 above, where Satan is the subject: ἧς ὑπερ-
οπλίῃσι φάος καὶ κῦδος ὀλέσσας. Again, the language of this pas-
sage anticipates that of the Fall in *Arc.* 6. 65–7. In the event, man did
not suffer a complete loss of divine light, despite the Fall. But,
whereas in his original state he was meant to live in continuous
light, in his fallen state he became open only to particular acts of
illumination.

84. ἀντιθέοιο: there is a similar instance in Didym. *Trin.* 2. 15 (M. 39.
544 A) = 'rivalling God', though the precise theological issue is dif-
ferent. Greg. several times employs the word substantivally; cf. *orr.*
30. 5 (p. 114. 4, M. 36. 108 C), 31. 26 (p. 179. 9, 164 A).

85. Texts disagree on whether to read ὀπάζει, ὀπάζῃ, or ὀλέσσῃ as
the last word: (L has ὀλέσσῃ, Cu ὀπάζῃ). The basic meaning of the
passage is unaffected by the choice. What is affected is the balance

and the similarity to other lines. The real choice is between ὀπάζῃ and ὀλέσσῃ. A subjunctive is called for by ὄφρα ... μή. These appear to be the relevant considerations:

(i) In favour of ὀλέσσῃ it may be said that the correspondence with v. 47 has point. There would be more than a verbal reminiscence involved.

(ii) The sense is not harmed by ὀπάζῃ. If it were read we should have a sentence of two balanced clauses, saying much the same thing. But this is not alien to Epic style. Nor is the different sense of ὀπάζειν which would be required alien to Greg.'s style. Where ὀπάζειν in v. 83 means 'grant', ὀπάζῃ here would have the sense 'chase, pursue' (LSJ s.v. III). Yet a third sense occurs in *Arc.* 5. 16: 'to give as leader'.

(iii) Against κῦδος ὀπάζῃ it may be urged that it provides a meaning so similar to κύδεος ἱμείρουσα as to be pointless. The contrast of 'yearning for' and 'losing' is much more appropriate.

(iv) The argument from assimilation might be applied to either reading. A scribe could have been influenced by v. 83 to produce an unconscious homeoteleuton or by v. 47 to make a conscious 'improvement'. ὀλέσσῃ remains the attested and more telling text.

86. W. Ackermann discussed the way in which γνῶμαι appear in Greg.'s verse, *Die didaktische Poesie des Gregorius von Nazianz* (Leipzig, 1908), 82 ff.; the *Moralia* naturally contain a large proportion of the total. γνῶμαι in general and their place in Greek literature and philosophy are dealt with in *RE* Supp. vi. 74– 90. A classic example of μέτρον is given in Pindar, *P.* 2. 34 (the context is Ixion's attempt upon Hera): χρὴ δὲ κατ᾽ αὐτὸν αἰεὶ παντὸς ὁρᾶν μέτρον. In *or.* 43. 60 (M. 36. 573в) Greg. quotes the saying τὸ πᾶν μέτρον ἄριστον (attributed to Cleobulus, one of the Seven Sages: cf. DK i. 10. 3, i. 63. 1), claiming it as a favourite precept of Basil, and the thought occurs in *carm.* 2. 1. 11. 1239 (M. 37. 1114A) as: μέτρον τ᾽ ἄριστον, τῶν σοφῶν ἑνὸς λόγος.

87. Λόγος αἰπύς: the same words recur in *Arc.* 7. 55. The straightforward sense is that of the Logos 'on high'. But it is possible that Greg. intended also the meaning 'sheer', as Agathias speaks of 'sheerest wisdom' (αἰπυτάτης σοφίης, *AP* 11. 354. 2).

88. ἀμφιθόωκον: a *hapax legomenon*.

89–92. Having shown the kinship of God, angels, and men, the poem now turns to the other essential teaching, the relationship of

Creator and created which places God on one side of a line and angels and men on the other. This is the reason why both must be kept at a distance from God. But soon a distinction made earlier (cf. v. 40) is again introduced. The boundaries are redrawn, with the angels standing on the side of God as ἁπλοῖ, and man placed on the other side, a composite being.

92. μιχθείσης: cf. *Arc*. 1. 24 n., *Arc*. 7. 1 n. Though I incline to the tr. 'mingled with', I accept L. R. Wickham's point that the words could be rendered 'mixed together by Godhead'.

93-100. *The two worlds, the heavenly and the mortal*

On the nature of the heavenly world, cf. vv. 67-74 n.

93. ἄλλος: for the pleonastic use of ἄλλος cf. e.g. H. *Il*. 15. 569 (νεώτερος ἄλλος).

94. θειοφόρων: cf. *Arc*. 3. 55-6 n. The word here has a fuller meaning than in that passage: the heavenly beings 'possess' God continuously.

μόνοις . . . θεητόν may be a reminiscence of Pl. *Phdr*. 247C: οὐσία . . . ψυχῆς κυβερνήτῃ μόνῳ θεατὴ νῷ. But there is a significant difference in that the 'minds' in Greg. are complete beings.

95-6. These lines return to the subject of deification. Something of what this means was expressed in the 'mingling' language of *Arc*. 1. 24 (see n.). More direct reference was made in *Arc*. 3. 4, where the Holy Spirit was said to make man God through baptism. Here we are told that a mortal may reach heaven, νόον καὶ σάρκα καθήρας. Putting these passages together, we may take it that Greg. is thinking of the 'deification' of baptism in a proleptic sense, as the 'mingling' on earth is an anticipation of the heavenly communion. The completion of the gift of 'becoming God' takes place in the world beyond the present.

τελέθῃσι means 'comes into being as, becomes'. Cf. also the middle in Ps.-Phocylides 104: Θεοὶ τελέθονται.

νόον καὶ σάρκα καθήρας: νόον and σάρκα are the direct objects of καθήρας. It is by the cleansing of both that man is deified. Some years before, in the panegyric on his brother Caesarius, Greg. had outlined his belief in the future life *or*. 7. 21 (M. 35. 781B ff.). The soul of the good Christian finds in death an immediate sense of exultation in being released from the body and perceives something of the blessedness which awaits it. Greg. hesitates over the way of describing what happens to the body (he calls it τὸ ἐπισκοτοῦν). Should he say ἀνακαθαρθέντος or ἀποτεθέντος? In fact, he seems to say both. For he goes on:

μικρὸν δ᾽ ὕστερον, καὶ τὸ συγγενὲς σαρκίον ἀπολαβοῦσα, ᾧ τὰ ἐκεῖθεν
συνεφιλοσόφησε, παρὰ τῆς καὶ δούσης καὶ πιστευθείσης γῆς, τρόπον ὃν
οἶδεν ὁ ταῦτα συνδήσας καὶ διαλύσας Θεός, τούτῳ συγκληρονομεῖ τῆς
ἐκεῖθεν δόξης· καὶ καθάπερ τῶν μοχθηρῶν αὐτοῦ μετέσχε διὰ τὴν συμ-
φυΐαν, οὕτω καὶ τῶν τερπνῶν ἑαυτῆς μεταδίδωσιν, ὅλον εἰς ἑαυτὴν ἀναλώ-
σασα, καὶ γενομένη σὺν τούτῳ ἓν καὶ πνεῦμα καὶ νοῦς καὶ Θεός,
καταποθέντος ὑπὸ τῆς ζωῆς τοῦ θνητοῦ τε καὶ ῥέοντος.

(or. 7. 21, M. 35. 781 c f.)

The body which the soul 'receives back' has been both 'laid aside' and 'cleansed' before it is 'swallowed up' in deification. This, then, is the way in which we are to understand the purification of the body in the present passage. The mind, it may be thought, is purified by its increasing apprehension of destined divine happiness; cf. . . . καὶ οἷον ἤδη τῇ φαντασίᾳ καρποῦται τὴν ἀποκειμένην μακαριότητα, loc. cit. (781 c). Death and future life in Greg.'s understanding are fully treated in J. Mossay, *La Mort et l'au-delà dans saint Grégoire de Nazianze* (Louvain, 1966).

On the subject of deification, cf. J. Gross, *La Divinisation du chrétien d'après les Pères grecs* (Paris, 1938); pp. 239 ff. are concerned with the Cappadocians, with pp. 244–50 relating to Greg. in particular. The passage quoted above bears out Gross's conclusion that deification for Greg. means not identification so much as assimilation (p. 249). Cf. also Mersch, *Le Corps mystique du Christ*, i. 447; M. Lot-Borodine, 'La doctrine de la déification dans l'Église grecque jusqu'au xie siècle', *RHR* 105 (1932), 5–43; 106 (1932), 523–74; Ruether, *Gregory*, pp. 150 ff.; Althaus, *Heilslehre*, 4–5, 71 ff., 79 ff., 141–2, 166, 179, 191 ff.; Winslow, *Dynamics*, 73–199, esp. 171–99.

97–9. The mortal world.

97. Greg. permits a false quantity in θνητός. Even if θνατός were read, this would not mend matters, as the α here is long in the Doric form. Cf. Jungck edn. of *De vita sua*, pp. 34–6; C. U. Crimi, 'Il problema delle "false quantities" di Gregorio Nazianzeno', *Siculorum Gymnasium*, NS 25 (1972), 1–26.

πάγη: cf. *Arc*. 5. 1 n.

98. χάρις: the word here has the meaning of 'beauty', or, as in Pi. *O*. 1. 18, 8. 57, 80, 'glory'. κῆρυξ perhaps continues the sense of the first part of the line in being associated particularly with the heavenly bodies. In Pss. 18. 2 (19. 1 Heb.), 49. 6 (50. 6 Heb.), 96. 6 (97. 6 Heb.) it is the heavens which are spoken of as especially 'proclaiming' God. In *or.* 44. 3 (M. 36. 609c), however, the whole world is called God's κήρυκα.

99. εἰκόνος ἐμβασίλευμα turns to the earth. It is a 'royal palace' because it is the appointed home of man, who is formed in the image of the King of Creation. ἐμβασίλευμα is a *hapax legomenon*: cf. the verb ἐμβασιλεύειν in v. 63. For εἰκών, cf. *Arc.* 7. 74–5 n.

100. The line summarizes the purposive, voluntary, *ex nihilo* creation teaching of the poem and prepares for the doctrine of continuing Providence which is advanced in the following poem.

5. On Providence

Title and purpose

The title Περὶ Προνοίας is agreed. It accurately indicates content. After a brief assault on chance as the sole arbiter of fortune, the poem settles to its central task of refuting astral determinism. The place of the poem in the sequence is clear. Just as, in Greg.'s world picture, it makes most sense to hold that the God who ordered the elements is the same God who made them (*Arc.* 4. 14–15), so now it is obvious to him that there is continuity between the Creator and the power which governs the established universe, the continuity of complete identity.

There were many people in Greg.'s time who would have given an affirmative answer to the question 'Do you believe in Providence?' but who would have proved, at best, embarrassing allies and, at worst, blunt enemies of Greg.'s position. The followers of Plotinus could point to the section of the *Enneads* which deals exclusively with Providence (3. 2. 3), while Stoics could claim belief in Providence as one of their most distinctive tenets; cf. e.g. Epictetus, *Diatr.* 1. 14, 16 ed. H. Schenkl (Leipzig (Teubner), 1916), 56 ff.; M. Pohlenz, *Die Stoa: Geschichte einer geistigen Bewegung* (Göttingen, 1964), i. 98 ff. But Plotinus' treatment, starting as it does with an attack upon the automatic theory in terms which Greg. could well echo (3. 2. 1), quickly shifts to a defence of the eternal existence of the universe. Having explicitly dismissed any theory of creation out of non-existence, Plotinus shows that he can have little help to give Greg. in his formulation of a doctrine of Providence. The kind of Providence which operates in a world which is produced by necessity rather than purpose (ἐξ ἀνάγκης ὄντος αὐτοῦ καὶ οὐκ ἐκ λογισμοῦ γενομένου, 3. 2. 3. 3–4) is not what Greg. would recognize as Providence; cf. Pinault 103 ff.; Moreschini, 'Platonismo', 1374, 1382, 1386. Nor would the Stoics' rejection of chance governance of the universe be enough to counterbalance their rigid determinism of Fate and their acceptance of astral influence (cf. below vv. 15b ff.). Again, Aristotle gains a slighting reference from Greg. because of what he takes to be the philosopher's quite inadequate teaching on Providence, *or.* 27. 10 (p. 19. 1–2, M. 36. 24B f.). Cf. notes in the edns. of Mason, Barbel, and Norris (pp. 100–1). Greg. himself defines Providence in *carm.* 1. 2. 34. 265 (M. 37. 964A): ἡ δ᾽, οἰακισμός, ᾧ φέρει τὸ πᾶν Θεός.

Writing of the early Empire, R. MacMullen in *Enemies of the Roman*

Order (Cambridge, Mass., 1967), 141 pointed to 'a world dedicated to astral fatalism', a world in which astrologers could hope to rise to positions of influence. Though the Christian emperors set their face against these, there is little doubt that the power of fatalistic systems endured.

At the other extreme from Greg. we might place Carneades, the 3rd–2nd c. sceptic. He would have dismissed almost everything for which Greg. stood, being contemptuous of all dogmatic pronouncements and, deriding all concepts of divinity, would have no dealing with any notion of prophecy or providence. Yet such is the nature of Greg.'s eclectic plundering that he has no qualms about taking over wholesale for his own very different purposes the arguments Carneades used against the possibility of making astral predictions (cf. 15b–33 n.).

Among Christian writers Origen had given a central place to the Providence of God and the free will of created rational beings, while Nyssen defended similar views in his *contra fatum* (M. 45. 145 ff.). Nazianzen himself writes a somewhat parallel poem in iambics, 1. 1. 6 (M. 37. 430A–438A).

In *Systematic Theology* i. 294, Paul Tillich wrote: 'In the late ancient world fate conquered providence and established a reign of terror among the masses; but Christianity emphasized the victory of Christ over the forces of fate and fear just when they seemed to have overwhelmed him at the cross. Here faith in providence was definitively established.' This poem has some part in that establishment.

1–52. *The world is ruled by the Creator, not by chance nor by stars*

1. εὐρυθέμειλον: if N's εὐρυθέμεθλον, read by Caillau, were accepted (*PGL* marks it [*]), this, with *carm.* 1. 2. 1. 531 (M. 37. 562A), would be its only occurrence, apart from a *v.l.* in Call. *Dian.* 248, reported by E. Cahen (Paris, 1942), εὐρὺ θέμειλον (ABE) or εὐρυθέμειλον (Bergk). References to the foundation of the earth are frequent in the OT, e.g. Pss. 17 (18 Heb.). 16 (τὰ θεμέλια τῆς οἰκουμένης); 81 (82 Heb.). 5 (τὰ θεμέλια τῆς γῆς); Prov. 8. 29; Isa. 14. 15, 40. 21.

ἐπήξατο: two established meanings of πήγνυμι fit here equally well, neither excluding the other. The sense may be that of fastening together different parts or that of fixing, establishing (where there is often a thought of the permanence of what is established).

ἀπείρων: the Ep. form carries all the meaning of ἄπειρος. This is a word with a long philosophical history stretching back to Anaximander. (Cf. Guthrie, *History*, i. 77 ff.) In Christian literature it is a natural epithet of God (cf. e.g. *or.* 38. 8, M. 36. 320A) or of the Logos (*PGL* s.v. 3). N's reading ἄπειρον makes sense, though Billius found it difficult. Supposing that it must mean 'infinite' and hesitating to apply this to the visible world, he suggested that Greg. was here talking of two worlds, visible and invisible. But, as Caillau recognized, this has no support in the text. However, ἄπειρον need not have this meaning. Guthrie holds that as early as Xenophanes a weaker sense was possible (op. cit. 381). We should then have the world described as 'immense', the English word providing an exact parallel for the weakened sense.

There is a valuable discussion of the concept in Nyssen's writings by E. Mühlenberg, *Die Unendlichkeit Gottes bei Gregor von Nyssa* (Göttingen, 1966).

2. The idea that the origin of the world is to be traced to the action of νοῦς is found as early as Anaxagoras: καὶ ὁποῖα ἔμελλεν ἔσεσθαι καὶ ὁποῖα ἦν, ἄσσα νῦν μὴ ἔστι, καὶ ὁποῖα ἔστι, πάντα διεκόσμησε νοῦς. (fr. 12; DK ii. 38. 10–11). He is reported to have used the words νοῦν κοσμοποιόν; cf. Ἀναξαγόρας νοῦν κοσμοποιὸν τὸν θεόν (DK ii. 19. 36). When, however, Greg. writes the similar κοσμογόνος νοῦς in *Arc.* 4. 68, he is outlining a very different conception of the relationship of the Divine Mind to the world. Plato (*Phd.* 97C–99D) and Aristotle (*Metaph.* 985ᵃ, 988ᵇ) criticized Anaxagoras for positing mind and later abandoning it in favour of physical causes. (Cf. n. on v. 4 below.) Greg. sees the providential action of the Divine Mind as continuous from eternity. For God as νοῦς cf. *Arc.* 1. 29 and *PGL* s.v. F. 1.

ἐντὸς ... ὕπερθεν: cf. *Arc.* 2. 5–6 n.

3. The argument of this line is closely linked with that of the previous one. The thought of the two lines is: 'The Divine Mind contains all possibilities (cf. *Arc.* 4. 70 n.). It transcends everything. (If it did not, it would be contained within the universe.) But how can the immensity of the unlimited be contained?' This differs from Billius' interpretation. He takes it that Greg. is saying that the Divine Mind is beyond human comprehension. (Caillau's 'comprehendi' is amenable to either understanding.) Now it is true that one of the meanings of ἀχώρητος is 'incomprehensible' (cf. *PGL* s.v.). But there are two difficulties with Billius' tr. The passage is not concerned with man's understanding but with God's relationship with the universe. Second, λαβέσθαι is middle, meaning 'to lay hold of, to obtain possession of'. The lexica cite no instance of the middle that would correspond with the active 'to apprehend with the mind, to understand' (LSJ s.v. I. 9b).

4–6. God sets the world in motion.

4. πρώτης ὑπὸ ῥιπῆς: ὑπὸ ῥιπῆς is a Homeric expression, as in *Il*. 12. 462 (the whirled force of a stone) or 15. 171 (the force of the North Wind). The reading ῥοπῆς (cf. Caillau's n.) seems less likely: it is difficult to think of it as meaning 'momentum' without some qualifying word (as it has in Philo Mechanicus, *Bel*. 69. 21).

πρώτης: in writing about God's giving the world its first impetus Greg. is emphasizing again the place of divine initiative. He is very far from the notion often associated with initial impetus, that once the world had been given its first 'push' it was left to run on its own. (Cf. Guthrie's description of Anaxagoras: 'In Anaxagoras's system mind simply set the wheels going and then withdrew, leaving the cosmos to continue under its own momentum, subject to purely mechanical laws.' *History* i. 326.) Yet there is a sense in which the world might be thought to run by itself. In a passage closely parallel to the present one, Basil describes how the plant-world has continued to follow its own course season after season, without the need of God to repeat the initial command 'Let the earth bring forth': ὡς γὰρ οἱ στρόβιλοι ἐκ τῆς πρώτης αὐτοῖς ἐνδοθείσης πληγῆς τὰς ἐφεξῆς ποιοῦνται περιστροφάς, ὅταν πήξαντες τὸ κέντρον ἐν ἑαυτοῖς περιφέρωνται ... *hex*. 5. 10 (G. 1. 49C f., M. 29. 116C f.). He is drawing on Plat. *Rep*. 436D ὡς οἵ γε στρόβιλοι ὅλοι ἑστᾶσί τε ἅμα καὶ κινοῦνται, ὅταν ἐν τῷ αὐτῷ πήξαντες περιφέρωνται. The figure of the ball rolling down the slope is used to similar effect in *hex*. 9. 2 (G. 1. 81B,˙M. 29. 189B f.). (Cf. further J. F. Callahan, *DOP* 12 (1958), 34 f.) In the thought of the Cappadocians this apparent independence of nature is itself part of divine Providence and very far from leaving the world 'subject to *purely* mechanical laws'.

5–6. ῥόμβον: of the meanings of ῥόμβος given in LSJ only that of the 'magic wheel' could possibly fit here. But closer examination of the lines shows the difficulty of this meaning. Such a wheel would be driven by torsion, not by a 'blow'. In any case, A. S. F. Gow doubts whether the word ever did mean 'magic wheel', in his n. on Theocritus, *Idyll* 2. 30, *Theocritus*, ii (Cambridge, 1952), 44. Caillau tr. 'trochum', giving a picture similar to that in Hor. *Od*. 3. 24, 27. But if we are to look for an otherwise unattested meaning for ῥόμβος, there are strong reasons for choosing 'spinning-top'.

(i) The close resemblance to *hex.* 5. 10 (quoted in the previous n.) suggests this tr.

(ii) The word ῥόμβος is very similar to the Homeric στρόμβος (cf. *Il.* 14. 413: στρόμβον δ' ὡς ἔσσευσε βαλών), which means 'spinning-top', but which is metrically impossible at this point in the line.

(iii) The picture of an object 'driven on its whirling course by a blow' suits a top rather than anything else.

The suggestion that a spinning-top is meant is not new. A. Patin tr. ῥόμβον here as 'Kreisel' in *Herakleitische Beispiele* (Pr. Neuberg, 1891–2), 84 n. 11, and the tr. was repeated by J. Dräseke in *Zeitschrift für wissenschaftliche Theologie*, 49 (1906), 243 n. Again, 'toupie' is Gallay's rendering (p. 131, repr. Devolder 70). But the tr. is nowhere discussed. Some justification such as that attempted above is called for.

The picture of the top appealed to Vergil and to Tibullus. Cf. *A.* 7. 378: 'ceu quondam torto volitans sub verbere turbo' and Tib. 1. 5. 3: 'namque agor, ut per plana citus sola verbere turben.'

6. κινύμενον: cf. *Arc.* 1. 31.

ἀκινήτοισι: a double reference may be seen here, to Aristotle's τὸ πρῶτον κινοῦν ἀκίνητον αὐτό (*Metaph.* 1012ᵇ31) and to the 'fixed' nature of God's purposes in Creation and continuing Providence.

7–9. The automatic theory of the universe.

In denying that some automatic activity is responsible for the creation and operation of the universe Greg. is taking up a well-worn argument. Eusebius, having set out extracts of some length from Diodorus Siculus (*p.e.* 1. 6–7, 18d ff., 21. 49c ff.) and Plutarch (1. 8, 22b ff., 56c ff.), takes as the majority opinion of Greek physical philosophers: οὐ δημιουργόν, οὐ ποιητήν τινα τῶν ὅλων ὑποστησαμένων, ἀλλ' οὐδ' ὅλως θεοῦ μνήμην ποιησαμένων, μόνῃ δὲ τῇ ἀλόγῳ φορᾷ καὶ τῇ αὐτομάτῳ κινήσει τὴν αἰτίαν τοῦ παντὸς ἀνατεθειμένων, 1. 8 (25c, 61β). Cf. 1. 7 (21d f., 56β): most Greek philosophers accept this view, he claims. Theophilus of Antioch associates it specifically with Euhemerus. By his damaging writings about the gods he has left himself without any gods at all, Theophilus says ἀλλὰ τὰ πάντα αὐτοματισμῷ διαδοκεῖσθαι βούλεται, *Autol.* 3. 7 (M. 6. 1129c).

Generally, however, the tendency is to hold that αὐτόματος and related words are the specific hall-mark of the Epicureans. Hippolytus states that Epicurus denies Providence and believes πάντα κατὰ αὐτοματισμὸν γινέσθαι, *haer*. 1. 22 (p. 26. 19, M. 16. 3049B). Cf. Methodius *res*. 2. 10 (p. 349. 10 ff.), where Democritus and Epicurus are associated in the atomic theory: σμικρότατα καὶ εἴδη ἐξ ἀτόμων ἢ ὄγκων ἢ ἀμερῶν ἢ ὁμοιομερῶν αὐτομάτῳ καὶ ἀπροαιρέτῳ φιλίᾳ. Providence has no place in their system.

In the surviving literature Epicurus himself does not use αὐτόματος or derivatives, preferring to speak of τύχη and ἀνάγκη. Cf. the comment of C. Bailey, *Epicurus: The Extant Remains* (Oxford, 1926), 341 (on *Ep*. 3. 133): 'Epicurus' conception of "chance" seems to be of a force co-ordinate with necessity. Natural law causes the inevitable sequence of events, but it is chance that rules the production of particular causes: e.g., ἀνάγκη causes the motions and meetings of atoms, but chance causes them to fall into the positions which create our world.' But Aristotle appears to associate τὸ αὐτόματον with Democritus and his followers, among whom Epicurus is rightly numbered, and the term became established to characterize this philosophy; cf. Arist. *Ph*. 196ᵃ24 ff., with the note in W. D. Ross's edn., *Aristotle's Physics* (Oxford, 1936), 515. Athanasius, for instance, gives it as an Epicurean opinion that the world came into being αὐτομάτως, καὶ ὡς ἔτυχε, *inc*. 2. 1 (M. 25. 97C f.); cf. Cyr. *Jul*. 2 (47B, M. 76. 572D). In *or*. 25. 6 (M. 35. 1205A) Greg. writes τὸ αὐτόματον Ἐπικούρου μετὰ τῶν ἀτόμων καὶ τῆς ἡδονῆς. For the thought of Epicurus see further A. A. Long, *Hellenistic Philosophy* (London, 1974), ch. 2. Text and commentary are well presented in A. A. Long and D. N. Sedley, *The Hellenistic Philosophers* (Cambridge, 1987), i. 25 ff., ii. 18 ff.

In vv. 7–9 Greg. is making the transition to the Cosmological Argument, pointing to the splendour of the universe (τοσούτου καὶ τοίου) as a tacit witness of design.

10–13. Examples in support of the Cosmological Argument. On this stock defence of the doctrine of Creation, cf. the art. 'Cosmological Argument', in *ODC* 347. Greg. uses it in *or*. 28. 6 (pp. 29. 3 ff., M. 36. 17C ff.), taking a lyre as his example.

12–13. These lines do little if anything for the argument. If one could imagine that the universe could come into existence without a maker, one would surely find in its continued existence no great problem.

ἀνηγεμόνευτος: the word occurs in a similar context in Marcus Aurelius, where he is discussing the same questions of fate, providence, or chance operating in the universe. One of the possibilities he considers is that the universe is φυρμὸς ἀνηγεμόνευτος (*Med.* 12. 14).

14. σημάντορα: 'leader, commander', as Zeus is called θεῶν σημάντορι πάντων in Hes. *Sc.* 56.

15b-33. *Astrology*

The argument switches from attacking those who deny purposive government in the universe to arraigning people who accept the notion of control but assign it to the stars.

On the general subject of astrology in the ancient world reference may be made to: A. Bouché-Leclercq, *L'Astrologie grecque* (Paris, 1899); F. Cumont, *Astrology and Religion among the Greeks and Romans* (New York, 1912); id., *Les Religions orientales dans le paganisme romain* (Paris, 1929); A. J. Festugière, *La Révélation d'Hermès Trismégiste*, i: *L'Astrologie et les sciences occultes* (Paris, 1944); W. Gundel (rev. H. G. Gundel), *Sternglaube, Sternreligion und Sternorakel*, id., 'Astrologie', *RAC* i (1950), 817-31. The place of astrology in the whole pattern of ancient thinking on fate is fully traced by E. Amand de Mendieta in *Fatalisme et liberté dans l'antiquité grecque* (Louvain, 1945). The Cappadocians are discussed on pp. 383-439, Nazianzen most briefly on pp. 401-4.

The specifically Christian attitude to astrology is dealt with in U. Riedinger, *Die hl. Schrift im Kampf der griechischen Kirche gegen die Astrologie* (Innsbruck, 1956); J. Bidez, 'Le traité d'astrologie cité par saint Basile dans son Hexaéméron', *L'Antiquité classique* 7 (1938), 19-21; M. L. W. Laistner, 'The Western Church and Astrology during the Early Middle Ages', *HTR* 34 (1941), 251-75. (The influence of Eastern Fathers, including Gregory, is discussed.)

The Christian attack on astrology may be traced, for example, through Tatian, *orat.* 8 ff. (Schwartz, pp. 8 ff., M. 6. 821 A ff.), Hippolytus, *haer.* 4. 1-27 (pp. 32 ff., M. 16. 3056 c ff.), Tertullian, *idol.* 9 (CSEL 20. 38 ff.; M. *PL* 1. 671 B ff.), Eusebius, *p.e.* 6 (236a ff., M. 21. 404 A ff.). Many other passages might be cited, but these are representative. Most Christian writers make a straightforward attack upon astrology, if they have occasion to mention it, or dismiss it outright. (Tatian, e.g., brands it as a demonic invention.) But Origen, *more suo*, discusses astrology in a wide theological context, relating it to free will, biblical revelation, prophecy, and divine powers in the universe.

He insists on the distinction between thinking that the stars may give indications of events and believing that they are the causes of events. He sets out his subjects of enquiry thus: πῶς, προγνώστου ὄντος ἐξ αἰῶνος τοῦ θεοῦ περὶ τῶν ὑφ᾽ ἑκάστου πράττεσθαι νομιζομένων, τὸ ἐφ᾽ ἡμῖν σώζεται· καὶ τίνα τρόπον οἱ ἀστέρες οὐκ εἰσὶ ποιητικοὶ τῶν ἐν ἀνθρώποις, σημαντικοὶ δὲ μόνον. He goes on to show that human attempts to reach knowledge are misguided. Biblical accounts show that the stars are signs (cf. Gen. 1. 14, Jer. 10. 2). But they are signs for the divine powers only. Man's free will is maintained because the stars, like prophecies, indicate, without determining, events; see *comm. in Gen.* = Eus. *p.e.* 6. 11 (281a ff., M. 21. 477B ff.) = *philoc.* 23. 6 ff. (Robinson, pp. 194. 6 ff.), cf. M. 12. 61B. Origen mentions astrology also in *princ.* 3. 3. 2–3 (pp. 257. 10 ff., M. 11. 314C ff.). The suggestion was made by Koetschau, the GCS editor, that Rufinus has omitted a compromising passage (only his Latin version survives), surmising that Origen's real views might be close to those attributed to him by Theophilus of Alexandria, *ep.synod.* 2 (M. *PL* 22. 764, CSEL 55. 150. 5 ff.):

Praescientiam quoque futurorum, quae soli Domino nota est, stellarum motibus tribuit, ut ex earum cursu et varietate formarum daemones futura cognoscant et vel agant aliqua vel ab his agenda demandent. ex quo perspicuum est eum idolatriam et astrologiam et varias Ethnicorum fraudulentae divinationis praestigias approbare.

But there is no evidence that these were Origen's views. Quite the contrary. What we have of Origen makes it plain that for him foreknowledge 'soli Domino nota est': if the stars are signs, it is solely because God makes them so. As for the Powers who are able to read the signs, they are directly appointed by God for that purpose and they are to use their ability to interpret him to other superhuman beings and to the souls of those who have escaped the bonds of this present life: *comm. in Gen.* (M. 12. 81C ff.) = *Philoc.* 23. 20 (Robinson, p. 208. 22 ff.). Far from being able to manipulate events, the Powers are limited by God to certain areas prescribed for action (84B = *Philoc.* p. 209. 16 ff.). The sentence which Koetschau cites from Photius *cod.* 117 (M. 103. 396A), to the effect that astrology is ποιητική, is surely a misunderstanding or a misrepresentation of Origen (cf. the passage from the Genesis commentary quoted above). Greg. clearly regarded Origen as an ally in the battle against astrology, as the *Philocalia* selection shows, and there is no evidence to show that he was mistaken in his belief. Among Greg.'s Christian contemporaries both Basil and

Nyssen wrote on astrology. The importance of the former's Sixth Homily on the *Hexaemeron* throughout the Middle Ages is brought out by Y. Courtonne, *Saint Basile et l'hellénisme* (Paris, 1934), 99 ff. (Cf. Riedinger 47 ff.) Nyssen devoted his *Contra Fatum* to the defence of free will against astrological determinism (M. 45. 145 C ff.). See further J. Gaïth, *La Conception de la liberté chez Grégoire de Nysse* (Paris, 1953).

Astrology was, however, opposed by many who were not Christians. Among the philosophers, Panaetius (*c*.185–109 BC) had stood apart from most of his fellow Stoics in rejecting it. Eusebius cites the Cynic Oenomaus in the 2nd c. AD as one who would have no dealings with astrology, *p.e.* 6. 7 (255b ff., M. 21. 433A ff.) and the 3rd-c. Peripatetic Alexander of Aphrodisias agreed with him (cf. *RE* i. 1453). The position of Plotinus is of interest. For, though he can be very scornful of the notion that the stars actively spend their time causing events in human life, thus taking the place of the One who controls the universe (2. 3. 6), and though he realizes the incredible difficulties involved in the supposed interrelations of different people's astral influences (3. 1. 5), yet he does not deny that stars have a function in announcing the future. They are to take their place with other forms of augury as σημαντικὰ . . . τῶν ἐσομένων. He goes on: ἔστω τοίνυν ὥσπερ γράμματα ἐν οὐρανῷ γραφόμενα ἀεὶ ἢ γεγραμμένα καὶ κινούμενα, ποιοῦντα μέν τι ἔργον καὶ ἄλλο (2. 3. 7). Plotinus agrees with Origen in seeing the stars not as effective agents but merely as σημαντικά and, like Origen, attributes this power of signification to the dispensation of a single divine controlling force. Where Plotinus differs from Origen is in allowing that this form of augury is accessible to men. Cf. J. W. Trigg, *Origen*, 90–1.

Astrology met with political as well as philosophical opposition, (cf. v. 19 n.). Diocletian had forbidden the practice in 294 (Cod. Iust. 9. 18. 2), and Greg. could look back on a series of laws enacted by Christian emperors in a vain attempt to wipe out all trace of the art. Constantius, for instance, had issued an edict in 357 banning all astrological practices (Cod. Theod. 9. 16. 4), followed by further legislation in 358 (ibid. 6). Yet further laws were passed in 370 and 373, but still astrology flourished. (Cf. Cumont, *Astrology and Religion*, 177.)

For one thing, if there were pagans who rejected astrology, there were Christians who were attracted by it. The vehemence with which Christian writers assailed astrology may show a certain uneasiness about its effects upon members of the Church. As Bidez showed, 'Au temps de Saint Basile, assurément l'astrologie ne manquait pas d'adeptes chez les chrétiens' ('Le traité', 21). Bouché-Leclercq 616 cites the 5th-c. Eusebius of Alexandria as witness to the continuing temptation which astrology held out to Christians.

There can be no doubt that, in addressing himself to astrology, Greg. was attacking a contemporary problem. The Manichees associated themselves with the practice (cf. Widengren, *Mani and Manichaeism*, 69 ff.) and Lieu, *Manichaeism*, 141–3. The time was not so distant that people had forgotten the Emperor Julian's championing of astrology or Greg.'s resultant onslaught on him in *or*. 5. 5 (M. 35. 669B f.). Astrological literature was increasing. Before his conversion to Christianity Firmicus Maternus had written his *Mathesis*, in which he dealt with the subject in eight books (ed. by W. Kroll, F. Skutsch, and K. Ziegler, Leipzig (Teubner), 1897–1913). The date *c*.336 is given by B. Altaner, *Patrology* (ET Freiburg i. B., 1960), 422. Cf. T. Mommsen, *Hermes*, 29 (1894), 468–9. Nearer to the time when Greg. was writing there appeared works on astrology by Paulus Alexandrinus, cf. *RE* xviii/4 (1949), cols. 2376 ff. (W. Gundel), ed. E. Boer, Leiden, 1958), and Hephaestion of Thebes (cf. *RE* 8 (1913), cols. 309–10); ed. D. Pingree, 2 vols. (Leipzig, 1973–4). These are learned treatises, making their appeal to educated men. Particular support came from the Stoics, who, as Bouché-Leclercq stresses, gave to astrological speculation an intellectual respectability which they might otherwise have lacked (544–5; cf. v. 66 n.).

Riedinger, in his assessment of Greg.'s place in the history of Patristic writings on astrology (pp. 42 ff.), while agreeing with Laistner's statement ('Western Church', 258) that *Arc*. 5 was not widely known to later writers, points out that it was known to a number of those most concerned with the specific problems of astrology. Yet at the time of its writing the importance of this poem was quite different. Riedinger shows that the material on which Greg. draws is not uncommon, but that it is not often found outside monographs. The value of *Arc*. 5 lies precisely here. By attempting to integrate arguments on a rather specialized subject in a sequence of poems on basic Christian belief, Greg., unoriginal as he is, assists in giving that faith more comprehensive expression.

A further reference to astrology will be found in *Arc*. 8. 15–17, where its origin is touched on.

15. ἡγεμονῆας picks up v. 13. Is having the wrong 'guides' any better than having none at all?

COMMENTARY ON *ARC*. 5. 16-19

16. ὀπάζων: ὀπάζειν is common in Homer in the sense 'give as a leader'. For other meanings, cf. *Arc*. 4. 85 n.

17. οὐρανόν here means both the physical heaven in which the stars are set and heaven as the seat of divine authority.

ἑλίξεις: cf. *Arc*. 3. 43 n. Here there may be a play on the sense of 'revolving in the mind' and 'setting in circular motion' (of the stars in heaven). Cf. *or.Sib*. 3. 82 οὐρανὸν εἱλίξῃ, 8. 233 οὐρανὸν εἱλίξει, 8. 413 οὐρανὸν εἱλίξω.

18. Like Plotinus, Greg. sees in the claims of astrology the negation of unitary authority in the universe. Each star is made to exercise an individual influence which can result only in fragmentation, a pluralism of authority. But where Plotinus sees this as a reason for a reinterpretation of astral divination along with other forms, within a monistic system, Greg. holds that the entire system is condemned by its failure to provide a single governing principle. (On Plotinus cf. the edn. of E. Bréhier, *Plotin: 'Ennéades'*, ii (Paris, 1924), 24 ff., introd. to 2. 3).

19-24. *Practical criticisms, drawn from traditional observation.* Astrology is criticized on the ground that it does not 'work', in that people born under the same star follow different destinies, whereas the same fate overtakes those born under different stars; this and similar objections go back certainly as far as Carneades. Cf. e.g. Cic. *De divinatione* 2. 47, 97 and S.E. *M*. 5. 91-3. Further references are given in Bouché-Leclercq, *L'Astrologie grecque*, 381, 388 and in Amand, *Fatalisme*, 51-5 (Carneades' arguments) and 401-4 (Greg.'s use of them in this passage). The latter deals also with Nyssen's approach in *Contra Fatum* (M. 45. 165 ff.) on pp. 423 ff.

There was to be a classic summary of arguments in Aug. *de civ. Dei* 5. 1-8 (CSEL 40/1. 209-22; CCSL 47. 128-36).

19. βασιλεύς: Basil reverses the question in *hex*. 6. 7 (G. 1. 56D f., M. 29. 133 A), asking how a king can ensure that his son is born under a royal star.

These references to kings have an importance which goes beyond the obvious contrast which they present to beggars in the social scale. For it was the connection between royal personages and astrologers which frequently brought suspicion upon the latter. The use of the stars to predict the death of an emperor could well be regarded as disturbing, not to say subversive. Legislation may be thought often to issue from this concern rather than from any abstract consideration of the philosophical or religious principles involved in astrology. (Cf. Bouché-Leclerq, 566; F. H. Cramer, *Astrology in Roman Law and Politics* (Philadelphia, 1954), 248-83; MacMullen, *Enemies of the Roman Order*, ch. 4.) Diocletian outlawed all divination (*Cod. Theod.* 9. 18. 2) and Christian emperors were to follow him. Greg. would have known of the laws of Constantius under which it was a capital crime, *Cod. Theod.* 9. 16. 4, 8, 12.

συνάστερος: the word is not found in LSJ and *PGL* cites only this occurrence. But the form σύναστρος is found in *Testamentum Salomonis* 1321A and the noun συναστρία is a regular astrological term in Ptolemy, *Tetrabiblos* 4. 7. 6 (p. 193 Camerarius). Cf. also *Cat. Cod. Astr.* V/1. 180. 10 and LSJ and *PGL* s.vv. συναστρία and συναστρέω. Nyssen uses συναστρία in *Contra fatum* 168B.

21. **ὑπέρφρονα:** the commonest meaning is 'arrogant'. If βασιλεύς = 'emperor' the epithet 'arrogant' may be thought to indicate that Greg. is thinking of his old enemy Julian. In *or.* 5. 38 (M. 35. 713B) Julian is coupled with Tantalus, Tityus, and Ixion, for any of whom ὑπέρφρων would appear a mild description. It is unlikely that Greg. would call the emperors in general 'arrogant'. His respectful tone towards Constantius is very marked in *carm.* 1. 2. 25. 290 ff. (M. 37. 833A f.), and Theodosius is treated with no less respect in 2. 1. 11. 1278 ff. (M. 37. 1117A f.), cf. 1305 ff. (1119A f.). For Greg.'s dealings with the emperors cf. M.-M. Hauser-Meury, *Prosopographie zu den Schriften Gregors von Nazianz* (Bonn, 1960), 56 ff., 167 ff.; Plagnieux 429 ff.; and K. M. Setton, *Christian Attitude towards the Emperor in the Fourth Century* (New York, 1941), 104-5. On the other hand, it is not likely that Greg. would allow such a specific reference as Julian would provide to intrude on a general discussion. Two suggestions may be made: (*a*) to take βασιλεύς of any monarch and retain the meaning 'arrogant'; (*b*) to understand ὑπέρφρονα not in its usual verse meaning, but give it a sense found in prose, 'justifiably proud' (cf. Thuc. 2. 62, D.C. 45. 43).

21-2. The picture of disaster at sea touched Greg. closely, as his own experience left a deep mark on him; cf. *carm.* 2. 1. 11. 112-201 (M. 37. 1037-1043A); *or.* 18. 31 (M. 35. 1024B ff.).

22. **ἀλλογενέθλοις:** a *hapax legomenon*.

ὁμὸς μόρος: cf. Homer's ἰσόμορον καὶ ὁμῇ πεπρωμένον αἴσῃ (*Il.* 15. 209).

23-4. **συνέδησας ... συνέδησε:** Greg. may here be alluding to the term σύνδεσμος, which was used in both astronomy and astrology. It meant a node, the point of intersection of the paths of planets in astronomy, and a connection of heavenly bodies in astrology; cf. LSJ s.v. VI. Here the verb refers to the supposed 'connection' of subjects of the same star and their actual joining together in death.

Greg.'s rejection of the astrological use of συνδέω is made the more pointed by its positive use in Christian theories of creation. When Athanasius is writing of the way in which the creator Lord brought together what would appear to be opposed elements, he calls him ὁ συνδήσας αὐτά, *gent*. 37 (M. 25. 73A). Cf. Greg. in 2. 2. 7. 65 (M. 37. 1556A): ἢ τόδε πᾶν συνέπηξε καὶ ἁρμονίῃ συνέδησεν. (The subject is divine τέχνη.) Elsewhere συνδέω is used to express God's action in binding soul or spirit and flesh, e.g. 1. 2. 3. 16 (M. 37. 634A).

25–7. The argument is that those who hold to stellar influence must make a choice between individual and corporate determination. If there is some overriding (ἀρείων) necessity which determines the fate of a group of men, such as a ship's crew, then personal ἀνάγκη is a meaningless idea. Any power which could arbitrate between opposing stars would introduce a quite new principle.

27. ὁ μίξας: Greg. uses the same expression in *Arc*. 7. 80 to refer to the work of the Logos in forming man as a composite being. Here the meaning is 'bringing into connection', with the auxiliary sense of 'ordering'.

28. συνέδησε, picking up vv. 23–4, could mean connecting stars in astrological relationships or connecting human beings with the stars which affect their destiny. The point of the line is that such overall control would remove from the stars any effective power. For the line as a whole, cf. *carm*. 1. 1. 6. 13 (M. 37. 431A).

29. Caillau's understanding of this line rests on the assumption that it is exactly parallel to *carm*. 1. 1. 6. 12 (M. 37. 431A); εἰ μὲν Θεοῦ, πῶς πρῶτον, ὃ στρέφει Θεός; cf. his n. ἐξετίναξεν must thus be made to correspond in some way to στρέφει. But it is difficult to support Caillau's 'agitavit' as a tr. of ἐξετίναξεν. Billius, despite the metrical weakness of ἐκτινάσσει, had the merit of trying to preserve a recognized sense of ἐκτινάσσω, that of 'throwing out' ('excutitur'). Greg.'s use of the same ἐξετίναξεν in *carm*. 2. 1. 15. 17 (M. 37. 1251A) favours this sense. If we follow the reading of Cu, θεὸν ἐξετίναξεν, comparing Nicetas' ὃ μοι τὸν θεὸν ἐκτινάσσει, the sentence makes very good sense: 'But if it is God (*sc.* who makes and breaks connections at will), why bring in the first explanation, which, as I see it, threw God out?' God cannot be introduced at this late stage merely to resolve astrological difficulties.

30. For Greg. this is the ultimate absurdity. Again the favourite ἐλίσσω appears (cf. *Arc*. 3. 43 n.). Both Billius and Caillau produce here very weak (and, in fact, unjustifiable) translations, with 'subdere' and 'subjicere'. ἐλίξῃς surely means 'make God revolve' subject to the stars. For the suggestion that God is subject to determination cf. *carm*. 1. 1. 6. 17–18 (M. 37. 431 A).

31. This is another form of the argument which Greg. used against polytheism: multiple sources of authority amount to anarchy. Cf. *Arc*. 3. 81–2 n.

32. Cf. v. 29.

33. MSS vary between ἢ γὰρ δὴ and ἤδη γὰρ. The first gives a simple 'either . . . or' disjunction. The second implies the disjunction, but states it in a less direct way: 'For thus God really is in control, unless of course you believe that the stars are.'

33–44. Positive teaching on God's Providence.

34. κυβεϱνᾷ: the astrological use of κυβερνῶ is shown in Zodiol. cod. Mosq. gr. 186, cited by Bidez, 'Le traité', 20. Though it was not uncommon to find κυβερνῶ in Christian usage, e.g. Ath. *gent*. 36 (M. 25. 72 B) (of God: κυβερνῶν τὰ πάντα) the astrological connection gives the word particular point here. (Cf. *Arc*. 1. 5 n.) We may note also the Stoic use of the word, e.g. Ζεῦ, φύσεως ἀρχηγέ, νόμου μέτα πάντα κυβερνῶν . . . δίκης μέτα πάντα κυβερνᾷς, Cleanthes, *Hymn to Zeus*, vv. 2 and 35 (*SVF* i. 537; Powell, *Coll. Alex*., pp. 227–8).

35. νωμῶν is a well-established figure of government; cf. A. *Th*. 3 and, in Greg., *carm*. 2. 1. 1. 573 (M. 37. 1013 A).

The Logos carries out the providential government of the world he brought into being (cf. *Arc*. 4. 58, 7. 55 ff. n.).

36. It is unnecessary to look for a meaning such as σήμασι in νοήμασι (cf. Billius and Caillau's nn.). The word has a straightforward meaning as in *Arc*. 4. 68. The exercise of divine thought is directed towards the providential ordering of the universe.

37. ἁϱμονίην: the harmony of the heavenly world has here no connection with the Pythagorean notion of the harmony of heavenly bodies, the celebrated 'harmony of the spheres'. (For this cf. e.g. Pl. *Rep*. 617B, Arist. *Cael*. 290ᵇ13, *Metaph*. 986ᵃ, together with Guthrie, *History*, i. 167, 295 ff.) There is here a contrast between the calm order of the heavens and the uncertainties of earthly life. A not dissimilar sense is found in *Corp. Herm*. 1. 14, where W. Scott, *Hermetica* (London, 1924–36), i. 121, tr. ἁρμονίας as 'the structure of the heavens', remarking in his note (ii. 1–2): 'The writer seems to have adopted the Pythagorean phrase "the harmony of the spheres"; but he employs it in an altered sense. He is thinking, not of music, but rather of carpentry; the heavens are compared to the framework of a roof or dome fitted together by a builder.' Cf. the Budé edn. of A. D. Nock and A. J. Festugière (Paris, 1945–54), i. 21 n. 39, where the tr. 'composite framework' is given (in English). It is this providential 'fitting together' of all the parts of the cosmic system, contrasted with the multiplicity of astrological government, which produced metaphorical 'harmony'; cf. *carm.* 1. 1. 6. 2 (M. 37. 430A).

δρόμον: cf. Procl. *Par. Ptol.* 136 οἱ δρόμοι τῶν ἀστέρων.

39 ff. So far is man from knowing the secrets of the heavens that he does not yet know those of the earth.

39–40. ἐν κευθμῶσι ... ἧς σοφίης is a striking figure, recalling remote mountain fastnesses or the depths of the earth. Cf. *carm.* 2. 1. 62. 4 (M. 37. 1405A) κευθμῶν᾽ ἐς ᾄδου. κευθμών is found in Apoll. † *Met. Ps.* (Teubner p. 91. 45, M. 33. 1373B = κρύφια (*Ps.* 43. 22).

41. For the temporal sense of ἐνθάδε, 'now', cf. S. *OT* 488, *OC* 992.

42–3. Two ideas of harvest are combined in these lines: that it comes at its own due season, that it is a time of judgement. The biblical association of harvest and judgement is seen in such passages as Joel 3. 13, Matt. 13. 24–30, Rev. 14. 15–16.

κείρει is a violent word, more appropriate to the figurative than to the literal harvest. When used of crops it means 'ravage', e.g. Hdt. 5. 63.

γεημόρος is a *hapax legomenon*, formed on the analogy of γεηπό-νος. The forms cited in LSJ are γημόρος, γαμόρος, and γεωμόρος. For ὥρια πάντα cf. H. *Od.* 9. 131.

44. This poetical form of ἄναστρος, ἀνάστερος, is found also in Arat. 349, Ps.-Maneth. 4. 528. But the word here has an extended sense, meaning 'free from astrology'.

45–52. *The moral effects of belief in astrology and details of its technical language.* Riedinger, *Die hl. Schrift im Kampf der griechischen Kirche*, 44, points to two lines of attack upon astrology to be found in Greg. Man is incapable of grasping such a subject: it is a basic absurdity to attribute to inanimate objects like stars knowledge and power to determine events. But there is a third consideration which weighs with Greg., a moral one. He objects to astrology because he finds morally repugnant a system which destroys the meaning of human choice, which causes the disappearance of moral 'laws', it being a law, for instance, that the guilty should ultimately be punished and the good finally rewarded. Dependence on the stars levels all distinctions of good and evil. (Cf. Amand, *Fatalisme*, 62 ff.)

45-6. *PGL* records ὡροθέτης as a *hapax*, offering the tr. 'sign in the ascendant at the hour of birth'. This is curious. Surely ὡροθέτης is a person, a 'caster of horoscopes'; cf. the vb. ὡροθετέω in *AP* 11. 160 (Lucill.). The use may have been suggested by such common parallels as νομοθέτης and νομοθετέω.

λεπταλέας: 'fine, delicate.' There is probably a play on the term λεπτόν, found in writers on astronomy and astrology = 'division of a degree' (LSJ s.v. III. 4). μοῖρα here is a degree of arc, rather than the twelfth part of the zodiac (LSJ s.v. I. 5), W. Gundel, cf. *RAC* 1 (1950), 819. Taken together the words appear to mean minutes and seconds of arc, the implication that the divisions are too fine for accurate calculations to be made from them. Basil objects to these tiny divisions. By the time the midwife has announced the birth of a child to the Chaldaean, the position of the influencing star has altered: εἶπε τῷ Χαλδαίῳ τὸ γεννηθέν. Διὰ πόσων, βούλει, θῶμεν τῶν λεπτο-τάτων τῆς μαίας τὴν φωνὴν παρελθεῖν κτλ., *hex.* 6. 5 (G. 1. 54E f., M. 29. 129A). The stock nature of this argument may be seen in Amand 49 ff., who includes references to Sextus Empiricus, Philo, Hippo-lytus and Nyssen.

ζωοφόρους τε κύκλους: the zodiac is meant. Cf. Bas. *hex.* 6. 5 (G. 1. 54D, M. 29. 128C): τὸν ζωοφόρον λεγόμενον κύκλον.

μέτρα πορείης: Caillau tr. 'vitae mensuras'. But is this what the Greek means? It is much more likely that the words continue the astrological terminology. πορεία is used for the course of the sun in *Hymn. Is.* 32, Eudox. *Ars* 2. 15 and for that of other heavenly bodies in Pss. Sol. 19. 2, Aristeas *apol.* 4. 2 (Goodspeed, p. 6). μέτρα fits well with this view, for it is precisely the measurement of the distances covered by the heavenly bodies which interested astrologers. A similar list of terms is found in *or.* 28. 29 (p. 67. 3 ff., M. 36. 68B).

49. φέρει: the meaning here is 'carries along'. Soph. writes in *OC* 1693: τὸ φέρον ἐκ θεοῦ. The n. in Jebb's edn. is valuable (Cambridge, 1889). He offers as one explanation of τὸ φέρον '*That which carries*' or '*leads*' us forward in a course which we cannot control (cf. ἡ ὁδὸς φέρει ἐκεῖσε and like phrases). We may compare the use of φορά 'chance' in *carm.* 1. 1. 6. 9 (M. 37. 430A) and the association of φορά with the stars in *or.* 7. 7 (M. 35. 761C): οὐ τῇ φορᾷ τῶν ἄστρων διδοὺς τὰ ὄντα καὶ τὰ γινόμενα.

περιωγῇ: the lexica report this form περιωγή (= περιαγωγή) only here and in *Arc*. 6. 2. Metrical considerations may be thought to have produced this coinage: the initial tribrach of περιαγωγή could not be accommodated in a hexameter. For the use of περιαγωγή = 'revolution, rotation' cf. LSJ s.v. II. 1.

50. ῥοιζοῦμαι: 'whirled', like an arrow and with as much power of self-determination. Cf. Lycophron 1426: ἰῶν τηλόθεν ῥοιζουμένων.

51. ῥοπή: it was the power to incline (ῥέπειν) in the direction of good or bad which was given man at his creation (*Arc*. 7. 103). The word here indicates a settled disposition or propensity, as Nyssen ascribes to the devil an inclination towards evil, following his fall (*or. catech*. 6, p. 35. 10, M. 45. 29A). ῥοπή carries with it considerable associative powers, suggesting as it may the contrast in Pl. *Phdr*. 247B between the chariots of the gods in their perfect equipoise (ἰσορρόπως) and the chariots of mortals. There the vicious horse is depicted as ἐπι τὴν γῆν ῥέπων τε καὶ βαρύνων. Cf. Plot. 4. 8. 5. 26: ῥοπῇ αὐτοεξουσίῳ, with J. M. Rist, *Plotinus: The Road to Reality* (Cambridge, 1967), 120–1, who cites (n. 10) H. Lewy, *Chaldaean Oracles and Theurgy* (Cairo, 1956; 2nd edn. Paris, 1982), 295 n. 136 on the equivalence of ῥέπω and νεύω in discussion of the fall of souls. See also H. F. R. M. Oosthout, 'Wijzgerig taalgebruik in de redevoeringen van Gregorius van Nazianze tegen de achtergrond van de Neoplatoonse metafysica' (diss. Nijmegen, 1986), 215 ff.

53-71. *The star at Christ's nativity*

It is clear that the story of the Magi (Matt. 2. 1–12) could cause difficulty to Christians anxious to disavow all influence of the stars on human life. Bouché-Leclercq wrote (*L'Astrologie grecque*, 611): 'Le cas des Mages ... fut pour ces exégètes et polémistes chrétiens un embarras des plus graves.' He lists a number of places where attempts were made by Christians to answer charges of inconsistency or special pleading. To that list our present passage may be added. It repeats established arguments.

53. μέγα κλέος: L. Sternbach, 'De Gregorio Nazianzeno Homeri interprete', in *Stromata in honorem Casimiri Morawski* (Kraków, 1908), 177, suggested that the reading here should be μεγακλέος. He cites a number of instances of the adjective μεγακλής in Greg. It is found also in Opp. *C*. 2. 4 (μεγακλέα). In defence of the division μέγα κλέος we may point to κλέος as a title of Christ in *Arc*. 2. 9.

54. ἀντολίηθε: cf. Matt. 2. 1. There is perhaps a play on ἡγεμονεύ-
σας. In v. 33 Greg. has denied that the stars are ἡγεμονῆες ('control-
ling'). He does not make an exception here: the star is a 'guide'.

56–62. *The nature of the star.* Greg. takes his place in a line of Christian
interpreters who assert the novelty of the Bethlehem star. It was not
subject to astrological calculation, as it appeared solely to announce
the birth of Christ. Cf. Ignatius, *Eph.* 19. 2, where it is said: ἀστὴρ ἐν
οὐρανῷ ἔλαμψεν ὑπὲρ πάντας τοὺς ἀστέρας, καὶ τὸ φῶς αὐτοῦ
ἀνεκλάλητον ἦν, καὶ ξενισμὸν παρεῖχεν ἡ καινότης αὐτοῦ . . . (Bihl-
meyer, p. 87. 27 ff., M. 5. 660A f.). The words ξένος and καινός
appear in the description of the star given by Clem. Alex. in *exc.
Thdot.* 74. 2 (GCS 3. 130. 18 ff., M. 9. 693A). Its purpose was to over-
throw astrology and turn men from belief in fate to acceptance of
Providence. Origen stressed the distinction between the Bethlehem
star and ordinary stars in *Cels.* 1. 58–9 (pp. 109–10, M. 11. 768A ff.)
and *Jo.* 1. 26 (24) (p. 32. 30 ff., M. 14. 72A).

58 ff. Christian thought was determined that the Magi should be seen
to have derived their knowledge from sources which went back to
OT revelation. The question is dealt with by J. Bidez and F.
Cumont, *Les Mages hellénisés* (Paris, 1938), i. 48 ff. Here are cited a
number of passages which attempt to show that Balaam is the
source of the skill possessed by the Magi: cf. Or. *Cels.* 1. 60 (p. 111.
11 ff., M. 11. 769D ff.). Origen thought of the prophecies of Balaam,
as recorded by Moses, circulating in Mesopotamia and thus known
to the Magi who recognized their fulfilment in the star; cf. *hom. 13 in
Num.* 7 (p. 116. 28 ff., M. 12. 674A ff.).

Origen distinguished the Magi from the Chaldaeans, attacking
Celsus for confusing them, in *Cels.* 1. 58 (p. 109. 22 ff., M. 11. 768B).
Photius reported that Diodore of Tarsus made the same distinction
when he said that the Magi learned from the Chaldaeans the
prophecy which they had received from Balaam (*cod.* 223, M. 103.
877A f.). Bidez and Cumont 33 ff., 51 show that most Christian
writers think of the Magi as Persian, some as Arab, others as Chal-
daean. Whether Greg. is committing himself to the last view in v. 59
is difficult to say. The term 'Chaldaean' had come into use as a
generic word for 'astrologer', as in the passage of Basil quoted
above on vv. 45–6; cf. further *cod. Theodos.* 9. 16. 4 (AD 357), 3. 16. 8 (AD
358) and Bouché-Leclercq, *L'Astrologie grecque,* 556. Certainly in *or.*
4. 109 (M. 35. 645A) Greg. writes: τὸ δὲ μαγεύειν οὐ Περσικόν; Cf. v.
63 n.)

COMMENTARY ON *ARC.* 5. 59-69

59. ἀστροπολεύειν is a *hapax legomenon*. ἀστροπόλος finds equally
thin attestation, *PGL* citing only Antiochus Monachus ('obiit post
619') *hom.* 84. (M. 89. 1688C). The derivation is from πολεύω/
πολέω. The first has an astrological sense (of the planet presiding
over a day), the second means 'to range over, revolve'.

61. ἀρτιφαῆ: the only other author recorded as using the word ἀρτι-
φαής is Nonnus, in this sense of 'newly shining' in *D.* 5. 165, and
with the meaning 'newly seeing' in *par. Jo.* 9. 17 (M. 43. 828A).

τροχάοντα: cf. Aratus' description of the Ram, οὐδὲν ἀφαυρό-
τερον τροχάει Κυνοσουρίδος Ἄρκτου (227).

63-4. The adoration is taken as an abrogation of astrological claims.
Cf. Ign. *Eph.* 19. 3 (Bihlmeyer, p. 88. 1 ff., M. 5. 660B), Tert. *idol.* 9
(M. *PL.* 1. 672A f., CSEL 20. 38. 23 ff.): 'at enim scientia ista usque
ad evangelium fuit concessa, ut Christo edito nemo exinde nativi-
tatem alicuius de caelo interpretetur.' Cf. also the passage of Clem.
Alex., cited on vv. 56–62 above. Greg. elsewhere refers to this idea in
carm. 1. 2. 34. 198–9 (M. 37. 959A) and *or.* 2. 24 (M. 35. 433B).

μήδεα: if the Magi are thought of as Persian (cf. vv. 58–9 n.),
there may be a play on Μῆδοι.

65-71. Stars and men both have allotted courses to follow, but they
are independent of each other.

66. ἀείδρομοι: ἀείδρομος is a *hapax legomenon*. Greg. coined also
ἀειπλανής, ἀεισθενής, ἀειστρεφής, and ἀειφλεγής.

67. παλίμποροι: Sophocles glosses 'retrograding', a technical term
in astronomy to describe the actual or apparent motion of heavenly
bodies 'backward' in the zodiac, i.e. from east to west. Planets are
here referred to, moving as they may against the general direction of
the constellations of the zodiac. Though he does not refer to it much
in his writings, Greg. may be thought to have had a fair knowledge
of astronomy derived from the years in Athens when he was study-
ing probably under Himerios. (Cf. Y. Courtonne, *Saint Basile et
l'hellénisme,* 7–9.; Gallay, *La Vie de saint Grégoire de Nazianze,* 51.)

68-9. *The nature of the stars.* Two theories are mentioned: (*a*) The stars
consist of self-maintaining fire; (*b*) The stars are composed of a
'quintessence'.

(*a*) The entry under ἄτροφος in *PGL* cites this passage, glossing
'*ill-fed, under-nourished,* met. *growing no larger, constant in size,* of stars'.
But is this the point? What is being discussed in both parts of the
εἴτε ... εἴτε is the substance of the stars. The Stoics thought of
this substance as fiery. It was not fire in the ordinary sense, what

Zeno called τὸ . . . ἄτεχνον καὶ μεταβάλλον εἰς ἑαυτὸ τὴν τροφήν, but τὸ . . . τεχνικόν, αὐξητικόν τε καὶ τηρητικόν (Stob. *Ecl.* 1. 25. 5). Yet the stars were still composed of a fire which needed nourishment. Cicero, having said in *ND* 2. 40 'sidera tota esse ignea', goes on in 2. 118:

sunt autem stellae natura flammeae; quocirca terrae, maris, aquarum vaporibus aluntur eis, qui a sole ex agris tepefactis et ex aquis excitantur, quibus altae renovataeque stellae atque omnis aether refundunt eadem ut rursum trahunt indidem, nihil ut fere intereat aut admodum paullum, quod astrorum ignis et aetheris flamma consumat.

Cf. also *Tusc.* 1. 43, Diog. Laert. 7. 139, 145. Plotinus, however, argued against the need of the heavenly bodies for any kind of τροφή. Cf. 2. 1. 4 and 2. 1. 8: οὐδὲν δεῖ τοίνυν ἄλλου σώματος τῷ οὐρανῷ, ἵνα μένῃ . . . (ll. 15–16) . . . οὐ τοίνυν οὐδὲ τροφῆς δεῖσθαι φατέον τὰ ἐκεῖ, . . . (ll. 19–20). This, then, is the reason for the choice of ἄτροφος: constant size is only a secondary attribute here. In the other passage cited in *PGL*, Gr. Nyss. *hex.* 5 (M. 44. 68A), the constant size of the stars is indicated. But there is no mention of fire.

(*b*) The idea of a πέμπτον σῶμα appears in Aristotle (perhaps earlier: cf. Guthrie, *History* i. 270 ff.). In *Cael.* 270ᵇ21, *Mete.* 341ᵃ2, *An.* 418ᵇ9, it appears as an alternative to fire as the substance of which the stars are composed. This element is αἰθήρ, which, argues Aristotle, has a circular motion which fits it for the circumference of the universe. Fire, on the other hand, moves naturally in straight lines. The πέμπτον σῶμα idea came to have diverse application. Origen, for example, denies its relevance to the question of the resurrection body in *princ.* 3. 6. 6 (p. 288. 21 ff., M. 11. 339B f.). Greg. here relates the 'quintessence' to its original Aristotelian connection with the stars. (Cf. Basil *hex.* 1. 11. (G. 1. 10E f., M. 29. 25B f.). In *or.* 28. 8 (p. 33. 5 ff., M. 36. 36A) he examines the possibility that God may be identified with this πέμπτον σῶμα, thus perhaps taking up another side of Aristotle's teaching, that the 'quintessence' was the substance of minds as well as stars. (This is certainly the way in which Cicero states the doctrine in *Acad. Post.* 1. 26.) See further Kertsch, *Bildersprache*, 164.

70–1. As far as the sense goes, there is little to choose between ἄνιμεν and ἄνομεν. (For ἴομεν cf. Caillau's n. It is also the reading of L.) The notion of ascent (ἄνιμεν) goes well with οὐρανίην. As Dronke noted (*Carmina Selecta*, 203), ὁδὸν ἄνω is a good

Homeric expression (cf. *Od.* 3. 496), in the sense of 'completing a journey'.

The lines show a tension familiar in Greg., the tension between the divine and the earthly elements in man. In saying that man is to hasten to the attainment of a 'rational' and 'heavenly' nature, Greg. means that man will come to a nature which is wholly so. Already, in his earthly state, man shares some of the divine characteristics, holding an intermediate place between the mortal and the immortal. Cf. *Arc.* 7. 65 ff.

δέσμιον: whether we read δέσμιοι or δέσμιον, the sense is the same: we are, our nature is, 'bound' to the earth. It is characteristic of Greg. that he should take a straightforward expression in Lam. 3. 34 and give it a metaphorical meaning. The Heb. *'ăsîrê 'āreṣ* and the Greek δεσμίους γῆς refer simply to 'prisoners in a country' (Jerusalem Bible, cf. New English Bible).

6. On Rational Natures

Title and purpose

The app. crit. reveals a variety of ways in which a title may be ascribed. As the titles have little claim to definitive standing (cf. Intro.) the reader may feel free to choose. Almost all of those on offer give an accurate characterization. The poem is about 'beings' or 'natures' which may equally well be called 'intellectual' or 'rational'. This means that the only inappropriate title (cited by Caillau) is περὶ ἀσωμάτων φύσεων. Human beings as well as angels are intended. The poem picks up the subject of creation in dealing with the relationship to God of beings created rational, touching on Satan's responsibility for evil in the world and introducing human history in the Eden story.

1–26. *Degrees of illumination among rational beings*

1–5. *The image of the rainbow.* G. Soutar, *Nature in Greek Poetry* (London, 1939), 112 ff. remarks that the Greeks (he is speaking of Classical Greek poetry) make little of the rainbow, showing 'faint appreciation' of its colours and lacking the symbolic meaning which the Hebrews found in it. Nazianzen cannot be said to have added much to the stock of rainbow imagery, but both he and Nyssen find a certain illustrative value in it. Nyssen uses the rainbow in a Trinitarian argument as an instance of distinction without separation, attempting an explanation in terms of refraction (οἷόν τις καμπὴ καὶ ἐπάνοδος, *diff. ess.* int. opp Bas. *ep.* 38. 5, M. 32. 222B ff.) Earlier discussions of the rainbow will be found, e.g. in Arist. *Mete.* 371ᵇ18 ff.; Epicurus *Ep.* 2. 109–10; Sen. *NQ* 1. 3. Greg. gives little explanation, being content with a simple point (vv. 6 ff.).

1. Cf. Aratus 899: Διὸς εὐδιόωντος.

2. **ἀποκρούστοις:** Nicander (*Th.* 270) has the word to describe a small boat driven back in a wind: εἰς ἄνεμον βεβίηται ἀπόκρουστος λιβὸς οὔρῳ. Here, and here only, the word has the sense 'refracted'. For a similar meaning Arist. uses ἀνάκλασις and cognates (*Mete.* 372ᵃ ff.). He discusses the way in which he thinks that condensed air acts as a mirror in 373ᵇ2. Nyssen uses similar language, explaining more fully than Nazianzen does how the sunbeam strikes obliquely the cloud formation (M. 32. 333B f.).

περιωγαῖς: the word is found only here and in *Arc.* 5. 49, where see n. Dronke was mistaken in printing as the text of Cu περιωπαῖς (*Carmina Selecta*, 203). (Cf. also Caillau's n.) The MS clearly reads περιωγαῖς; a comparison of the way in which the scribe writes γα here and in αὐγαῖς v. 7 will confirm this (fo. 78). Nicetas has in his paraphrase the regular form περιαγωγαῖς (cf. *Arc*. 5. 49 n.). The ἀπόκρουστοι περιωγαί are circular motions of sunlight, refracted in such a way that the rays bend back upon themselves, as in Nyssen, loc. cit.

3. Cf. Verg. *A*. 4. 701: (of Iris) 'mille trahens varios adverso sole colores' and the similar 5. 89.

ἑλίσσει: cf. *Arc*. 3. 43 n. Here the meaning is 'makes to curve', or possibly 'makes to turn back (in a circle)' as Homer uses ἑλισσέμεν of rounding the post in a chariot-race (*Il*. 23. 309).

4. σελαγίζεται: the -ίζω form is not common outside Nonnus. LSJ lists only the 3rd-c. AD hymn in *Papyri russischer und georgischer Sammlungen*. *PGL* adds citations from Nonnus and Sozomen, together with (in middle and passive) the present passage and the 9th–10th cent. Arethas, *Apoc*. 16. 17 (M. 106. 712 D). We may compare Greg.'s use of σέλας in *Arc*. 4. 65.

There is a close parallel in the image of the pebble thrown into the water, with the concentric circles of ripples corresponding to the rainbow circles, in *carm*. 1. 2. 2. 283 ff. (M. 37. 600A). The words ἔκτοθι λυομένοισι occur (v. 286). This figure is found also in *or*. 18. 19 (M. 35. 1008B). The passages are discussed in Kertsch, *Bildersprache*, 182 ff., cf. vv. 51–2.

For αἰθήρ cf. vv. 50–2 n.

5. The form ἔκτοθε (edd.) is not found in the lexica. It is better to read ἔκτοθι than to suppose ἔκτοθε equivalent to the metrically impossible ἔκτοθεν. The meaning is clear: the outer rings fade away, dissolve, melt into the surrounding air.

6–7. *The application of the figure.* The degree of mental or spiritual illumination depends on distance from the source of light. The application itself uses figurative language with the physical and mental senses of 'light' merging.

ἀποστίλβοντος: cf. Clem. *prot*. 11 (p. 81. 24, M. 8. 236A) for a metaphorical use.

8–12. These lines appear also in *carm*. 1. 2. 1. 15–19 (M. 37. 523A), except that in v. 11 τεινώμεσθα is read for ἑλκώμεσθα.

8. πηγή: cf. *Arc*. 4. 81 n. Perhaps the association of light and life in Ps. 35 (36 Heb.). 10 may be the origin of the expression:

ὅτι παρὰ σοὶ πηγὴ ζωῆς,
ἐν τῷ φωτί σου ὀψόμεθα φῶς.

Cf. ἡ πηγὴ τοῦ φωτός in Serap. *Euch*. 13. 5. There is in Kertsch, *Bildersprache* an extensive study of the background and development of πηγή as a philosophical and religious term: see pp. 87, 116, 119, 122 ff., 135, 138 ff., 145 ff., and 205 and for πηγάζειν pp. 148 ff.

9a–11. The theme of the opening lines of *Arc*. 1 recurs: knowledge of God is unattainable by minds less than his own. But this is not a reason for despair. On the contrary, it is seen as part of the dispensation of providence that God should lead on, always encouraging the desire for deeper knowledge.

11b–26. *Angels.* On the subject of angels in the Fathers, the following may be consulted: J. Turmel, 'Histoire de l'angélologie des temps apostoliques à la fin du ve siècle', *RHL* 3 (1898), 299–308, 407–34, 533–52; A. Vacant and G. Bareille, 'Anges', *DTC* 1 (1903), cols. 1189–1222 together with *DTC, Tables générales* (1951), cols. 153d–7; J. Michl, 'Engel. IV (christlich)', *RAC* v (1962), 109–200; J. Daniélou, *Les Anges et leur mission d'après les Pères de l'Église* (Gembloux, 1952). Cf. also K. W. A. Pelz, *Die Engellehre des hl. Augustinus* (Münster, 1913), where an account is given of Augustine's predecessors; A. Recheis, *Engel, Tod und Seelenreise* (Temi e Testi, 4; Rome, 1958), esp. 132 ff.; J. Rousse, 'Les anges et leur ministère selon saint Grégoire de Nazianze', *MSR* 22 (1965), 133–52. (Cf. vv. 22–6 n.) See also Barbel 78 ff. n. 26. Among places where Greg. deals with angels are *orr*. 28. 31 (p. 69. 16 ff., M. 36. 69D ff.), 31. 15 (p. 163. 9 ff., 149B f.). Origen's place in the shaping of Greg.'s thought is explored by Moreschini, 'Influenze', 54–7, which may be taken with his comment on *or*. 38. 10 (SC p. 122 n. 2 and pp. 64–5).

12. δεύτερα: the angels' status as second only to the Trinity is emphasized in the view that they were created before all other creatures; cf. *or*. 38. 9–10 (M. 36. 320C ff.) = 45. 5 (629A ff.). This is a common Christian Greek view. Cf. e.g. Or. *princ*. 2. 9. 1 ff. (p. 163. 24 ff., M. 11. 255B ff.); Bas. *hex*. 1. 5. (G. 1. 5C ff., M. 29. 13A ff.); Pelz, 6. Cf. *or*. 6. 12 (M. 35. 737B) for δεύτερα.

13. αἰγλήεντες: cf. *Arc*. 3. 28 n.

ἀειδέες: contrast this with the application of the word in v. 36: θεότητος ἀειδέος. There the word ἀειδής has the full meaning given in *PGL* (s.v. 7): 'both as above form and as without visible form'. Cf. Greg. Nyss. *Eun*. 1 (p. 94. 20, M. 45. 321A). Here the word has a diminished sense. The angels are invisible, but, as creatures, they are formed after an εἶδος in the mind of God.

13-14. θόωκον ἀμφί: a variant of ἀμφιθόωκος (*Arc.* 4. 88). In Homer, *Il.* 8. 439, θῶκος is found as the throne of a god. (Cf. A. *Pr.* 831.) Rousse, 'Les anges', 141, sees here a picture of troops of angels dancing round the throne 'des farandoles sacrées', after the manner of angels in Fra Angelico. It must be said, somewhat prosaically, that we are not here told what the angels are doing as they circle the throne. In the passage which Rousse claims as parallel to this we read: καὶ σὺν ἀγγέλοις χορεύσεις τὴν ἄπαυστον χορείαν *carm.* 1. 2. 3. 95 (M. 37. 640A). Here, indeed, one might argue, is a reference to dancing. But as early as the Platonic corpus we find χορείαν ... χορῶν used of the circling motion of the stars (*Epin.* 982e) and it could well be that no more is meant here.

ἐλαφροί: they are airy and nimble, as messengers (or dancers) should be. Cf. *or.* 28. 31 (p. 71. 8, M. 36. 72B). The angels form a κόσμος νοητός, not in the common understanding of a world of pure ideas, but as individual minds they constitute a realm of God's power and rule.

15-16. A reminiscence of Ps. 103 (104 Heb.). 4 ὁ ποιῶν τοὺς ἀγγέλους αὐτοῦ πνεύματα, καὶ τοὺς λειτουργοὺς αὐτοῦ πῦρ φλέγον. Cf. Heb. 1. 7 and 1 *Clem.* 36. 3 (Bihlmeyer, p. 55. 12 ff., M. 1. 281A). Greg. does not follow the line of Hebrews, where 'winds' and 'fire' are taken as marks of the instability of the angelic nature when contrasted with that of the Son. Here the thought concentrates solely on the light, refined angelic nature and its suitability to rapid motion in carrying out God's commands; cf. Ps. 102 (103 Heb.). 20. In *or.* 28. 31 (p. 70. 5 ff., M. 36. 72A), Greg. interprets πνεῦμα as νοητὴ φύσις and fire as referring to the angelic power of purification.

ἠέρος: are we to distinguish ἀήρ from αἰθήρ, as in v. 52? It seems unlikely that Greg. is being so precise as to differentiate between the αἰθήρ, the natural element of angels, and the lower ἀήρ through which their commissions might take them in their concern for the world. More probably ἠέρος means the whole realm of air, contrasted with earth.

ὑποδρήσσουσιν: cf. Greg.'s ὑποδρηστήρ in *carm.* 2. 1. 16. 11 (M. 37. 1255A) and ὑποδρήστειρα *Arc.* 4. 79 (with n.). For the form ὑποδρήσσω cf. A.R. 3. 274, Musae. 13.

17. Man resembles the angels in being νοερός, but is distinguished from them by not being ἁπλοῦς. Cf. *Arc.* 4. 40 n., 77 n. and 89-92 n.

διαυγέες: radiant, as creatures of light, and translucent as being incorporeal (or nearly so, cf. v. 60 n.).

οὔτ' ἀπὸ σαρκῶν: cf. the use of ἄσαρκος in *carmm.* 1. 2. 4. 8 (M. 37. 641 A), 1. 2. 10. 892 (744 A), referring to angels.

It will be noted that, though Greg. calls the angels ἄσαρκοι, this does not mean that they are ἀσώματοι. Origen had taught that the Persons of the Trinity alone are incorporeal, *princ.* 1. 6. 4 (p. 85. 14 ff., M. 11. 170B f.). However refined the angelic body may be, there is something distinguishable as a σῶμα; cf. Turmel, *RHL* 3 (1898), 407 ff., together with id. ('P. Coulange'), *The Life of the Devil*, 44 ff. ET (London, 1929); Michl, *RAC* v (1962), 121. Greg. shows that he appreciates the distinction between ἄσαρκος and ἀσώματος in *or.* 28. 31 (p. 70. 10, M. 36. 72A), where he says that angelic nature may be relatively incorporeal (compared with human nature), but in absolute terms he does not venture beyond ἢ ὅτι ἐγγύτατα.

18. πάγεν: for the form cf. H. *Il.* 11. 572. There is here an allusion to the belief that all composite entities must ultimately suffer breakdown and destruction. Cf. the application of ἄπηκτος to God in *Arc.* 2. 16. Pl. *Phd.* 78C provides a classic statement of the view that only that which is uncompounded (ἀσύνθετος) can escape dissolution.

20-1. Greg. seems to realize that he is in danger of making the angelic nature almost indistinguishable from God's. But it is doubtful which precise attribute of divinity is in his mind when he draws back from calling the angels ἀτειρέες. There are two possibilities:

(i) ἀτειρέες means 'indestructible', as, e.g., ἀτειρής describes bronze in H. *Il.* 5. 292. The only reason why Greg. might hesitate to call the heavenly beings 'indestructible' is the implied doubt on the omnipotence of God. Could he not, if he wished, destroy part of his creation, albeit the highest part?

(ii) The word means 'stubborn, unyielding' (cf. LSJ s.v. II), in this case to evil (as Nicetas interprets). These lines would then be directly linked with the thought of v. 53 and the fall of Lucifer in the following lines. (Again, this appears in Nicetas.) Certainly the meaning would have been clearer if there had been some such specifying dative as κακίᾳ (cf. *AP* 12. 175. 3-4 (Strat.): ἀτειρὴς οἴνῳ). But the sense emerges fairly clearly and, in the absence elsewhere of any suggestion that Greg. was exercised over the possibility of the destruction of the heavenly beings, this interpretation is to be preferred. (Cf. Gallay's tr. 'absolument fermes et inébranlables', p. 132, repr. Devolder 71.)

The figure of the horse which needs restraint is a common one. Cf. e.g. Meth. *symp.* 5. 3 (p. 56. 9, M. 18. 101 A): Plato talks of relaxing such restraint in *Prt.* 338A: χαλάσαι τὰς ἡνίας τοῖς λόγοις. Greg. reaches a similar point in *or.* 28. 31 (p. 70. 10 ff., M. 36. 72A ff.). He feels 'dizzy' with speculation, ἰλιγγιῶμεν, p. 70. 11 (72A) and contents himself with a bare summary of the titles applied to angelic powers.

22–6. *The functions of angels.* Origen had dealt with this in *princ.* 1. 8. 1 (pp. 94 ff., M. 11. 176A ff.), maintaining that angelic functions correspond to merit displayed. Greg. is content to list functions without trying to account for diversity. He contemplates the possibility of some kind of rank structure in *or.* 28. 4 (p. 27. 8 ff., M. 36. 32A): some angels may have a clearer understanding of God than others κατὰ τὴν ἀναλογίαν τῆς τάξεως. But he offers no explanation of the distinction; cf. also *or.* 40. 5 (M. 36. 364B). On the varying ministries of angels in Greg. cf. Rousse, 'Les anges', 140 ff. Greg. alludes in these lines to most of the functions specified by Rousse. The others relate specifically to Christ, baptism, and eschatology.

22. παραστάται: cf. Dan. 7. 10. For the angels who remain in contemplation and praise cf. *or.* 28. 31 (p. 70. 15 ff., M. 36. 72 B), *carmm.* 1. 2. 10. 923 ff. (M. 37. 747A), 2. 1. 1. 280 ff. (M. 37. 991A).

23–6. Other angels are allotted various parts of the universe as their charge. It is these angels who hold together the universe in harmony, as Greg. describes them in *or.* 28. 31 (p. 71. 10–11, M. 36. 72C): πάντα εἰς ἓν ἀγούσας, πρὸς μίαν σύννευσιν τοῦ τὰ πάντα δημιουργήσαντος.

24. ἐπιστασίην: this is a regular term for an angel's office (cf. *PGL* s.v. Surely the present passage should there be cited under 1.c, 'of office of angels in caring for the created order', rather than 1.a?)

25. ἄνδρας: belief in personal guardian angels rests on such passages as Ps. 90 (Heb. 91). 11–12 (cited in Luke 4. 10–11), Tob. 5. 6, 22, Matt. 18. 10, Acts 12. 15, Heb. 1. 14. Origen makes a good deal of the idea in e.g. *princ.* 2. 10. 7 (p. 181. 19 ff., M. 11. 240A), 3. 2. 4 (pp. 250 ff., M. 11. 308C ff.), *Cels.* 1. 61 (p. 112. 9 ff., M. 11. 772C), 8. 27 (p. 243, M. 11. 1556C ff.), 8. 34 (pp. 249–50, M. 11. 1565C ff.), *or.* 11. 3 (p. 323, M. 11. 449B ff.), *comm. in Mt.* 13. 5. (pp. 190 ff., M. 13. 1104C ff.).

πτόλιας: pagan thought took it that each city had its own presiding deity (cf. LSJ s.v. πολιοῦχος). Greg. may be offering a Christian alternative to this view (cf. below), or perhaps he is associating churches with their cities (cf. Rev.).

ἔνθεα: the angels of the nations play a big part in Origen: cf. e.g.
princ. 1. 5. 2 (pp. 70. 28 ff., M. 11. 158B f.), where Deut. 32. 8-9 is
cited), *Cels.* 5. 30 (pp. 31-2, M. 11. 1225C ff.), together with J. Danié-
lou, *Origen*, ET (London, 1955), 224 ff. Notice how this contrasts
with the beliefs expressed by Julian, who reaffirms the pagan view
that the beings who exercise authority over nations and cities are
gods, (*Gal.* 115d ... ἐθνάρχαις καὶ πολιούχοις θεοῖς).

26. The line probably refers to the charge given to angels of assisting
men in prayer, cf. *carm.* 1. 2. 1. 83 ff. (M. 37. 528A f.). The language
reflects Rom. 12. 1: θυσίαν ζῶσαν ... τὴν λογικὴν λατρείαν ὑμῶν,
and is similar to *Corp. Herm.* 1. 31: δέξαι λογικὰς θυσίας ἁγνάς. (Cf.
the n. in Scott's edn.: 'an act of worship which consists in verbal
adoration, as opposed to material offerings.' See also Nock–Festu-
gière, i. 27-8.) As Origen wrote in *or.* 11. 4-5 (p. 323. 14 ff., M. 11.
449D ff.), angels are able to use their special knowledge (cf. ἐπι-
ίστορες) to assist men to pray fittingly. Cf. *Cels.* 8. 64 (p. 280, M. 11.
1612C ff.).

27-46. *Hesitation about going farther with the subject*

We have already seen Greg.'s hesitation in approaching his theme (cf.
Arc. 3. 1). Undoubtedly there is a rhetorical element in his reluctance,
but there is still genuine perplexity in Greg.'s mind. Not only is he
overcome by the thought of the heavenly splendour (vv. 27 ff.). He is
perplexed by the possible moral effects on his readers of having to
admit that sin is possible among these heavenly beings.

28. ἀχλὺς brings associations of the mistiness which comes over the
eyes of a dying Homeric warrior (*Il.* 5. 696), or the effect of strong
emotion (Archil. 191. 2 West), or, most aptly here, the temporary
blurring of the vision which the appearance of a god can produce
(H. *Il.* 20. 321). Cf. the 'dizziness' passage cited in n. on vv. 20-1.

30-5. *The image of the river-crossing.* Greg. likens himself to a traveller
who, crossing a river, experiences a sudden moment of panic but
decides that the only thing he can do is go on. Imagery from swollen
streams is found several times in Homer, e.g. *Il.* 4. 452-6, 13. 136-46,
but Greg.'s simile is more like *Macbeth* 3. 4. 138: 'Returning were as
tedious as go o'er.'

30. τρηχαλέος is a form of τραχύς which is not recorded in literature
earlier than the 2nd c. AD, when it appears in the epic poet Pancrates
(*P. Oxy.* 1085. 11) and in the medical poet Marcellus Sidetes. Later it

COMMENTARY ON *ARC*. 6. 30–8

occurs in the Greek Anthology. Plutarch describes a river as τραχύς in *Alex*. 60. Cf. *carm*. 1. 2. 9. 78–9 (M. 37. 673A).

31. ἀνέπαλτο: the sense is not 'recoils' or 'falls back' as Billius' and Caillau's 'resilit' must be tr. The meaning is 'leaps, is borne upwards', an accurate description of the sensation of being suddenly swept out of one's depth. (Cf. H. *Il*. 23. 694 for the form ἀνέπαλτο and 692 ff. for the picture of a fish leaping up and suddenly disappearing.)

ἱέμενός περ. Cf. H. *Od*. 1. 6.

32. Cf. H. *Il*. 21. 551: πολλὰ δέ οἱ κραδίη πόρφυρε μένοντι. *Od*. 4. 427, 572; 10. 309: πολλὰ δέ μοι κραδίη πόρφυρε κιόντι. The middle is found in Himerios (who was probably Greg.'s teacher: cf. *Arc*. 5. 67 n.), *or*. 31. 2, and in Agathias (*AP* 10. 14).

The artistry of this line deserves attention. πορφύρω is skilfully chosen as a word which depicts equally well the swelling emotion of the heart (cf. the Homeric exx.) and the swelling rush of the stream. (It is used of surging waves in *Il*. 14. 16, *al*.) But in the brief compass of the verse the second meaning is only hinted at.

33. Cf. Antipho 3. 2. 1: αἱ χρεῖαι τολμᾶν βιάζονται.

35. χάσσατο: this is the point at which the traveller 'falls back'.

34–46. *The application of the simile.* The poem picks up the thought from v. 20. Though Greg. fears to go further in his approach to the heavenly beings, he believes that, having come so far, he must continue.

36. ἀειδέος: cf. v. 13 n.

ὑψιμέδοντα: a title of Zeus in Hes. *Th*. 529, the word ὑψιμέδων was appropriated for Jewish or Christian use in *or. Sib*., where θεὸν ὑψιμέδοντα appears in 1. 347, 2. 309, 8. 355. Cf. *Arc*. 8. 3 and *carm*. 1. 2. 1. 6 (M. 37. 522C).

38. κεκορημένον: this appears to be a reference to Origen's teaching on the reason for the Fall of the angels: they had become sated with goodness. Origen writes thus of Satan in *Cels*. 6. 44 (p. 115. 16 ff., M. 11. 1368A): καὶ ὢν "ἀποσφράγισμα ὁμοιώσεως καὶ στέφανος κάλλους" ἐν τῷ παραδείσῳ τοῦ Θεοῦ οἱονεὶ κορεσθεὶς τῶν ἀγαθῶν ἐν ἀπωλείᾳ ἐγένετο κατὰ τὸν εἰπόντα μυστικῶς πρὸς αὐτὸν λόγον· "ἀπώλεια ἐγένου καὶ οὐχ ὑπάρξεις εἰς τὸν αἰῶνα." (Cf. Ezek. 28. 12–13, 19). Similarly, if the text which Koetschau reconstructed from the anathemas against Origen at the Second Council of Constantinople (553) is near to Origen's original teaching, then he spoke of the rational creatures in these or similar terms: κόρον δὲ αὐτοὺς (*sc. νόας*) λαβεῖν τῆς θείας ἀγάπης καὶ θεωρίας, καὶ πρὸς τὸ χεῖρον τραπῆναι κατὰ τὴν ἑκάστου ἀναλογίαν τῆς ἐπὶ τοῦτο ῥοπῆς, *princ*. 2. 8. 3 (p. 159. 7 ff.).

Greg. here adapts the teaching to fit his emphasis on light as the characteristic of the angelic world and perhaps also to avoid the harshness of an outright assertion that the angels became sated with goodness.

39. στορέσαιμι: the verb is used of paving a road in *IGRom*. 4. 1431. 5, *al*.; cf. the passive in Hdt. 2. 138. The suggestion that even angels are open to sin might 'pave the way' for others.

40–1 show Greg.'s dilemma. How can he assert that the nature of angels is unchangeably good, when he thinks of the fallen angel, Satan?

41. Cf. *Arc*. 8. 36 n.

42–5. The connection of thought is: 'It must be Satan who contrives evil, for it is out of keeping with the mind of a good God to plant evil in man and thus set up enmity in the creature he loves. Nor is it the will of a good God that evil should subsequently arise as a rival or that it should have an eternal (or independent) existence.' Greg. is thus preparing the way, through the Fall of Satan, for the Fall of man. The two Falls are very closely linked, each being a reason for believing in the other. God did not create evil in either Satan or man. Man's Fall must therefore be attributed to Satan. But the ability of one who was created good to contrive evil shows that he has changed, has himself fallen.

Vv. 44–5 may be compared with the arguments of *Arc*. 4. 24 ff.

44. ἀντιθόωκον is a *hapax legomenon*. Cf. ἀντίθρονον in *Arc*. 4. 25.

45. ἄναρχον: a word which Greg. reserves for God, in particular God the Father: cf. *Arc*. 1. 25 n., 2. 19 n., 21 n.

46. As in *Arc*. 1. 16–24, 3. 36, 3. 90, Greg. is claiming a measure of inspiration for what he writes.

47–55. *The three ranks: God, angels and men*

47–9. God.

47. πρώτη gives more direct emphasis than πρῶτον.

ἄτροπος: the word is applicable only to Godhead: cf. *carm*. 1. 2. 1. 145 f. (M. 37. 533A), where Christ is called ἄτροπος οὐρανίοιο εἰκών. Cf. v. 40 n. and see vv. 53–4. Moreschini, 'Platonismo', 1377, parallels it as a word of Platonist background with ἄτρεπτος in *orr*. 18. 42 (M. 35. 1040C) and 39. 13 (M. 36. 349A).

48a. Unity is here associated with changelessness, multiplicity with instability. There is here a glance at what A. H. Armstrong referred to as 'perhaps the central and most important theme of all traditional philosophy', the problem of the One and the Many (*An Introduction to Ancient Philosophy* (London, 1965), 8). Appearing in Orphic writers and among Milesians like Anaximenes (cf. Guthrie, *History*, i. 132), it became a classic subject in Platonism. Plato meets the issue as it was raised by Parmenides in the dialogue named after him and in *Sophist* 244B ff. (cf. Guthrie, v. 148 ff.); the problem recurs in *Philebus* 14C–18D (ibid. 206 ff.). The segment of the question which we encounter is more moral than epistemological, the contrast between the unity of virtue and the multiple forms of evil, as found, say, in *Rep.* 4. 445C ff. Origen took up the idea in *or.* 21. 2 (p. 345. 17 ff., M. 11. 481A), where 'one' is applied to 'virtue', 'truth', 'the wisdom of God', 'the word of God', and suitable contrasts are drawn. Cf. the n. in J. E. L. Oulton and H. Chadwick, *Alexandrian Christianity: Selected Translations of Clement and Origen* (LCC ii; London, 1954), 353.

48b–49. God, by definition good, could change only for the worse. Cf. Ath. *Ar.* 1. 18 (M. 26. 49B), Greg. Nyss. *Ep.* 3 (M. 46. 1020B).

τὸ δὲ πλέον ὄντος ἄλυξις is a tightly-packed expression: it is small wonder that Caillau expands it in his tr. The meaning may be explained in this way. As God is the sum of all good, if it were possible to add any qualities to him they could be only evil ones. Such apparent additions would be, in effect, a diminution. Now the word ἄλυξις means 'escape'. It describes Cassandra's escape in A. *Ag.* 1299 and Greg. gives it this sense in v. 85 (cf. also Q.S. 12. 212). ὄντος ἄλυξις is then literally 'an escape from what is', a departure from absolute being.

50–2. *Angels and human beings.* The distinction between the second and the third grades of beings is expressed in terms of αἰθήρ and ἀήρ, the upper and lower atmosphere, nearer or farther from the sun. This is a traditional Greek contrast, going back to Heraclitus. The αἰθήρ is pure, often fiery (cf. αἴθω), heavenly substance, 'living and divine' (W. K. C. Guthrie, 'The Presocratic World-Picture', *HTR* 45 (1952), 87–104 at 93. Cf. also id., *History*, i. 471). The ἀήρ round the earth is less pure. In Christian thought it came to be thought of as the element of the demonic powers. Cf. Eph. 2. 2 (also *Asc.Is.* 11. 23). Further references in Arndt–Gingrich, s.v. ἀήρ, p. 20 and for the Greek Fathers *PGL* s.v. ἀήρ A. 6.

COMMENTARY ON *ARC*. 6. 52-5

52. ἠέρες: Greg. identifies men with the earthly 'climates', more distantly affected by the sun. (For the plural in this sense cf. Hippocrates, and Pl. *Phd*. 98c–d.)

53-5. *The nature of angels.* The position of God and man is clear: they stand at opposite ends of the scale of change. It is the nature of the angels which is in doubt. Caillau's n., implying that there is a distinction between the original state of the angels and their later state, cannot be justified in the text ('De prima angelorum creatione haec sunt intelligenda'). There is no differentiation between the original and any later state. Lucifer fell. As his nature was no different from that of the other angels, angelic nature must include some possibility of change. Greg.'s problem is that, seeing the continuity between the nature of Lucifer and that of the other angels, he cannot resist the conclusion that angels are still liable to turn to evil. Origen mentions the possibility in *hom. 4 in Ezech*. 2 (p. 363. 11 ff., M. 13. 698d ff.). Cyril of Jerusalem taught his catechumens that, as 'one alone is without sin', the angels needed forgiveness, though he declined to speculate on the reasons, *cat.* 2. 10 (M. 33. 393b). In *hom. in Ps.* 32 Basil is unwilling to go beyond δυσμετάθετος in characterizing the nature of the angels:

ἀλλ' ἐν τῇ πρώτῃ συστάσει καὶ τῷ οἱονεὶ φυράματι τῆς οὐσίας αὐτῶν συγκαταβληθεῖσαν ἔσχον τὴν ἁγιότητα. διὸ καὶ δυσμετάθετοί εἰσι πρὸς κακίαν, εὐθύς, οἱονεὶ βαφῇ τινι, τῷ ἁγιασμῷ στομωθέντες καὶ τὸ μόνιμον εἰς ἀρετὴν τῇ δωρεᾷ τὸ μόνιμον εἰς ἀρετὴν τῇ δωρεᾷ τοῦ ἁγίου Πνεύματος ἔχοντες

(G. 1. 136b, M. 29. 333c f.)

Greg. himself uses δυσκίνητος in *or.* 28. 31: καθαρὰς φύσεις καὶ ἀκιβδήλους, ἀκινήτους πρὸς τὸ χεῖρον ἢ δυσκινήτους (p. 70. 14–15, M. 36. 72b). Cf. 6. 12 (M. 35. 737b). Mason and Barbel offer no comments in their editions, but Caillau wished to restrict the meaning to the Fall of Lucifer. He continues: 'Nunc enim ad malum immobiles sunt angeli per concessam ipsis constantiae ac perseverentiae gratiam.' But, again, the text lacks anything which would justify the interpretation. Greg. is talking about angelic nature in general. Probably, as in the present passage, it was the fall of Lucifer which made him modify his ἀκινήτους. But it is the result for all angelic nature which concerns him. Again in *or.* 38. 9 (M. 36. 321A. = 45. 5. 629b) we find Greg. showing precisely the same hesitation as in the present passage: Lucifer and the rebel angels compel him to call all angels δυσκινήτους, though his inclination is for ἀκινήτους.

He makes it clear that the fall of Lucifer is not analogous to the Fall of Adam, inasmuch as Lucifer's defection affected only those angels who chose to follow him. The others lost none of their glory, any more than the disciples lost theirs when Judas turned traitor, *carm.* I. 2. I. 680 ff. (M. 37. 574A), cf. I. 2. 3. 47–8 (636A). In *or.* 40. 7 (M. 36. 365B f.) we find Greg. groping towards an equation of sinlessness and simple, uncompounded nature, with sin adhering to the composite being. But there is an unexplained qualification which makes the simple angelic nature 'very nearly' sinless, a qualification which, if pressed, destroys the argument. If sin in any degree is attributable to the simple angelic beings, then it cannot be composite nature as such which causes sin. (Cf. Michl, *RAC*, v. 126 ff.)

Turmel discussed Greg.'s teaching on angels in *RHL* 3 (1898), 459–60. He saw Basil and Greg. as providing a link between earlier views of the angels' susceptibility to sin (pp. 457 ff.) and Augustine's assertion of their sinlessness. 'Il était réservé à Augustin d'aller jusqu'au bout de la voie frayée par les Cappadociens, et de proclamer la stabilité des anges dans le bien.' But it should be noticed that the difference between Augustine and the Cappadocians is a very important one. Indeed, it could be argued that Augustine's view is not simply the next step from the Cappadocian position. For the real dividing-line comes between ἄτροπος and δύστροπος. Here is a difference of kind. All that separates δύστροπος and εὔτροπος is a difference of degree. Though Greg. was obviously reluctant to admit it, the angels stood on the same side of the line as man in being subject to change, with God alone on the other side. Greg. does not talk about actual sins for which the angels must be purified, as did the Priscillianists whom Augustine attacks in *Ad Oros*. 8. 10 (M. *PL* 42. 674 f.), but he does leave open the possibility of change, which must include change for the worse, sin.

56–66. *The Fall of Lucifer*

56. τοὔνεκεν: because evil could not exist close to God's light, Lucifer had to be banished to distant darkness.

Ἑωσφόρος: one of the passages which Basil and Greg. included in the *Philocalia*, I. 25 (Robinson, p. 31. 22 ff.) = *princ.* 4. 3. 9 (p. 336. 4 ff., M. 11. 392A) speaks of the impossibility of identifying with Nebuchadnezzar the figure who fell from heaven and who is called ἑωσφόρος (Isa. 14. 12 πῶς ἐξέπεσεν ἐκ τοῦ οὐρανοῦ ὁ ἑωσφόρος ὁ πρωὶ ἀνατέλλων;). In *princ*. I. 5. 5 (pp. 75 ff., M. 11. 163A ff.) Origen

COMMENTARY ON *ARC.* 6. 56–9

makes clear the identification of the 'Lucifer' of Isaiah with the Satan who, in Luke 10. 18, fell 'like lightning from heaven'; cf. also *philoc.* 26. 7 (Robinson, p. 240. 14 ff.); *hom. 12 in Num.* 4 (p. 105. 3 ff., M. 12. 655A ff.). This connection was quite widely accepted; cf. Turmel ('Coulange'), *The Life of the Devil*, 1 ff. Methodius, who differed from Origen on the reason for Satan's Fall, agreed with him in seeing in Isa. 14. 12 ff. a key text; *res.* 1. 37 (p. 279. 1 ff., M. 41. 1104B).

57–9. The background to the present passage will be found in Isa. 14. 13 ff.: εἰς τὸν οὐρανὸν ἀναβήσομαι, ἐπάνω τῶν ἀστέρων τοῦ οὐρανοῦ θήσω τὸν θρόνον μου . . . ἔσομαι ὅμοιος τῷ ὑψίστῳ; see too Ezek. 28. 12 ff. Cf. Jerome, *in Ezech.* lib. 9 c. 28 (M. *PL* 25. 266C f.). Theodoret, considering the common application of the title ἑωσφόρος to Christ, an exegesis of Ps. 109 (110 Heb.). 3 found from Justin, *dial.* 45. 4 (M. 6. 572D; Goodspeed, p. 142) onwards, explains: Ἑωσφόρον αὐτὸν καλεῖ οὐχ ὡς τοῦτο ἀληθῶς ὄντα, ἀλλ᾽ ὡς τοῦτο εἶναι φαντασθέντα καὶ δεῖξαι βουληθεὶς τὴν ἀθρόαν τῆς περιφανείας μεταβολήν, ἀπείκασεν Ἑωσφόρῳ ἐκ τοῦ οὐρανοῦ εἰς γῆν πεσόντι, *Is.* (S. 2. 268, M. 81. 333C); cf. also id., *Ezech.* (S. 2. 916, M. 81. 1097A f.), on *Ezech.* 28. 16. Greg., however, nowhere applies the title to Christ, though Basil, for instance, did so in *Eun.* 2. 17 (G. 1. 252D, M. 29. 608A). There is a passing reference to Lucifer in *or.* 36. 5 (M. 36. 269C), but no discussion of the title. (Cf. the passage cited on v. 59.)

βασιληίδα τιμὴν is a Homeric reminiscence: δῶκε δέ οἱ τιμῆς βασιληΐδος ἥμισυ πάσης (*Il.* 6. 193, the story of Bellerophon).

αἴγλην: cf. *Arc.* 3. 28 n. and v. 96 below.

59. ὅλον σκότος ἀντὶ Θεοῖο: the only possible sense is 'total darkness instead of God (as he aspired to become)'. Cf. *or.* 36. 5 (M. 36. 269C): οὗτος (sc. φθόνος) καὶ τὸν Ἑωσφόρον ἐσκότισε καταπεσόντα δι᾽ ἔπαρσιν· οὐ γὰρ ἤνεγκε, θεῖος ὤν, μὴ καὶ Θεὸς νομισθῆναι. In *or.* 6. 13 (M. 35. 737C) there is the simpler contrast σκότος ἀντὶ φωτός. Cf. also *or.* 38. 9 (M. 36. 321A). 'Darkness', as is clear from *Arc.* 4. 24 ff., is, in Greg. as in the Fathers generally, a realm of total negativity and deprivation. Denied positive power of motivation, σκότος may stand for ignorance, falsehood, the evil desires of the mind or, as here, for the demonic world of Satan. It is the domain of evil spirits in magical papyri (*PGM* 36. 138) and in Matt. 8. 12, 22. 13, 25. 30 'the outer darkness' is the place of punishment. In the Johannine literature σκοτία comes to stand for all evil powers opposing God, as in John 1. 5, 8. 12, 12. 35, 46 and 1 John 1. 5, 2. 8–9, 11. σκοτία is the place where demons live in *Hom. Clem.* 20. 9 and *Const. App.* 5. 16. 6.

When patristic writers are seeking a more positive evaluation of darkness, as we find it in Exod. 20. 21 where it is God who inhabits the darkness of a thick cloud, they tend to use γνόφος the LXX tr. for '*ărāpel* in the Exod. passage, as distinct from the regular Heb. word for 'darkness', *ḥōšek*, for which σκότος or σκοτία are used. Cf. e.g. Nyssen, *hom. I in Cant.* (M. 44. 773 B). When the human soul is able to discard reliance on rational processes it may progress through γνόφος to a true mystical experience of God (*hex.* M. 44. 65 C; *v.Mos.* M. 44. 376 D). γνόφος is the apt locus of contemplation and, indeed, may be equated with it. There is discussion of this aspect of Nyssen in Lossky, *Vision*, 70 ff., Louth, *Origins*, 80 ff. and Williams, *Wound*, 52 ff.

60–72 describe Lucifer's resultant state. Greg. thinks of the substance of Lucifer in quasi-physical terms. As being κοῦφος he would naturally ascend to the upper air. It is despite his constitution (which apparently remains unchanged) that Lucifer descends to the lower world.

χθαμαλὴν indicates what is low both physically and in status.

ὀλισθάνω has both literal and figurative usages in Classical Greek (cf. Ar. *Ra.* 690 for the sense of a moral fall).

61–6. *Lucifer's envy of men.* In a number of earlier writers it is this that is the reason for his Fall, Iren. *haer.* 4. 40. 3 (M. 7. 1113 C); see Turmel, *RHL* 3 (1898), 289 ff., *The Life of the Devil*, 8 ff. Nyssen writes in this vein in *or. catech.* 6 (p. 32. 9 ff., M. 45. 28 B). Satan is the angel in charge of earthly creatures who falls through his envy of man's godlike status. Now in Nazianzen Satan's primary envy is aroused by God's glory and his Fall results from the proud spirit which sets itself up against God. In this view he follows Origen and is in line with such writers as Eusebius, Chrysostom, and Theodoret. (Cf. Turmel, *The Life of the Devil*, 12 ff.) Satan's enmity with man follows from his enmity with God. It is as an act of spiteful revenge that Satan shows his envy for man, God's favoured creature. The envy of man is secondary.

62. For λώβην cf. *Arc.* 4. 52 n.

64. **Πλάσμα Θεοῦ:** cf. Gen. 2. 7: καὶ ἔπλασεν ὁ Θεὸς τὸν ἄνθρωπον χοῦν ἀπὸ τῆς γῆς. Justin had applied the word πλάσμα to Adam, *dial.* 40. 1 (p. 137, M. 6. 561 B). For Greg.'s use of the expression cf. *or.* 24. 9 (M. 35. 1180 B), 31. 11 (p. 158. 7, M. 36. 144 D).

65. τὸ: here in the sense of 'wherefore' as in Epic (LSJ s.v. ὁ ἡ τό A VIII. 2 and 3).

For similar language in Greg. cf. *carm.* 2. 1. 54. 6–7 (M. 37. 1398A). In Gen. 3. 24 the subject of ἐξέβαλεν is God, but the meaning is not necessarily altered if, to lay stress on Satan's part, he is said to have been the instrument of man's expulsion. Cf. Iren. *dem.* 16. 'man he [Satan] caused to be cast out of Paradise', tr. J. A. Robinson, *St. Irenaeus: The Demonstration of the Apostolic Preaching* (London, 1920), 84.

66. βάσκανος: cf. *M. Polyc.* 17. 1 (Bihlmeyer, p. 129. 7). Greg. has the same expression in *carm.* 1. 1. 27. 8 (M. 37. 499A). Gigante cites the passages of Greg. as the probable origin of βάσκανος in Eugenius Panormitanus 20. 8 (*Versus Iambici*, 196).

67–81. *The origin of demonic powers on earth*

Lucifer inspired other angels with the same pride and took them with him at his Fall to become demonic tempters of men.

67. οὐρανίης ἐξ ἄντυγος: cf. *AP* 9. 806 (anon.), 11. 292 (Palladas, 4th c. AD), Ps.-Manetho, 2(1). 68.

70. Greg. writes as a loyal citizen of the Empire to whom anyone who attempted to disrupt the Emperor's power would appear 'sinful' (cf. *Arc.* 5. 21 n.). If Greg. is thinking in specific, rather than general, terms, he may be remembering his old enemy Julian who detached his army from its allegiance to Constantius, an emperor much venerated by Greg.

ἀπορρήξας: Josephus has the passive in the sense of breaking allegiance (*BJ* 2. 14. 3).

71–2. Lucifer provided himself with subjects to rival those of the supreme God.

73–81. *Catalogue of the evils introduced by the fallen angels.* Lists of evils are not uncommon in Christian literature. In the NT we may find precedents in Mark 7. 21–2, Rom. 1. 29 ff., 1 Cor. 6. 9–10, Gal. 5. 20. Cf. also among verse writers the lists given in *orac. Sib.* 1. 175–9 (GCS, p. 14), 2. 255–83 (pp. 40 ff.) and by Ps.-Manetho 2(1) 301 ff. Athanasius provides a comprehensive catalogue of the sins and evils which assail mankind (*inc.* 5. 3–4, M. 25. 105B ff.), but makes them dependent on the Fall of Adam. Here the influx of evil into the world is a direct result of the Fall in heaven. In Greg., cf. *carm.* 2. 1. 13. 75 ff. (M. 37. 1233A f.).

COMMENTARY ON *ARC*. 6. 73–8

73. ἐβλάστησαν: the word is well tr. by Caillau's 'pullularunt'.

74. ἀνδροφόνοιο: cf. *Arc*. 4. 49 n.

ἀδρανέα: they are weak when compared with their former angelic power. Greg. has no doubt of their strength when compared with men.

σκιοέντα . . . φάσματα: the Epic form comes into an expression which looks back to Pl. *Phd*. 81 D, where σκιοειδῆ φαντάσματα refers to the souls which are still unable to escape completely from their bodies.

φάσματα νυκτός: cf. Soph. *El*. 501 τόδε φάσμα νυκτὸς.

76. ψεῦσται: cf. (of their leader) John 8. 44.

διδάσκαλοι ἀμπλακιάων: demons were thought to have taught men such evil practices as worshipping idols, cf. Athen. *leg*. 26. 1 (p. 292, M. 6. 94 D ff.) and believing in fate, cf. Tat. *orat*. 9 (p. 9. 23 ff., M. 6. 825 A ff.).

77. πλάγκται: only here and in 1. 2. 2. 318 (M. 37. 603A) is the form πλάγκτης (= πλαγκτήρ, 'deceiver') found.

ζωροπόται: they encouraged 'hard' drinking, i.e., of unmixed wine.

φιλομειδέες: Homer uses the form φιλομμειδής of Aphrodite in *Il*. 3. 424, *Od*. 8. 362, but the tone of the present passage is better represented by *AP* 9. 524. 22 (anon.) where Dionysus is so described (also in the φιλομμειδής form). Though Greg. may be thinking of the roistering laughter which Eph. 5. 4 calls εὐτραπελία, we form the impression that he was not much given to laughter in any of its forms. In *or*. 8. 9 (M. 35. 800A) he praises his sister Gorgonia for thinking that even the ghost of a smile was something of an event, cf. *carmm*. 1. 2. 34. 111 (M. 37. 953A); 1. 2. 33. 77 ff. (933A f.). The μηδ-form is a curiosity, recalling perhaps a confused memory of Hes. *Th*. 200.

ἐγρεσίκωμοι: here again is an epithet applied to Dionysus in the same poem (*AP* 9. 524. 6): Εὔιον, εὐχαίτην, εὐάμπελον, ἐγρεσίκωμον.

78. χρησμολόγοι: here too we may have a word whose choice is influenced by its possible connection with a Greek god, this time Apollo, the god of the Delphic oracle. There is a contemptuous ring here in a word which early became associated with the dubious profession of oracle-monger.

It may not be coincidence that Greg. turns to epithets which had been or might be applied to Greek gods. There is a long patristic

210

tradition of equating heathen gods with demons, going back certainly as far as the Apologists; cf. *PGL* s.vv. δαιμόνιον 3. c and δαίμων C. 1–3. Origen, for instance, cites Ps. 95 (96 Heb.). 5 as evidence: ὅτι πάντες οἱ θεοὶ τῶν ἐθνῶν δαιμόνια, *Cels.* 3. 2 (p. 204. 25 ff., M. 11. 921D ff.) In 3. 28 (p. 225. 20–1, M. 11. 956A f.) he calls Apollo a δαίμων.

λοξοί: it is possible that λοξοί is to be taken with χρησμολόγοι. If Greg. could break the strict pattern of four independent words in v. 76, there is no reason why he should not do so here also. λοξός describes the ambiguous character of oracles in Lycophron 14 and 1467, Luc. *Alex.* 10 and elsewhere; cf. Λοξίας as an epithet of Apollo.

φιλοδήριες: *PGL* cites φιλόδηρις as a *hapax*.

αἱματόεντες: either as inciting men to violence or as encouraging sacrifice. For the second cf. Athenag. *leg.* 26. 1 (M. 6. 949D; Goodspeed, p. 246): (sc. 'demons') οἱ προσεστηκότες τῷ ἀπὸ τῶν ἱερείων αἵματι καὶ ταῦτα περιλιχμώμενοι.

79. Ταρτάρεοι: this is perhaps an allusion to the view that some of the demons are in Hades while others inhabit the air. Cf. Eus. *p.e.* 7. 16 (p. 329B ff., M. 21. 556C), a passage which sees the majority of the fallen angels as condemned immediately to Tartarus, with only a small number left on earth and in the lower air to provide good men with the necessary elements of conflict. But the epithet may mean no more than 'horrible' (cf. E. *HF* 907).

μυχόεντες: μυχόεις is a *hapax legomenon*. The word is suggested by the preceding Ταρτάρεοι, the noun μυχός being regularly associated with Tartarus. Cf. Hes. *Th.* 119 Τάρταρά τ᾽ ἠερόεντα μυχῷ χθονός; *or. Sib.* 4. 186 (GCS p. 102) Τάρταρά τ᾽ εὐρώεντα μυχοὶ στύγιοί τε γεένης, 8. 362 (GCS p. 165) οἶδα μυχοὺς γαίης καὶ Τάρταρα ἠερόεντα; Greg. *carm.* 2. 2 (epit.), 40. 5 (M. 38. 31A) Ταρτάρεοί τε μυχοί, 2. 2 (poem.). 5. 125 (M. 37. 1530A) ζοφερούς τε μυχούς, καὶ Τάρταρον αἰνὸν (cf. also for similar expressions E. *Supp.* 926, *Tr.* 952). We might perhaps take Ταρτάρεοι and μυχόεντες together as giving a picture of demons living in murky, underground holes in the earth but, differently from the opinion of Eusebius, emerging to harry mankind. The whole concern of the passage is with the effect the demons have upon men and it is unlikely that Greg. would here be interested in any that were immobilized in Hades.

ἀρχιγόητες: ἀρχιγόης is again a *hapax legomenon*. *PGL* glosses 'arch-impostor'. But it is also possible that a reference to magic is intended. γόης has the regular meaning of 'sorcerer' as well as 'impostor'. Demons are associated with magic in Justin, *I Apol*. 26. 2 (Goodspeed, p. 42; M. 6. 368A), Origen, *Cels*. 1. 60 (pp. 110–11, M. 11. 769B ff.), *hom. 16 in Num*. 7 (p. 147. 24 ff., M. 12. 698A).

80. This line gives some support to the suggestion that magic is referred to in the previous one, for καλέω means to summon by use of a magic formula. Cf. Origen, *Cels*. 1. 60 (p. 110. 23–4, M. 11. 769B) ὅτι μάγοι δαίμοσιν ὁμιλοῦντες καὶ τούτους ἐφ᾽ ἃ μεμαθήκασι καὶ βούλονται καλοῦντες ποιοῦσι κτλ.

81. λοχόωντες: cf. H. *Od*. 16. 369.

82–95. *Christ and the demons*

There was no arbitrary exercise of force against the devil, in whose continued existence Christ demonstrated divine purpose. The thought here is in line with what earlier Fathers had said about God's consistent desire to avoid the use of tyrannical force. Cf. e.g. *Diogn*. 7. 3 ff. (Bihlmeyer, p. 145. 25 f., M. 2. 1177A); Iren. *haer*. 4. 59. 3 (M. 7. 1110D ff.), 5. 1. 1 (1121B ff.); Orig. *hom. 20 in Jerem*. 2 (p. 177. 27 ff., M. 13. 501B ff.).

85. Cf. Nah. 1. 6. Here ἄλυξις is found in its normal meaning of 'escape' (cf. v. 48 n.).

86–7. *The status of Satan*. Greg. emphasizes the subordinate position of Satan in the divine economy, over against any dualistic notion, by using of him the same formula which he applied to man's position: οὔτ᾽ ἀνέηκεν ἐλεύθερον (*Arc*. 7. 100). In calling Satan μέσον, Greg. is using the word in a different way from that in which Eusebius applies it to Christ, *d.e*. 4. 10 (p. 167. 34, M. 22. 280B), who is μέσος in that he participates in both Godhead and manhood; cf. Ath. *Ar*. 2. 24 (M. 26. 200A). Satan does not mediate between good and evil men, as Christ mediates between God and man, being himself both, but is intermediary only in the sense that, being totally committed to one side, he has access to the other. He may be compared to an ambassador of an unfriendly power.

88–9. Where there is conflict between good and evil, it occurs as part of God's plan, not as existent in its own right. Contrast this with the Manichaean dualism of *Arc*. 4.

91. The common figure of refining may be illustrated from such passages as Pl. *Rep*. 413D f., 503A; Isa. 48. 10; Zech. 13. 9; Mal. 3. 2–3;

1 Cor. 3. 13; 1 Pet. 1. 7; Rev. 3. 18. For the part which purification played in Greg.'s thought cf. *Arc.* 1. 8b–15 n.

92-5. *The punishment of Lucifer.* Billius took it that Lucifer's punishment was to be eternal ('poenas dabit ille perennes'). But this distorts the meaning. ἀτειρής is not an adverb describing the manner of the punishment: it is an adjective depicting the character of the sufferer, as in *carm.* 2. 1. 1. 540 (M. 37. 1010A). Greg. is asking, albeit tentatively, whether the devil, for all his stubborn resistance (ἀτειρής), may not ultimately complete his punishment.

On this issue of the possibility of Satan's redemption, Nazianzen contrived to be something less than definite. Origen had been strongly inclined to believe in the final restoration of the devil; cf. Kelly, *Doctrines*, 474: '. . . the doctrine is insinuated, if not actually taught, in his writings as well as taken for granted by his adversaries.' Nyssen shows the same tendency. He writes, for instance, in *or. catech.* 26 (p. 98. 17 ff., M. 45. 68D) (*sc.* Christ) οὐ μόνον τὸν ἀπολωλότα διὰ τούτων εὐεργετῶν, ἀλλὰ καὶ αὐτὸν τὸν τὴν ἀπώλειαν καθ᾿ ἡμῶν ἐνεργήσαντα. Basil went quite the other way, holding out for the eternal punishment of all sinners, let alone Satan; cf. e.g. *Spir.* 16. 40 (G. 3. 34B ff., M. 32. 141A ff.), Kelly, *Doctrines*, 483–4. But Nazianzen does not go beyond the τάχα of the present passage or the possibility that there is a milder interpretation than the eternal fire of punishment: πάντα γὰρ ταῦτα τῆς ἀφανιστικῆς ἐστι δυνάμεως· εἰ μή τῳ φίλον κἀνταῦθα νοεῖν τοῦτο φιλανθρωπότερον, καὶ τοῦ κολάζοντος ἐπαξίως, *or.* 40. 36 (M. 36. 412A f.). There is no doubt that he takes this alternative to eternal fire seriously and ἐπαξίως appears to show some sympathy for it. But more than that cannot be said.

93-5. Satan's punishment takes place in two stages: through seeing the distresses of his subordinates and in his own person.

93. δαπτομένης: this reading is to be preferred to Caillau's δ᾿ ἁπτομένης. The sentence certainly runs more easily without the δέ. Indeed, it is difficult to see how the particle could be fitted into the grammar of the genitive absolute. If δαπτομένης is read, we have an equally good verb for consuming fire (cf. H. *Il.* 23. 183). Cf. Greg.'s own πυρὶ δαπτόμενος in *carm.* 1. 2. 14. 128 (M. 37. 765A) and *Arc.* 7. 8 n.

ὕλης here represents the gross element in Lucifer. It is not matter in the physical sense, of course. But neither is it something purely spiritual. Greg., as we have seen (v. 17 n.), is not prepared to dissociate σῶμα from the nature of the noetic beings. This corporeal element, however refined its nature, must still be accounted sufficiently substantial to be affected by fire. (Cf. Turmel, *The Life of the Devil*, 71 ff., who shows that as long as the demons were thought to have their substance of, say, air, there was no problem about their punishment. It was the assertion of complete spirituality which produced the difficulty.)

ἄμειψις = 'requital'. Cf. *Inscr. Prien*. 105. 18, where the word means 'repayment'.

95b. Cyril of Jerusalem's description of the devil as γεννήτωρ τῶν κακῶν may be compared, *catech*. 2. 4 (M. 33. 385 B).

96–9. *Conclusion*

For the claim to inspiration, cf. *Arc*. 1. 16–24 n.

97. Caillau's tr. 'primo et posteriore' is preferable to his interpretation of 'good' and 'bad' angels. What Greg. has been describing is precisely the contrast between the 'first' splendour shared by all the angels and the 'last' in which only the unfallen participate.

97b–98. μέτρον here has a different sense from that found in *Arc*. 4. 86. As, e.g., in Pl. *Tht*. 183 C, μέτρον means 'standard of judgement'. Whether in the heavenly or the earthly worlds, the standard is God. Cf. the words of Plotinus concerning the One, μέτρον γὰρ αὐτὸ καὶ οὐ μετρούμενον (5. 5. 4).

98b–99. God is the fixed point, the central light, and all judgement of worth is based upon proximity to, or distance from, him. The final words of the poem recapitulate the thought of its opening.

7. On the Soul

Title and purpose

Περὶ ψυχῆς is the agreed title. The Creation of man is linked with the nature of the divine element in him, the abstract discussion of the soul leading to the account of his Creation and Fall. In structure, the poem resembles *Arc.* 4, with an introduction devoted to an attack on opposing opinions leading to an exposition of Greg.'s own views.

Writing about Tertullian's *De Anima*, J. H. Waszink remarked that 'this work is not in the first place a scientific treatise but a refutation of heretical doctrines about the soul' (edn. p. 7*.) This is even more true of Greg.'s much slighter Περὶ ψυχῆς. Though Greg. would not have known Tertullian's work, comparison is instructive in reflecting a mass of common material.

Nyssen's *Dialogus de anima et resurrectione qui inscribitur Macrinia* (M. 46. 11–160) offers a survey of ideas, often in the form of contrasts with 'Greek' views. He dismisses Stoics and Epicureans in 21 B ff. Going farther afield, he attacks Manes, along with Greeks he claims hold a similar position (93). Transmigration attracts a fairly lengthy rebuttal (108 B ff.). The positive claims made for a Christian understanding of the soul include kinship to God through its status of being in God's image, coming into life and leaving it simultaneously with the body and the hope that all souls will finally be cleansed of all impurity and return to their primal state.

J. M. Mathieu has discussed certain aspects of Greg.'s treatment in his article 'Remarques sur l'anthropologie de Grégoire de Nazianze (*Poemata dogmatica*, VIII, 22–32; 78–96) et Porphyre', *Stud. Patr.* 17/3 (1982), 1115–19. He places Greg. within a context of writers who tackle similar themes, particularly showing affinities with Porphyry and Iamblichus, giving a good account of Greg.'s precise understanding.

1–52. *False theories of the soul*

The poem begins with a brief definition of the true nature of the soul, an earnest of the treatment to follow in vv. 53 ff. But the pattern quickly settles: from v. 36 on we find a series of traditional opinions processing before the reader to be controverted.

1. **ἄημα Θεοῦ:** cf. *carm*. 1. 2. 15. 151–2 (M. 37. 777A):

> ψυχὴ δ᾽ ἔστιν ἄημα Θεοῦ, καὶ κρείσσονα μοίρην
> αἰὲν ἄγαν ποθέει τῶν ὑπερουρανίων.

The present passage specifies the condition (μίξιν ἀνέτλη) of the soul which so aspires. Gen. 2. 7 reads: καὶ ἔπλασεν ὁ Θεὸς τὸν ἄνθρωπον χοῦν ἀπὸ τῆς γῆς· καὶ ἐνεφύσησεν εἰς τὸ πρόσωπον αὐτοῦ πνοὴν ζωῆς, καὶ ἐγένετο ὁ ἄνθρωπος εἰς ψυχὴν ζῶσαν. Greg's ἄημα is no more than a stylistic variation of πνοή. 'Flatus', the tr. of Billius and Caillau, is apt: it may mean either 'blowing' or 'breath'. If, however, we are reminded of Tertullian's use of *flatus* in *De Anima* 11 (M. *PL* 2. 664B, CCSL 2. 796. 7 ff., CSEL 20. 315. 3 ff.) or *adflatus* in *adv. Marc*. 2. 9 (M. *PL* 2. 294C, CCSL 1. 484. 22 f., CSEL 47. 345 ff.), we should notice that the intention of the two writers is different. Tertullian finds in *flatus/adflatus* a convenient distinction from *spiritus*, a distinction which he believes to correspond to a difference between πνοή and πνεῦμα; cf. Iren. *haer*. 5. 12. 2 (M. 7. 1152A ff.); see Waszink, *Tertulliani 'De Anima'*, 10*–14*, 193–5. But Greg. equates πνοή and πνεῦμα in vv. 73–4.

Though, in the instances cited by LSJ, ἄημα means 'blast, wind', the sense 'breath' may be readily derived from the verb ἄημι, which means either 'breathe' or 'blow'.

μίξιν: cf. v. 79 n.

3. **ἄφθιτος:** the view that the soul is mortal and destined to perish in the death of the body was a common Epicurean one. Cf. e.g. Epicurus *Sent*. II, *ap*. D.L. 10. 139 (71. 6–7 U.) and the passage of Lucretius beginning:

> nil igitur mors est ad nos neque pertinet hilum,
> quandoquidem natura animi mortalis habetur. (3. 830 f.)

Among the Stoics, Panaetius makes the same assertion (cf. Cic. *Tusc*. 1. 79): 'volt enim, quod nemo negat, quidquid natum sit interire; nasci autem animos, quod declaret eorum similitudo qui procreentur, quae etiam in ingeniis, non solum in corporibus appareat.'

4–6. Does εἰκόνα here mean the soul or the whole man? Either sense is possible in Greg. The first appears in *or*. 38. 11 (M. 36. 321D) = 45. 7 (M. 36. 632A), where he may be influenced by the thought of Origen. In *Cels*. 6. 63 (pp. 133–4, M. 11. 1393B ff.), distinguishing between the Logos who is the image and man who is κατ᾽ εἰκόνα, he dismisses the view that 'being in the image of God' refers either to the human body or to a combination of body and soul. That which is made in the image of God is the inner man. He concludes: ὅτε καὶ "ναός" ἐστι τοῦ ἐν τῷ "κατ᾽ εἰκόνα" ἀνειληφότος τοῦ Θεοῦ τὰ τοῦ Θεοῦ "τὸ σῶμα", τοῦ τοιαύτην ἔχοντος ψυχὴν καὶ ἐν τῇ ψυχῇ διὰ τὸ "κατ᾽ εἰκόνα" τὸν Θεόν. (p. 134. 10 ff. 1396Α). Indeed, this is in the general Platonic tradition of seeing the soul as the man; cf. *or.* 14. 6, M. 35. 865Α, together with J.-M. Szymusiak, *Éléments de théologie de l'homme selon saint Grégoire de Nazianze* (Rome, 1963), 32. n. 25. On the other hand, in v. 75 below εἰκών means the whole man, the composite. There is good reason for thinking that the second is the sense intended here. It is not the soul which is made mortal by sin, but man, the composite being made 'in the image', and called simply 'the image'. The soul does not perish with the body and, thus, the 'image' does not suffer complete dissolution.

5. The ignorance of the beasts contrasted with man is a commonplace in Greek, as also in Hebrew, e.g. Ps. 72 (73 Heb.). 22. Shakespeare and the Book of Common Prayer continue the tradition: 'a beast that wants discourse of reason' (*Hamlet*, I. ii. 150), 'like brute beasts that have no understanding' (Solemnization of Matrimony, Exhortation).

7–8. *The soul as fire.* This idea is found in varying forms in Heraclitus, Leucippus, Democritus, and the Stoics, with roots in popular belief (cf. Guthrie, *History*, i. 466).

(i) *Heraclitus*. Fire was for Heraclitus the first principle of the universe, as can be seen from DK i. 109. 5 ff., etc. It may well be that Philoponus was right in his interpretation: πῦρ δὲ οὐ τὴν φλόγα· . . . ἀλλὰ πῦρ ἔλεγε τὴν ξηρὰν ἀναθυμίασιν· ἐκ ταύτης οὖν εἶναι καὶ τὴν ψυχήν, *Comm. in Arist. De Anima* 405ᵃ25 (p. 87. 11 ff.). Cf. Ross's edn. of Aristotle's *De Anima* (Oxford, 1961), 181. But clearly Greg. does not credit Heraclitus with any such sophisticated thought about the nature of the fiery soul-substance. For him it is simply the fire which burns. Cf. the distinctions drawn by Nemesius in *nat. hom.* 2 (M. 40. 536Β). For further texts and discussion, cf. Kirk, Raven and Schofield, *The Presocratic Philosophers*, 198–9, 203–5.

(ii) *Leucippus and Democritus*. In *De Anima* 403ᵇ20 ff. Aristotle discusses the position of Democritus, linking the idea that the soul is fire or heat with the view that it is closely connected with respiration (cf. vv. 8–9 below, with n.). Taking as the characteristic of soul its ability to initiate motion (Cf. Ross, *Comm.*, p. 174 n. on κίνησις), Democritus holds that it is the spherical atoms of soul or fire which are best suited by their shape to set other atoms in motion.

ὅθεν Δημόκριτος μὲν πῦρ τι καὶ θερμόν φησιν αὐτὴν (sc. ψυχὴν) εἶναι·
ἀπείρων γὰρ ὄντων σχημάτων καὶ ἀτόμων τὰ σφαιροειδῆ πῦρ καὶ ψυχὴν
λέγει . . . ὧν τὴν μὲν πανσπερμίαν στοιχεῖα τῆς ὅλης φύσεως, . . . τούτων δὲ
τὰ σφαιροειδῆ ψυχήν, διὰ τὸ μάλιστα διὰ παντὸς δύνασθαι διαδύνειν τοὺς
τοιούτους ῥυσμοὺς καὶ κινεῖν τὰ λοιπά, κινούμενα καὶ αὐτά, ὑπολαμβά-
νοντες τὴν ψυχὴν εἶναι τὸ παρέχον τοῖς ζῴοις τὴν κίνησιν (403ᵇ31 ff.).

The initial ὅθεν connects with the primary characteristics of soul as motion. Whether Democritus meant to say that soul *is* fire or that it is *like* fire may be debated (cf. Aët. 4. 3. 5, Diels *Dox.* 388. 5 ff., and Guthrie, *History*, ii. 430 ff.); but again, it is unlikely that Greg. considered such refinements or went beyond Aristotle's account. For Democritus the soul was destructible and could be broken up into its component parts in the same way as the body in death. (Aët. 4. 7. 4, DK ii. 110. 24–5). Cf. v. 3 n.

Aristotle refers to Leucippus as 'agreeing' with Democritus (405ᵃ5). He would now generally be given a more original role. For the spherical atom which is both soul and fire cf. Kirk, Raven and Schofield, *The Presocratic Philosophers*, 427.

(iii) *The Stoics.* The Stoic view, as given by Zeno, is reported in Cicero *Tusc.* 1. 19: 'Zenoni Stoico animus ignis videtur' (cf. 1. 42; *N.D.* 2. 41–2; *Fin.* 4. 12; *Acad. Post.* 1. 39). Diogenes Laertius writes: Ζήνων δὲ ὁ Κιτιεὺς καὶ Ἀντίπατρος ἐν τοῖς Περὶ Ψυχῆς καὶ Ποσειδώνιος πνεῦμα ἔνθερμον εἶναι τὴν ψυχήν· τούτῳ γὰρ ἡμᾶς εἶναι ἐμπνόους καὶ ὑπὸ τούτου κινεῖσθαι (7. 157). Stoic thought was able to combine the doctrine of the fiery soul with a belief in the survival of the soul. At least, some Stoics were able to do so: Panaetius did not (cf. v. 3 n.). Cleanthes believed that all souls would survive the life of the body until the ἐκπύρωσις, when everything returns to God. Chrysippus restricts survival to the souls of the 'wise' (D.L. 7. 157). Cf. M. Pohlenz, *Die Stoa*, 3rd edn. (Göttingen, 1964), i. 229 ff.

Tertullian's treatment of the subject may be compared. When, writing in support of the corporeality of the soul, he cites Zeno, he does so without making any reference to fire: 'denique Zeno consitum spiritum definiens animam hoc modo instruit', *De An.* 5. 3 (M. *PL.* 2. 653 A, CCSL 2. 786. 13–14, CSEL 20. 304. 19–20). It is to

Hipparchus and to Heraclitus alone that he attributes the idea that the soul is 'ex igni', ibid. 5. 2 (653 A = p. 786. 5 ff; p. 304. 9 ff.), wrongly in the first case (cf. Waszink, edn. 127 ff.).

The corporeal nature of fire made the Stoic doctrine of the soul unacceptable to many, not least Neoplatonists. Plotinus thinks of fire as almost escaping the realm of corporeal things (cf. 1. 6. 3, 3. 6. 6), but the Stoic fire is consistently material. A good deal of Neoplatonic polemic was thus directed against the Stoics on the nature of the soul. (Cf. R. A. Norris Jr., *Manhood and Christ*, 23.)

μαλερός is in Homer a conventional epithet of fire. (Cf. *Il.* 9. 242, *al.*) By concentrating on the destructive element of fire Greg. is able to make the point that the body which is liable to be consumed has at its 'heart' the very element which would consume it. But the philosophers who connected fire with soul intended to draw attention to other characteristics of fire—its heat, for instance, which has a clear connection with life (cf. Guthrie, *History*, ii. 432).

δάπτον δαπτομένοιο: cf. *Arc.* 6. 93 n.

For κέαρ cf. vv. 19–20 n. It may here have the double sense of καρδία = 'soul' (*PGL* s.v. καρδία C) and καρδία = 'pith, core, heart' (LSJ s.v. καρδία III).

8b–9. *The soul as air* (ἀήρ is here to be distinguished from αἰθήρ, with its affinities to fire). The connection between the soul and the air which is breathed is very ancient and very widespread. 'That the air which we breathe should be the life itself which animates us is a common idea, and the breath-soul a world-wide conception' (Guthrie, *History*, i. 128; cf. the ensuing discussion and id., *The Greeks and their Gods* (London, 1950–4), ch. 5). This is the background against which the philosophers' teachings must be set. Anaximenes is reported thus: Ἀναξιμένης δὲ ὁ Μιλήσιος ἀρχὴν τῶν ὄντων ἀέρα ἀπεφήνατο, ἐκ γὰρ τούτου πάντα γίνεσθαι καὶ εἰς αὐτὸν ἀναλύεσθαι. οἷον ἡ ψυχή, φησιν, ἡ ἡμετέρα ἀὴρ οὖσα συγκρατεῖ ἡμᾶς, καὶ ὅλον τὸν κόσμον πνεῦμα καὶ ἀὴρ περιέχει (fr. 2; DK i. 95. 15 ff.); cf. the opinion of his follower Diogenes of Apollonia: ἄνθρωποι γὰρ καὶ τὰ ἄλλα ζῷα ἀναπνέοντα ζώει τῷ ἀέρι, καὶ τοῦτο αὐτοῖσι καὶ ψυχή ἐστι καὶ νόησις (fr. 4; DK ii. 60. 20–1). See further Pl. *Phd.* 96 B 4, Arist. *De An.* 405ᵃ21–2.

In Diogenes ἀήρ is held to be divine and, consequently, the human soul is μικρὸν . . . μόριον τοῦ Θεοῦ (Theophr. *de Sensu* 8. 42). The Orphic poets are cited by Aristotle for the notion of the soul breathed in from outside: φησὶ γὰρ τὴν ψυχὴν ἐκ τοῦ ὅλου εἰσιέναι ἀναπνεόντων, φερομένην ὑπὸ τῶν ἀνέμων (*An.* 410ᵇ28 ff.; the subject of φησὶ is a λόγος found in the Orphics). Among the Stoics the identification of soul and life-breath occurs in Chrysippus, according to Chalcidius, *comm. in Timaeum*, 220 (*SVF* ii. 879), and Tertullian expounds the opinion that soul and life-breath cannot be separated in *De An.* 10 (M. *PL* 2. 661 B ff., CCSL 2. 794 ff., CSEL 20. 312 ff.). Aristotle associates Diogenes with 'some others' in thinking of the soul as air (*De An.* 405ᵃ21). As Ross notes, Aëtius identifies these as Anaximenes, Anaxagoras, and Archelaus (*Plac.* 4. 3. 2), while Theodoret includes Anaximander (*Graec. Aff. Cur.* 5. 18).

ἀποπνευστοῦ: a *hapax legomenon*. The only other recorded instance of πνευστός is in Greg.'s 2. 2 (poem.) 5. 71 (M. 37. 1526A).

ἰσταμένοιο: motion might be associated with the soul in two ways. The soul might be that which initiates motion (cf. vv. 7–8 n.; *Democritus*), or that which is in constant movement, as air was to Anaximenes (*Dox.* 579. 21 ff.). The words are here taken in a pejorative sense, implying instability (cf. LSJ s.v. ἵστημι B. II. 2).

10. *The soul as blood.* As is the case with breath, there is a primitive association of the soul with blood. Plato includes both in the possibilities mentioned in *Phd.* 96B4. At the time when the *Phaedo* was written, the name most firmly linked with the theory of the soul as blood was that of Empedocles, whose thought is preserved in these lines:

αἵματος ἐν πελάγεσσι τεθραμμένη ἀντιθορόντος,
τῇ τε νόημα μάλιστα κικλήσκεται ἀνθρώποισιν·
αἷμα γὰρ ἀνθρώποις περικάρδιόν ἐστι νόημα

(Stob. *Ecl.* 1. 49, p. 424; fr. 105, DK i. 350, 13 ff.). The idea continued to be mainly associated with him, cf. Thphr. *de Sensu* 2. 10; Cic. *Tusc.* 1. 19 ('Empedocles animum esse censet cordi suffusum sanguinem.'); Eusebius (citing Plutarch) *p.e.* 1. 8 (24D, M. 21. 60D). See further Guthrie, *History* ii. 226, 228 ff. However, Aristotle assigns it to Critias (*An.* 405ᵇ6; DK i. 375. 24–6) and is followed in this by Nemesius 2. 67 (p. 16. 16 Morani, M. 40. 53b B), who unlike Greg. takes the trouble to argue against it (2. 73–5, 541 B ff.). Blood is no more an indispensable part of the body than bile or liver. Why not call them 'soul'? Again, he claims, as some animate creatures are bloodless there is a further proof that blood and soul are not to be identified.

But the question is given a more than doxographic interest by the connection in Hebrew thought also of blood with the soul. Gen. 9. 4

makes clear the link between *nepeš* and *dām* (LXX: πλὴν κρέας ἐν
αἵματι ψυχῆς οὐ φαγέσθαι.) Cf. Lev. 17. 14, 18 and Deut. 12. 23
(with the n. of S. R. Driver in *ICC* (Edinburgh, 1896), 148-9). On the
link in Hebrew thought between blood and soul one might mention
A. R. Johnson, *The Vitality of the Individual in the Thought of Ancient
Israel* (Cardiff, 1964), 8-9, 69 ff., 87-8.

Clement had rejected the Greek version of the doctrine in *paed*. 1.
6 (pp. 113 ff., M. 8. 296 B ff.), but Origen records that Lev. 17. 14 had
been used to support a theory of two souls in man, a higher and a
lower, the lower being present in the blood and being subject to
bodily desires, *princ*. 3. 4. 2 (p. 265. 4 ff., M. 11. 320 C ff.). The *Dia-
logus cum Heraclide* shows Origen again faced with the question of
identifying the soul and blood. Origen's reply makes a distinction
between the physical blood and the blood of the inner man, a
spiritual interpretation which removes the issue entirely from its
original context; see J. Scherer, *Entretien d'Origène avec Héraclide et les
évêques ses collègues sur le Père, le Fils, et l'Âme* (Cairo, 1949), 144-5; cf.
J. W. Trigg, *Origen* (Atlanta and London, 1985), 175-6.

11-17. *The soul as harmony.* The basic image is that of a lyre in tune
(ἡρμοσμένη). We must distinguish two ways in which the term
ἁρμονία might be, and was, applied to the soul: (*a*) the soul is a
harmony of corporeal parts or of physical opposites; (*b*) the soul is a
harmony of its own internal parts (a Pythagorean view which influ-
enced Plato, cf. Arist. *Metaphys*. 985^{b}26 ff. and Guthrie, *History*, i.
316-17). It is with the first that we are here concerned. This is the
form of the theory discussed in Pl. *Phd*. 85 E 3-86 D 4, 88 D 2-E-2,
91 C 6-95 A 3 and in Arist. *An*. 407^{b}27-408^{a}28. In Plato Simmias is
made to argue that the soul is the 'blending or attunement' (Hack-
forth's tr. of κρᾶσιν . . . καὶ ἁρμονίαν) of the four elements, the hot,
the cold, the dry, the moist. He deduces that the soul is destroyed
with the destruction of these opposites in death. The counter-
arguments of Socrates show that this reasoning is inconsistent with
the idea of the pre-existent soul which Simmias accepts and go on
to claim that, on this understanding, the soul must be subject to, not
master of, the elements. Aristotle's reasons for rejecting the attune-
ment theory centre on the contention that it does not answer to what
we know of the soul's functions. For instance, the soul initiates
movement where harmony does not; harmony cannot account for
the soul's active and passive experiences. Plotinus in his turn writes
against the soul-harmony notion in 4. 7. 8[4].

Of this theory in Greg.'s time and earlier R. A. Norris Jr. has observed that it 'does not seem to have been in any sense a live option. It was known largely through the doxographic tradition of the schools, and there is no indication that it was seriously maintained by any philosopher of the imperial period' (*Manhood and Christ*, 22).

Yet, though Greg. may be indulging in a rather antiquarian form of polemics, his argument is not without interest. His objections are both anthropological and moral. His anthropology assumes an essential gulf between the soul and the parts of the body. The human body is not basically different from animal bodies. Why then should the human soul differ from that of a well-attuned beast? But it is Greg.'s moral objection which takes the real weight. His arguments, while showing affinities with those of Plato and Aristotle, differ noticeably from theirs. Greg.'s distinction of the φύσις of flesh and soul depends on the kind of dichotomy which made Plato insist on the governing function of soul (*Phd.* 94 c 9 ff.). (Cf. Aristotle on the soul's inauguration of movement in *An.* 407ᵇ34–5.) Greg., however, approaches the question of good and evil in a different way. Plato argued that a harmony is an absolute (*Phd.* 94 A 1–4) and that the application of the theory would mean that all souls would be equally good (94 A 8–10). Greg., on the other hand, appears to admit at least the theoretical existence of different attunements, perhaps on the analogy of different instruments which, through their varying physical components, produce varying attunements. Greg. objects, not to the possibility, but to the morality, of applying such an analogy to the soul. To make the soul in any way dependent on the flesh is hard for Greg. To make it entirely so is unthinkable. Moral distinctions which rest upon physical constitution would be quite illusory.

11. A unifying principle should be separate from, not a function of, the diverse bodily elements.

12–13a. According to the accepted text, the soul is called εἶδος ἀθά-νατον. It is possible that what produced this expression is Aristotle's way of using εἶδος in relation to the soul; cf. *An.* 412ᵃ19 ff. ἀναγκαῖον ἄρα τὴν ψυχὴν οὐσίαν εἶναι ὡς εἶδος σώματος φυσικοῦ δυνάμει ζωὴν ἔχοντος. ἡ δ᾽ οὐσία ἐντελέχεια· τοιούτου ἄρα σώματος ἐντελέχεια; ibid. 412ᵃ27–8 διὸ ἡ ψυχή ἐστιν ἐντελέχεια ἡ πρώτη σώματος φυσικοῦ δυνάμει ζωὴν ἔχοντος. What Aristotle intended by this terminology has been much debated. (Cf. the note in Ross's edn., pp. 166–7 and R. A. Norris Jr., *Manhood and Christ*, 22–3.) But what concerns us here is the meaning which Greg. and his contemporaries were likely to place upon Aristotle's words. If we go back earlier, to Plotinus, we find that he goes straight from discussing the soul as harmony to attacking Aristotle's entelechy (4. 7. 8⁴, 8⁵). He attacks on the ground that, to make the soul the εἶδος of the material body by making it inseparable from the body (Arist. *An.* 413ᵃ4), is tantamount to destroying all its independent experience. His conclusion is this: οὐκ ἄρα τῷ εἶδος εἶναί τινος τὸ εἶναι ἔχει, ἀλλ᾽ ἔστιν οὐσία οὐ παρὰ τὸ ἐν σώματι ἱδρῦσθαι, τὸ εἶναι λαμβάνουσα, ἀλλ᾽ οὖσα πρὶν καὶ τοῦδε γενέσθαι, οἷον ζῴου οὐ τὸ σῶμα τὴν ψυχὴν γεννήσει (4. 7. 8⁵. 40 ff.).

There is no evidence that the Neoplatonists altered their views on this interpretation and Greg. may well have been acquainted with it as a standard assessment of Aristotle's position, one which is, it may be remarked, not necessarily an unfair one. For there is some point in Plotinus' treatment of the εἶδος theory immediately after that of ἁρμονία. It is not an ancient, but a modern, commentator, Sir David Ross, who points out that Aristotle may have had the ἐντελέχεια idea suggested to him by the Pythagorean teaching on the harmony of the body; cf. p. 15 of his edn. of *De Anima*, together with 407ᵇ27–408ᵃ28 n. (p. 195), where a remark of R. D. Hicks on the affinity of the two ideas is noted. Greg.'s εἴδεος ἀθανάτοιο would come as a direct contradiction to the entelechy of body. The eternal εἶδος is opposed to the transient one which would depend on physical constitution. Cf. Nemesius' understanding of Aristotle. He takes it that Aristotle taught that soul was merely something latent in matter. Cf. *nat. hom.* 2. 93–102 (pp. 26. 10–29. 18 Morani, M. 40. 560ʙ ff.), esp. 94–6.

The *v.l.* εἴδεος ἀνθρώποιο (cf. Caillau n.) is possible as an alternative periphrasis for 'soul'. For εἶδος here might mean 'essence', as it does in Arist. *Metaph.* 1032ᵇ1–2: εἶδος δὲ λέγω τὸ τί ἦν εἶναι ἑκάστου καὶ τὴν πρώτην οὐσίαν. This agrees with the Platonic tradition of thinking that the soul *is* the man (cf. vv. 4–6 n. above). Cf. Plotinus 4. 7. 1. 22 ff.: τὸ δὲ κυριώτατον καὶ αὐτὸς ὁ ἄνθρωπος· εἴπερ τοῦτο, κατὰ τὸ εἶδος ὡς πρὸς ὕλην τὸ σῶμα ἢ κατὰ τὸ χρώμενον ὡς πρὸς ὄργανον· ἑκατέρως δὲ ἡ ψυχὴ αὐτός. On the other hand, Nicetas read εἴδους ἀθανάτου in his paraphrase, and the attestation of ἀνθρώποιο is slight.

14. κρᾶσις: this short α form with acute accent is otherwise unattested. The simplest explanation is to assume a false quantity; cf. Introd. IV(*c*). κρᾶσις is associated with ἁρμονία in Pl. *Phd* 86ᵇ9, as was seen above. But we see here also a possible reference to that identification of the four elements, the hot, the cold, the dry, and the moist, with the four humours of the medical writers. This idea clearly influenced Nemesius. He accepted an anthropology in which man's material body is formed of the same four elements as animal bodies and, indeed, as inanimate objects, *nat. hom*. 1. 38 (p. 2. 13–17 Morani, M. 40. 505 B ff.). Cf. W. Telfer, 'The Birth of Christian Anthropology', *JTS*, NS 13 (1962), 347–54. But in rejecting the identification of the soul with the 'temperament' of these four elements, Nemesius does not mean to dissociate the soul entirely from bodily influence. He accepts the view that virtue and vice are related to bodily temperament and answers the question why vices come naturally to men in these words: τοῦτο ἀληθῶς ἐκ τῆς τοῦ σώματος κράσεως γίνεται. ὡς γὰρ φυσικῶς ὑγιεινοὶ καὶ νοσώδεις εἰσὶν ἐκ τῆς κράσεως, οὕτω τινὲς φυσικῶς πικρόχολοι ὄντες ὀργίλοι εἰσίν, ἄλλοι δειλοί, ἄλλοι κατωφερεῖς (2. 91, p. 25. 21–3 Morani, M. 40. 560 A). But, he goes on, the soul can control bodily temperament, as the body is the soul's instrument (ὄργανον, l. 26). As W. Telfer, *Cyril of Jerusalem and Nemesius of Emesa*, (LCC 4; London, 1955), 275 remarks, Nemesius shows a surprising awareness, 'so unique among early ecclesiastical writers, that the spiritual life of man is essentially conditioned by the body, with its functions and limitations.' Greg. clearly goes beyond Nemesius in his rejection of κρᾶσις. While agreeing with Nemesius on the impossibility of identifying any kind of κρᾶσις with soul, he would dispute also the interaction of soul and body envisaged by Nemesius. He sees the soul as much more independent of the body. The body is thought of in negative terms as that which weighs down and retards the soul or keeps it in bondage. Examine, for instance, Greg.'s preoccupation with the struggle of soul against body in *carm*. 1. 2. 14. 63 ff. (M. 37. 760 A ff.), a lament which sees the development of character as the conquest of the body, and compare it with the view of Nemesius that variation in character arises both from the kind of control that the soul exercises and from the particular physical temperament on which it has to work. Elsewhere Greg. uses κρᾶμα for the union of soul and body or 'breath and dust', contrasting angelic state with the low, heavy composite existence of the human being, *orr*. 27. 7 (p. 12. 7, M. 36. 20 C), 28. 3 (p. 26. 11, 29 B), 38. 5 (316 C), 45. 7 (632 A).

κρᾶσις itself, parallelled by μίξις, takes on a Christological sense in *or.* 38. 13 (M. 36. 325 c), indicating a strong union of the natures.

15–17. Again Nemesius may be compared. In seeking a principle of differentiation, he argues that a temperament of elements would apply equally to inanimate objects and to living creatures, *nat. hom.* 2. 87 (p. 24. 4–7 Morani, M. 40. 556A f.). Greg. argues similarly that κρᾶσις provides no basis for distinction, but limits himself to animate creatures, finding in κρᾶσις no adequate explanation of the phenomenon of reason in some and not in others.

17. εὐκραέες: εὐκραής corresponds to none of the meanings given in LSJ, but = 'of good temperament'. For this εὐκρασία may be compared, a technical term for the proper adjustment of the body elements (Arist. *PA* 673ᵇ25, Gal. 6. 31, *al.*).

18–19. *The soul's connection with bodily life.* Greg. characterizes the theories he has mentioned by saying that they equate soul with physical life. Soul is thus neither more nor less than that which distinguishes a living body from a corpse. (Cf. the summary of Arist. *An.* 412ᵃ17 ff. given in Ross's edn., p. 215: 'Soul cannot be body, because it is that the possession of which distinguishes a living body from a lifeless one.') In other words, Greg. criticizes all these views for reducing soul to a function of body, instead of treating it as a self-existent entity.

κέαρ. The tragic κέαρ takes over the meanings of καρδία as it was used by biblical and patristic writers to mean, amongst other things, 'the organ of natural and spiritual enlightenment' (Arndt–Gingrich, s.v. 1.'b), the 'seat of divine presence and grace' (*PGL* s.v. C. 4).

20–1. This higher element in man, Greg. argues, cannot be treated as mere fodder to keep the body's strength up.

22–31. *Individual and common soul.* The background of the kind of belief to which Greg. now turns is to be sought far back in Greek philosophy. W. K. C. Guthrie writes: '*Psyche* for a thinker of the fifth century meant not only *a* soul but soul; that is, the world was permeated by a kind of soul-stuff which is best indicated by the omission of the article ... Portions of this soul-substance, Alcmaeon thought, inhabit the human body, and in particular the brain...' (*History*, i. 355–6). Something of the sort was taught by the Stoics, with the notion that human souls are of fiery breath which is part of the divine universal soul. Cf. the following passages: αἱ ψυχαὶ συναφεῖς τῷ Θεῷ ἅτε αὐτοῦ μόρια οὖσαι καὶ ἀποσπάσματα (Epictetus, *Diss.* 1. 14. 6); εἰς μὲν τὰ ἄλογα ζῷα μία ψυχὴ διῄρηται·

εἰς δὲ τὰ λογικὰ μία νοερὰ ψυχὴ μεμέρισται (Marc. Aurel. Ant. 9. 8); μία οὐσία κοινή, κἂν διείργηται ἰδίως ποιοῖς σώμασι μυρίοις· μία ψυχή, κἂν φύσεσι διείργηται μυρίαις καὶ ἰδίαις περιγραφαῖς (id. 12. 30).

μεριστὴ has here not the meaning found in Arist. *An.* 402ᵇ1 (of the internal division of the soul), but means 'separated, individual' (cf. Jul. *or.* 4. (11). 151C); it emphasizes the separate nature of the individual soul and at the same time its connection with the common soul of which it is a μέρος. But the Manichees may also be in Greg.'s mind. For one of the complaints which Nemesius made against them was that they divided up the one soul of the world into fragments which were joined alike to animate and inanimate things. This supposed division of the one soul into parts strikes Nemesius as a gross error, *nat. hom.* 2. 112–17 (pp. 33. 20–34. 17 Morani, M. 40. 577A f.).

24. **πλαζομένη ... δι᾽ ἠέρος**: these words suggest a Pythagorean account of the departure of the soul in death, as given by Diogenes Laertius (8. 31): ἐκριφθεῖσάν τ᾽ αὐτὴν (sc. τὴν ψυχὴν) ἐπὶ γῆς πλάζεσθαι ἐν τῷ ἀέρι ὁμοίαν τῷ σώματι. (He is drawing his information from Alexander Polyhistor.) But, though the language is similar, the intention in Greg. is quite different. For πλαζομένη here is meant to describe not the supposed fate of the soul after physical death, but the unstable, inconstant nature of a soul which is interacting with some undifferentiated, universal soul.

24b–27. Connect these lines with vv. 8–9 above, with n. Criticism of the soul–air view took varying forms. Nemesius, for example, argues on biological grounds similar to these used to combat the equation of blood and soul: many living creatures do not breathe air, but they possess soul; therefore air is not soul, *nat. hom.* 2. 76 (p. 20. 6–11 Morani, M. 40. 544B ff.; the line is much the same as that in Arist. *An.* 410ᵇ27 ff.). Greg.'s approach has greater affinity with another of Aristotle's arguments when, in *An.* 411ᵃ16 ff., he contrasts the undifferentiated quality of air with the distinctions within soul: εἰ δ᾽ ὁ μὲν ἀὴρ διασπώμενος ὁμοειδής, ἡ δὲ ψυχὴ ἀνομοιομερής, τὸ μέν τι αὐτῆς ὑπάρξει δῆλον ὅτι, τὸ δ᾽ οὐχ ὑπάρξει, ἀναγκαῖον οὖν αὐτὴν ἢ ὁμοιομερῆ εἶναι ἢ μὴ ἐνυπάρχειν ἐν ὁτῳοῦν μορίῳ τοῦ παντός (20–3).

μεταπνείοντες: for the meaning 'to breathe in and out, to breathe' *PGL* cites only this passage. LSJ record only one instance of the verb (Opp. *H.* 5. 314), where the sense is 'to recover breath'.

26. ἔκειντο: there is little likelihood in the suggestion of Nicetas that the word refers to death. The same interpretation is given by Leunclavius in his tr. 'et simul exspirantes morerentur' (1018c). Why should the mutual involvement of the souls of living creatures be a cause of immediate death? The straightforward meaning is: 'all would be placed (i.e. present) in all.' ἄν must be understood with ἔκειντο to complete the unfulfilled condition.

27. Tr.: '(and this will be true) even if it is the nature of air to flow (or vary) from time to time and from person to person.' The point is that, unless there is a fundamental principle of distinction, differences of time and place will be irrelevant. Such variation as is implied by χυτή does not alter the homogeneous nature of air as maintained by Aristotle *An.* 411ª20 ff.

28-31. These lines present the theory in a modified form. The soul becomes permanent in the body, not fluctuating as the outer air does. But it still resembles air in being drawn into the body from outside in the first place.

28-9 are awkward in grammar if Caillau is right in taking τεκοῦσα (understood from the following τεκούσης) as the subject of ἔσχε. But equally good sense and simpler grammar come from taking ψυχὴ as subject of ἔσχε. The meaning is then: 'If the soul is permanent, what is it that it occupies, what is it that is already alive in the mother's womb, if she draws me in from outside?'

It should be noted that Greg. is not denying that the soul comes from without. All he denies is that the mother breathes it in from the outer air. Greg. goes on to assert that the soul enters the body of the unborn child from without, coming directly from God (cf. below, vv. 80-1, with n.).

The soul here is identified with the total person (cf. above, vv. 4-6 n.).

προέσπασεν: προσπάω is a rare word. LSJ record only a middle use by Diodorus Siculus, and Soph. and *PGL* mention only the present passage.

32-52. *Transmigration of souls and cycles of reincarnation.* We are not here directly concerned with tracing the history of the notions encompassed by the Greek words παλιγγενεσία, μετεμψύχωσις, and μετενσωμάτωσις, with their associations with Empedocles, the Pythagoreans, Orphics, and Platonists. (Cf. W. Stettner, *Die Seelenwanderung bei Griechen und Römern* (Stuttgart and Berlin, 1934); J. H. Waszink, 'Beseelung', *RAC* ii (1954), 176-83.) What is here of particular concern is the question whether Greg. is merely producing a set-piece from a doxographic repertoire (cf. vv. 11–17 n.), or whether he is intent on controverting a living belief. There are several reasons for suggesting the second alternative.

Justin felt it worth while to distance Christianity from Platonic belief in transmigration, *dial.* 4 (p. 95, M. 6. 484B). Clement's view is characterized by H. Chadwick as 'obscure', though his judgement tilts against the charge of Photius that he accepted a form of transmigration (*CHLGEMP* 172–3, *Early Christian Thought and the Classical Tradition* (Oxford, 1966), 49). Origen's opinions have been much debated. One can point to *Cels.* 5. 29 (p. 31. 6 ff., M. 11. 1225B) for a denial that the binding of soul to body involves reincarnation; cf. 3. 75 (p. 267. 11 f., M. 11. 1020A) for τὴν περὶ μετενσωματώσεως ἄνοιαν.

The Rufinus version of *princ.* 1. 8. 4 (p. 105. 1 ff., M. 11. 180B ff.) is explicit in its denial of transmigration. Koetschau, on the other hand, assembles texts of Nyssen, Jerome, and Justinian to suggest that Origen might really have tended to, even if he did not precisely state, some form of belief in transmigration (GCS 5. 102. 12 ff., 104. 8 ff.). Whether or not one accepts Koetschau's attempted reconstruction (it is, at best, questionable), it is hard to dispute Chadwick's conclusion: 'Yet his own system presupposes a picture of the soul's course which is strikingly similar.' (*CHLGEMP* 191, cf. *Early Christian Thought*, 115–16). Greg. may feel it necessary to go beyond the position which Jerome attributed to Origen, that of offering ideas akin to transmigration as a basis for speculation: 'et ad extremum ne teneretur Pythagorici dogmatis reus, qui asserit μετεμψύχωσιν, post tam nefandam disputationem, qua lectoris animum vulneravit, "haec", inquit, "iuxta nostram sententiam non sint dogmata, sed quaesita tantum atque proiecta, ne penitus intractata viderentur."' (*Ep. ad Avit.* 4: M. *PL.* 22; *Ep.* 104. 4. 1063).

Transmigration was a living issue among Neoplatonists. Plato had thought that the souls of gross men might in a subsequent reincarnation pass into animals, the doctrine of 'metensomatosis' (*Phd.* 81 D 6 ff., *Rep.* 620A ff.). Plotinus repeats the view in 3. 4. 2. But Porphyry modifies it to produce the teaching of 'metempsychosis' in which the souls of rational men pass only into other rational men and the irrational souls of animals are likewise limited to passage into other animals (cf. Porphyry ap. Stob. *Ecl.* 1. 49. 60, Wachsmuth, p. 445. 15 ff.). This is what Iamblichus also holds (*Myst.* 1. 8;

Parthey, p. 24. 2) and Sallustius follows in the same line (*De dis* 20; Nock, p. 34. 25 ff.). The latter argues that metempsychosis explains such facts as blindness at birth and claims that this doctrine alone saves one from having to believe in an infinite number of souls (cf. vv. 50–2 n.). In the following century Proclus was to continue the contention of Porphyry in opting for an allegorical interpretation of such passages as the reincarnation of Orpheus in a swan (*Rep*. 620A) when he wrote on the subject in his work *In Remp*. 2. 312. 10 ff., 313. 7 ff. But for the souls of men he maintained a constant 'cyclic reinstatement'; cf. E. R. Dodds, *Proclus: the Elements of Theology* (Oxford, 1963), 175, who gives this tr. of ἀποκατάστασις. The majority of Neoplatonists would have been with him; cf. P. Courcelle, 'Anti-Christian Arguments and Christian Platonism: from Arnobius to St. Ambrose', in A. Momigliano (ed.), *The Conflict between Paganism and Christianity in the Fourth Century* (Oxford, 1963), 151–92. However, Greg.'s reference in *or*. 27. 10 (p. 18. 2 ff., M. 36. 24B) to the transmigration theory (μετενσωματώσεις καὶ περιόδους) mentions only Plato, and that without discussion.

Again, there was a place for transmigration in Mani's system. (Cf. A. V. Williams Jackson, *Journal of the American Oriental Society*, 45 (1925), 246–68; Widengren 65–6.) Nemesius connected the doctrine with the Manichees in these terms: φάσκοντες γάρ, ἀνατρέχειν τὰς μεμολυσμένας ψυχὰς ἐπὶ τὰ στοιχεῖα καὶ συγκαταμίγνυσθαι ἀλλήλλαις, πάλιν αὐτὰς ἐν ταῖς μετενσωματώσεσί φασι τιμωρεῖσθαι, κατὰ τὸ μέγεθος τῶν ἁμαρτημάτων, ἑνοῦντες αὐτὰς καὶ πάλιν χωρίζοντες καθ᾽ ὑπόστασιν (*nat. hom*. 2. 111–12, p. 33. 13–16 Morani = M. 40. 577B).

In the chapters which Tert. allows himself for discussion of *metempsychosis* and *metensomatosis* (28–31; M. *PL* 2. 686A–702B; CCSL 2. 815–29; CSEL 20. 335–52), in addition to attacking Platonic theory and the claims of Empedocles and of Pythagoras (that he reincarnated Euphorbus), he singles out as 'heretics' in the Christian era Simon Magus (c. 34) and Carpocrates (c. 35).

Nemesius, in reviewing the Platonist and Manichaean positions on transmigration, concludes that this idea is at the root of all Greek belief in the immortality of the soul (2. 115, p. 34. 18–19 Morani = M. 40. 581A). Whether this is a fair judgement or not, it is clear that the views which Greg. is attacking have theological importance as well as contemporary significance. We may point to the strong ethical character which the doctrine had in its Platonic form, where adjustment of soul to body involved the moral question of reward and punishment. Greg. chooses to direct his irony mainly against a primitive form of metensomatosis (perhaps he could not resist the oratorical effect), rather than against the more developed, more ethical, forms of metempsychosis. But he might well argue that, in so doing, he was not guilty of a genetic fallacy. For, if he could show the basic impossibility of the whole idea of transmigration, he obviates the need to discuss its supposed ethical content. If it is thought that the introduction of Empedocles' supposed reincarnations gives to this polemic an archaic, unreal effect, it must be remembered that no more tenable evidence on the doctrine had ever been offered. This kind of anecdote, coupled with the theory of recollection (cf. vv. 47 ff.), was all that could be produced to support transmigration teaching.

33. Pl. *Rep.* 617D ff. gives examples of the way in which souls between one earthly existence and the next are given choices of lives to be followed. Plato envisages a correspondence between the acquired characteristics of souls and the choices they make.

34. αἰὲν: cf. vv. 44–5 n.

35. ἀμπλακίης has an ancient ring, ἀμπλακίη occurring in one of the early Greek transmigration documents, Empedocles fr. 115 (DK i. 357. 17).

36. εἵμασιν: cf. the use of χιτών in representing the body as the garment of the soul in Empedocles fr. 126 (DK i. 362. 9); *IG* 14. 2241 (σῶμα χιτὼν ψυχῆς); Proclus, *Inst.* (*Elem.*), 209.

37. ἐτώσια μοχθίζοντες is a reminiscence of Theocritus. Cf. 1. 38, 7. 48 ἐτώσια μοχθίζοντι (the first of hopeless lovers, the second of those who waste their time attacking Homer).

38. The cycle of reincarnation is likened to the unending punishment of a prime sinner of Greek literature, Ixion, who having attempted to rape Hera, is represented in poetry and art as eternally bound to a wheel. Cf. Pi. *P.* 2. 21 ff.:

> θεῶν δ' ἐφετμαῖς Ἰξίονα φαντὶ ταῦτα βροτοῖς
> λέγειν ἐν πτερόεντι τροχῷ
> παντᾷ κυλινδόμενον·

Himerius (*Ecl.* 3. 11) takes Ixion as the type of θράσος. Greg. alludes to him in *or.* 5. 38. (M. 35. 713C): ῥοιζουμένῳ τροχῷ συγκυκλού-μενος.

The idea of a 'wheel of rebirth' was found in Orphic literature.

Cf. O. Kern, *Orphicorum Fragmenta* (Berlin, 1922), 32b6 (p. 106), 229 (p. 244), 230 (pp. 245 f.), 231 (p. 246).

39. The doctrine is here presented in its most ludicrous form, yet it cannot be accounted an unfair presentation. For Empedocles had claimed that he could recall previous incarnations as a boy, a girl, a shrub, a bird, and a fish:

ἤδη γάρ ποτ᾽ ἐγὼ γενόμην κοῦρός τε κόρη τε
θάμνος οἰωνός τε καὶ ἔξαλος ἔλλοπος ἰχθύς

(fr. 117; DK i. 359. 1 f.).

The celebrated passage in *Rep.* 617D ff. gives Plato's description of how the souls of men pass into animals and from animals into men. Despite attempts made in both ancient and more recent times to show that Plato did not intend this to be taken literally, no one could blame Greg. for seeing a straightforward sense in this and other passages of Plato where transmigration is discussed. The onus of proof still rests with those who would discount the literal interpretation: cf. J. Adam's edn., rev. D. A. Rees (Cambridge, 1963), ii. 456, on 618A3. The transmigrations mentioned include the passage of souls from man to swan, nightingale, eagle, lion, and monkey as well as from human male to female. *Phd.* 82A speaks of wolves, hawks, and kites as the recipients of souls previously in men. (Plato did not envisage the migration of the soul into plants in the way in which Empedocles had.) A more credible form of transmigration (metempsychosis) was represented by the claims of Pythagoras to be the reincarnation of the Homeric Euphorbus: cf. E. Rohde, *Psyche: the Cult of Souls and Belief in Immortality among the Greeks*, ET W. B. Hillis (London, 1925), App. X, pp. 598 ff. But this claim also came in for both ridicule and reasoned criticism. An example of the second will be found in Tertullian's *De Anima*, where the arbitrary nature of this reincarnation is emphasized. It could certainly not be justified on grounds of fitting correspondence: 'ecce enim Euphorbum militarem et bellicam animam satis constat vel de ipsa gloria clipeorum consecratorum. Pythagoran vero tam residem et inbellem, ut proelia tunc Graeciae vitans Italiae maluerit quietem geometriae et astrologiae et musicae devotus, alienus studio et affectu Euphorbi.' (*De An.* 31. 4: M. *PL* 2. 701B; CCSL 2. 828. 21 ff.; CSEL 20. 351. 15 ff.) But Pythagoras is firmly associated also with metensomatosis (cf. Guthrie, *History*, i. 186–7, 306): the souls of animals and men are kindred and interchangeable.

The cycle of reincarnations in this line is a composite from several sources. φυτόν, ὄρνιν, and ἰχθὺν refer explicitly to the Empedocles fr. quoted above. βροτόν could apply to any reincarnation theory. κύνα reflects a notable satirical comment on Pythagoras which appeared in his own lifetime. Xenophanes makes him recognize a friend's voice in the howl of a dog which is being beaten:

καί ποτέ μιν στυφελιζομένου σκύλακος παριόντα
φασὶν ἐποικτῖραι καὶ τόδε φάσθαι ἔπος·
"παῦσαι μηδὲ ῥάπιζ᾽, ἐπεὶ ἦ φίλου ἀνέρος ἐστὶν
ψυχή, τὴν ἔγνων φθεγξαμένης ἀίων."

(fr. 7; DK i. 131. 1 ff., from D.L. 8. 36).

I can trace no specific reference behind ὄφιν. It might well have been added simply to complete the zoological range, but whether by Greg. or in some source I am unable to say.

40. Greg. intends repetition of the same cycle of birth to signify futility, as well it might. Reincarnation, of course, might have purpose, as it does in Pl. *Phdr.* 249A: the souls which choose the philosophic life in three successive incarnations gain 'remission' from the long series of reincarnations. Greg.'s description most naturally fits not the Platonic conception, but the Pythagorean, with its rigid pattern of cyclic repetition in which the whole of history will be repeated again exactly. Cf. Eudemus ap. Simplic. *Phys.* 732. 26 (fr. 8. 88 Wehrli, p. 41. 18 ff.): εἰ δέ τις πιστεύσειε τοῖς Πυθαγορείοις, ὥστε πάλιν τὰ αὐτὰ ἀριθμῷ, κἀγὼ μυθολογήσω τὸ ῥαβδίον ἔχων ὑμῖν καθημένοις οὕτω, καὶ τὰ ἄλλα πάντα ὁμοίως ἕξει, καὶ τὸν χρόνον εὔλογόν ἐστι τὸν αὐτὸν εἶναι. Cf. further Porphyry, *Vita Pythagorae*, 19 (DK 14. 8a; i. 100. 37 ff.):

... πρῶτον μὲν ὡς ἀθάνατον εἶναί φησι (sc. Pythagoras) τὴν ψυχήν, εἶτα μεταβάλλουσαν εἰς ἄλλα γένη ζῴων, πρὸς δὲ τούτοις ὅτι κατὰ περιόδους τινὰς τὰ γιγνόμενά ποτε πάλιν γίγνεται, νέον δ᾽ οὐδὲν ἁπλῶς ἐστι, καὶ ὅτι πάντα τὰ γιγνόμενα ἔμψυχα ὁμογενῆ δεῖ νομίζειν. φαίνεται γὰρ εἰς τὴν Ἑλλάδα τὰ δόγματα πρῶτος κομίσαι ταῦτα Πυθαγόρας.

Men are thus involved in a twofold cycle, a cycle of rebirth in human, animal, or plant form, and a second which is an exact repetition of the first.

41-2. μέχρι τίνος; an expression of some impatience: 'How long does this continue?' or 'Where does this take us?' Cf. D.S. 14. 65:

μέχρι τίνος καρτερήσομεν ταῦτα πάσχοντες; Greg. cannot conceive of the rational element in soul as remaining dormant during the supposed manifestation in animal or plant form.

θάμνον: cf. the fr. of Empedocles quoted on v. 39.

λακέρυζα κορώνη: these words are found in Hes. *Op.* 747, fr. 171, and Ar. *Av.* 609. In the second and third of these passages the crow is taken as a type of longevity, an association which may carry over into the present passage. Here the main stress falls on λακέρυζα: senseless, inarticulate croaking is all that it ever achieves. But perhaps the implication 'for all its long life' may also be present.

It is possible to see in κορώνη a further reference. In his satire *Gallus*, Lucian had made Pythagoras, reincarnated as a cock, detail his previous lives, one of which was that of a jackdaw, κολοιός (*Gall.* 20). The jackdaw, the frog, and the cock are taken by Lucian as three types of pretentious chatterers, suitable to express his own opinion of the reincarnation theory (4). It may be that the 'croaking crow' contains a side-reference to the 'chattering jackdaw'. (Cf. Courcelle, 'Anti-Christian Arguments', 164, where these and connected passages are discussed.)

43. ἄναυδος: the epithet for fish in A. *Pers.* 577.

44–52. *Reward and punishment.* The question here is not the interim punishment of the soul in being placed in the body of an inferior animal, but the ultimate punishment at the end of the cyclic process. Greg. argues that the advocates of transmigration can find no logical place for a final, as opposed to an intermediate, punishment. Punishment cannot be severed from a body, and which of the successive bodies is to be chosen? We must then look at the teaching of transmigrationists on final judgement.

As far as the Orphics and Pythagoreans were concerned, there was no punishment apart from reincarnation itself. Reward consists in escape, through purification, from the cycle, while punishment is neither more nor less than absence of reward, the continuing bondage of the soul to the wheel of reincarnation. (Cf. Guthrie, *History*, i. 202 ff.) In the *Phaedrus*, however, Plato contemplates reward and punishment between successive incarnations, with souls despatched for punishment beneath the earth or reward in heaven (249A). In the Myth of Er he writes of incurable sinners who are to suffer everlasting punishment (*Rep.* 614B ff., cf. *Phd.* 113D ff., *Grg.* 523A ff.). Other souls, though evil, are curable by punishment

(*Grg.* 525 A f., *Phd.* 113 E, *Rep.* 615 A f.). But the nature of this punishment of souls is not at all easy to determine. For, while stressing that the souls in judgement are stripped of all physical concomitants (they are 'naked', *Grg.* 523 E), Plato describes punishments which seem to presuppose bodies. He writes of hanging up in prison (*Grg.* 523 E), binding hand and foot, flaying, impaling on thorns (*Rep.* 615 E f.). This may be in Greg.'s mind when he writes on the difficulty of imagining punishment for a soul which was ἄσαρκος.

This is the kind of problem which Origen was trying to meet in *princ.* 2. 10. 1 ff. He takes up a position against fellow Christians ('nonnullos nostrorum' 2. 10. 3: p. 175. 11 = M. 11. 235 B) who accept a purely physical view of the resurrection body which is to receive punishment. But his concern to preserve continuity with the earthly body may be seen from the account of Origen given in Methodius *res.* 1. 22. 3–5 (p. 244. 20 ff.). The form of the resurrection body will not be at the same stage as the physical body upon earth, but it will continue its εἶδος in a way analogous to that in which the εἶδος of the child's body is continued in that of the man in old age. The Transfiguration also is cited as an example of continuity in change. (Cf. the valuable discussion of Origen's views in H. Chadwick, 'Origen, Celsus and the Resurrection of the Body', *HTR* 41 (1948), 83–102.) The nature of punishment accordingly must be thought of as that which is appropriate to a spiritual body; cf. 1 Cor. 15. 44; Or. *Cels.* 5. 19. (pp. 19. 30 ff., M. 11. 1208 B ff.). In *princ.* 2. 10. 3 (pp. 175. 11 ff., M. 11. 235 B ff.) Origen writes that the worthy will have a refashioned spiritual body which can live in heaven and those of lesser merit will have correspondingly graded bodies, 'ita tamen ut etiam eorum, qui ad "ignem aeternum" vel ad "supplicia" destinandi sunt, per ipsam resurrectionis permutationem ita corpus incorruptum sit quod resurgit, ut ne suppliciis quidem corrumpi valeat ac dissolvi' (p. 176. 16 ff., 236 B).

The punishing fire Origen locates within the soul, the flames of conscience rather than flames external to the soul (2. 10. 4: pp. 177. 1 ff., M. 11. 236 C ff.) and he compares the flames of love, jealousy, and the like (2. 10. 5: p. 178. 15 ff., 237 B f.). Origen conceives of a punishment of the soul which is analogous to the rending apart of the limbs of the body, thinking of the state of a soul 'extra ordinem atque compagem vel ad eam harmoniam, qua⟨e⟩ ad bene agendum et utiliter sentiendum a deo creata est' (p. 179. 3 ff., 238 A). For Origen, then, as for those whom Greg. attacks, the punishment of a soul which was ἄσαρκος would not seem so strange. On the contrary, Origen would find strange the presence of flesh in the spiritual world.

When we turn to Greg.'s own view we see that the principle of punishment in the flesh is the same whether it comes after one life or many. He appears to think of resurrection as, initially at least, a reconstitution of the physical body. Consider the passage in the panegyric on Caesarius, where he describes the destiny of a good soul as escaping in death from the bonds of the body and going to meet its Lord. He goes on:

μικρὸν δ᾿ ὕστερον, καὶ τὸ συγγενὲς σαρκίον ἀπολαβοῦσα, ᾧ τὰ ἐκεῖθεν
συνεφιλοσόφησε, παρὰ τῆς καὶ δούσης καὶ πιστευθείσης γῆς, τρόπον ὃν
οἶδεν ὁ ταῦτα συνδήσας καὶ διαλύσας Θεός, τούτῳ συγκληρονομεῖ τῆς ἐκεί-
θεν δόξης· καὶ καθάπερ τῶν μοχθηρῶν αὐτοῦ μετέσχε διὰ τὴν συμφυΐαν,
οὕτω καὶ τῶν τερπνῶν ἑαυτῆς μετεδίδωσιν, ὅλον εἰς ἑαυτὴν ἀναλώσασα καὶ
γενομένη σὺν τούτῳ ἓν καὶ πνεῦμα καὶ νοῦς καὶ θεός, καταποθέντος ὑπὸ τῆς
ζωῆς τοῦ θνητοῦ τε καὶ ῥεόντος (*or.* 7. 21, M. 35. 781 C ff.).

Now although the resurrection body of the good Christian is to be, in Pauline language (cf. 2 Cor. 5. 4), 'swallowed up by' or 'absorbed into' life, there does seem to be a stage when it is in a real sense identifiable with the earthly human body: note the use of ἀπο-λαμβάνειν, the word found in Justin *1 Apol.* 18. 6 (Goodspeed, p. 239, M. 6. 356B) for receiving back the physical body in resurrection. Greg. is in agreement with Origen in thinking of the body as being in a constant state of change during its earthly lifetime (*or.* 31. 15: p. 164. 2, M. 36. 149B), but he gives no sign of having followed up the idea of continuing adaptation when he was dealing with the resurrection body. The latter is identified with some unspecified phase of the earthly body. It seems reasonable to suppose a connection between Greg.'s insistence on the presence of the flesh in the final punishment and his teaching on the survival of a reconstituted body. Origen had shown the justice of punishing a soul in a body which preserves the εἶδος of the earthly body in which sin had been committed (cf. Jerome, *adv. Joh. Hier.* 26. 376C, quoted by Chadwick, 'Origen', 99). Greg. would appear to maintain the same justice with a different belief about the nature of the body which is to share the punishment.

There is a full discussion of Greg.'s belief on soul and body and on the meaning of resurrection in Mossay, *La Mort et l'au-delà*, chs. 5–6.

46. If the principle of punishment after death in a physical body is once accepted, the transmigrationist might argue, there is no fundamental difficulty in supposing it to take place in the body in which the soul had sinned most.

47–52. *How could the soul 'forget' previous existences?* The transmigrationist was open to attacks from two sides. If he admitted that he could remember no previous existences, his theory might be dismissed as gratuitous speculation. If he claimed that he could remember previous lives, his 'memories' were likely to be treated as a joke. Plato's λήθη theory in *Rep.* 621A was an attempt to make feasible supposed forgetfulness of previous existence. But even if the mind can be induced to 'recollect' items of knowledge, one thing which it does not recall is detail of previous existence.

The point of vv. 47–50 is blunted if one ignores the comparative in πλεόνων. The successive incarnations must have given the soul a wider range of knowledge. It is thus all the more surprising that it should be denied the basic knowledge of what these incarnations were.

50. δορή is an otherwise unattested (Ionic) form of δορά, 'skin, hide'.

50–2 ironically suggest that the reason for transmigration might be shortage of souls which would compel the repeated use of the same ones over and over again. A passage in Sallustius is a valuable comment, showing how some contemporary supporters of metempsychosis argued against a doctrine which involved belief in an infinite number of souls or the continual creation of souls:

εἰ γὰρ μὴ πάλιν αἱ ψυχαὶ εἰς σώματα φέροιντο, ἀνάγκη ἀπείρους εἶναι ἢ τὸν Θεὸν ἀεὶ ἑτέρας ποιεῖν. ἀλλ' οὐδὲ ἄπειρόν τι ἐν τῷ Κόσμῳ· ἐν γὰρ πεπερασμένῳ ἄπειρόν τι οὐκ ἂν γένοιτο. οὐδὲ ἄλλας γίνεσθαι δυνατόν· πᾶν γὰρ ἐν ᾧ τι γίνεται καινόν, καὶ ἀτελὲς εἶναι ἀνάγκη. τὸν δὲ κόσμον ἐκ τελείου γενόμενον τέλειον εἶναι πρόσηκει. (*De Dis* 20. 3; Nock, p. 36. 5 ff.).

Greg. may be parodying that kind of reasoning.

51. δέτης is a *hapax legomenon*.

θυλάκοισι picks up δορή (v. 50), the skin containing the soul being likened to a bag. (Cf. the connection of the δορή root with θύλακος in Ar. *Eq.* 370 δερῶ σε θύλακον κλοπῆς.) The distinction is made between the 'sacks' (bodies) which would decay and whose number would thus be unimportant and the immortal souls which, on this theory, must be of an unvarying number.

53–129. *Greg.'s doctrine of Man*

On the background of discussion on the nature of Man, see H. Karpp, *Probleme altchristlicher Anthropologie* (Gütersloh, 1950); R. A. Norris Jr., *Manhood and Christ*, esp. 21–78; J. M. da Cruz Pontes, 'Le problème de l'origine de l'âme de la patristique et la solution thomiste', *Recherches de théologie ancienne et médiévale*, 31 (1964), 175–229; A. W. Argyle, 'The Christian Doctrine of the soul'. *SJT* 18 (1965), 273–93; Waszink, *RAC* ii. 176–83; C. Tresmontant, *La Métaphysique du christianisme* (Paris, 1961), 249 ff.

For direct discussion of Greg., see Ullmann 289–313; K. Weiss, *Die Erziehungslehre der drei Kappadozier* (Freiburg i. Br., 1903), 6 ff.; Pinault 45 ff.; Portmann, *Die göttliche Paidagogia*, 7 ff., 63 ff.; J.-M. Szymusiak, *Éléments de Théologie de l'homme selon saint Grégoire de Nazianze* (Rome, 1963); id., 'Grégoire de Nazianze et le péché', *Stud. Patr.* 9 (= *TU* 94; Berlin, 1966), 288–305; Ruether, *Gregory of Nazianzus*, 130–6; T. Špidlík, *Grégoire de Nazianze* (Rome, 1971); Althaus, *Heilslehre*; Winslow, *Dynamics*; Moreschini, 'Platonismo'; id., edn. of *orr.* 38–41 (SC 358; Paris, 1990), 45–61. Cf. also G. B. Ladner, 'The Philosophical Anthropology of St. Gregory of Nyssa', *DOP*, 12 (1958), 59–94.

On Greg.'s teaching on the deification of man cf. *Arc.* 4. 95–6.

54. ἔνθεν ἑλών: cf. H. *Od.* 8. 500, 'Hear my account, picking it up at that point.'

τέρψιν: the idea of making more pleasurable a didactic theme is familiar from Lucretius 1. 933 ff. (= 4. 8 ff.) 'carmina, Musaeo contingens cuncta lepore'. He goes on to use the picture of children who are persuaded to drink healing wormwood by the honey smeared on the rim of the cup.

55–60. *The creation of the universe.*

55. The first four words recapitulate the point of *Arc.* 4: the world was not always in existence, but was created at a precise point in time. The words recall what Arius said about the Son (*Symb. Nic.* (325), anath. 1; Opitz 3. 52. 2; M. 20. 1540C), surely intentionally. It is right to talk in this way about the origin of the physical universe, just as it is wrong to use this language of the Son.

νοῦ Λόγος: in *or.* 30. 20 (p. 139. 3 ff., M. 36. 129A) Greg. discusses the relationship of Father and Son in these terms: λόγος δέ, ὅτι

237

οὕτως ἔχει πρὸς τὸν πατέρα, ὡς πρὸς νοῦν λόγος (cf. the n. in Mason's edn.).

αἰπύς: cf. *Arc*. 4. 87 n.

59–77 occur also in *carm*. 1. 2. 1. 81–99 (M. 37. 528A f.). Cf. also *or*. 38. 11 (M. 36. 321C ff.) = 45. 7. 629D ff., closely parallel to this section.

59–60. *Reasons for the creation of man.* The second reason, that man should control animal creation, comes from Gen. 1. 26. The first, that man is to have knowledge of God's wisdom, is to be connected with the teaching on man in God's image (cf. v. 75) and the belief that man was made to ascend to more perfect knowledge, in time (cf. 107 ff.).

σοφίης ἐπιίστορα: the same words are found in *IG* iii. 946 (*Inscriptiones Atticae aetatis Romanae*, ed. Dittenberger = *CIA* 3).

The association of Wisdom with knowledge of the created order is an established one. Cf. Prov. 3. 19, 8. 30, Sap. 7. 22, 9. 9, 14. 2, together with Chrysostom's interpretation of 1 Cor. 1. 21 (at *hom. 4 in I Cor*. 2 (Field 2. 31 ff., M. 61. 29 ff.). Despite the close connection of Wisdom with the Logos, Greg. can still personify Wisdom as μητρὸς. (Cf. *Arc*. 3. 57 n.)

60. βασιλῆα represents the sense of ἀρχέτωσαν in Gen. 1. 26.

θεουδέα: two translations are possible, 'God-fearing' or 'God-like'. The first is the Homeric meaning, found also in later authors. (*PGL* cites Paulus Silentarius and Nonnus, together with a 4th-c. source (*Monumenta Asiae Minoris Antiquae*, i. 171) and a line of Greg. (*carm*. 1. 2. 1. 82, M. 37. 528A) which is identical with the present line (cf. 59–77 n.). But 'Godlike' is also open to us, as Caillau saw ('Deo similem') and as Gallay tr. by 'à la ressemblance de Dieu' (p. 134, repr. Devolder 72). Support for this understanding comes from Quintus Smyrnaeus 1. 65, 3. 775, and Chrysostom has this sense (of God's image in man) in *fr. Job* 1. 1 (M. 64. 509C). Both attestations and sense are delicately balanced. 'Godlike' shows man's fitness to govern and the source of his authority: 'God-fearing' points to man's intermediate status, the lord of the animal creation, and the servant of the God of all creation. Perhaps the second is favoured by the parallel passage in *or*. 38. 11 (M. 36. 324A) = 45. 7 (632B) βασιλευόμενον ἄνωθεν.

61–9. The speech of the Logos sets out the reasons for the creation of man.

62. For νόες cf. *Arc*. 6. 17 n.

64. ἀγάλλεται: the verb combines the ideas of joy and abundance, rather like 'laetari'.

65–6. Cf. *Arc*. 4. 35 n. In *or*. 38. 11 (M. 36. 321 C) = 45. 7 (632 A) Greg. speaks of this union as the κρᾶμα and μίξις of νοῦς and αἴσθησις, elements in creation which had hitherto stood apart. Nyssen writes in a similar way in *or*. *catech*. 6. (pp. 28 ff., M. 45. 25 B ff.). Divine Wisdom effected a harmony of opposites, giving man a special place in Creation as the μίγμα which ensures that the whole of Creation may be accepted by God and share his fellowship. In both Gregories, man maintains continuity between the higher and the lower forms of Creation; cf. Weiss, *Erziehungslehre*, 9: 'Der Mensch erscheint demnach als Mittel- und Bindeglied der beiden Welten.' For νοήμονα cf. 75 n.

67–8. ἐχέφρονα means more than the Homeric 'prudent': it indicates man's possession of that which the animals lack, φρήν.

μύστην / οὐρανίων: cf. *or*. 38. 11 (M. 36. 324 A) = 45. 7 (632 A): ἄγγελον ἄλλον, προσκυνητὴν μικτόν, ἐπόπτην τῆς ὁρατῆς κτίσεως, μύστην τῆς νοουμένης. Here, as J. Gross observes (*La Divinisation du chrétien*, 246; cf. the tr. of C. G. Browne and J. E. Swallow, *St. Gregory of Nazianzus: Select Orations and Letters* (LNPF 7; Oxford and New York, 1894), 348), there is a distinction to be made between the initiate (μύστης) into the heavenly mysteries and the advanced initiate (ἐπόπτης) into the secrets of the visible, physical world. Cf. μύσται in *or*. 28. 3 (p. 24. 8, M. 36. 29 A), where it is clear that the initiates are only in the early stages of divine knowledge. For *or*. 38. 11, see the notes in Moreschini, SC edn.

68–9. ἄγγελον ἄλλον / ἐκ χθονός: man is 'another kind of angel' in that he shares angelic νοῦς and joins the angels in their function of praise (cf. ὑμνητῆρα).

The form ὑμνητήρ comes in the Greek Anthology (*AP* 7. 19. 1, Leonidas) and in Opp. *H*. 3. 7.

70–7. *The creation of Adam.*

71. The unexpressed contrast is clear: the immortal hands of the Logos formed the mortal shape of man. Where Irenaeus had spoken of the 'two hands of God' to make at once a Trinitarian affirmation and a declaration of the direct nature of God's creative action against suggestions of intermediary creators, Greg. has a simpler image of divine activity. For Iren. cf. *dem*. 11, p. 80 Robinson, and ibid. 51 for other passages. The language has a straightforward biblical ring. Cf. Job 10. 8: αἱ χεῖρές σου ἔπλασέν με καὶ ἐποίησάν με.

But Greg., no less than Irenaeus, has a need to assert the direct-ness of divine creative intent in Adam, over against Manichaean mythology in which Adam is the result of intercourse between the male and female demons Asqalūn and Namrāel. (Cf. A. V. W. Jack-son, *Researches in Manichaeism* (New York, 1932), 248–9; Widengren 59 ff.)

72. μοιϱήσατο: 'allotted', 'gave as his share'. Man's μοῖρα is the sharing of eternal life. Contrast the epic and tragic concentration in μοῖρα on the transience of human life.

73. ἀποϱϱώξ: cf. *Arc*. 4. 32 n. There is an analogous use of the word in orac. ap. Luc. *Alex*. 40: ἡ δὲ προφητείη δίης φρενός ἐστιν ἀπορρώξ. But the gift of which Greg. is thinking is a permanent one.

ἀειδέος: it is the God who is himself 'without form' who gives shape or form to human beings (v. 71).

74. Cf. Gen. 2. 7.

75. Cf. above, vv. 4–6 n. Man has been called νοήμονα in v. 66. The present line raises the question 'What part has νοῦς in Greg.'s anthropology?' Any attempt to impose absolute regularity upon Greg.'s doctrine of human nature is likely to fail. In Pinault's words, it is 'assez flottante' (p. 47; cf. Szymusiak, 'Grégoire de Nazianze et le péché', 291, esp. n. 2). In trying to decide the meaning of this line we must be prepared to limit the area of its relevance and accept it as merely one of several ways in which Greg. tried to express his understanding of the nature of man; cf. *Arc*. 4. 32 n.

There is in this line a tripartite division of man: whatever is the relationship between νοῦς on the one hand and body and soul on the other, it is meant to stand over against them as a third entity. This is true whether we tr. with Szymusiak 'car la nature princière de l'esprit (νοῦς) est commune à tous deux' or, as Gallay does (cf. also Caillau), 'car l'esprit commande en moi aux deux' (p. 135, repr. Devolder 73). Greg. was to give expression to a clear tripartite view in his answer to Apollinarius in *carm*. 1. 1. 10. 56 ff. (M. 37. 496A):

> ἐπεὶ δ᾽ ἄμικτός ἐστι σαρκίῳ Θεός,
> ψυχὴ δὲ καὶ νοῦς οἷον ἐν μεταιχμίῳ,
> σαρκὸς μὲν σύνοικος, ὡς δ᾽ εἰκὼν Θεοῦ.

Here the image of God in man is specifically the mind: it is the qual-ity of being νοερός which man shares with God and with the angels. (Cf. *Arc*. 4. 77 n.) The soul stands on the side of the flesh. Yet there is not complete separation of mind and soul. For where does the mind come from, if it is not part of what God breathed into man at his creation? While holding the soul together as a unity, Greg. maintains its affinities both with the intellectual and with the physical worlds. There is thus a sense in which the soul in its function of animating the body can be said to stand on the fleshly side of the compound, man. Yet when the contrast is drawn between the visible flesh and its invisible content, it may be thought to be directly connected with the invisible world of mind. A similar kind of relativity appears in *ep.* 101 (M. 37. 185 A f.). Human mind is at once perfect and imperfect: perfect when compared with soul and body, imperfect when compared with God, to whom it is subject. In *or.* 2. 23 (M. 35. 432 B f.) the soul is spoken of as having a mediating function between God and flesh: διὰ τοῦτο Θεὸς σαρκὶ διὰ μέσης ψυχῆς ἀνεκράθη, καὶ συνεδέθη τὰ διεστῶτα τῇ πρὸς ἄμφω τοῦ μεσιτεύοντος οἰκειότητι. The same thought is present here, but Greg. chooses to mark off mind as that part of man which communicates directly with God, rather than treating it as the upper end of the spectrum of soul. (Cf. Ladner, 'Philosophical Anthropology', 61 ff.; R. A. Norris Jr., *Manhood and Christ*, 35 ff.)

76–7. Greg. here returns to a twofold view of man in which the flesh is contrasted with that which is breathed into man, the soul being identified with εἰκών as it is in *or.* 38. 11 (M. 36. 321 C f.) = 45. 7 (632 A): παρ' ἑαυτοῦ δὲ πνοὴν ἐνθείς (ὃ δὴ νοερὰν ψυχὴν καὶ εἰκόνα Θεοῦ οἶδεν ὁ λόγος).

στέργω here has the strong sense 'have affection for', rather than the weaker 'acquiesce in'. There is a tension, with strong force likely to be exerted in both directions.

βιότων: this reading, over against βίοτον, gives excellent sense, contrasting the two forms of life.

78–96. *The continuance of the race of Adam.* The continuance of the race raised few problems on the purely physical side, with physical flesh propagating its like. But the continuance of the human soul from generation to generation caused considerable difficulty in patristic times. Four major views emerge: (*a*) souls pre-exist and are drawn at need from their own world to occupy human bodies; (*b*) God creates a new soul for every child conceived (creationism); (*c*) souls pass from parents to children as part of the same process as physical generation (traducianism); (*d*) souls pass from parents to children in a way analogous to the generation of flesh from flesh, but not as part of the physical process (generationism or spiritual traducianism). These ideas were all current in the 4th c.; cf. Karpp, *Probleme altchristlicher Anthropologie*, 240; Argyle, 'Christian Doctrine', 286 ff.

Greg. in these lines takes up a creationist position. Material flesh from material flesh is no different in principle from flesh from material dust. But, just as soul in Adam was breathed into him from without by God, so does soul enter Adam's descendants. A passage very closely parallel to the present one (the passages in fact have two lines in common) is *carm.* 1. 2. 1. 392 ff. (M. 37. 551 A f.). The human father is said to be father only of the flesh and blood, the mortal part of man.

$$\psi\upsilon\chi\grave{\eta}\ \delta\grave{\epsilon}\ \Theta\epsilon o\hat{\upsilon}\ \kappa\rho\alpha\tau\acute{\epsilon}o\nu\tau o\varsigma\ \ddot{\alpha}\eta\mu\alpha$$
$$\ddot{\epsilon}\kappa\tau o\theta\epsilon\nu\ \epsilon\grave{\iota}\sigma\pi\acute{\iota}\pi\tau o\upsilon\sigma\alpha\ \pi\lambda\acute{\alpha}\sigma\epsilon\iota\ \chi oo\varsigma.\ o\hat{\iota}\delta\epsilon\nu\ \acute{o}\ \mu\acute{\iota}\xi\alpha\varsigma$$
$$\pi\hat{\omega}\varsigma\ \tau\grave{o}\ \pi\rho\hat{\omega}\tau o\nu\ \ddot{\epsilon}\pi\nu\epsilon\upsilon\sigma\epsilon\ \kappa\alpha\grave{\iota}\ \epsilon\grave{\iota}\kappa\acute{o}\nu\alpha\ \mu\acute{\iota}\xi\alpha\tau o\ \gamma\alpha\acute{\iota}\eta.$$

(Caillau reads $\mu\acute{\iota}\xi\alpha\tau o$ for $\delta\acute{\eta}\sigma\alpha\tau o$ of the present passage, but there is a *v.l.* $\delta\acute{\eta}\sigma\alpha\tau o$.)

78-9. Billius saw the confusion in Nicetas' words $\psi\upsilon\chi\grave{\eta}\ \delta\grave{\epsilon}\ \beta\lambda\alpha\sigma\tau o\hat{\upsilon}\sigma\alpha\ \grave{\epsilon}\kappa\ \psi\upsilon\chi\hat{\eta}\varsigma$, contradicting as they do the correct interpretation a line or two below in the paraphrase.

ἀρχεγόνοιο: cf. *Arc.* 2. 53 n.

ἐπιμίσγετ': Greg. makes considerable use of the idea of 'mixing' in describing the nature of the union of body and soul in man. Cf. e.g. *Arc.* 4. 91–2, vv. 1 above and 84 below, *orr.* 20. 11 (M. 35. 1077C), 38. 11 (M. 36. 321C) = 45. 7 (629D f.). In this language Greg. doubtless shows Stoic influence, intending to stress the reality of the union of the elements without losing the individuality of the constituent elements and their retention of their specific characteristics. (Cf. Portmann, *Die göttliche Paidagogia*, pp. 64–5, together with vv. 65–6 n.)

ἀΐστως: the only other instances of the adverb (cf. LSJ) have the meaning 'utterly', but here the meaning is 'in an unseen manner'.

80-1. The pattern of original creation is preserved: matter produces matter and soul enters from without. For $\epsilon\grave{\iota}\kappa\acute{\omega}\nu$ = 'soul' cf. vv. 4–6 n.

82-90. *The traducianist alternative.* Though Greg. does not accept any form of traducianism, it is noticeable that he details the theory at some length without offering any detailed criticism of it, a sharp contrast to his normal way with ideas which he does not accept. The suggestion of adverse criticism may be present in $\theta\alpha\rho\sigma\alpha\lambda\acute{\epsilon}\omega\varsigma$, a word which tends to suggest audacity, excessive confidence, but otherwise disapproval is not explicit. Nazianzen may be influenced in this tolerance by Nyssen's tendency to a form of traducianism or generationism. He would be familiar with the traducianism of *De hominis opificio* 29 (Forbes 1. 282 ff.; M. 44. 233 D ff.) and *De anima et resurrectione* M. 46. 125 C, dated respectively 379 and 380. (Cf. Daniélou, 'Chronologie', 162–3.) Nyssen himself finds difficulty in maintaining a consistent position and some scholars have detected creationist tendencies in him. (Cf. Weiss, *Erziehungslehre*, 15; Karpp, *Probleme altchristlicher Anthropologie*, 240 ff., esp. 243 n. 3.) It is, therefore, no surprise that Nazianzen, while putting forward the creationist view, should feel disinclined to assail traducianism.

82. ἀρήγων has perhaps an ironical ring.

83. πλεόνεσσιν: for the prevalence of traducianist views, cf. Karpp, loc. cit.

85. ῥύσις indicates the flowing of the human race from its source in Adam, perhaps with a suggestion of the instability of the flesh when contrasted with soul; cf. the association of ῥευστός with the perishable nature of the body, noted by Chadwick, 'Origen', 87–8. Cf. *Arc.* 2. 14 n., 8. 67 and Kertsch, *Bildersprache*, 115.

87–90. On this view the soul continues by a process of natural reproduction, being divided and distributed to the human race in the same process by which the flesh is continued, or by an analogous process.

88. ἀρτιγένεθλος: MSS vary between this reading and αὐτογένεθλος. The former occurs elsewhere only in Orph. *A.* 388, where it has the literal sense of 'new-born'. In this traducianist context the soul is understood to be a fresh creation in the same sense as the body, in contrast, say, with notions of pre-existence. On the other hand, αὐτογένεθλος, though lexically better attested, gives doubtful sense. It is difficult to believe that Greg. would call 'self-originated' something which, for all its independence of body, is clearly created.

89. σπέρματος admits of two interpretations, (*a*) the semen of Adam, (*b*) the figurative sense of 'origin' (cf. LSJ s.v. I. 2). If the second is accepted, we have a parallel to the use of ῥίζα in v. 86. The traducianist position would then be represented in very general terms. The soul of Adam would be transmitted to following generations, apportioned out, but whether through the act of physical generation or by an analogous, but in some sense independent, process would remain undecided. But σπέρματος surely suggests that Greg. is being more specific. The question of what precisely was transmitted in the sperm of the father was one which inevitably produced discussion in traducianist circles. Cf. e.g. Tertullian, *De Anima* 27 (M. *PL* 2. 694c ff.; CCSL 2. 822 ff.; CSEL 20. (344. 27 ff.), where it is firmly stated that the semen contains both 'corporeal' and 'psychic' elements to form the body and soul of the child. (The background of this belief and its developments are fully investigated by Waszink, edn., 343 ff.) In 27. 5 Tertullian writes: 'Unico igitur impetu utriusque toto homine concusso despumatur semen totius hominis habens ex corporali substantia umorem, ex animali calorem.' Some such debate is likely to lie behind the use of σπέρματος here.

90. μένον εἶδος: in referring εἶδος to the soul Greg. is using language reminiscent of Aristotle (cf. *An*. 412ᵃ19). But there is a notable distinction. Aristotle wrote that the soul *was* the εἶδος of the body; Greg. says merely that the soul *has* an εἶδος, a continuing form which outlasts the temporal body.

91-6. *The meaning of rationality in the soul.* Greg. now leaves traducianism to return to pursuing his own speculations on the soul. He picks up from the traducianist argument a point which he accepts for different reasons, the eternal nature of the soul. He continues from there.

91. ἡγεσίη is a *hapax legomenon* and ἡγεσία is found only in Hesychius (glossed as ἥγησις). In Stoic thought τὸ ἡγεμονικόν is reason, the part of the soul in authority, looking back to ἡγεμοῦν in Pl. *Tim*. 41c7 and Ar. *EN* 1113ᵃ6, τὸ ἡγούμενον. (Cf. Guthrie, *History*, iii. 469 n. 2). In Zeno the Stoic form appears in *SVF* 1. 39 *al*. Greg. uses it in *or*. 38. 7 (M. 36. 317c), 41. 11 (44B), *al*.

91b-96. *The analogy of the flute and the flute-player.* Nicetas took it that the point of the analogy was to contrast the behaviour of the rational soul in the child with its behaviour in the adult. On this understanding the problem is how to reconcile the statement that the soul is meant to exercise rational control with the observation that in small children it appears to do no such thing. As the skilled flautist is constricted by an inadequate instrument, so even a potentially noble soul is hampered by a child's body.

Another possible interpretation might see Greg. attacking a more fundamental issue, the way in which the soul may at any time be affected by the health or weakness of the body. Nemesius, as we have seen (v. 14 n.), was prepared to accept considerable interaction of soul and body. He, too, uses a musical figure, showing how the soul may be distorted (συνδιαστρέφεται) by the body, as the musician may be thrown off tune by a faultily tuned lyre (*nat. hom.* 2. 96 = 1. 26. 3–4 Morani). If this is Greg.'s meaning, it will be seen that he stops short of Nemesius in that he thinks only of limitation of the soul's self-expression and not of its being damaged.

92. The adjective **ἔκτροπος** is very much a Cappadocian word, being attested in *PGL* only in Nyssen and Nazianzen. Otherwise only the adverb is found, once in the grammarian Erotianus (1st c. AD). The meaning 'inharmonious' is easily derived from ἐκτρέπω and ἐκτροπή.

94. **εὐρύπορος** has a very literal sense 'having a wide pipe, tube'. In Homer and Aeschylus it refers to the broad paths of the sea.

95. **ἅψεσιν**: Caillau's 'membris' apparently takes it that Greg. is equating ἅψις (which elsewhere means 'contact') with ἁφή, which has the same connection with 'touch' and can also mean 'contact', but which came to mean 'ligament' in Col. 2. 19 and Eph. 4. 16. This looks very likely.

97–129. *The status of man and his relation to Adam.* Cf. *or.* 38. 11–12 in SC edn.

97–106. *Adam before the Fall.*

97. If νέον points to the close relationship of the Son with man (cf. vv. 61 ff.), the close collocation of βροτός and ἄφθιτος stresses the divine-human distinction (cf. A. *Eu.* 724: ἀφθίτους θεῖναι βροτούς). For ἄφθιτος cf. *Arc.* 2. 83 n.

98–9 contain a clear statement of the purpose of man's creation: he is to progress to the divine life of heaven. Cf. *Arc.* 3. 4 n., 4. 95 ff. n.

100–4. Man is set in an intermediary position, a position which is the mark of his temporary, earthly status, as distinct from his eternal destiny. He is in a middle position between freedom and control. Man's freedom is limited, not in the sense that he is denied free will, but because he is limited in the area in which he may exercise his choice. God is free in being subject to no external law. Man's freedom is limited to the acceptance or rejection of a law, the framing of which is beyond his competence. Cf. *carm.* 1. 2. 10. 120 ff. (M. 37. 689A f.).

101–2. **χαράξας / ἐν κραδίῃ**: the language may be influenced by Jer. 38. 33 (31. 33 Heb.). Cf. also the version of Prov. 3. 3 in Cod. Alex.: γράψον δὲ αὐτὰς ἐπὶ τὸ πλάτος τῆς καρδίας σου. Greg. substitutes the more forceful χαράσσω.

103. ἀμφιτάλαντος is a rare word, being attested only once in the lexica outside Greg., as a neuter substantive at Anon *ep*. (J. A. Cramer, *Anecdota Graeca* (Oxford, 1836), iii. 169. 4). Greg. himself finds a use for it several times: *carmm*. 1. 2. 9. 69 (M. 37. 672A); 2. 1. 13. 172 (1241A), *s.v.l*.; *ep*. 4 (25C). Cf. ῥοπή *Arc*. 5. 51 n., ἀμφιρεπής *Arc*. 8. 86; ῥέπω is found in a similar context in Thphl. Ant. *Autol*. 2. 27 (M. 6. 1096A).

Pellegrino, *La Poesia di S. Gregorio Nazianzeno*, 60, finds in this line a prosaic quality which abruptly breaks in upon the contemplation of the groves of Paradise. But this is rather harsh criticism and seems to attack Greg. for doing what he set out to do. For his purpose is not to draw word-pictures of Paradise but to show Paradise as the place of choice. The close juxtaposition of the idyllic miniature and the sharp reality of moral choice may count in favour of Greg.'s skill, rather than against it. Who can say that ἀμφιτάλαντος is prosaic? P. Gallay conjectured that it is a word of Koine Christian provenance, but offered no evidence (*Langue et style de S. Grégoire de Nazianze dans sa correspondance* (Paris, 1933), 76). But if ἀμφιδέξιος is suitable for verse, or ἀμφιθάλασσος, why not ἀμφιτάλαντος?

104. γυμνόν both literally and figuratively. ἄτερ repeats the sense which γυμνὸν could have carried by itself. Cf. *Hom. Clem*. 6. 16: νοῦς . . . πάσης κακίας γυμνός.

ἀμφιθέτοιο: cf. *carm*. 1. 2. 29. 298 (M. 37. 906A). This is a word which Greg. appears to have taken up in a figurative sense, adapting its literal meaning in referring to a double-ended or double-handled object (LSJ). Here the word is concerned with double-dealing or, *PGL* suggests, the falsity of artificial addition.

105. For discussion of the varying patristic notions of Paradise and man's primal state see A. Slomkowski, *L'État primitif de l'homme dans la tradition de l'Église avant S. Augustin* (Paris, 1928). For Greg.'s views in particular, cf. J. Gross, *Entstehungsgeschichte des Erbsündendogmas*, i (Munich and Basle, 1960), 143 ff., Althaus, *Heilslehre*, Winslow, *Dynamics*, C. Moreschini, SC edn. of *orr*. 38–41, pp. 45 ff.

οὐρανίη means that Adam's status allowed him to share the life of the heavenly beings. There is no suggestion of an extra-terrestrial site for Paradise. Greg. treats this as a real place, though this does not preclude his elsewhere finding in it also allegorical interpretations. (Cf. *or*. 38. 12 (M. 36. 324B ff.) = 45. 8 (632C ff.), together with F. K. Hümmer, *Des hl. Gregor von Nazianz, des Theologen, Lehre von der Gnade* (Kempten, 1890), p. 38; Kelly, *Doctrines*, 348.)

106. Cf. Gen. 2. 15.

δοηστῆρα, poised between λόγων and γεωργόν, plays on two senses. Adam is to be a 'labouring' farmer (cf. H. *Od.* 16. 248) and a 'doer' of God's commands.

107-29. *The Fall and its effects.* In addition to the literature noted in v. 105 n., cf. the following: Tennant, *The Sources of the Doctrines of the Fall and Original Sin* (Cambridge, 1903); N. P. Williams, *The Ideas of the Fall and of Original Sin* (London, 1924), 282-92 esp. on Greg.); Kelly, *Doctrines*, 344 ff.

Discussion of Greg.'s position is found also in Portmann, *Die göttliche Paidagogia*, 75 ff.; B. Otis, 'Cappadocian Thought as a Coherent System', *DOP* 12 (1958), 95-124 at 110 ff.; Szymusiak, 'Grégoire de Nazianze et le péché'. Once the fall of Lucifer is accepted, the fall of man is readily explicable as temptation by a stronger power. The real problem, a problem to which Greg. has offered no answer, is to explain how a fall was possible for Lucifer.

107-11. The tree of the knowledge of good and evil is interpreted through Heb. 5. 12-14: the fruit of the tree was too strong for Adam, who needed the food of a child. Cf. 1 Cor. 3. 2.

107. τελειοτέροιο applies both to the tree itself, which is more perfect, more developed, than the others, and, as a proleptic transferred epithet, to Adam. It is the tree intended for the developed Adam.

108. Cf. Heb. 5. 14.

109-10. Perhaps Greg. is here conflating two figurative oppositions, child ~ adult and the catechumen ~ mature believer. The second idea may be linked with the μύστης of v. 67 above. (For ἀρχόμενοι cf. *Arc.* 3. 19 n.)

ἀεξομένοισι may be compared to the τέλειοι of Heb. 5. 14.

111. Cf. Heb. 5. 13, 1 Cor. 2. 6, 3. 1 f.

νηπιάχοισι suggests the belief developed by Irenaeus that Adam was created a child in mental, moral, and spiritual capacity. (Cf. the references collected by Szymusiak, 'Grégoire de Nazianze et le péché', 297 n. 2.)

112-18. *The Fall and its effects on Adam.*

112-13. Satan's part in the Fall of man has been commented on in *Arc.* 6. 61-6.

παραιφασίῃσι: παραιφασίη, which elsewhere means 'comfort,

consolation' (cf. LSJ s.v.), here corresponds to one of the meanings of παραίφασις, 'beguilement' (*AP* 5. 284. 7 (Agathias); *APl.* 5. 373.). Eve's place in the Fall is emphasized in *orr.* 18. 8 (M. 35. 993 B), 36. 5 (M. 36. 269 C).

114. The tragedy of the Fall as Greg. sees it is expressed in προώριος. Unlike Lucifer, who tried to seize a glory which could never have been his, Adam prematurely grasped at, and lost, something which God had intended that he should one day possess. In *or.* 2. 25 (M. 35. 436 A) Greg. talks of the work of Christ as restoration of the old Adam, in that he takes man to the tree of life from which he had been estranged by the tree of knowledge.

προώριος: only Nonnus is cited by LSJ for this form.

ἡδυβόρος is found only here and in *carm.* 1. 1. 27. 96 (M. 37. 505 A).

115–16. Though he never discusses the idea, Greg. thinks that man originally possessed a body of more subtle constitution than the present human body. Cf. *or.* 38. 12 (M. 36. 324 C) = 45. 8 (633 A) καὶ τοὺς δερματίνους ἀμφιέννυται χιτῶνας, ἴσως τὴν παχυτέραν σάρκα καὶ θνητὴν καὶ ἀντίτυπον. This flesh of finer consistency could not be different in kind from the flesh of animals, if man was to be a link between the worlds of sense and of mind, but different in degree from their flesh and that of fallen man. βαρεῖαν contains also the proleptic sense 'which was henceforth to be a burden to him'.

Allegorical interpretation of the coats of skin is found elsewhere in the Fathers. Irenaeus, for instance, reports a Gnostic belief that the coats mean bodies, *haer.* 1. 5. 5 (M. 7. 501 A), and Clem. Al. *str.* 3. 95. 2 (GCS 2. 239. 26 ff., M. 8. 1196 A f.) confirms this. Methodius claimed that this was Origen's view, *res.* 1. 4. 2 (pp. 223. 28 ff.) but *sel. in Gen.* (M. 12. 101–2) presents the notion merely as a possibility. Nyssen takes the coats of skin to represent the mortal element in man (*or.catech.* 8 (pp. 42. 14 ff., M. 45. 33 B f.)); etc. (Cf. Holl, *Amphilochius von Ikonium*, 202–3; Szymusiak, 'Grégoire de Nazianze et le péché', 298 n. 3.) The coats of skin replace the 'garments of light' in which man was clothed before the Fall. Cf. *SC* edn. of *or.* 38, pp. 130–1 n. 2.

116. νεκροφόρος: Adam became his own corpse-bearer, the meaning found in Polyb. 35. 6. 2, Plu. *Cato Ma.* 9. 2. Cf. also Philo's description of the soul as νεκροφοροῦσα *Agr.* 25 (i. 304, M.; ii. 95. 4 C.–W.). But Adam is νεκροφόρος in a wider sense in that he brought death into the world; cf. the similar application of θανατηφόρος to the tree of knowledge in † Dion. Al. *fr.* (Feltoe, p. 200. 3).

ἔκερσεν: I am unable to find a parallel for the form ἔκορσα = ἐκόρεσα (the form behind H. *Il.* 16. 747). The reading ἔκερσεν has considerable probability. ἔκερσα is a recognized Homeric form (cf. *Il.* 13. 546) and ἔκερσεν makes good sense. The idea that Christ 'cut short' sin by death fits closely with the thought of v. 122. The sense thus moves from punishment (Billius, Caillau) to providence. Nicetas makes it clear that he read ἔκερσεν and understood the passage this way when he paraphrases: διακέκοπται μὲν ἡ ἁμαρτία τῷ θανάτῳ, ὡς μὴ διαιωνίζειν τὸ κακόν, καὶ τοῦτο δὲ ἔργον ἀγαθότητος θεοῦ.

117. **ἄλσος** has traditional religious associations as a sacred grove or holy place (*LSJ s.v. II*). Cf. *Arc.* 8. 23–4 n.

118. Cf. Gen. 3. 17–19.

118b–119. Gen. 3. 24b reads: καὶ ἔταξεν τὰ χερουβὶν καὶ τὴν φλογίνην ῥομφαίαν τὴν στρεφομένην φυλάσσειν τὴν ὁδὸν τοῦ ξύλου τῆς ζωῆς. Perhaps ζῆλον appears through association with passages such as Zeph. 1. 18, 3. 8; Is. 26. 11; Ps. 78 (Heb. 79). 5; Heb. 10. 27. All link ζῆλος with fire and judgement.

120. The meaning would appear to be that given by Billius and Caillau: God provides against the approach of any second human being like Adam. But it is not easy to see how 'primi more parentis' or 'Adamus, ut ante' emerges from ὁ πρόσθε. The only explanation which fits the grammar is to suppose ὁ πρόσθε to be parenthetic. 'Lest any Adam (the former Adam, I mean) . . .' The distinction is thus made between the first and the Second Adam, as in *carm.* 1. 1. 10. 4 (M. 37. 465 A).

121. The *v.l.* φαγεῖν (cf. Caillau's n.) is easily explained by the proximity of ἐδωδήν. But φυγεῖν gives the obvious meaning. Man must learn the obedience of shunning the tree of good and evil before he may safely approach the tree of life (cf. v. 122 n.).

δαπτρείαν: if the -εῖος form is correct, it occurs only here. Dronke, following the reading of Cu, δαπτρίαν, supported it by pointing to other instances where Greg. lengthens a short syllable, the closest parallel being the ι of χθόνιος. δάπτριος itself is found only in Greg. *carmm.* 2. 2 (poem.). 3. 33 (M. 37. 1482A); 2. 1. 50. 15 (1386A).

122. The sting of the line is in **κακός**. Later generations of men are to be prevented from approaching the tree of life for the very reasons which, e.g. Irenaeus, gave for Adam's expulsion. To eat of the tree of life in a state of sin would be to gain eternity, but an eternity of evil:

'eiecit eum de paradiso et a ligno vitae longe transtulit: non invidens ei lignum vitae, quemadmodum quidam audent dicere, sed miserans eius, ut non perseveraret semper transgressor', *haer*. 3. 23. 6 (M. 7. 964A). Cf. Methodius, *res*. 1. 39 (pp. 283. 14 ff.) and G. von Rad, *Genesis*, ET J. H. Marks (London, 1961; German edn. 1956), 94; '. . . and we are also to learn that the severe denial of eternal life also has a merciful reverse side, namely, the withholding a good which for man would be unbearable in his present condition.' In Greg., cf. *or*. 38. 12 (M. 36. 324c f.) = 45. 8 (633A f.).

122b–127. *Man's return to Paradise*. Paradise is the port to which man will return after a stormy voyage.

123. ἁλίπλοος: cf. Call. *Del*. 15, A.R. 3. 1329.

124–5. πετάσσας / ἱστίον: cf. H. *Od*. 5. 269. For ἐρέτης = 'oar' cf. *AP* 6. 4. 6 (Leonidas).

126. The Cusanus reads ἀποτῆλε πλέοντες. Nicetas, however, appears to support ἀπὸ τῆλε πεσόντες, reading ἐκπεσόντες. There is much more point in ἀπὸ τῆλε πεσόντες than in ἀποτῆλε πλέοντες. Taking ἀποπεσόντες as tmesis, we find a use parallel to that in *or*. 39. 6 (M. 36. 341A): τῆς τοῦ Θεοῦ δόξης ἀποπεσεῖν. (πλέοντες, it might be conjectured, is the work of a scribe who wished, unnecessarily, to read nautical language at every point.)

127. The figure need not be pressed too closely. The sailor's return to port depends either on his adjusting the sails to a favourable change of the wind or on a hard pull on the oars. But the implication of οὐκ ἀμογητὶ is not that man, by a similar expenditure of energy, can regain Paradise. Greg.'s doctrine of the work of Christ is too central for any such adumbrations of Pelagianism. The Fall laid man open to a life of rigorous struggle, physical and moral. His return to Paradise will not take place without this struggle. But neither will it be accomplished as a result of it.

128–9. *The effects of the Fall*. As Szymusiak observes, Greg. offers no explanation of the way in which the effects of Adam's fall are transmitted to his descendants ('Grégoire de Nazianze et le péché', 299 ff.). In particular, it will be noted that there is no attempt to relate the questions of participation in Adam's sin and sharing in the soul of Adam (cf. v. 89 n.).

ἄτη . . . στάχυς: is there a half-reminiscence of A. *Pers*. 821–2?

> ὕβρις γὰρ ἐξανθοῦσ' ἐκάρπωσεν στάχυν
> ἄτης, ὅθεν πάγκλαυτον ἐξαμᾷ θέρος.

8. On the Testaments and the Coming of Christ

Title and purpose

The several titles, of varying degrees of fullness, show the content to be the two Testaments and the coming of Christ. This is straight-forward enough. The only problem is to decide what the limits of the poem are. Is *Arc.* 8 the 99 lines which are printed by Caillau and by Migne? Or should we regard vv. 82–99 as a separate poem? Again, are we to admit as an integral part the 60 lines found in L between vv. 18 and 19, the lines printed by Wyss? I have to say that I am inclined to change the opinion which I expressed in *JTS* 1970, 'The *Poemata Arcana*', 35–6 and 'Some Literary Questions'. Without questioning that these are genuine lines of Greg. and that the thought they contain is germane to the present poem, I would now doubt the correctness of placing them where they appear in L. The MS evidence is not strong and the subject-matter could well be thought an encouragement to interpolation. The lines, I would continue to hold, are of theological and literary interest and certainly fill out the argument by detailing Israel's idolatry of the Golden Calf, apostasy which led to the giving of the Sinai Law by Christ as a necessary but temporary expedient. But the poem can proceed quite easily from v. 18 to v. 19 without their intervention. Billius suspected a hiatus, as Nicetas had done when he added a generalizing paraphrase:

οὕτως εἰδωλολατρεία τῷ τῶν ἀνθρώπων ἀπ' ἀρχῆς παρεισεφθάρη βίῳ. καὶ οὐ μόνον οἱ ἐκ τῶν ἄλλων ἐθνῶν τοῖς εἰρημένοις τρόποις κατεφθείροντο, ἤδη δὲ καὶ Ἑβραίων ἱερὸν ἔθνος διὰ τὸν Ἀβραὰμ νομισθὲν ὅλον ἀπολωλεκὸς βουλήν ἐστιν οὐχ ὑπεῖκον θείοις προφήταις ὀδυρομένοις καὶ ἐξιλασκομένοις τὴν ὀργὴν τοῦ θεοῦ ὑπὲρ αὐτῶν, οἳ πολλάκις πρότερον διὰ τὰς εἰδωλολατρείας αὐτῶν ὡς Μωσῆς καὶ Ἠλίας κατεκτέννυσαν αὐτούς.

But, as Wyss pointed out, 'Zu Gregor von Nazianz', in *Phyllobolia für Peter Von der Mühll* (Basle, 1946), 153–83 at 171 ff., there can be no suggestion that Nicetas had the L lines in front of him: he merely suspected a hiatus. We may be allowed to think he was wrong.

We may also question whether Wyss is right in being hesitant about the connection of vv. 82–99 with the rest of the poem. He writes, com-menting on the introduction by the scribe of Ox. Clark. 12 (C) of separate titles before vv. 31 and 82: 'Was περὶ διαθηκῶν anlangt, ist es völlig ausgeschlossen, daß Vers 31 den Anfang eines Gedichtes bildet; dagegen halte ich es für denkbar, daß die Verse 82–99 ursprünglich ein selbständiges Gedicht über die Taufe ausgemacht haben' (p. 172 n. 1). Yet what good reason is there for believing that the Clarkianus' scribe was more justified in his second insertion of a title? (That he had a propensity for adding unnecessary titles may be seen from his introduction of Περὶ ἀγγέλων in *Arc*. 4, before v. 89.) V. 81 speaks of redemption: vv. 82 ff. discuss the nature of man and his proneness to the sin which made Redemption necessary. Again, the reference to baptism in vv. 78b ff. is picked up and the thought carried on in the closing lines of the poem. Finally, it may be held that the anaphora of vv. 97–9 provides a fitting conclusion to the entire sequence of eight poems, as Keydell argued in 'Ein dogmatisches Lehrgedicht Gregors von Nazianz', 317–18. The argument is not weakened by Greg.'s use of a similar anaphora elsewhere in the middle of a poem, *carm*. 2. 1. 13. 96–8 (M. 37. 1235A); it is sufficient that there is particular point in its use here. Finally, if we accept the continuity between vv. 18 and 19 we are spared consideration of Keydell's suggestion (loc. cit.) of further hiatus between v. 18 and L 1 and again between L 60 and v. 19.

1–8. *The unity of the Old and the New Laws*

The alleged discrepancy between the provisions of the Old and the New Testaments formed an important part of 4th-c. anti-Christian polemic, cf. Courcelle, 'Anti-Christian Arguments', 159–60.

2. ἐξεφαάνθη: cf. *Arc*. 2. 9–10 n.

4. πείρασιν αἴης: cf. πείρατα γαίης in L 14 Wyss.

5. This and the following lines dispose of any ambiguity in δισσοῖο (v. 1): for δισσός may mean 'diverse, at variance', as well as 'twofold'.

6–7. δόγμασιν: 'divine decrees' (see *PGL* s.v. D). Two possibilities are mentioned to be dismissed. If the Testaments conflict, either the inconsistency is a divine oversight or it implies a change of mind.

  παλιμβούλοισιν: perhaps the presence of the form παλίμβουλος, in a line where metre guarantees the -βουλος rather than the -βολος ending, may cause second thoughts about LSJ's dismissing παλίμβουλος as a *falsa lectio* for παλίμβολος. The latter carries with it the sense of unreliability, rather than of wiser reconsideration (cf. exx. in LSJ).

9–18. *The historical results of the Fall of Adam*

The poem here picks up the thought of *Arc.* 7. 128–9. But, again, there is no explanation of the way in which subsequent generations are affected by Adam. Something is transmitted which is more than mere bad example, but precisely what we are not told. Instead, Greg. illustrates the effects from history. Adam's fall has laid his descendants open to all the evils which entered the world with the Fall of Lucifer (cf. *Arc.* 6. 73–81 n.).

9. λυσσήεις: apart from its occurrence in Greg., the form λυσσήεις is found only in Hesychius, where it is glossed μανιώδης. Soph. mentions the present passage. The word is not in *PGL*. Having, as it would appear, coined the word, Greg. uses it with δαίμων as subject in *carm.* 2. 1. 1. 52 (M. 37. 974A) and at *carm.* 2. 1. 13. 43 (1230A) of the devil. M. Schmid called it 'ein Lieblingswort Gregors' ('Gregor von Nazianz und Hesychios', *RhM*, NF 21 (1866), pp. 489–97 at 494). The λύσσα association is a powerful one. In Classical literature the word may describe a fearful, supernaturally caused madness or it may refer to the raging of the Furies; cf. e.g. A. *Ch.* 288; E. *Ba.* 977. Euripides once personifies Λύσσα as the goddess of madness (*HF* 823). In the Fathers it may refer to the follies of paganism or heresy; cf. *PGL* s.vv. λύσσα, λυσσάω.

βάλεν ἐκ: cf. *Arc.* 6. 65 n.

11–12. Adam is compared to a defeated military commander. A similar figure is found in *carm.* 2. 1. 34. 137 (M. 37. 1317A). For ἡγητήρ = 'leader' cf. Pi. *P.* 1. 69 ἀγητήρ.

ἔγχεϊ: this reading, over against αἴσχεϊ, is supported by Nicetas' paraphrase κοντοῖς καὶ βέλεσι καὶ πᾶσιν ὅπλοις.

κακὸν καὶ κῆρα φυτεῦσαι: cf. H. *Il.* 15. 134 κακὸν μέγα πᾶσι φυτεῦσαι and *Od.* 2. 165 φόνον καὶ κῆρα φυτεῦσαι. Cf. *Arc.* 4. 53–4 n.

13 appears to contain a reminiscence of *h. Merc.* 413 Ἑρμέω βουλῇσι κλεψίφρονος. The only other recorded instance is in Ps.-Man. 1(5). 93 (Köchly, p. 88).

14–18 begin to detail man's religious deviations. Cf. Ath. *inc.* 11 (M. 25. 116B f.), *gent.* 8 (M. 25. 16C ff.). For the practice of astrology cf. *Arc.* 5. In *or.* 28. 14 (p. 44. 6 ff., M. 36. 44C f.) Greg. describes how pictures and images of the dead came to be worshipped. He may also have in mind the divinization of emperors, the subject of attack in e.g. Ath. *gent.* (M. 25. 20B f.).

14. Here the conventional epithet ceases to be conventional, taking the weight of meaning.

17. The meaning appears to be 'reliable (only) in bringing evil on his own kind', his followers or, possibly, 'reliable in bringing (all too) familiar evils'. The devil, who is supremely faithless, is represented as to be trusted only to produce evil.

19–30. *The religious failure of the Hebrews*

19. For Israel as a holy people cf. Exod. 19. 6, Deut. 7. 6, *al.*

20. λιταζομένοισιν: the prophets either entreated God to spare his people (cf. e.g. Joel 2. 17) or begged the people to repent. λιτάζομαι is a by-form of λίσσομαι, not common, but found in Oppian (*C*. 2. 373) and Orph. fr. 333 (Kern, p. 332), as well as in several inscriptions (cf. LSJ). Greg. uses the form in *carm*. 2. 2 (epigr.) 65. 1 (M. 38. 116A, *AP* 8. 192. 1).

21. μῆνιν ἀεί: is this a curious play on H. *Il*. 1. 1?

ὤλλυον is the imperfect of the form ὀλλύω and is found in Archil. 27 and *Com. Adesp.* 608. For Israel's killing of the prophets cf. Matt. 23. 27, Luke 13. 34, Acts 7. 52.

23–4. οἱ πλέονες κακίους: cf. H. *Od*. 2. 277, where the words are part of a γνώμη expressing decline, each generation being worse than the preceding:

> παῦροι γάρ τοι παῖδες ὁμοῖοι πατρὶ πέλονται,
> οἱ πλέονες κακίους, παῦροι δέ τε πατρὸς ἀρείους.

ἄλσεα: ἄλση regularly tr. 'āšērîm in LXX.

ὀρέων κορυφὰς represents such expressions as βουνὸν ὑψηλόν (Heb. *gib'ā gǝbōhā*): e.g. 4 Kgds. 17. 10, Jer. 2. 20.

αἱματόεντας: demanding human sacrifices. Cf. *Arc*. 6. 78 n.

25. *PGL* misprints ζηλήμονα as ζηγήμονα.

26. ἐκ δ' ἐτίναχθεν: cf. H. *Il*. 16. 348 (of the knocking out of teeth). Caillau appears to make the word refer to the Exile ('e terra sua eiecti sunt'), but the second half of the line makes it more probable that Greg. is thinking of the displacement of the Hebrews from their unique position.

26b–30. *The Gentiles and the New Covenant.* Greg. writes of himself as the representative Gentile.

27. ζήλοιο: cf. Rom. 11. 11.

ποδηγεσίη is a *hapax legomenon*.

29. Greg. here envisages the final conversion of the Jews, who will one day repent. The question of the place of the Jews in Divine

Providence was one which exercised a number of the Fathers, and some of their interest takes the form of anti-Jewish apologetic. Cyril of Jerusalem appears to believe that the repentance of the Jews will come too late to be of any avail, *catech.* 13. 41 (M. 33. 822A f.). His namesake of Alexandria, in many ways his inferior in charity, here displays a softer temper and looks for the ultimate conversion of the Jews, *Joel* 14 (3. 213B, M. 71. 353C ff.), *glaph. Gen.* 6 (1. 200E, M. 69. 320B ff.), *Jo.* 2. 5 (4. 208D, M. 73. 340C f.). Greg. clearly distinguishes the final repentance of the Jews from their present position, to which he shows some hostility. He expresses delight that Julian was unable to carry out a plan to resettle the Jews in Jerusalem, ascribing the failure in graphic terms to divine intervention. Cf. *or.* 5. 3–4 (M. 35. 668A ff.), also H. Lietzmann, *A History of the Early Church*, iii: *From Constantine to Julian*, ET B. Lee Woolf (London, 1953), 282.

Origen had earlier taken a firm line against Judaism, as may be seen from N. de Lange, *Origen and the Jews* (Cambridge, 1976). The whole question is fully surveyed in M. Simon, *Verus Israel: Études sur les relations entre chrétiens et juifs dans l'empire romain (135–425)*, 2 edn. (Paris, 1964).

ἀνίης: the fall of Jerusalem in AD 70 and the subsequent scattering of the Jews were taken as clear signs of their punishment for the death of Jesus. Cf. e.g. Eus. *h.e.* 1. 1. 2 (p. 6. 9 ff., M. 20. 49A).

30. βασκανίη: the story of the evil which envelops man begins with ὁ βάσκανος (*Arc.* 6. 66). The final dispensation of God's grace will use βασκανία as a means of accomplishing divine purpose.

31–59. *The purpose of the Incarnation*

V. 31 picks up from v. 24. The Incarnation follows the depravity of the broken Law.

Vv. 32–52 are substantially the same as *carm.* 1. 2. 1. 137–54 (M. 37. 535A f.). V. 40 from ἀθανάτοιο to v. 45 are not found in the *moralia* passage and there are minor verbal differences elsewhere.

32. ἔμμορε τιμῆς: the same words are found in H. *Il.* 1. 278, 15. 189, *Od.* 5. 335, 11. 338, Hes. *Op.* 347, Call. fr. 373.

34–9a. As a result of the Fall the divine element in man was being destroyed and needed to be reasserted.

34. μοίρης: cf. *Arc.* 7. 72, 77.

35. θυμοβόροιο: cf. LSJ. Here the θυμός element indicates the soul of man which was being eaten away by evil. (Cf. *PGL* s.v. θυμοκτόνος and θυμοφθόρος).

36. σκολιόν ... δράκοντα: cf. *Arc.* 6. 41, *carmm.* 1. 1. 2. 141 (M. 37. 533A), 2. 1. 45. 101 (1360A).

δράκοντα identifies the devil with the serpent of Gen. 3 (it is a natural synonym for ὄφιν) and also with the whole complex of evil which is associated with the dragon in Daniel, Rev. 12. 3, *al.* σκολιόν points at once to the twisting, sinuous motion of the snake (cf. Milton, *P.L.* 9. 499: 'Fold above fold, a surging maze; ...'), and to his crooked, evil ways.

The suggestion was made by A. Ludwich, 'Nachahmer und Vorbilder des Dichters Gregorios von Nazianz', *RhM* NF 42 (1887), 233–8 at 238, that σκολιόν ... δράκοντα is a reminiscence of Aratus 70, where the words σκολιοῖο Δράκοντος refer to the constellation Draco. But equally well one might cite Isa. 27. 1 ἐπὶ τὸν δράκοντα ὄφιν σκολιόν. The figure appealed to verse writers. Cf. *or. sib.* 8. 116 σκολιοῦ ... δράκοντος and Nonnus, *D.* 12. 319 σκολίῃσι δράκων δινωτὸς ἀκάνθαις.

37. λάχος: the association of the word is here not with 'lot' or 'chance'. Rather does it mean 'possession' (cf. LSJ s.v. λαγχάνω II). It thus approximates to the meaning κλῆρος in L 45 and 47 Wyss. By their sin men were passing into the power of the devil: Christ came to reassert inalienable rights over the human race.

37b–39a. The figure changes. Man is diseased with sin which Christ alone can cure. Cf. *Arc.* 2. 57, 61 n.

39b. κενώσας: for the doctrine of 'kenosis' in the writings of the Cappadocians cf. P. Henry, 'Kénose', *Dictionnaire de la Bible*, Suppl. v (Paris, 1957), 79–85 (79–80) referring specifically to Greg.; Sellers, *Two Ancient Christologies*, 70–1; Barbel, *Fünf theol. Reden*, 160–1 n. 40 on Greg. in particular. Cf. *or.* 29. 18 (p. 101. 15 ff., M. 36. 97C). What becomes clear from these is that nothing approximating to modern 'kenotic' theories emerges in the Cappadocians, or, indeed, in the Fathers generally.

Phil. 2. 7 contains the words ἑαυτὸν ἐκένωσε, μορφὴν δούλου λαβών, ἐν ὁμοιώματι γενόμενος. Greg. here defines the element of limitation in the Incarnation. The Logos limits a characteristic manifestation of Godhead, its 'glory'. This is very much in line with what Greg. wrote in *or.* 37. 3 (M. 36. 285B): ἀλλ᾽ ἐπειδὴ κενοῦται δι᾽ ἡμᾶς, ἐπειδὴ κατέρχεται (κένωσιν δὲ λέγω τὴν τῆς δόξης οἷον ὕφεσίν τε καὶ ἐλάττωσιν), διὰ τοῦτο χωρητὸς γίνεται.

40–1. ἀμήτωρ ... δίχα πατρός: cf. Heb. 7. 3: ἀπάτωρ, ἀμήτωρ.

COMMENTARY ON *ARC*. 8. 40–52

Greg. explains in *or*. 30. 21 (p. 143. 8–9, M. 36. 132C): Μελχισεδὲκ δέ, ὡς ἀμήτωρ τὸ ὑπὲρ ἡμᾶς, καὶ ἀπάτωρ τὸ καθ᾽ ἡμᾶς.

41–2. ξένος ... οὐ ξένος: this is not a correction but a paradox (cf. ἄμβροτος ... βροτωθείς). In human terms, Christ was an unprecedented son through the Virgin Birth. Yet he 'came to his own' (John 1. 11) and took normal human form.

βροτωθείς: βροτόω is attested in the lexica only here and in *Christus Patiens* 511 (Ps.-Gr.Naz., M. 38. 177A).

43–4. ὅλον ... ὅλος ... ὅλος: cf. *or*. 30. 6 (p. 116. 3–4, M. 36. 109C): ὅλον ἐν ἑαυτῷ ἐμὲ φέρων. This position was capable of development in an anti-Apollinarian direction, but, as is argued in Introd., the words are not here used explicitly against Apollinarius.

48–9. The two natures of Christ. Cf. Introd. to *Arc*. 2. Greg. insists on the unity of Christ: he is ἕν. But it is open to us to ask what this 'one' is. Greg. gives little direct answer. ἀγείρας is a colourless word ('bringing together') which gives no hint of the relationship of the two natures. The same is true in *or*. 30. 8 (p. 120. 10 f., M. 36. 113B), where see Mason's n.: εἰ γὰρ καὶ τὸ συναμφότερον ἕν, ἀλλ᾽ οὐ τῇ φύσει, τῇ δὲ συνόδῳ τούτων.

κευθομένην: for the hidden divine nature cf. *Arc*. 3. 92 n. ἀμφαδίην means 'obvious' (cf. *PGL* s.v. ἀναφανδόν), rather than 'revealed'. The contrast, as in *Arc*. 3, is between the man Jesus who could be seen by any casual onlooker and the divine Logos who was concealed from many. The revelation consisted in the whole Person of Christ.

51–2. A passage from *or*. 29. 19 (p. 102. 12 ff., M. 36. 100A) is of value for understanding the present passage: διὰ μέσου νοὸς ὁμιλήσας σαρκί, καὶ γενόμενος ἄνθρωπος, ὁ κάτω Θεός· ἐπειδὴ συνεκράθη Θεῷ, καὶ γέγονεν εἰς, τοῦ κρείττονος ἐκνικήσαντος, ἵνα γένωμαι τοσοῦτον θεός, ὅσον ἐκεῖνος ἄνθρωπος. Christ is one and he is divine because Godhead comes in the Incarnation not from outside to an alien community but to humanity which is akin to Godhead. κερασθείς should be taken closely with βροτός. The affinity of God and man stems from the creation of man when he was 'mixed with Godhead'. Christ is divine 'on both sides', fully divine as Logos and partly divine as man. Cf. Norris, pp. 154–5; cf. *ep*. 101 (M. 37. 180A): τὰ γὰρ ἀμφότερα ἓν τῇ συγκράσει, θεοῦ μὲν ἐνανθρωπήσαντος, ἀνθρώπου δὲ θεωθέντος, ἢ ὅπως ἄν τις ὀνομάσειε.

The ending of ἀμφοτέρωθεν should not be pressed. Greg. clearly intended it to mean that the two natures existed side by side, not that any composite nature was made 'from' both. We are a long way from the misunderstanding over ἐν δύο φύσεσιν and ἐκ δύο φύσεων which followed Chalcedon. (Cf. Bindley–Green, *The Oecumenical Documents of the Faith*, 197.) Cf. also *or*. 2. 23 (M. 35. 429C), 30. 8 (M. 36. 113B, p. 120. 10–11), 38. 3 (313C).

ὑπέστη: the emphasis is here on a fundamental meaning of ὑφίστημι, reality of existence. As Grillmeier observes of Hipp. *haer.* 1. 8. 2 (GCS 3. 13. 15; M. 16. 3032D), it may be taken as synonymous with ὑπάρχειν (*Christ in Christian Tradition*, i. 117 n. 31).

53–9. *Christ as the Second Adam.* Cf. *carm*. 1. 1. 10. 4 (M. 37. 465A), *or*. 2. 25 (M. 35. 433C ff.), 24. 9 (1180B), 39. 2 (M. 36. 336B), 41. 4 (433A), with 1 Cor. 15. 45.

54. ἐξακέσαιτο: cf. 37b–39a n.

πετάσματι: cf. *Arc*. 3. 91 n. Again the word = καταπετάσματι, this time alluding to Heb. 10. 20. Access to God, prevented by human sin, is made possible through the veil of Christ's flesh.

55. χωρητός: it is remarkable that a word which does not appear in LSJ should call for the best part of a column's entry in *PGL*, with meanings ranging over 'passable', 'finite', and 'comprehensible', in the case of the second and third in contexts of theological sensitivity. Here we find the straightforward meaning 'capable of'.

56–9. *The meeting of Christ and Satan.* The language is that of direct conquest, of the 'overthrow' of the devil. Yet, as in *or*. 39. 13 (M. 36. 349A), there is the suggestion that the devil, for all his cunning, has been outwitted: ἐπειδὴ γὰρ ᾤετο ἀήττονος εἶναι τῆς κακίας ὁ σοφιστής, θεότητος ἐλπίδι δελεάσας ἡμᾶς, σαρκὸς προβλήματι δελεάζεται.

Cf. also *or*. 30. 6 (p. 116. 14 ff., M. 36. 112A) and Mason, edn. 117 n. The interplay of conquest and deception is discussed in the SC edn. of *or*. 38–41, pp. 59, 176–7.

There is perhaps a double sense in ἀέλπτως. It might mean 'beyond man's reasonable expectation' (cf. A. *Pers*. 261), as well as 'unexpectedly for Satan', cf. Gr. Nyss. *or. catech*. 26 (p. 97. 5, M. 45. 68B): παρὰ τὸ ἐλπισθέν.

59. This is an apt simile in that the elements go beyond mere picturesque imagery. The rock is a traditional OT figure for strength and stability, as the sea may be a symbol of the chaotic and demonic. One is reminded also of the Homeric picture of Hector, whose attack upon unbroken ranks of the enemy is likened to that of waves beating upon a rock (*Il*. 15. 605–22, esp. 618 ff.).

For ἁλίκτυπον cf. S. *Ant.* 953, Nonn. *D.* 31. 113, and ἠλίβατος in *Il.* 15. 619.

τρηχείην gives the picture of a jagged rock.

OT imagery of the rock is generally different. The land-locked desert rock of Exod. 17. 6 *al.*, identified by Paul with the pre-existent Christ in 1 Cor. 10. 4, is a symbol not of strength but of physical or spiritual refreshment. The most common use, of course, does concentrate thought on strength, that of refuge and salvation, but it is the symbol of God's provision for human need and weakness, not of the divine power to withstand an evil power. Again, the great white rock which is identified with the Son of God in Hermas is one which towers above a mountain range (*sim.* 9. 2. 1–2, *al.*, interpreted in 9. 12. 1).

60–71. *The Coming of Christ*

60–4. The birth (Luke 2. 13, Matt. 2. 1 ff.).

60–1. There is no need to suppose that Greg. believed that the earth had literally shaken at the birth of Christ as a parallel to the earthquake recorded in Matt. 27. 51. Both heaven and earth are in a state of commotion and excitement (cf. Matt. 21. 10). In *or.* 31. 25 (M. 36. 160D; p. 176. 3 ff.), with Heb. 12. 27 in mind, he writes of the two great changes which affected human life, the two Testaments, comparing them to σεισμοὶ γῆς, like the words used in Matt. 27. 51. (See the SC edn., p. 323 n.)

62. Cf. *Arc.* 5. 54 n.

63. **λάτρις** here = λάτρης, 'worshipper'.

64. The 'newborn' child had a new, unprecedented birth.

65–6. The suggestion that birth involved uncleanness is simply an extension of the view that flesh is by nature unclean. Cf. e.g. Celsus in Or. *Cels.* 6. 73 (p. 142. 18 ff., M. 11. 1408C). Greg. appears to go beyond Origen in his answer. The latter contented himself with denying that the contact was of the kind to affect the divine nature, drawing the stock comparison of light unaffected by dirt; cf. H. Chadwick, tr. of *Contra Celsum* (Cambridge, 1965), 387 n. 2. Greg. does not concede as much, avoiding the imputation of shame, not by minimizing the contact with the body, but by limiting the occasion of shame to sin.

ἐπεὶ Λόγος αὐτὸν ἔπηξεν. It would be more usual to say that the Logos formed the *body*; cf. e.g. Ath. *inc.* 8. 3 (p. 12. 29, M. 25.

109C). But αὐτοπαγὴς βροτὸς in v. 69 comes closer to the idea of producing a human body.

67. ῥύσει: cf. 2. 14, 7. 85 nn. The present use combines the senses of the 'flow' of human life through the process of physical birth and instability of mortal life.

68. ἀνύμφέα: this is the only certain instance of ἀνυμφής recorded in the lexica (LSJ note a cj.). Cf. Luke 1. 35.

69. αὐτοπαγὴς: comparison with the examples in LSJ will show Greg., as often, giving a new twist to the word. Caillau comments on αὐτοπαγὴς 'Communius hoc Spiritui sancto tribuitur'. But in the passage of Athanasius cited on vv. 65–6 n. it is the Logos who is subject: ἐν τῇ Παρθένῳ κατασκευάζει ἑαυτῷ ναὸν τὸ σῶμα. The close connection of the Logos with man is reasserted. He formed man in the first place and it is fitting that he should form the human body in which he comes as man.

καθήρατο: Caillau shows in his note, against Billius' application of the word to Christ's baptism, that the reference is to Luke 2. 22, the Purification.

70. θρεπτήρια: Christ repays the Law for being brought up in its nurture by submitting to its purificatory requirements. (Is not LSJ's tr. 'return made by children for their rearing' (s.v. θρεπτήριος III. 2) more apt than the *PGL* tr. 'price for rearing a child'? The second would suggest that the child is other than the person paying the price.)

71. πεμπτήριος is a word peculiar to Greg. See *carmm.* 2. 2 (poem.) 5. 264 (M. 37. 1540A), 2. 2 (poem.). 6. 1 (1542A), 2. 1. 11. 1795 (1155A). Christ's respect for the Law is a parting gift.

72–7a. *Christ and John the Baptist*

72. φάους . . . λύχνῳ: the Baptist was a true lamp, but still secondary, deriving his light from Christ, the True Light; cf. John 1. 6–9. The explicit contrast of λύχνος and φῶς is found in Origen, e.g. fr. 17 *in Jo.* (p. 496. 23).

73–4. Cf. Mark 1. 1–8; Matt. 3. 1–12; Luke 1. 5–25, 57–80; 3. 1–18; John 1. 6–9, 15–18.

75–7a. In these lines Isa. 57. 19 is alluded to (τοῖς μακρὰν καὶ τοῖς ἐγγὺς οὖσιν) and taken, as in Eph. 2. 17, to mean Gentiles and Jews. Combined with this is an interpretation of the 'Christ cornerstone' motif (cf. Eph. 2. 20, 1 Pet. 2. 6, Isa. 28. 16, Ps. 117 (118 Heb.). 22) in which Christ is the stone which joins the two walls, Jewish and

COMMENTARY ON *ARC*. 8. 75–81

Gentile; cf. Cyr. *Is*. 3. 2 (2. 397E, M. 70. 632D); Jo.D. *hom*. 4. 30 (M. 96. 632C). The form ἀκρόγωνος is found also in *carm*. 2. 1. 14. 15 (M. 37. 1246A).

Greg.'s epic vocabulary allows him a play on λαός/λᾶας.

77b–84. *The twofold cleansing*

Christ brought purification through baptism (cf. *PGL* s.v. καθάρσιος C. 2 for examples of this connection) and through the shedding of his blood. Cf. *Arc*. 2. 2 n.

ἀενάοιο: ἀέναος is applied to the Holy Spirit in *Hom. Clem*. 3. 12. It is particularly apt here for another of its associations, with the water of baptism (*Hom. Clem*. 11. 35) and also for its suggestion of 'living water' (*PGL* s.v. 1.b). Greg. treats baptism extensively in *or*. 40 (M. 36. 360B ff.), see SC edn.; cf. also *Arc*. 3. 44 ff. n., and below, vv. 86b–99.

79. αἵματος ἡμετέροιο: in *or*. 45. 29 (M. 36. 661D) Greg. identifies the blood of Christ shed at the Crucifixion as the human element, the water as the divine: αἷμα καὶ ὕδωρ τῆς πλευρᾶς χεόμενον· τὸ μὲν, ὡς ἄνθρωπον, τὸ δὲ, ὡς ὑπὲρ ἄνθρωπον.

80. ἐξεκένωσε: here used of 'pouring out', as in Theoc. 16. 40.

81. ῥύσιον is here used in much the same way as λύτρον (cf. Mark 10. 45). Cf. *AP* 6. 274, 7. 605, and ῥῦσις in Sir. 51. 9.

ἀρχεγόνων: the reference is to Adam. Cf. *carm*. 1. 1. 18. 3 (M. 37. 481A), which speaks of Christ's physical descent ἀφ᾽ αἵματος ἀρχε-γόνοιο 2. 2 (poem.), 1. 346 (1476A).

ἄποινον: Greg. here uses the sg. (found only in *IG* xiv. 1389 i 10) of a regular Classical word (in pl.) for 'ransom', 'atonement', 'compensation', or 'rescue'. Homer, Aeschylus, and Euripides may be cited along with 'rare' (LSJ) prose usages by Herodotus and Plato.

It would not be possible to tell from these lines what meaning Greg. attached to the 'ransom' idea. Elsewhere, however, he is more explicit. It is true that in *orr*. 1. 5 (M. 35. 400A), 29. 20 (p. 105. 5 ff., M. 36. 101A), and 30. 20 (p. 141. 7 ff., 132A) we are met by general statements, yet in *or*. 45. 22 (M. 36. 653A ff.) Greg. is quite precise in rejecting the view that the ransom was paid to the devil and is no less firm in refuting any payment to the Father; cf. *carm*. 1. 1. 10. 65–72 (M. 37. 470A). The locus of salvation is the divine οἰκονομία through which the Father accepts a sacrifice he has not demanded, a sacrifice made within the sphere of Godhead by the Son who acts out an integral divine purpose. There is full discussion of Greg.'s position in Winslow, *Dynamics*, 108 ff., Althaus, *Heilslehre*, 133 ff., Holl, *Amphilochius von Ikonium*, 180 ff., Turner, *Redemption*, ch. 3, esp. pp. 58 ff.

82–4 touch on the reasons for man's Fall. It is because man is τρεπτός that he could be seduced from keeping God's command, thus necessitating redemption. It is difficult to see what purpose is served by these lines. If man is τρεπτός it is because God created him so. If he were ἄτρεπτος, he would not be man but God (cf. *Arc.* 6. 54 n.), and the question of keeping God's command would not arise. The only point at which speculation takes on meaning is when it asks whether man, being τρεπτός, might still have avoided sin.

τρεπτός is very much a word of the Christian era, as it takes on the idea of mutability in the direction of sin. A determined opponent of Arianism like Greg. would be very much aware of its heretical application to the Son (e.g. in Ar. ap. Ath. *Ar.* 1. 9 (M. 26. 29B). In Greg.'s understanding, salvation is possible precisely because of the Son's immunity from this mortal weakness.

84. The three verbs in the imperfect (ἄεξε unaugmented is an attested early form) depict the human state as it might have been. In omitting ἄν or κεν Greg. appears to be extending the idiom discussed at *Arc.* 3. 49 n.; however, καί may be a corruption of κεν.

85–7a deal with man's actual condition. Apparently realizing that the speculation of the preceding lines would assimilate man to God, Greg. returns to his account of historical man and the means of his salvation, through baptism.

86. ἀμφιρεπῆ is a *hapax legomenon*. The double ρ form is found later in commentaries and in scholia on Eur. Cf. ἀμφιτάλαντον in *Arc.* 7. 103.

κλιτόν is also a *hapax legomenon*.

87b–99. *Baptism*

87b–90a. *The 'seal' of the Exodus.* The 'seal' of baptism is likened to the 'sealing' or marking of the Israelites' doorposts in Exod. 12. 21 ff. This typology may be traced through a number of the Fathers. Cf. e.g. Justin, *Dial.* 111. 3 (Goodspeed, p. 227; M. 6. 732C); Or. *sel. in Ex.* 12. 7 (M. 12. 284C f.); Bas. *hom.* 13. 4 (G. 2. 117B; M. 31. 432C); for discussion, and further references, see Lampe, *The Seal of the Spirit*, 116, J. Ysebaert, *Greek Baptismal Terminology*, 424. Cf. Greg. *or.* 1. 3 (M. 35. 479A) for the connection of the Exodus text and the seal with the death and resurrection of Christ and *or.* 40. 15 (M. 36. 377A f.) for the association with baptism: εἰ δὲ προκαταλάβοις σεαυτὸν τῇ σφραγῖδι, καὶ τὸ μέλλον ἀσφαλίσαιο τῷ καλλίστῳ τῶν βοηθημάτων καὶ στερροτάτῳ σημειωθεὶς καὶ ψυχὴν καὶ σῶμα, τῷ χρίσματι καὶ τῷ Πνεύματι, ὡς ὁ Ἰσραὴλ πάλαι τῷ νυκτερινῷ καὶ φυλακτινῷ τῶν πρωτοτόκων αἵματι, τί σοι συμβήσεται καὶ τί σοι πραγμάτευται; cf. *carm.* 1. 2. 34. 237 (M. 37. 962A). The present passage links cleansing and sealing both with baptism and with the death of Christ. It is appropriate that the Son who is Σφρηγὶς κινυμένη πατρῷος (*Arc.* 1. 31) should be closely linked with bestowing the seal of baptism.

90. N. P. Williams found difficulty with the length of the second syllable of νυκτὶ (*The Ideas of the Fall and of Original Sin*, 290 n. 1). But a long vowel in a dative singular is quite normal in Homer (cf. Monro, *Homeric Grammar*, §373).

90b–96. *The 'seal' of Christian baptism.*

91. σφρηγὶς: cf. Lampe, *The Seal of the Spirit*, 239–40.

ἀλεξικάκοιο: a word associated with the pagan gods Hermes and Zeus (e.g. Ar. *Pax* 422) is taken over for Christian use.

91–2. νηπιάχοις ... ἀεξομένοισι: these contrasts have suggested that Greg. is here foreshadowing a form of Pelagianism. It must be admitted that the charge is here more difficult to ward off than any which might be implied by *Arc.* 7. 122 ff. (cf. n.). It is difficult, however, to see how original sin could be dissociated from Greg.'s position. What has happened in Adam has clearly affected man, although, as we have seen, Greg. has no very clear notion of how this has happened. This passage may be taken as another facet of Greg.'s uncertainty. He does not think of adult baptism as superior; this he makes clear in *or.* 40. 29 (M. 36. 400C ff.). But he is, apparently, here pointing to the 'cure' of actual sin committed by one who has reached maturity. This need not mean that there was nothing in the child's condition which called for cure. But certainly there is something more obvious done in the case of the adult. (Cf. N. P. Williams, *The Ideas of the Fall and of Original Sin*, 289 ff., 345, 552; Kelly, *Doctrines*, 349 ff.) Cf. also *or.* 40. 7 (M. 36. 365C).

93. φωτοδόταο: the word glances at an ancient notion of baptism, enlightenment. Cf. *Arc.* 3. 44 n., and Ysebaert, *Greek Baptismal Terminology*, 173 ff., Moreschini, 'Luce'.

θεόρρυτος emphasizes again that the seal is the blood of Christ.

Oppian in *Hal.* 5. 9 writes of λύθροιο θεορρυτοῦ in reference to the blood of Titans.

94–5. Here we have imagery drawn from the baptismal ceremony, with its symbolic sense of plunging into the deep waters of distress and emerging unburdened to a new life.

There is probably a play on ἄκος/ἄχος, as there is in S. *Tr.* 1037.

97–9. As Keydell pointed out ('Lehrgedicht', 317–18), the anaphora provides a very fitting conclusion to the entire sequence of eight poems, though it is true that Greg. uses a similar device, with a line and a half in common, in *carm.* 2. 1. 13. 96–8 (M. 37. 1235A), in the middle of a poem.

Baptism is one of the great common gifts to man. The same idea appears in expanded form in *or.* 40. 8 (M. 36. 368C f.). The notion that there are great 'common gifts' of Nature is found in Menander 740 (531). 7–8 τὸν ἀέρα τὸν κοινόν and 416 (481). 4: τὸν ἥλιον τὸν κοινόν. Cf. 737 (611). Greg. refers to the idea in *or.* 32. 22 (M. 36. 200B f.). In talking of it in *or.* 33. 9 (M. 36. 225B) he claims: ἀρχαίως ἔχω καὶ φιλοσόφως. Is there perhaps in v. 98 a half-reminiscence of A. *Pr.* 1091–2 ὦ πάντων | αἰθὴρ κοινὸν φάος εἱλίσσων?

Kertsch (*Bildersprache*, 21–2), in a context referring to influences of Maximus of Tyre, cites as parallels *orr.* 14. 25 (M. 35. 889C), 19. 11 (1056C), and 4. 96 (629C), comparing also Clem. *str.* 3. 6 (p. 216. 30 ff., M. 8. 1148C f.) He is quoting from *Concerning Righteousness* by the Gnostic Epiphanes, who is delightfully characterized by H. Chadwick as 'an intelligent but nasty-minded adolescent of somewhat pornographic tendencies' (LCC ii; *Alexandrian Christianity*, 25).

99. The poem closes with the transition from the natural order established by God to the means of salvation appointed within the order of history.

σαόβροτον: would be a *hapax*. The form σαόμβροτον is found in Procl. *H.* 7. 40.

Select Bibliography

A. PRIMARY SOURCES

(i) Editions of or including the Arcana (including translations and scholia)

BILLIUS (De Billy, J.), *Gregorii Nazianzeni opuscula quaedam* (Paris, 1575).

—— *Gregorii Nazianzeni omnia opera* (Paris, 1583).

BOLLIG, P. J. (vol. i), and GISMONDI, H. [= E.] (vol. ii), *S. Gregorii Nazianzeni liber carminum iambicorum versio Syriaca antiquissima*, 2 vols. (Beirut, 1895–6).

CAILLAU, A. B. = vol. ii of Maurist edn., *Gregorii Nazianzeni opera omnia*, 2 vols. (Paris, 1778, 1840).

CANTARELLA, R., *Poeti bizantini* (Milan, 1948).

CUMONT, F., in *Catalogus codicum astrologorum Graecorum*, viii/3, ed. P. Boudreaux (Brussels, 1912), 120–2 [Cosmas' scholion on *Arc* 5. 46].

DEVOLDER, E., *Saint Grégoire de Nazianze: Textes choisis* (Namur, 1960) [repr. of Gallay's trans. of *Arcana*].

DRONKE, E., *De Niceta Davide et Zonara interpretibus carminum S. Gregorii Nazianzeni* (Koblenz, 1839).

—— *S. Gregorii Nazianzeni Carmina Selecta* (Göttingen, 1840).

GALLAY, P., *Grégoire de Nazianze: Poèmes et Lettres choisies* (Paris 1941) [cf. Devolder].

HOESCHEL, D., *S. Gregorii Nazianzeni Theologi Arcana seu De Principiis versus CCCCXXCII, cum paraphrasi Graeca* (Leiden, 1591).

HORNSCHUH, M. J., *S. Gregorii Nazianzeni Theologi Ἀπόρρητα seu Arcana* (Leipzig, 1645).

LEUNCLAVIUS, F., *Opera Gregorii Nazianzeni* (Basle, 1591).

MCGUCKIN, J. A., *St. Gregory Nazianzen: Selected Poems* (Oxford, 1986, repr. 1989).

MAI, A. *Spicilegium Romanum*, ii (Rome, 1839), 1–373 of second sequence [Cosmas' scholia].

MIGNE, J. P., *Patrologia Graeca*, 35–8 (Paris, 1857–8).

MORELLI, F., *Gregorii Nazianzeni opera omnia*, 2 vols. (Paris, 1609–12; repr. Paris, 1630; Leipzig and Cologne, 1690).

MORESCHINI, C., *Gregorio Nazianzeno: I cinque discorsi teologici* (Rome, 1986) [contains a tr. of the *Arcana*, with footnotes].

—— and COSTA, I., *Niceta David: Commento ai 'Carmina Arcana' di Gregorio Nazianzeno* (Naples, 1992).

VÁRI, R., 'Sancti Gregorii Nazianzeni codicis Mediceo-Laurentiani celeberrimi collatio', *Egyetemes philologiai közlöny*, 20 (1896), 759–72.

(*ii*) *Editions of other works of Gregory*

BARBEL, J., *Gregor von Nazianz: Die fünf theologischen Reden* (Testimonia, 3; Düsseldorf, 1963).

BERNARDI, J., S. *Grégoire de Nazianze: Discours 1–3* (SC 247; Paris, 1978).

—— S. *Grégoire de Nazianze: Discours 4–5, Contre Julien* (SC 309; Paris, 1983).

BLACKETT, B. P., *Translations from Gregory Nazianzen, Aurelius and Prudentius* (London, 1937)

BOYD, H. J., *Select Poems of Synesius and Gregory Nazianzen* (London, 1814).

BROWNE, C. G., and SWALLOW, J. E., *St. Gregory of Nazianzus: Select Orations and Letters* (LNPF vii. 187–498; Oxford and New York, 1894).

CHATFIELD, A. W., *Songs and Hymns of the Earliest Christian Greek Poets Translated into English Verse* (London, 1876).

DAVIDS, H. L., *De Gnomologieën van Sint Gregorius van Nazianze* (Amsterdam, 1940).

GALLAY, P., *Gregor von Nazianz: Briefe* (GCS 53; Berlin, 1969).

—— S. *Grégoire de Nazianze: Lettres*, 2 vols. (Paris, 1964, 1967).

—— and JOURJON, M., S. *Grégoire de Nazianze: Discours théologiques 27–31* (SC 250; Paris, 1978).

—— —— S. *Grégoire de Nazianze: Lettres théologiques* (SC 208; Paris, 1974).

JUNGCK, C., *Gregor von Nazianz: De vita sua* (Heidelberg, 1974).

LANGUS, JOANNES, *Gregorii Nazianzeni Graeca quaedam et sancta carmina* (Basle, 1567).

MANUTIUS, ALDUS, *Gregorii ep. Nazianzeni carmina* (Venice, 1504).

MASON, A. J., *The Five Theological Orations of Gregory of Nazianzus* (Cambridge, 1899).

MORESCHINI, C., and GALLAY, P., S. *Grégoire de Nazianze: Discours 38–41* (SC 358; Paris, 1990).

MOSSAY, J., S. *Grégoire de Nazianze: Discours 24–26* (SC 284; Paris. 1981).

NORRIS, F. W., *Faith Gives Fullness to Reasoning: The Five Theological Orations of S. Gregory Nazianzen* (Leiden, 1991) [with tr. by F. Williams and L. Wickham].

PALLA, R., *Gregor von Nazianz: Carmina de Virtute Ia/Ib* (Graz, 1985) [tr. and comm. M. Kertsch].

WERHAHN, H. M., *Gregorii Nazianzeni Σύγκρισις βίων* (Wiesbaden, 1953).

B. SECONDARY SOURCES

(*i*) *Works of reference*

ARNDT, W. F., and GINGRICH, F. W., *A Greek–English Lexicon of the New Testament and Other Early Christian Literature* (Chicago and Cambridge, 1952).

CHANTRAINE, P., *Grammaire homérique*, 2 vols. (Paris, 1958, 1963).

DENNISTON, J. D., *The Greek Particles*, 2nd edn. (Oxford, 1954).

SELECT BIBLIOGRAPHY

EBELING, H., *Lexicon Homericum*, 2 vols. (Leipzig, 1880–5).

GEERARD, M., *Clavis Patrum Graecorum*, ii (Turnhout, 1974), 179–209, nos. 3010–3125.

GOODWIN, W. W., *Syntax of the Moods and Tenses of the Greek Verb* (London and New York, 1889).

MONRO, D. B., *A Grammar of the Homeric Dialect* (Oxford, 1891).

MÜLLER, G., *Lexicon Athanasianum* (Berlin, 1944–52).

ROSCHER, W. H., *Ausführliches Lexikon der griechischen und römischen Mythologie*, 6 vols. and 4 suppls. (Leipzig, 1884–1937).

SCHNEEMELCHER, W., *Bibliographia Patristica* (Berlin, 1959–).

SCHWYZER, E., rev. DEBRUNNER, A., *Griechische Grammatik* (Munich, 1953).

SOPHOCLES, E. A., *Greek Lexicon of the Roman and Byzantine Periods* (New York and Leipzig, 1893).

STEPHANUS, H., *Thesaurus Graecae Linguae*, ed. K. Hase, W. and L. Dindorf (Paris, 1831–65).

(*ii*) *Works on Gregory* (*or in large part concerned with him*)

ACKERMANN, W., *Die didaktische Poesie des Gregorius von Nazianz* (Leipzig, 1908).

ALTHAUS, H., *Die Heilslehre des heiligen Gregor von Nazianz* (Münsterische Beiträge zur Theologie, 34; Munster, 1972).

ARMSTRONG, A. H., 'The Theory of Non-Existence of Matter in Plotinus and the Cappadocians', *Stud. Patr.* 5 (= TU 80; Berlin, 1962), 427–9.

ASMUS, I. R., 'Gregor von Nazianz und sein Verhältnis zum Kynismus', *Theologische Studien und Kritiken*, 67 (1894), 314–38.

BELLINI, E., *La chiesa nel mistero della salvezza in S. Gregorio Nazianzeno* (Venegono Inferiore (Varese), 1970).

—— 'Bibliografia su San Gregorio Nazianzeno' (*La Scuola Cattolica*, supplemento bibliografico 1971), 165–81.

—— 'Il dogma trinitario nei primi discorsi di Gregorio Nazianzeno', *Augustinianum*, 13 (1973), 525–34.

BENOÎT, A., *S. Grégoire de Nazianze: Sa vie, ses œuvres, et son époque* (Marseille and Paris, 1876; repr. Hildesheim and New York, 1973).

BERNARDI, J., *La Prédication des Pères cappadociens: Le Prédicateur et son auditoire* (PFLS 30; Montpellier, 1968).

CALLAHAN, J. F., 'Greek Philosophy and the Cappadocian Cosmology', *DOP* 12 (1958), 29–57.

CATAUDELLA, Q., 'Le poesie di Gregorio Nazianzeno', *Atene e Roma*, 8 (1927), 88–96.

—— 'Gregorio Nazianzeno', *Enciclopedia Cattolica*, vi (1951), 1088–96.

CORSARO, F., 'Gregorio Nazianzeno poeta', *MSLC* 6 (1956), 5–21.

CRIMI, C. U., 'Il problema delle "false quantities" di Gregorio Nazianzeno alla luce della tradizione manoscritta di un carme, I,2,10: *De virtute*', *Siculorum Gymnasium*, 25 (1972), 1–26.

267

CUMMINGS, J. T., 'Towards a Critical Edition of the *Carmen de Vita Sua* of St. Gregory Nazianzen', *Stud. Patr.* 7 (= TU 92; Berlin, 1966), 52–9.

DEMOEN, K. 'The Attitude towards Greek Poetry in the Verse of Gregory Nazianzen', in J. den Boeft and A. Hilhorst (eds.), *Early Christian Poetry: A Collection of Essays* (Supplements to *Vigiliae Christianae*, 22; Leiden and New York, 1993), 235–52.

DONDERS, A., *Der hl. Kirchenlehrer Gregor von Nazianz als Homilet* (Münster, 1909).

DRÄSEKE, J., 'Neuplatonisches in des Gregorios von Nazianz Trinitätslehre', *BZ* 15 (1906), 141–60.

DUBEDOUT, E., *De D. Gregorii Nazianzeni carminibus* (Paris, 1901).

DZIECH, J., *De Gregorio Nazianzeno Diatribae quae dicitur alumno* (Poznań, 1925).

ELLVERSON, A., *The Dual Nature of Man: A Study in the Theological Anthropology of Gregory of Nazianzus* (Acta Univ. Upsal., Studia doctrinae Christianae, 21; Stockholm, 1981).

FLEURY, S., *Hellénisme et christianisme: S. Grégoire de Nazianze et son temps* (Paris, 1930).

FOCKEN, J., *De Gregorii Nazianzeni orationum carminum dogmaticorum argumentandi ratione* (Diss. Nuremberg, 1912).

FRANGESKOU, V. A., 'Gregory Nazianzen's Usage of the Homeric Simile', Ἑλληνικά (Thessaloniki), 36 (1985), 12–26.

GALLAY, P., *Langue et style de S. Grégoire de Nazianze dans sa correspondance* (Paris, 1943).

—— *La Vie de S. Grégoire de Nazianze* (Lyon, 1943).

GOTTWALD, R., *De Gregorio Nazianzeno Platonico* (Berlin, 1906).

GREGG, R. C., *Consolation Philosophy: Greek and Christian* Paideia *in Basil and the Two Gregories* (Patristic Monograph Series, 3; Cambridge, Mass., 1975).

GRENIER, A., *La Vie et les poésies de S. Grégoire de Nazianze* (Clermont-Ferrand, 1858).

GRONAU, C., *De Basilio, Gregorio Nazianzeno Nyssenoque Platonis imitatoribus* (Göttingen, 1908).

GUIGNET, M., *S. Grégoire de Nazianze et la rhétorique* (Paris, 1911).

HAUSER-MEURY, M., *Prosopographie zu den Schriften Gregors von Nazianz* (Diss. Basel: Theophaneia, 13; Bonn, 1960).

HERGENRÖTHER, J., *Die Lehre von der göttlichen Dreieinigkeit nach dem hl. Gregor von Nazianz, dem Theologen* (Regensburg, 1850).

HENRY, R. DE L., *The Later Greek Optative and its Use in the Writings of Gregory Nazianzen* (Washington, DC, 1943).

HOLL, K., *Amphilochius von Ikonium in seinem Verhältnis zu den großen Kappadoziern* (Tübingen, 1904).

KERTSCH, M., *Bildersprache bei Gregor von Nazianz: Ein Beitrag zur spätantiken Rhetorik und Popularphilosophie* (Graz, 1978).

KEYDELL, R., 'Ein dogmatisches Lehrgedicht Gregors von Nazianz', *BZ* 44 (1951), 315–21.

—— 'Die literarhistorische Stellung der Gedichte Gregors von Nazianz', *Atti dell'VIII Congresso internazionale di studi bizantini* (Rome, 1953), i. 134–43.

KNAACK, G., 'Zu Gregorios von Nazianz', *Neue Jahrbücher für Philologie und Pädagogik*, 135 (1887), 619–20.

LEFHERZ, F., *Studien zu Gregor von Nazianz: Mythologie, Überlieferung, Scholiasten* (Bonn, 1957).

LUDWICH, A., 'Nachahmer und Vorbilder des Dichters Gregorios von Nazianz', *RhM*, NF 42 (1887), 233–8.

McGUCKIN, J. A., 'Perceiving Light from Light in Light: The Trinitarian Theology of St. Gregory Nazianzen', *Acts of the International Colloquium Commemorating the 16th Centenary of St. Gregory Nazianzen, Brookline, 1991 = Greek Orthodox Theological Review*, 39/1–2 (1994), 7–32.

MATHIEU, J. M., 'Remarques sur l'anthropologie de Grégoire de Nazianze (*Poemata dogmatica*, VIII, 22–32; 78–96) et Porphyre', *Stud. Patr.* 17/3 (1982), 1115–19.

MEEHAN, D., 'Editions of St. Gregory of Nazianzus', *Irish Theological Quarterly*, 3 (1951), 203–19.

MEIJERING, E. P., 'The Doctrine of the Will and of the Trinity of the Orations of Gregory Nazianzen', *Nederlands Theologisch Tijdschrift*, 27 (1973), 224–34; repr. id., *God Being History* (Amsterdam, 1975), 103–13.

MISIER, A., 'Origine de l'édition de Bâle de S. Grégoire de Nazianze', *Revue de philologie*, 27 (1903), 125–38.

MORESCHINI, C., 'Luce e purificazione nella dottrina di Gregorio Nazianzeno', *Augustinianum*, 13 (1973), 534–49.

—— 'Il platonismo cristiano di Gregorio di Nazianzo', *Annali della Scuola Normale Superiore di Pisa*, 3rd ser., 4/4 (1974), 1347–92.

—— 'Influenze di Origene su Gregorio Nazianzeno', *Atti e memorie dell'Accademia Toscana di Scienze e Lettere 'La Colombaria'*, 44 = NS 30 (1979), 35–57.

—— 'La parafrasi di Niceta David ai Carmina Arcana di Gregorio Nazianzeno', Κοινωνία, 9/2 (1985), 101–14.

—— 'Poesia e cultura in Gregorio Nazianzeno', in S. Felici (ed.), *Crescita dell'uomo nella catechesi dei Padri (età postnicena): Convegno di studio e aggiornamento, Facoltà di lettere cristiane e classiche (Pontificium Institutum Altioris Latinitatis), Roma, 20–21 marzo 1987* (Biblioteca di scienze religiose, 80; Rome, 1988), 51–63.

MOSSAY, J., *La Mort et l'au-delà dans S. Grégoire de Nazianze* (Louvain, 1966).

—— 'Gregor von Nazianz', *Theologische Realenzyklopädie*, xiv (Berlin and New York, 1985), 164–73.

—— and COULIE, B., with DETIENNE, C., and CETEDOC, *Thesaurus Sancti Gregorii Nazianzeni: Enumeratio lemmatum: Carmina, Christus Patiens, Vita* (CC, Thesaurus Patrum Graecorum: Turnhout, 1991).

—— (ed.), *Symposium Nazianzenum (Louvain-la-Neuve, 25–28 août, 1981): Actes du Colloque International* (Studien zur Geschichte und Kultur des Altertums, Reihe 2: Forschungen zu Gregor von Nazianz, II; Paderborn, 1983).

NARDI, C., 'Note al primo carme teologico di Gregorio Nazianzeno', *Prometheus* (1990), 155–74.

OOSTHOUT, H. F. R. M., 'Wijsgerig taalgebruik in de redevoeringen van Gregorius van Nazianze tegen de Achtergrond van de Neoplatoonse Metafysica' (Diss. Nijmegen, 1986).

OTIS, B., 'Cappadocian Thought as a Coherent System', *DOP* 12 (1958), 95–124.

—— 'The Throne and the Mountain: An Essay on St. Gregory of Nazianzus', *Classical Journal*, 56/4 (1961), 146–65.

PATIN, A., *Herakleitische Beispiele* (Programm Neuberg, 1891–2)

PELLEGRINO, M., *La poesia di S. Gregorio Nazianzeno* (Milan, 1932).

PINAULT, H., *Le Platonisme de saint Grégoire de Nazianze: Essai sur les relations du christianisme et de l'hellénisme dans son œuvre théologique* (La Roche-sur-Yon, 1925).

PLAGNIEUX, J., *Saint Grégoire de Nazianze théologien* (Paris, 1951).

PORTMANN, F. X., *Die göttliche Paidagogia bei Gregor von Nazianz: Eine dogmengeschichtliche Studie* (Sankt Ottilien, 1954).

ROUSSE, J., 'Les anges et leur ministère selon saint Grégoire de Nazianze', *MSR* 22 (1955), 133–52.

RUETHER, R. R., *Gregory of Nazianzus: Rhetor and Philosopher* (Oxford, 1969).

SAJDAK, J., *De Gregorio Nazianzeno poetarum christianorum fonte* (Archiwum Filologiczne Akademji Umiejętności w Krakowie, 1; Kraków, 1917).

SCHEIDWEILER, F., 'Zu den Gedichten Gregors von Nazianz bei Cantarella und Soyter', *BZ* 49 (1956), 345–8.

SCHMID, M., 'Gregor von Nazianz und Hesychios', *RhM*, NF 21 (1866), 489–97.

SCHUBACH, M., *De b. patris Gregorii Nazianzeni Theologi carminibus commentatio patrologica* (Koblenz, 1871).

SCHUPART, J. G., *Gregorius Nazianzenus Theologus* (Giessen, 1721).

SICHERL, M., MOSSAY, J., and LAFONTAINE, G., 'Vers une édition critique de Grégoire de Nazianze', *RHE* 74 (1979), 626–40.

SINKO, T., 'Chronologia poezji św. Grezgorza z Nazjianzu', *Sprawozdania z Czynności i Posiedzeń Akademii Umiejętności w Krakowie*, 48/5 (1947), 147–56.

SÖLL, G., 'Die Mariologie der Kappadozier im Lichte der Dogmengeschichte', *ThQ* 131 (1951), 163–88, 288–319, 426–57.

ŠPIDLÍK, T., *Grégoire de Nazianze: Introduction à l'étude de sa doctrine spirituelle* (Rome, 1971).

STEPHAN, L., *Die Soteriologie des hl. Gregor von Nazianz* (Vienna, 1938).

STERNBACH, L., 'De Gregorio Nazianzeno Homeri interprete', in *Stromata in honorem Casimiri Morawski* (Kraków, 1908), 171–8.

—— 'Prolegomena in carmina Gregorii Nazianzeni', *Sprawozdania z Czynności i Posiedzeń Akademji Umiejętności w Krakowie*, 30/5 (1925), 2.

STOPPEL, P., *Quaestiones de Gregorii Nazianzeni poetarum scaenicorum imitatione et arte metrica* (Rostock, 1881).

SYKES, D. A., 'The *Poemata Arcana* of St. Gregory Nazianzen', *JTS*, NS 21 (1970), 32–42.

—— 'The *Poemata Arcana* of St. Gregory Nazianzen: Some Literary Questions', *BZ* 72 (1979), 6–15.

—— 'The Bible and Greek Classics in Gregory Nazianzen's Verse', *Stud. Patr.* 17/3 (1982), 1127–30.

—— 'Gregory Nazianzen as Didactic Poet', *Stud. Patr.* 16/2 (= TU 129; Berlin, 1985), 433–7.

—— 'Gregory Nazianzen, Poet of the Moral Life', *Stud. Patr.* 22 (1989), 69–73.

—— 'Reflections on Gregory Nazianzen's *Poemata quae spectant ad alios*', *Stud. Patr.* 18/3 (1989), 551–6.

SZYMUSIAK, J.-M., *Éléments de théologie de l'homme selon saint Grégoire de Nazianze* (Rome, 1963).

—— 'Grégoire de Nazianze et le péché', *Stud. Patr.* 9 (= TU 94; Berlin, 1966), 288–305.

—— 'Pour une chronologie des Discours de Saint Grégoire de Nazianze', *VC* 20/3 (1966), 183–9.

TRISOGLIO, F., 'Gregorio di Nazianzo, scrittore e teologo in quaranta anni di ricerche (1925–1965)', *Rivista di storia e letteratura religiosa*, 8 (1972), 341–74.

—— *Gregorio di Nazianzo in un quarantennio di ricerche (1925–1965) = Rivista lasalliana*, 40/1–4 (1973).

—— 'La poesia della Trinità nell'opera letteraria di S. Gregorio di Nazianzo', in *Forma Futuri: Studi in onore di M. Pellegrino* (Turin, 1975), 712–40.

—— 'La figura dell'eretico in Gregorio di Nazianzo,' *Augustinianum*, 25 (1985), 793–832.

ULLMANN, C., *Gregorius von Nazianz, der Theologe* (Gotha, 1866).

WEISS, H., *Die großen Kappadozier Basilius, Gregor von Nazianz und Gregor von Nyssa als Exegeten* (Braunsberg, 1872).

WEISS, K., *Die Erziehungslehre der drei Kappadokier* (Freiburg im Breisgau, 1903).

WERHAHN, H. M., 'Dubia und Spuria bei Gregor von Nazianz', *Stud. Patr.* 7 (= TU 92; Berlin, 1966), 337–47.

WINSLOW, D. F., *The Dynamics of Salvation: A Study in Gregory of Nazianzus* (Cambridge, Mass., 1979).

WYSS, B., 'Zu Gregor von Nazianz', in *Phyllobolia für Peter Von der Mühll zum 60. Geburtstag* (Basle, 1946), 159–83.

—— 'Gregor von Nazianz: Ein griechisch-christlicher Dichter des vierten Jahrhunderts', *Museum Helveticum*, 6 (1949), 177–10.

—— 'Gregor II (Gregor von Nazianz)', *RAC* xii (1983), 794–863.

(iii) Other works

ABRAMOWSKI, L., 'Eunomios', *RAC* vi (1966), 936–47.

ADAM, A., *Texte zum Manichäismus* (Berlin, 1969).

ALTANER, B., *Patrology*, ET H. Graef (Freiburg im Breisgau, 1960).

AMAND DE MENDIETA, E. A., *Fatalisme et liberté dans l'antiquité grecque* (Louvain, 1945).

ARGYLE, A. W., 'The Christian Doctrine of the Soul', *SJT* 18 (1965), 273–93.

ARMSTRONG, A. H., 'Studies in Traditional Anthropology I. Plato: A. The Soul of Man', *Downside Review*, 65/201 (1947), 237–45, 'B. The Form of Man', 65/202 (1947), 363–73, 'C. Individual and Community', 66/204, (1948), 148–64; 'II. Plotinus: A. 'Man's Higher Self', 66/206 (1948), 405–18, 'B. The Relevance of Plotinus', 67/208 (1949), 123–33, 'C. Soul and Body', 67/210 (1949), 406–19.

—— 'Platonic Elements in St. Gregory of Nyssa's Doctrine of Man', *Dominican Studies*, 1 (1948), 113–26.

—— 'The Nature of Man in St. Gregory of Nyssa', *ECQ* 8/3 (1949), suppl. 2–9.

—— 'The World of the Senses in Pagan and Christian Thought', *Downside Review*, 68/213 (1950), 305–23.

—— 'Plotinus's Doctrine of the Infinite and its Significance for Christian Thought', *Downside Review*, 73/231 (1954–5), 47–58.

—— 'The Background to the Doctrine "That the Intelligibles are Not Outside the Intellect"', *Les Sources de Plotin* (Entretiens Hardt, 5; Vandœuvres-Geneva, 1960), 393–425.

—— *An Introduction to Ancient Philosophy* (London, 1965).

—— (ed.), *The Cambridge History of Later Greek and Early Medieval Philosophy* (Cambridge, 1967).

BALTHASAR, H. VON, *Présence et pensée: Essai sur la philosophie religieuse de Grégoire de Nysse* (Paris, 1942).

BARDENHEWER, O., *Geschichte der altchristlichen Literatur*, 5 vols. (Freiburg im Breisgau, 1912–31; vols. i–ii rev. edn. 1913–14).

BARDY, G., 'Manichéisme', *DTC* ix (1926–7), 1841–95.

BARNES, M. R., and WILLIAMS, D. H. (eds.), *Arianism after Arius* (Edinburgh, 1993).

BAUDRY, J., *Le Problème de l'origine et de l'éternité du monde* (Paris, 1931).

BECK, H.-G., *Kirche und theologische Literatur im byzantinischen Reich* (Munich, 1977).

BIDEZ, J., 'Le traité d'astrologie cité par Saint Basile dans son Hexaéméron', *L'Antiquité classique*, 7 (1938), 19–21.

—— and CUMONT, F., *Les Mages hellénisés* (Paris, 1938).

BINDLEY, T. H., rev. GREEN, F. W., *The Oecumenical Documents of the Faith* (London, 1950).

BISSINGER, M., *Das Adjektiv μέγας in der griechischen Dichtung* (Munich, 1966).

BOUCHÉ-LECLERCQ, A., *L'Astrologie grecque* (Paris, 1899).

CAMPENHAUSEN, H. VON, *The Fathers of the Greek Church*, ET (London, 1963).

CATAUDELLA, Q., *Critica ed estetica nella letteratura greca cristiana* (Turin, 1928).

CHADWICK, H., 'Origen, Celsus and the Resurrection of the Body', *HTR* 41/2 (1948), 83–102.

—— *Early Christian Thought and the Classical Tradition* (Oxford, 1966).

SELECT BIBLIOGRAPHY

Coulange, *see* Turmel.

COURCELLE, P., 'Anti-Christian Arguments and Christian Platonism: from Arnobius to Ambrose', in A. Momigliano (ed.), *The Conflict between Paganism and Christianity in the Fourth Century* (Oxford, 1963), 181–92.

COURTONNE, Y., *Saint Basile et l'hellénisme* (Paris, 1934).

CRAMER, F. H., *Astrology in Roman Law and Politics* (Philadelphia, 1954).

CUMONT, F., *Astrology and Religion among the Greeks and Romans* (New York, 1912).

—— *Les Religions orientales dans le paganisme romain* (Paris, 1929).

DANIÉLOU, J., *Sacramentum Futuri* (Paris, 1950); ET W. Hibberd, *From Shadows to Reality* (London, 1960).

—— *Les Anges et leur mission d'après les Pères de l'Église* (Gembloux, 1952).

—— *Origen*, ET W. Mitchell (London and New York, 1955).

—— *A History of Christian Doctrine*, ET J. A. Baker, 3 vols. (London, 1964–77).

—— 'La chronologie des œuvres de Grégoire de Nysse', *Stud. Patr.* 7 (= TU 92; Berlin, 1966), 159–69.

DODDS, E. R., *The Greeks and the Irrational* (Berkeley, Los Angeles, and London, 1951).

DÖLGER, F. J., *Sphragis* (Studien zur Geschichte und Kultur des Altertums, 5; Paderborn, 1911–12).

—— 'Christophorus als Ehrentitel für Martyrer und Gläubige im christlichen Altertum', *AC* 4 (1934), 73–80.

FESTUGIÈRE, A. J., *La Révélation d'Hermès Trismégiste*, i: *L'Astrologie et les sciences occultes* (Paris, 1944), ii: *Le Dieu cosmique* (Paris, 1949).

FLOROVSKY, G., 'The Idea of Creation in Christian Philosophy', *ECQ* 8/3 (1949), suppl. 53–77.

FREND, W. H. C., *The Rise of Christianity* (London, 1984).

GAÏTH, J., *La Conception de la liberté chez Grégoire de Nysse* (Paris, 1953).

GALTIER, P., *Le Saint Esprit en nous d'après les Pères grecs* (Rome, 1946).

GERLITZ, P., *Außerchristliche Einflüsse auf die Entwicklung des christlichen Trinitätsdogmas* (Leiden, 1963).

GREEN, F. W., 'The Later Development of the Doctrine of the Trinity', in A. E. J. Rawlinson (ed.), *Essays on the Incarnation and the Trinity* (London, 1928).

GREGG, R. C. (ed.), *Arianism* (Cambridge, Mass., 1985).

GRILLMEIER, A., *Christ in Christian Tradition*, i, rev. edn. ET J. Bowden (London, 1975).

GROSS, J., *La Divinisation du chrétien d'après les Pères grecs* (Paris, 1938).

—— *Entstehungsgeschichte des Erbsündendogmas*, i (Munich and Basle, 1960).

GUNDEL, W., 'Astrologie', *RAC* i (1950), 810–31.

—— (rev. H. G. Gundel) *Sternglaube, Sternreligion und Sternorakel* (Heidelberg, 1959).

GUTHRIE, W. K. C., *The Greeks and their Gods* (London, 1950).

—— 'The Presocratic World-Picture', *HTR* 45 (1952), 87–104.

—— *A History of Greek Philosophy*, 6 vols. (Cambridge, 1962–81).

273

HANSON, R. P. C., *The Search for the Christian Doctrine of God: The Arian Controversy 318–381* (Edinburgh, 1988).

HENRY, P., 'Kénose', *Dictionnaire de la Bible*, suppl. v (Paris, 1957), 79–85.

HERMANN, A., 'Christophorus', *RAC* ii (1954), 1241–50.

HOCHSTAFFL, J., *Negative Theologie* (Munich, 1976).

HUSSEY, E., *The Presocratics* (London, 1972).

IVÁNKA, E. VON, *Hellenisches und christliches im frühbyzantinischen Geistesleben* (Vienna, 1948).

—— *Plato Christianus: Übernahme und Umgestaltung des Platonismus durch die Väter* (Einsiedeln, 1964).

JACKSON, A. V. W., *Researches in Manichaeism* (New York, 1932).

JAEGER, W., *Theology of the Early Greek Philosophers* (Oxford, 1947).

—— *Early Christianity and Greek Paideia* (Cambridge, Mass., and London, 1961).

JOHNSON, A. R., *The Vitality of the Individual in the Thought of Ancient Israel* (Cardiff, 1964).

KARPP, H., *Probleme altchristlicher Anthropologie* (Gütersloh, 1950).

KELLY, J. N. D., *Rufinus: A Commentary on the Apostles' Creed* (ACW 20; London, 1955).

—— *Early Christian Doctrines* (London, 1977).

—— *Early Christian Creeds*, 2nd edn. (London, 1977).

KEYDELL, R., *Quaestiones metricae de epicis Graecis recentioribus* (Berlin, 1911).

KING, N. Q., *The Emperor Theodosius and the Establishment of Christianity* (London, 1961).

KIRK, G. S., RAVEN, J. E., and SCHOFIELD, M., *The Presocratic Philosophers*, 2nd edn. (Cambridge, 1983).

KOPECEK, T. A., *A History of Neo-Arianism*, 2 vols. (Cambridge, Mass., 1979).

KRETSCHMAR, G., *Studien zur frühchristlichen Trinitätstheologie* (Tübingen, 1956).

LABRIOLLE, P. DE, *La Réaction païenne: Étude sur la polémique antichrétienne du Iᵉʳ au VIᵉ siècle* (Paris, 1950).

LADNER, G. B., 'The Philosophical Anthropology of St. Gregory of Nyssa', *DOP* 12 (1958), 59–94.

LAISTNER, M. L. W., 'The Western Church and Astrology during the Early Middle Ages', *HTR* 34 (1941), 251–75.

—— *Christianity and Pagan Culture in the Later Roman Empire* (Ithaca, 1951).

LAMPE, G. H. W., *The Seal of the Spirit* (London, 1951).

—— *God as Spirit* (Oxford, 1977).

LANGE, N. DE, *Origen and the Jews* (Cambridge, 1976).

LEWY, H., *Chaldaean Oracles and Theurgy* (Cairo, 1956; 2nd edn. Paris, 1982).

LEYS, R., *L'Image de Dieu chez saint Grégoire de Nysse* (Brussels, 1951).

—— 'La théologie spirituelle de Grégoire de Nysse', *Stud. Patr.* 2 (= TU 64; Berlin, 1957), 495–511.

LIETZMANN, H., *A History of the Early Church*, iii: *From Constantine to Julian*, ET B. Lee Woolf (London, 1953).

LIEU, S. C., *Manicheism in the Later Roman Empire and in Medieval China* (Manchester, 1985).

LONG, A. A., *Hellenistic Philosophy: Stoics, Epicureans, Sceptics* (London, 1974).

—— and SEDLEY, D. N., *The Hellenistic Philosophers* (Cambridge, 1987).

LOSSKY, V., *The Vision of God* (London, 1963).

LOT-BORODINE, A., 'La doctrine de la déification dans l'Église grecque jusqu'au XIᵉ siècle', *RHR* 105 (1932), 5–43; 106 (1932), 523–74.

LOUTH, A., *The Origins of the Christian Mystical Tradition: From Plato to Denys* (Oxford, 1981).

MAAS, P., *Greek Metre*, ET H. Lloyd-Jones (Oxford, 1962).

MACMULLEN, R., *Enemies of the Roman Order* (Cambridge, Mass., 1967).

MAYOR, J. E. B., 'Darkness the Privation of Light, Night the Absence of Day', *Journal of Philology*, 28/56 (1903), 289–92.

MERKI, H., ʽΟμοίωσις Θεῷ: Von der platonischen Angleichung an Gott zur Gottähnlichkeit bei Gregor von Nyssa* (Fribourg, 1952).

MERSCH, E., *Le Corps mystique du Christ*, 2 vols. (Paris, 1951).

MEYENDORFF, J., *Byzantine Theology: Historical Trends and Doctrinal Themes* (New York, 1974).

MEYER, W., 'Zur Geschichte des griechischen und lateinischen Hexameters', *Sitzungsberichte der Königlich bayerischen Akademie der Wissenschaften, philosophisch-philologische Klasse*, 1884, 979–1087.

MICHL, J., 'Engel IV (christlich)', *RAC* v (1962), 109–200.

MORTLEY, R., *From Word to Silence*, 2 vols. (Bonn, 1986).

MÜHLENBERG, E., *Die Unendlichkeit Gottes bei Gregor von Nyssa* (Göttingen, 1966).

MURRAY, G., *Five Stages of Greek Religion* (Oxford, 1925).

NORRIS, R. A, Jr., *Manhood and Christ: A Study in the Christology of Theodore of Mopsuestia* (Oxford, 1963).

—— *God and the World in Early Christian Theology* (London, 1966).

ONIANS, R. B., *The Origins of European Thought about the Body, the Mind, the Soul, the World, Time, and Fate* (Cambridge, 1951).

OSBORN, E., *The Beginning of Christian Philosophy* (Cambridge, 1981).

PELIKAN, J., *The Christian Tradition: A History of the Development of Doctrine*, 5 vols. (Chicago and London, 1971–89).

—— *Christianity and Culture: The Metamorphosis of Natural Theology in the Christian Encounter with Hellenism* (New Haven and London, 1993).

PELZ, K. W. A., *Die Engellehre des hl. Augustinus: Ein Beitrag zur Dogmengeschichte* (Münster, 1913).

POHLENZ, M., *Die Stoa: Geschichte einer geistigen Bewegung*, 3rd edn. (Göttingen, 1964).

POLOTSKY, H. J., 'Manichäismus', *RE*, Suppl. vi (1935), 240–71.

PÖSCHL, V., GÄRTNER, H., and HEYKE, W., *Bibliographie zur antiken Bildersprache* (Heidelberg, 1964).

PRESTIGE, G. W., *God in Patristic Thought* (London, 1952).

PUECH, A., *Histoire de la littérature grecque chrétienne depuis les origines jusqu'à la fin du IVe siècle*, 3 vols. (Paris, 1928–30).

PUECH, H. C., *Le Manichéisme, son fondateur, sa doctrine* (Paris, 1949).

QUASTEN, J., *Patrology*, 4 vols. (i: Utrecht and Brussels, 1950; ii: Utrecht and Antwerp, 1953; iii: Utrecht, Antwerp, and Westminster, Md., 1960; vol. iv, with foreword by Quasten = A. Di Bernardino (ed.), *Patrologia*, iii (Turin, 1978), ET P. Solari, Westminster, Md., 86).

RAUSCHEN, G., *Jahrbücher der christlichen Kirche unter dem Kaiser Theodosius dem Großen* (Freiburg im Breisgau, 1897).

RICH, A. N. M., 'The Platonic Ideas as Thoughts of God', *Mnemosyne*, 4th ser., 7 (1954), 123–33.

RIEDINGER, U., *Die heilige Schrift im Kampf der griechischen Kirche gegen die Astrologie von Origen bis Johannes von Damaskos* (Innsbruck, 1956).

RIST, J. M., *Plotinus: The Road to Reality* (Cambridge, 1967).

—— 'Basil's "Neoplatonism": Its Background and Nature.' in P. J. Fedwick (ed.), *Basil of Caesarea, Christian, Humanist, Ascetic* (Toronto, 1981), 137–220; repr. *Platonism and its Christian Heritage* (London, 1985), no. XII.

RITTER, H., and PRELLER, L., *Historia philosophiae Graecae et Romanae ex fontium locis contexta* (Gotha, 1934).

ROHDE, E., *Psyche: the Cult of Souls and the Belief in Immortality among the Greeks*, ET W. B. Hillis (London, 1925).

SCHERMANN, T., *Die Gottheit des Heiligen Geistes nach den griechischen Vätern des vierten Jahrhunderts* (Freiburg im Breisgau, 1901).

SCHWYZER, H.-R., 'Plotinos', *RE* xxi/1 (1951), 471–592.

SELLERS, R. V., *Two Ancient Christologies* (London, 1940).

SETTON, K. M., *The Christian Attitude towards the Emperor in the Fourth Century* (New York, 1941).

SIMON, M., *Verus Israel: Études sur les relations entre chrétiens et juifs dans l'empire romain (135–425)* (Paris, 1964).

SIMONETTI, M., *La crisi ariana nel quarto secolo* (Rome, 1975).

SLOMKOWSKI, A., *L'État primitif de l'homme dans la tradition de l'Église avant S. Augustin* (Paris, 1928).

SOUTAR, G., *Nature in Greek Poetry* (London, 1939).

SPANNEUT, M., *Le Stoïcisme des Pères de l'Église de Clément de Rome à Clément d'Alexandrie* (Paris, 1957).

STÄHLIN, O., *Die altchristliche griechische Literatur*, in W. von Christ, *Geschichte der griechischen Literatur*, ii/2 (Munich, 1924).

STANFORD, W. B., *Greek Metaphor* (Oxford, 1936).

STETTNER, W., *Die Seelenwanderung bei Griechen und Römern* (Stuttgart and Berlin, 1934).

STUDER, B., *Trinity and Incarnation: The Faith of the Early Church*, ET M. Westerhoff, ed. A. Louth (Edinburgh, 1993).

TELFER, W., 'The Birth of Christian Anthropology', *JTS*, NS 13 (1962), 347–54.

TENNANT, F. R., *The Sources of the Doctrine of the Fall and of Original Sin* (Cambridge, 1903).

THRAEDE, K., 'Untersuchungen zum Ursprung und zur Geschichte der christlichen Poesie II', *JAC* 5 (1962), 128–31.

TIXERONT, J., *Histoire des dogmes dans l'antiquité chrétienne* (Paris, 1905).

TRESMONTANT, C., *La Métaphysique du christianisme et la naissance de la philosophie chrétienne* (Paris, 1961).

TRIGG, J. W., *Origen: The Bible and Philosophy in the Third-Century Church* (Atlanta and London, 1985).

TURMEL, J., 'Histoire de l'angélologie du temps apostolique à la fin du Vᵉ siècle', *RHL* 3 (1898), 299–308, 407–34, 533–52.

—— ('P. Coulange'), *The Life of the Devil*, ET S. H. Guest (London, 1929).

TURNER, H. E. W., *The Pattern of Christian Truth* (London, 1954).

UEBERWEG, F., , and PRAECHTER, K., *Grundriß der Geschichte der Philosophie* (Basle, 1923).

VILLEMAIN, A. F., *Tableau de l'éloquence chrétienne au IVᵉ siècle* (Paris, 1851).

VOGEL, C. J. DE, *Greek Philosophy: A Collection of Texts with Notes and Explanations*, 3 vols. (Leiden, 1950–9).

WALLIS, R. T., *Neoplatonism* (London, 1972).

WASZINK, J. H., 'Beseelung', *RAC* ii (1954), 176–83.

WEIGL, E., *Christologie vom Tode des Athanasius bis zum Ausbruch des nestorianischen Streites* (Munich, 1925).

WICKHAM, L. R., 'The *Syntagmation* of Aetius the Anomean', *JTS*, NS 19 (1968), 532–69.

WIDENGREN, G., *Mani and Manichaeism*, ET (London, 1965).

WIFSTRAND, A., *Von Kallimachos zu Nonnos: Metrisch-stilistische Untersuchungen zur späteren griechischen Epik und zu verwandten Gedichtgattungen* (Lund, 1933).

WILES, M. F., *The Making of Christian Doctrine* (Cambridge, 1967).

—— *The Remaking of Christian Doctrine* (London, 1974).

—— 'Eunomius: Hair-Splitting Dialectician or Defender of the Accessibility of Salvation?', in R. Williams (ed.), *The Making of Orthodoxy: Essays in Honour of Henry Chadwick* (Cambridge, 1989).

WILLIAMS, N. P., *The Ideas of the Fall and of Original Sin* (London, 1924).

WILLIAMS, R., *The Wound of Knowledge: Christian Spirituality from the New Testament to St. John of the Cross* (London, 1979).

WOLFSON, H. A., *The Philosophy of the Church Fathers*, i: *Faith, Trinity, Incarnation* (Cambridge, Mass., 1964).

YSEBAERT, J., *Greek Baptismal Terminology: its Origin and Development* (Nijmegen, 1962).

ZELLER, E., *Die Philosophie der Griechen*, 3 vols. (i/1–2: 6th edn. rev. W. Nestle, Leipzig, 1919–20; ii/1, 5th edn., Leipzig, 1922; ii/2, 4th edn., Leipzig, 1921; iii/1–2, 5th edn. Leipzig, 1923).

Index of Greek Words

*   to denote words not in LSJ
[*]   to denote words in a different form in LSJ

ἀγένητος 2.32
ἀδάμαστος 2.68, 8.82
ἀδήριτος 3.86, 4.39
ἀειδής 3.9, 6.13, 6.36, 7.73
*ἀείδρομος 5.66
ἄημα 7.1
ἀήρ 5.61, 6.1, 6.15. 6.52, 7.9, 7.24, 7.27,
    8.97
αἰθήρ 6.4, 6.52
αἰολόδωρος 3.5
ἀΐστως 7.79
ἀκέαστος 2.35, 3.73
ἀκίνητος 5.6, 6.53–5 n.
ἄκος 8.39, 8.92
ἄκοσμος 4.27
ἀκόσμως 7.4, 7.36
ἄκτιστος 3.42
ἀλλογένεθλος 5.22
ἄλλος 1.29–30, 2.17, 8.53
ἄλυξις 6.49. 6.85
ἀμάρυγμα 3.43
ἄμειψις 6.93
ἀμέτρητος 2.64
ἄμετρος 3.41
ἀμήτωρ 8.40
ἄμικτος 4.11
ἀμογητί 7.127
ἀμφίθετος 7.104
*ἀμφιθόωκος 4.88
[*]ἀμφιρεπής 8.86
*ἀμφιτάλαντος 7.103
ἀμφότερος 8.76
ἀμφοτέρωθεν 4.36, 7.65, 8.51
ἀνάγκη 2.2, 5.25, 5.7–9 n.
ἀναίτιος 1.25
ἄναρχος 1.31, 2.19, 3.58, 3.76, 3.81, 4.39,
    4.55, 5.12, 6.45
ἀνάστερος 5.44
ἀνείδεος 4.7
ἀνηγεμόνευτος 5.13
ἀντεισέρχομαι 8.26
ἀντίθεος 4.84

*ἀντιθόωκος 6.44
*ἀντίθρονος 4.25
ἄνυμφής 8.68
ἀπαθής 2.15
ἀπειρέσιος 4.33
ἀπείριτος 1.27
ἀπείρων 5.1
ἄπηκτος 2.16
ἀπήορος 2.6, pp. xiii–iv
ἁπλοῦς 4.40, 4.92, 6.17
ἄποινον 8.81
ἀπόκρουστος 6.2
ἀποξέω 2.60
*ἀπόπνευστος 7.8
ἀπόρρητος p. 51
ἀπορρώξ 4.32, 5.73
ἄπρηκτος 4.61
ἄρευστος 3.88
ἀρτιγένεθλος 7.89
ἀρτιφαής 5.61
ἀρχέγονος 2.53, 3.37, 7.78, 8.81
ἀρχέτυπος 2.8
ἀρχή 2.21
*ἀρχιγόης 6.79
ἀρχιερεύς 2.75
ἄσαρκος 2.37, 2.80, 7.45
ἀστατέω 3.66
ἄστατος 3.68
*ἀστροπολεύω 5.59
ἀσώματος 2.16
ἄσωμος 4.9
ἀτειρής 6.92
ἀτέλεστος 4.61
ἄτροπος 6.40. 6.47, 6.53
ἄτροφος 5.68
αὐγάζεσκω 3.25
αὔλος 4.7
αὐτοδάϊκτος 4.53
αὐτοδίδακτος 1.38
αὐτοκέλευστος 3.7
αὐτόματος 5.7, 5.9
αὐτοπαγής 8.69

279

σοφίη 3.57, 4.29, 5.40, 7.59
*συνάναρχος 4.4
*συνάστερος 5.19
συνδέω 5.23, 5.24, 5.28
σφρηγίς 1.31, 8.91, 8.92
σῶμα 2.57, 2.63, 5.68, 7.11, 7.19, 7.33, 7.48, 7.79, 7.84, 8.34

[*]Ταρτάρεος 6.79
τέμνω 3.2, 3.53, 3.59, 4.11
τεύχω 2.51
*τμῆξις 2.27
τομή 2.14
τρεπτός 8.82
Τριάς 3.60, 3.73, 3.87, 3.90, 3.93, 4.55, 4.88, 6.12
τρισάριθμος 3.74
τρισσός 2.68, 3.43, 3.46, 3.62, 3.71, 3.78
*τρισσοφαής 4.65
τρίτος 6.52, 6.54
τύπος 3.62, 4.67, 7.88
τυπόω 1.36, 8.16

ὕλη 4.3, 4.7, 4.19, 6.93
*ὕμνημα 3.5
ὑπαστράπτω 3.28
ὑπερέχω 2.67
ὑποδρήσσω 6.16

ὑποδρήστειρα 4.79
*ὑψιθέω 4.40
*ὑψιθόωκος 3.6
ὑψιμέδων 6.37, 6.71, 8.3

φαεσφόρος 3.46
φάος, φῶς 2.22, 3.21, 3.32, 3.45, 3.71, 3.78, 3.90, 4.25, 4.33, 4.39, 4.46, 4.47, 4.56, 4.78, 4.82, 4.85, 4.88, 4.98, 6.6, 6.8, 6.11, 6.38, 6.50, 6.81
φθονερός 4.54, 7.112
[φθόνος] 4.83 n.
*φιλάναρχος 4.18
*φιλόδηρις 6.78
φύσις 2.8, 2.17, 2.35, 3.2, 3.41, 3.68, 3.71, 3.73, 3.92, 4.10, 4.35, 4.36, 4.42, 4.51, 4.77, 4.83, 4.89, 4.92, 5.7, 5.68, 5.71, 6 title, 6.6, 6.42, 6.45, 6.53, 7.7, 7.13, 7.27, 7.75, 7.101, 8.48
φῶς 7.36, 7.66
φωτοδότης 8.93

*Χριστοφόρος 4.57

ψυχή 4.32, 7 title, 7.1, 7.19, 7.24, 7.31, 7.34, 7.44, 7.51, 7.53, 7.79, 7.87

*ὡροθέτης 5.45

Scripture Index

The version of the Bible which has been used is the Septuagint

38.31 (31.33 Heb.)   7.101–2
43.23 (36.23 Heb.)   1.16

Lamentations
3.34   5.71

Ezekiel
28.12 ff.   6.57–8
28.12–13   6.38
28.19   6.38

Joel
3.13   5.42–3

Nahum
1.6   6.85

Zephaniah
1.18   7.118–19
3.8   7.118–19

Zechariah
13.9   6.91

Malachi
3.2–3   6.91

Sirach
24.8   4.15

Tobit
5.6   6.25
5.22   6.25

Wisdom of Solomon
7.22   7.59–60
7.26   2.8
9.9   7.59–60
11.17   4.7–8
14.2   7.59–60

4 Maccabees
11.5   4.15

Matthew
2.1 ff.   8.60–4
2.1–12   5.53–71
2.2   2.65–6
2.9–11   2.65–6
3.1–12   8.73–4
3.13–17   2.70–1
4.1–11   2.68
8.12   6.59
9.2   2.73
12.41–4   1.6–7
13.24–30   5.42–3
14.13–21   2.69
15.32–9   2.69
16.28   4.49
18.10   6.25
21   5.54

21.10   8.60–1
22.13   6.59
23.27   8.21
25.30   6.59
26.24   3.49
27.51   8.60–1
28.10   3.47

Mark
1.1–8   8.73–4
1.9–11   2.70–1
1.12–13   2.68
4.35–41   2.72
6.30–44   2.69
7.71–2   6.73–81
8.1–10   2.69
9.1–11   4.49
10.45   8.81
13.14   1.19

Luke
1.5–25   8.73–4
1.35   8.68
2.7   2.65–6
2.13   8.60–4
2.22   8.69
3.1–18   8.73–4
3.21–2   2.70–1
4.1–13   2.68
4.10–11   6.25
8.22–5   2.72
9.10–17   2.69
9.27   4.49
13.34   8.21
16.26   3.71
21.1–4   1.6–7

John
1.5   6.59
1.6–9   8.72–4
1.11   8.41–2
1.15–18   8.73–4
1.18   1.28
2.1–11   2.69
3.2   3.7
4.14   4.81
6.1–14   2.69
6.27   1.31
8.12   6.59
8.35   6.59
8.44   4.49, 6.76
8.52   4.49
14.28   3.55
16.12   3.18

SCRIPTURE INDEX

General Index

Adam 2.62–3, 3.37–9, 4.48–50, 6.63–6,
  6.70–3, 6.97–129, 8.9–11, 8.44,
  p. 154 n.
  Second 8.53–9
affinity, divine–human 8.51–2
Albinus 4.67–74
Anaxagoras 5.2
angels 1.4–5, 2.2, 3.92–3, 4.77–92, 6.11b–
  26, 6.50–5, 6.96–7, 7.61–2, 8.61, p. 71
Apollinarius p. 67, pp. 93–4
Apollinarius Metaphrastes 3.1
Arians 1.14b–15, 1.28–30, 1.35b–9, 2.14,
  2.31–2, 2.42, 2.45–6, 2.49–50, 3.9,
  3.61–2, 3.72–3, 3.85
Aristotle 4.7–15, 4.55–74, 5 intro., 5.6–9,
  5.7–8, 7.11–17, 7.24b–90, p. 74, p. 146
astrology 5.15b–33, 5.45–52
Athanasius 3.3, 3.72–3, 8.65–6, p. 74
Augustine 4.51–4, 4.43b–6, 4.59b–62,
  4.83, 6.53–5
automatic theory of the universe 5.7–9

baptism 3.44–53, 4.95–6, 8.87b–99, p. 68
Basil 3.42, 4.24–54, 4.55–74, 5.15b–33,
  6.53–5, pp. 114–15
blood 2.1–2, 2.76, 7.10, 8.79, 8.88
burning bush 3.32

Callimachus 3.1
Carneades 5 intro.
Chaldaeans 5.58 ff.
chance 5.1–52
Christology see Godhead
coats of skin 7.115–16
coinherence 3.75
Constantinople, Creed of (381) 3.7, 3.42,
  p. 115
cosmic religion 4.55
cosmological argument 5.10–13
cosmology 4 passim
Covenant, New 8.26b–30
creatio ex aeterno 4.70–4
creatio ex nihilo 4.7–15, 4.100
Creation 4 intro.
Creationism 7.78–96
Crucifixion 8.79

darkness 4.23–31, 6.59
dating p. 66
deification 2.47–50, 4.95–6
Democritus 5.7–9
demons 6.82–95
didactic verse pp. 58–9
Diogenes 7.8b–9

Empedocles 7.10, 7.32–52
Epicurus, Epicureans 4.55–74, 5.7–9, 7.3
eternity of the world 4.55–74
Eunomius, Eunomians 1.28–30, 2.14,
  2.26–7, 2.31–2, 2.82–3, 3.42, 3.47,
  3.58, pp. 103–4
Eve 3.37–43
evil 4.43b–6, 4.51–4, 6.37–45, 6.73–81,
  7.104–9, 8.12–17, 8.34–8, 8.91
Exodus 8.87b–90

Fall:
  of Lucifer 4.46b–50, 6.56–66
  of Adam 4.48b–50, 7.112–29, 8.9–18
fire 3.32, 5.68–9, 7.7–8
form 4.7–8
freedom 3.42, 7.100–4
future life 4.95–6

Generationism 7.78–86
Gentiles 8.26b–30
Gnosticism 1.19, 4.3–4, pp. 151–2
Godhead 1.3–5, 1.25–39, 2.5–56, 3, 4.1–
  23, 4.51–100, 5.1–44, 6.1–26, 6.47–66,
  p. 68
  Father 1.25–34, 2.5–56, 3.24–5, 3.56–9,
    7.55–6, 8.31–3, 8.39–40, pp. 68–9
  Son, Word, Christ 1.10–15, 1.27–34, 2
    passim, 3.9, 3.16–17, 3.25–31, 3.54–6,
    4.76–92, 5.53–69, 6.82–95, 7.55–77,
    7.97–129, 8.26b–99, pp. 69–70
  Spirit 1.22–4, 1.34–9, 3 passim, 6.96–9,
    8.67–9, 8.77–9, pp. 70–1, 114–15
  Trinity 1.25–35a, 3.37–53, 3.71–93,
    4.55–89, 6.1–2, p. 68
grammar p. 61
Gregory Nyssen 4.24–54, 5 intro., 5.15b–
  33, 7.82–90

286

GENERAL INDEX